JUDGES

JUDGES:

God's War Against Humanism

James B. Jordan

Geneva Ministries
Tyler, Texas

Copyright © 1985
James B. Jordan

ISBN 0-939404-10-9
Library of Congress Catalog Card Number 85-070014
Printed in the United States of America

Unless otherwise indicated, Scripture quotations in the body of
the commentary are either the author's own, or are from the
New American Standard Bible, copyright 1971 by the Lockman
Foundation, and used by permission.

Typesetting by Thoburn Press, Tyler, Texas

Published by
Geneva Ministries
P.O. Box 8376
Tyler, Texas 75711

To my mother
Sarah Burrell Jordan

TABLE OF CONTENTS

INTRODUCTION

One of the best ways to communicate truth in such a way as to grip the hearts and minds of the hearer is by means of story telling. The Bible is full of stories, designed for just this purpose. The whole theology of story telling could use a treatment in itself. In this book, however, it is my intention to illustrate such a theology, rather than to write it systematically.

God is Himself the Great Story Teller. Being God, He can sovereignly superintend all events so as to bring His stories to life. His stories really happened. The fact that they are told as stories does not subtract one whit from their real historical character. Still, what gives them their thrilling power is not only that we know that they really happened in a certain year and at a certain place, but because they speak to us today.

Why do good stories speak to us today? Because, as students of literature would say, they embody universal characteristics, and deal with universal problems, hopes, fears, symbols, and so forth. This is exactly correct. Universal truths are not the same as abstract generalities, however. It is precisely in the specific events themselves that the most universal aspects of the stories are seen.

Images of God in Judges

There are in Biblical theology certain great universals. They derive from the fact that man is the image, the very symbol of God. Thus, throughout the Bible marches *The Seed*. He is the one born of *The Woman* who will crush the head of *The Serpent*. We shall meet him several times in the book of Judges. Indeed, the crushing of the head of the enemy is one of the most obvious themes in the book:

Ehud kills Eglon, political head.
Jael crushes Sisera's head with a tentpeg.
Gideon destroys the four political heads Zebah, Zalmunna, Oreb,
   and Zeeb.
Abimelech's head is crushed by a rock, again by a woman.
Samson destroys all five heads of the Philistine cities, by crush-
   ing them with rocks.

There is also *The Anointed One,* also known by his Hebrew name *Messiah.* He is the one who has had oil poured upon his head, making him a special priest or king over God's people. Or, apart from oil he has been given a special anointing of the Holy Spirit. He represents God's people, for better or for worse. We shall meet him in Judges as well, because each of the judges was anointed by the Spirit.

As mentioned above, there is *The Mother,* and we meet her in the persons of Deborah and her evil twin, the mother of Sisera, as well as in the mother of Samson. There is also *The Bride,* and we shall meet her in the wife of the Levite who is raped to death by the men of Gibeah. And since there is *The Bride,* we also see *The Groom.* We see him offering salvation to those outside the kingdom, in the person of the young Samson; and we find him faithlessly leaving *The Bride* to die, in the person of the Levite. And of course, if there is the mother and the bride, there must also be *The Whore,* and what better candidate than Delilah to fill that symbolic role?

Less familiar to us, perhaps, is *The Youth.* He is the young man who is offered the temptation to seize power prematurely, which was the sin of Adam and of Ham.[1] We meet him in the person of Gideon. Another character we meet frequently in Genesis, but only once in Judges, is *The Younger Brother.* When the older brother apostatizes, and is judged, the younger brother takes his place. We meet him in Judges in the person of Jotham, because the death of his older brothers was a sign to Israel that the old world order is under judgment.

And we have not exhausted the list. But are all these mere symbols, mere allegorical figures? Not at all. If you or I had

1. See James B. Jordan, "Rebellion, Tyranny, and Dominion in the Book of Genesis," in North, ed., *Tactics of Christian Resistance.* Christianity & Civilization No. 3 (Tyler, TX: Geneva Ministries, 1983).

written these stories, and had tried to make everything come out just so, we would have had to engage in a little judicious fiction (and there is nothing wrong with that, as Jesus' parables illustrate). But that is not what we have here. These were real flesh and blood people, who really lived. Their lives were so ordered by God, however, that everything did come out just so; and the history of their lives was written by the author in such a way as to bring out the universal meanings, without the need to distort a single fact.

Keys to Interpretation

Who was this author of Judges? Christians confess that God wrote this book, ultimately, as He wrote all of the Bible. I think the most likely candidate for human authorship is Samuel. As we shall see, one of the major themes in Judges is that there was no human king in Israel. The people were supposed to recognize the Lord as their king. When they did not, chaos ensued. It is Samuel who made the great speech against the tyranny of human kings in 1 Samuel 8, and it is very easy to believe that he might have been moved by God to prepare Judges as a tract for the times.

Judges, like all the so-called "history books" of the Old Testament, is really a prophecy. Judges is numbered among what are called the "Former Prophets." These books were called prophecies because the histories they recorded were regarded as exemplary. The histories showed God's principles in action, and thus formed prophetic warnings to the people. If we read Judges merely as a set of exciting stories, we miss this.

To get at the prophetic meaning, we need to know four "secrets" of interpreting Biblical narratives. First, we have to take seriously the universals, as mentioned above. The first enemy who invades Israel in the book of Judges is Cushan-of-Double-Wickedness from Aram-of-Double-River. This is Mesopotamia. What is the prophecy? If the people do not live righteously, the enemy will come from Mesopotamia. And so it was. First Assyria conquered Northern Israel, and later Babylon conquered Southern Israel, so that even the idea of a two-fold destruction came to pass.

Along these lines, we must confess with Genesis 1:26 that man, both individually and corporately (at various levels), is the very image of God. This means that human life inevitably and incessantly images the life of God, either properly (righteously) or improperly (sinfully). What this fact means is that there is a profound symbolic dimension to everything in human life. For instance, the interaction of people with one another shows the interaction among the Three Persons of God, either rightly or wrongly. Now, this is more particularly true of the stories recounted in the Bible, since they are designed as prophecy. In more pointed ways they show us how to image God, or how not to.

The symbolism or typology of Scripture is more or less *vague*. There is nothing wrong with vagueness. We have to have some vague words in our language as well as some more specific words. For instance, to tell someone that a room is "large" is vague compared to telling him that the dimensions of the room are $12 \times 120 \times 120$ feet—yet "large" conveys information better than the specifics would. Similarly, to say that the sun rose today around 6:00 A.M. is perfectly clear, yet it is relatively more vague than to say that the horizon of the earth lowered to reveal the sun at precisely 5:58:45 A.M., Eastern Daylight Time, as viewed from Athens, Georgia.

Some of the parables of Jesus are very specific, so specific as to be virtual allegories (such as the Parable of the Wedding Feast, Matthew 22:1-13), while others are more vague or general. This is also true of the stories of the Old Testament. Some events are clearly and pointedly symbolic and typological, while some are only vaguely and generally so.

We have to explain this in order to distance ourselves from the "interpretive minimalism" that has come to characterize evangelical commentaries on Scripture in recent years. We do not need some specific New Testament verse to "prove" that a given Old Testament story has symbolic dimensions. Rather, such symbolic dimensions are presupposed in the very fact that man is the image of God. Thus, we ought not be afraid to hazard a guess at the wider prophetic meanings of Scripture narratives, as we consider how they image the ways of God.

Such a "maximalist" approach as this puts us more in line with the kind of interpretation used by the Church Fathers. It seems dangerous, because it is not readily evident what kinds of checks and balances are to be employed in such an approach.

Do the five loaves and two fishes represent the five books of Moses and the Old and New Testaments? Almost certainly not. What, however, is our check on such an interpretation? We have to say that the check and balance on interpretation is the whole rest of Scripture and of theology. As time goes along, and we learn more and more, our interpretations will become refined. If we do not plunge in and try now, however, that day of refinement will never come.

Let me take an example now. In Judges 1:11-15 we have the story of Othniel and Achsah. The characters here are the Enemy (giants), the Father (Caleb), the Son (Othniel), the Daughter (Achsah), and two other factors: springs of water and a donkey. The Son destroys the Enemy in order to win the Bride from the Father. Can we see a *vague* image of the gospel here? Certainly; it fairly leaps off the page. After the marriage, we find the Bride asking the Father for springs of water. Can we see in this a *vague* image of the Church asking for and receiving the Spirit? Also, we see the Bride riding on an ass, an unclean beast. Given the fact that unclean animals signify the unconverted nations (Acts 10, 11), and that the false Bride of Revelation is seen riding on the back of the Beast (Rev. 17:3), can we see in this a *vague* picture of the Church riding on and dominating the heathen world? I think so.

These are *vague* images, snapshots of truth as it were. It would be stretching matters to try to make this story into a prophetic type in the full sense, but at the same time we ought not to blind ourselves to the possibility that a more general picture of the kingdom of God is presented here. Without any doubt, the story of Othniel and Achsah is designed to picture for us the winning of the kingdom, and the blessings that come to the righteous after the kingdom is won. In a general way, this is parallel to the work of Christ in winning the kingdom, and the blessings that come to the Church afterwards. Given this *general* truth, we are invited to inspect the passage more closely to see more specific parallels, as I did above.

One does not burn at the stake for interpretations such as this. At the same time, we would not be doing our duty to the text if we did not at least give some reflection to them. In this commentary, I shall be interpreting the text "maximally." The reader must consider the ideas I throw out, and if he finds that some are not really well supported, or not credible, that is fine. The important thing is to engage in the interpretive discussion, and strive for a fuller understanding of the prophecies before us.

The second "secret" is to keep an eye on the interaction between God and man. We ask three questions:

1. What is God's Word of promise and command?
2. What is man's response (rebellion or faithfulness)?
3. What is God's Word of evaluation (judgment or blessing)?

Every Biblical narrative contains all three elements, at least by implication. Sometimes the Word of promise/command is not expressed, because it is contained in the Law, which is the background for all the later books of the Bible. Every promise is a command, for the faithful man knows that he needs to pursue the blessing in the promise; and every command is a promise, for God will always bless those who submit to His commands. We then come to man's response. Men are either faithful or rebellious — sometimes a mixture of the two. Then, third, we come to God's evaluation or judgment, which entails either curse or blessing.

This threefold action underlies every narrative in Scripture. Adam was given a command/promise. He rebelled. God came to judge him. Humanity as a whole is given a command/promise from God. Human history as a whole is the response of humanity. The Last Judgment is the final evaluation made by God. Abram was given a command: move to Canaan. Abram obeyed. After he arrived in Canaan, God met him and blessed him — and gave him his next orders, which Abram obeyed, and God blessed him and then gave him his next orders, which he obeyed, etc., etc.

The third "secret" is to take note of the larger covenant-historical context of the book. The Bible presents one basic story over and over again, with variations each time, designed for our instruction. This is the story of creation, fall, decline, judgment, and re-creation. This pattern happens in three very large historical sweeps during the Old Covenant. The first occurrence is the creation of the world, the fall of Adam, the decline recorded in Genesis 6, the judgment of the Flood, and the re-creation in Noah.

The second occurrence of this pattern in its large form begins with the re-creation of the world after the Flood. This re-creation takes the same form as the first creation: First the wider world is made (Gen. 1; Gen. 10, the nations), and then the sanctuary is set up (Gen. 2, Eden; Gen. 12, call of Abram). The creation section continues until Israel is fully settled in the land, when David finally conquers all of it. Then comes the fall, with Solomon, and a progressive decline until the Exile, when the new Adams and Eves are once again cast out of God's sanctuary. The re-creation comes with Daniel and Ezra.

The third occurrence of this pattern begins with the re-creation of the world under Daniel, and the re-establishment of the sanctuary by Ezra. The big fall comes when God's people crucify the Lord of Glory. The decline continues until A.D. 70, and issues in the destruction of the sanctuary. The final, third re-creation is, thus, the Church, which is permanent.

I have identified these three large occurrences of the pattern by using the rule of the sanctuary. In spite of all the ups and downs in Israel's history, they were not cast out of the land until Nebuchadnezzar destroyed Jerusalem. Thus, from Abraham to Nebuchadnezzar is one large history. Accordingly, the first three "days" of history have at their centers three sanctuaries: Eden, the first Tabernacle/Temple, and the second (Ezra's) Temple. Christ's death in the third cycle (on the third "day") broke this cycle forever. In spite of her ups and downs, the history of the Church will be one of progressive re-creation and culmination.

Now, within the second great occurrence of this pattern (from Abraham to the Exile), there are three smaller manifestations of the pattern:

Basic pattern No. 2a:
  Creation: Abraham to Exodus
  Fall and Decline: Wilderness
  Judgment: Death of that generation
  Re-creation: Death of Aaron, as high priest, enabling people to leave wilderness "city of refuge" and once again take possession of their lands (Num. 20:29 and 21:1ff.)

Basic pattern No. 2b:
  Creation: Joshua and the conquest

Fall: Judges chapter 1
Decline: book of Judges
Judgment: capture of the Ark at the time of Samson,
    Samuel, and Ruth (I develop this in detail in chapter 12 of
    this book)
Re-creation: the return of the Ark

Basic pattern No. 2c:
    Creation: Samuel and David
    Fall: Solomon, who breaks all the laws for kings (compare
        Deuteronomy 17:16f. with 1 Kings 10:14ff., 26ff.; 11:1ff.)
    Decline: the two monarchies
    Judgment: the destruction of Jerusalem and the Exile
    Re-creation: Ezra, Nehemiah

Throughout the Bible, there are smaller manifestations of
this pattern as well. Our concern in this third "secret" of interpretation is to note the position of the book of Judges in the
overall sweep of redemptive history. Judges records the fall,
decline, and judgment of Israel, and also (in Samson and in the
last chapter) the beginnings of re-creation. This is an important
structure for understanding the book.

The fourth "secret" of interpretation is to pay close attention
to the specific details in the text. God does not waste words.
God has absolute superintendence of events, and every detail
recorded in the text is to be pondered for significance. Judges
9:53, for instance, does not say, "Someone threw a stone and it
hit Abimelech so that he was dying." Rather, it says, "A certain
woman threw an upper millstone on Abimelech's head, crushing
his skull." Every detail is important, as we shall see in chapter 8
of this study: that it was a woman, that it was a stone, that it
was a millstone, that it hit and crushed his head.

Similarly, numbers are usually important as symbols in the
text. Ancient writers always used numbers symbolically, and it
strains credulity to think that the writers of the Bible did not do
so. People today don't think of numbers symbolically, but in the
history of the world, modern man is a great exception on this
point. To be sure, the numbers are also literally true, but since
God superintends all events, we are certainly invited to consider
the deeper significance of the number patterns in the text.

The writings in the Bible are carefully constructed literary masterpieces. Failure to keep that fact in mind leads to sloppy interpretation. (Undoubtedly there is a fair share of sloppy work in this present commentary, but let us agree at the outset that we shall at least try to be as careful as possible.) If something is repeated in the text, it is repeated for a reason. If someone's name is given, or omitted (as with Samson's mother), there is a reason. If attention is called to specific numbers, there is a reason. In other words, a "host of 7000 men" is not interpretively the same as a "large host of men." Details are important.

By keeping these four "secrets" in mind, we can have a God-centered approach to the message of Judges. Primarily, after all, these are not moral tales of what men did rightly or wrongly. Primarily they are stories about how God deals with man, in judgment and redemption. The interplay between God and man is the heart of history.

So, as we retell these stories, we shall be looking at their prophetic meaning. What did they mean to the people of that time? What lessons were they supposed to draw from the text? And what lessons are we to draw, as well?

Overviews of Judges

Let us now turn to an overview of the book, in terms of its larger structure. There are several interlaced structuring devices in Judges.

First of all, the stories recounted in Judges come in five sets of pairs. My guess is that this arrangement is designed to exemplify the Biblical doctrine that any matter is established only "at the mouth of two or three witnesses" (Dt. 19:15). This type of pairing or doubling is quite common in the Bible, and probably for this reason. God is Three and One, and He always gives two or three testimonies to Himself.

The following is an outline and overview of Judges, in terms of these pairs.

    I. Two Introductions:
       A. From Conquest to Compromise (1:1–2:5)
       B. Principles of Chastisement (2:6–3:6)

   II. Two Exemplary Judges:
       A. Othniel (3:7-11)
       B. Ehud (3:12-30)

III. Two Unlikely Judges:
   A. Deborah, a woman (4:1–5:31)
   B. Gideon, a youth (6:1–9:57)
      1. Gideon's triumphs (6:1–8:28)
      2. Gideon's fall and the beginning of the polemic against kingship (8:29–9:57)

(Notice that Psalm 83:9-12 and Isaiah 9:1-4 put the Deborah and Gideon stories together.)

IV. Two Compromised Judges:
   A. Jephthah, the half-breed (10:1–12:15)
      1. Jephthah's sin of desiring the crown (11:1-40)
      2. Jephthah's righteous acts (12:1-7)
   B. Samson, the Nazirite (13:1–16:31)
      1. Samson's birth (13)
      2. Samson's evangelistic work (14–15)
      3. Samson's fall (16)

(Notice that the story of Jephthah is bracketed with notices about minor judges (10:1-5; 12:8-15), which illustrate the temptation to kingship. Notice also that the Jephthah and Samson stories are inversions one of another: Jephthah's righteous acts come after his fall, while Samson's fall comes after his righteous acts.)

V. Two Appendices
   A. The Levites fail to guard the worship of Israel (17–18) (See 3:7 — idolatry)
   B. The Levites fail to guard the morality of Israel (19–21) (See 3:6 — whoredom)

Such is the simplest way to outline the book. There is a second way to do it, which brings out the two-witness aspect even more fully. Beginning with Ehud, at least, each section introduces a theme that is taken up by the next section, as follows:

Ehud and Deborah: In both stories we have deliverance from the enemy by an assassinating hand. In both stories the head of the serpent is crushed by the Messianic hero or heroine, and then the armies of God follow after with a mopping up operation. (Cf. 3:27 and 4:14). Ehud recaptured the "City of Palm Trees," and Deborah sat as judge under a palm tree.

Deborah and Gideon: In both stories we have deliverance by subordinates when leaders default. In both stories, when the wicked are defeated, the sun rises (5:31; 8:13).

Gideon and Jephthah: Here we have two stories showing a desire to establish a false kingship; and both Abimelech and Jephthah were halfbreeds. A humanistic kingship grows out of a halfbreed faith.

Jephthah and Samson: In both stories, character flaws prevent effective leadership and social progress. In both stories we have rebellion against and betrayal of God's anointed leader.

Samson and Appendix 1: These two stories are linked by having the same setting, and by the betrayal either of the Lord Himself or of the Lord's Anointed for 1100 pieces of silver.

Appendices 1 & 2: In both of these the underlying problem is the default on the part of the Levite-guardians of Israel.

A third overall structure in Judges is seen in the middle section of the book. There is a progressive rebellion against God, seen in a progressive refusal to follow His Anointed:

Ehud: No problem following the Anointed.
Deborah: Barak must be persuaded to follow the Lord's command.
Gideon: Most of the tribes follow him, but Ephraim shows rebellion.
Jephthah: Ephraim rebels outright and is punished.
Samson: Judah is no better than Ephraim, and delivers the Messiah over to the enemy. In fact, as the royal tribe, Judah possesses higher privileges, and so her sin is greater than Ephraim's.

Fourth, there is a general parallel between the first section of Judges, and the outline of the rest of the book. As we shall see, the first introduction to Judges shows Israel beginning well, but progressively compromising until God judges them, and then grants them healing through sacrifice. Similarly, the rest of the book of Judges shows the same pattern: beginning well (Othniel, Ehud), progressive decline (as noted above), final judgment (the second appendix), followed by redemption and new life (the last chapter of the book). As we shall see when we get to it, the second appendix picks up on language and themes from the first introduction, so that these two sections bracket the book of Judges.

Theology of Judges

In terms of its "theology proper," the book of Judges presents God almost exclusively in two aspects. The first is as the LORD. God told Moses in Exodus 6:3, "I appeared to Abraham, Isaac, and Jacob, as God Almighty, but by My name, LORD, I did not make Myself known to them." This does not mean that the patriarchs did not use the name YHWH or LORD, but that God had not made clear to them its meaning. God appeared to the patriarchs as God Almighty, the God Who creates covenants and makes promises. At the exodus, God appeared to Israel as the LORD, the God Who continues ("establishes") His covenant and who keeps His promises. Exodus 6:6-8 gives a detailed exposition of the meaning of the name LORD: The LORD is the one who brings His people out of bondage (v. 6), who marries them (v. 7), and who gives them the land promised to them (v. 8).

The name LORD, then, has to do with God's faithfulness in the face of man's faithlessness. It has to do with the land God promised, and the conquest of that land. It has to do with God's marriage to Israel. It has to do with bondage and deliverance. These are all major themes in Judges, and this is why "LORD" is the name for God used here. Thus, the book of Judges as a whole is a large-scale exposition of the meaning of the name LORD.

The other term used to refer to God in Judges is "Angel of the LORD." According to Exodus 24:20ff., the Angel is the one who goes before the people, as Captain of the LORD's host, to lead them into the land. The Angel of the LORD, thus, appeared to Joshua at the beginning of the conquest (Joshua 5:13ff.). In Judges, God manifests Himself as Angel when He judges the people at Gilgal for their faithlessness in the conquest (Jud. 2:1-4), when He appears to Gideon to summon him to war for the land (Jud. 6:11-22), and when he appears to the wife of Manoah to announce the birth of Samson the deliverer (Jud. 13:3-21).

*   *   *   *   *   *   *   *   *   *

This material was originally presented to the Adult Sunday School Class at St. Paul Presbyterian Church, Jackson, Mississippi, in the summer and fall of 1978, while I was a student at

Reformed Theological Seminary. Before finishing the book, I transferred to Westminster Theological Seminary in Philadelphia. My studies in Judges were again presented, this time finishing the book, to the members of Trinity Presbyterian Church of Fairfax, Virginia, in the summer and fall of 1979. It was presented a third time to the Adult Sunday School Class of Calvary Presbyterian Church, Glenside, Pennsylvania, in the spring of 1980, but I graduated and left the area before I finished the book. A final complete presentation was made to the members of Westminster Presbyterian Church of Tyler, Texas, during 1980 and 1981. Tapes of these lectures have been available from Geneva Ministries, 708 Hamvasy Lane, Tyler, TX 75701. The reader should realize that I have changed my mind significantly at several points, and the tapes have now been withdrawn from circulation.

I hereby thank the rulers of these four churches for giving me the opportunity to lecture through Judges, and I here thank the members of each of those classes for their encouragement. Particularly, I thank Pastor and Mrs. Robert Thoburn, of Trinity Presbyterian Church, for giving me the time, during the summer of 1980, to write a first draft of this book, and for letting me use one of their offices and typewriters for my labors. Thanks also to David Chilton, Michael Gilstrap, and Gary North for reading the manuscript and making valuable specific suggestions. Finally I should like to thank Oakton Reformed Fellowship (Oakton, Virginia) for their help in the publication of this book.

This book is dedicated to my mother, Sarah Burrell Jordan, who read these stories to me as a child, and whom I regard as a Deborah, a mother in Israel.

CONQUEST, COMPROMISE, JUDGMENT, AND RESTORATION (Judges 1:1–2:5)

There are two introductions to the book of Judges. The first is an historical introduction, showing the great works of God, and the not so great works of man. The second introduction is a thematic one.

This first section in the Book of Judges displays very obviously the three-fold pattern of Biblical narrative. First, there is God's command to conquer Canaan. Then, there is a whole series of human responses. Finally, in 2:1-5, there comes the evaluation of the Lord, judgment and restoration:

I. The Command/Promise of the Lord (1:1-2)

II. The Response of Israel (1:3-36)
    A. Judah (1:3-21)
        1. Initial Faithfulness (1:3-17)
        2. Progressive Failure (1:18-21)
    B. Joseph (1:22-29)
        1. Initial Faithfulness (1:22-26)
        2. Progressive Failure (1:27-29)
    C. The Other Tribes: Progressive Failure (1:30-36)
        1. The First Degree of Compromise (1:30)
        2. The Second Degree of Compromise (1:31-33)
        3. The Third Degree of Compromise (1:34-36)

III. The Evaluation of the Lord (2:1-5)

The Command/Promise of the Lord (1:1-2)

1. And it came about after the death of Joshua that the sons of Israel inquired of the LORD, saying, "Who shall go up first for us against the Canaanites, to fight against them?"

2. And the LORD said, "Judah shall go up; behold, I have given the land into his hand."

As Judges opens, God has already commanded Israel to conquer Canaan. Judges is continuous with Joshua, as seen by the fact that it begins with the word "and." Now, at the beginning of the book, the people inquire as to which tribe should lead the war against the Canaanites. The Lord replies that Judah should go up first, "for I have given the land into his hand." (The procedure of this inquiry is set out in Numbers 27:18-21. They consulted with the high priest, who wore the "ephod." The ephod had a breastplate of jewels, one for each tribe. Scholars think that God caused a particular jewel to light up, or maybe heat up, in answer to a question about which tribe was to do this or that. Numbers 27:21 forbad Israel to go into battle without consulting the ephod first.)

Was it right for God to command the destruction of the Canaanites? Yes, because the iniquity of the Canaanites was by that time filled up, in accordance with the prophecy of Genesis 15:16, and it was time for them to be wiped off the face of the earth, just as the Flood had earlier done to a wicked civilization that had filled up its cup of wrath. God's command was that the Canaanites should be completely driven out or slaughtered; one way or another completely removed from the land (Ex. 23:27-33; Dt. 20:16-18). The initial conquest of the land under Joshua had been completed, and the land had been parcelled out to the tribes. What was left was an extended mopping-up operation, to clear the land completely of the human vermin of the Canaanites.

Thus, as the book of Judges opens, we have the Word of command/promise from God: "Destroy the Canaanites, take the land completely, and I will be with you to protect you and to ensure your success." How will Israel respond to this Word from God?

Predictably, God says that the royal tribe, Judah, should go up first (Gen. 49:10). The royal tribe, from which David and later Jesus would come, is to lead the fray. Indeed, the text says that the *land* has been given into his hand, indicating the preeminent place of Judah as the ruling tribe over all the land, through the coming King. Thus, we turn first to the activities of Judah, after the death of Joshua.

The Response of Israel:
Judah's Initial Faithfulness (1:3-17)

The Salvation of Simeon

3. Then Judah said to Simeon his brother, "Come up with me into my lot, that we may fight against the Canaanites, and I in turn will go with you into your lot."

Simeon goes along with Judah. There is a specific reason for this. Simeon and Levi had been cursed for their sin to be scattered throughout the land, and not to have their own special tribal land (Gen. 34; Dt. 22:22-29; Gen. 49:5-7). In the case of Levi, this curse was turned into a blessing, as they became the priests (guardians) of Israel and dwelt in the Levitical cities (Dt. 33:8-11); but to this point, no salvation has come for Simeon.

By identifying themselves with the royal tribe, however, Simeon finds salvation. The blessings that come to the tribe of Judah will come to Simeon as well. (Indeed, this had already been set out in Joshua 19:1-9, where it is stated that Simeon's land was taken out of Judah's territory.) Later in history, Simeon will be part of the southern kingdom of Judah, and thus will be spared the Assyrian captivity.

It is important to consider, however briefly, the specific nature of the sin committed by Levi and Simeon in Genesis 34. They took the sign of circumcision, which was a sign of their calling as priests to the nations, and turned it into a weapon against the nations. They turned the sword of wrath against members of the covenant. They put personal family feelings before their covenantal duties. Notice how Levi and Simeon are called to repent of these sins. In Exodus 32, Levi is called to put his covenantal duties before his feelings for his brethren (as this is pointed out in Deuteronomy 33:9). Here in Judges 1, Simeon is called upon to judge righteous judgment in fully destroying the Canaanite city of Hormah (v. 17, see our comments on this verse below).

The Conquest of the World

4. And Judah went up, and the LORD gave the Canaanites and the Perizzites into their hands; and they smote 10,000 men at Bezek.
5. And they found Adoni-Bezek [The Lord of Bezek] in

Bezek, and fought against him, and they smote the Canaanites and the Perizzites.

6. But Adoni-Bezek fled; and they pursued him and caught him and cut off his thumbs and big toes.

7. And Adoni-Bezek said, "Seventy kings with their thumbs and big toes cut off used to gather up scraps from under my table; as I have done, so God has repaid me." So they brought him to Jerusalem and he died there.

The first victory was over Adoni-Bezek. *Adoni* means Lord, so this was the Lord of Bezek. It is thought that *bezek* means "lightning flash" or even "sunrise." If so, then Adoni-Bezek was a Jovian figure, a picture of the Satanic ruler of this age.

This points to something that is fairly obvious in this paragraph as a whole, which is its typical/symbolic character. Adoni-Bezek ruled over seventy kings. The number seventy is used throughout Scripture as the number of the nations of the world (starting with the seventy nations listed in Genesis 10). Adoni-Bezek is here presented as a type of the world-ruler, later portrayed as a beast in Daniel and Revelation. The *initial* victory is over Satan; all else is a mopping up operation.

In connection with this, 10,000 men were slain. This is probably a round number. Its symbolic significance is apparent when we remember that ten is the number for totality in Scripture. Ten thousand indicates a total, complete defeat and liquidation of the forces of Adoni-Bezek.

Perfect retribution is measured out against Adoni-Bezek. According to the Biblical principle, "an eye for an eye" (Ex. 21:22-25; Lev. 24:17-22), just as he had done to others, so it was done to him. Adoni-Bezek is forced to confess to the justice of this: "As I have done, so God has repaid me." On the last day, every tongue will confess to the justice measured out by Jesus Christ, the greatest son of Judah. Sadly, most commentators on Judges present this as an act of unwarranted cruelty on Judah's part; but the Bible teaches it in principle, and the text says that it was an act of Divine justice. Let us beware of criticizing God!

Why chop off thumbs and big toes? Well, just try to pick up something with your fingers alone, and try to imagine what it would be like to try and walk without your big toe (since your foot is basically a flexible tripod). In order to symbolize his destruction of the dominion of the seventy kings, Adoni-Bezek had crippled their hands and feet. (Also, it is impossible to wield a spear or shoot a bow without your thumb.)

An additional message is seen here. Israel is the savior of the "seventy nations of the world." The gentiles are delivered from Satan's grasp by the actions of the priestly nation.

It was the Lord who gave the victory, according to verse 4, and thus it was to the Lord's city that Adoni-Bezek was brought to die. This brings us to the importance of Jerusalem.

The Conquest of Jerusalem

8. And the sons of Judah fought against Jerusalem and captured it and struck it with the edge of the sword and set the city on fire.

Jerusalem was already known to the people of Israel. Melchizedek had been king and priest there (Gen. 14:18ff.), and Abram had paid tithes to him. Thus, Abram had acknowledged the importance of Jerusalem, and its centrality as the home of the king. Judah, the royal tribe, could easily deduce from this that God intended them to take Jerusalem, and make it the capital of Israel. Thus, the text moves immediately to a description of the sack of Jerusalem.

Note that it is after the defeat of the world-ruler, the enemy of God, that God builds His city. This pattern shows up over and over in the Bible, and nowhere more fully than in the New Testament, when the New Jerusalem is built up after and upon the defeat of the dragon. For symbolic reasons, they brought Adoni-Bezek, defeated by God, to God's city in order that they might put him to death there.

Jerusalem, the royal city, was initially captured by Judah, the royal tribe, even though it was located in the territory of Benjamin (Josh. 18:28). Later on, Jerusalem would fall back into the hands of the Jebusites, and it would be David, the royal person from the royal tribe of Judah, who would finally conquer and hold Jerusalem (2 Sam. 5:6ff.).

The city was set on fire. Why? Because fire is the sign of the wrath of God. We shall see this more fully when we come to verse 17 below. For now, the use of fire brought about a whole burnt sacrifice, completely consuming the evil city, making room for the new city of God.

The Conquest of Hebron

9. And afterward the sons of Judah went down to fight against the Canaanites living in the hill country and in the south country and in the lowland.

10. So Judah went against the Canaanites who lived in Hebron (now the name of Hebron formerly was Kiriath-Arba); and they struck Sheshai and Ahiman and Talmai.

Verse nine is designed to impress upon us Judah's initial faithfulness. They fought Canaanites wherever they were: hill country, south country, lowlands. That they were not entirely successful appears only later. Right now, Scripture wants us to see that they started well, faithfully following out God's orders to the letter.

Verse ten shows three aspects of the conquest. First of all, Hebron was a sanctuary city. Abram had settled there, and it had been a place of sanctuary for him. Indeed, he had left Hebron to rescue Lot, and had brought him back there (Gen. 13:18–14:24). The Israelites, accordingly, were told to make Hebron one of the Cities of Refuge (Josh. 20:7). To conquer Hebron, thus, was to establish sanctuary, a place of refuge, in the land.

Second, the earlier name of Hebron is given: Kiriath-Arba. *Kiriath* means "city," and *Arba* means "four," and so this could mean "the four cities," indicating that Hebron was a metropolis that had engulfed four towns. Arba, however, was the personal name of the man who spawned the race of giants known as Anakim. In Joshua 14:15, Arba is called the greatest man among the Anakim, and in Joshua 15:13 he is called the father of Anak. So, Kiriath-Arba could also mean "the city of Arba." Puns are common in the Bible, however, and so possibly we should allow both meanings to stand. If Hebron were a metropolis, as we suppose, then the second aspect of the conquest shown in this verse is that Judah was taking the large cities.

The third aspect, then, is the destruction of giants. The three tribes mentioned, Sheshai, Ahiman, and Talmai, were descendants of Arba, and were giants (Num. 13:22). It was these very tribes that had frightened the Israelites when they came out of Egypt, so that the entire generation was prevented from entering the promised land (Num. 13:28ff.). No such fear stops faithful Judah now, however.

The association of giants with Hebron tells that if we want to have sanctuary, we have to destroy the giants. God gives no refuge to those who do not war against sin.

The Story of Othniel and Achsah

11. Then from there he went against the inhabitants of Debir. Now the name of Debir formerly was Kiriath-Sepher.

12. And Caleb said, "The one who attacks Kiriath-Sepher and captures it, I will even give him my daughter Achsah for a wife."

13. And Othniel the son of Kenaz, Caleb's younger brother, captured it; so he gave him his daughter Achsah for a wife.

14. Then it came about when she came to him, that she persuaded him to ask her father for a field. Then she alighted from her donkey, and Caleb said to her, "What do you wish for yourself?"

15. And she said to him, "Give me a blessing: Since you have given me the land of the south country, give me also springs of water." So Caleb gave her the upper springs and the lower springs.

Here is one of the famous, romantic love stories in the Bible, found also in Joshua 15:13-19, as if to tell us that it is so important that it should be told twice. The setting is Debir. *Debir* means "word." The city was formerly Kiriath-Sepher, which means "city of books." In other words, Debir was a large library city. It was where the clay tablets were stored. It was the repository for the philosophical books of the Canaanites, their genealogical records, their trading records, treaties, land ownership documents, and much more. To destroy this place was to destroy their entire civilization, as can well be imagined. Thus, Debir was well guarded, for an entire civilization depended on the preservation of its books.

Caleb and Joshua were the only two spies who had advocated conquering the land of Canaan (Num. 13, 14), and as a result, they and they alone were allowed to enter the land. It was the giants who had frightened the people away, and we can well imagine what was on Caleb's mind all those thirty-eight long, wearying years of wandering in the desert: Just wait until I get my hands on those giants! Thus, when Joshua offered to let

Caleb have the pick of the land, Caleb chose the land of the giants (Josh. 14:6-12), and gave as his reason that he had been thinking about it all those years (v. 12). Indeed, it was Caleb who led the conquest of Hebron (Josh. 14:13-15; Jud. 1:20).

Now we ought to note that Caleb was not a racial Israelite, but a convert from the Kenizzites (Gen. 15:19; Josh. 14:6). This is remarkable in itself, showing the plenteous grace of God. Like Uzziah later on, Caleb the convert was a better soldier of God than were many who had been born into the kingdom. Caleb's father was Jephunneh (Josh. 14:6). Jephunneh had a younger son, Kenaz, named apparently for the tribal ancestor, and his son, Caleb's nephew, was Othniel.

Caleb offered to marry his daughter Achsah to whoever conquered Debir. This was a shrewd move, ensuring a worthy son-in-law for himself and a worthy husband for Achsah. Caleb knew that only in the strength of the Lord could a man conquer Debir, and so he assured a Godly husband for his daughter.

And so, in a vignette, we have a great love story. Othniel, to win the bride, destroyed the city. No Medieval dragon-slayer ever did more for his princess. And of course, this romance is but an emblem of the gospel, for it was the Greater Othniel who conquered the wicked word of this world, in order to win His holy bride.

The destruction of Debir is one more revelation of what it means to conquer Canaan. The words, the philosophy, of the Canaanites must be destroyed, and replaced with the Word of God. In America today, as I write this, it is more and more the case that the City of Books is in the hands of the heathen. A few years ago the United States Supreme Court passed the Thor Power Tool Decision. The effect of this decision is that publishers must pay a tax on their book inventories each and every year, so that books are nowadays published in small amounts, and sold off as soon as possible. The only kinds of books that stay in print year after year are, for the most part, trash. This action on the part of the Federal Government is a tremendous attack on the true freedom of the press, yet there has been little outcry against it from the establishment. Recently, the Presbyterian and Reformed Publishing Company of Phillipsburg, N. J., had its non-profit status removed (since the government decided it was making "too much money"). The result is that this small, scholarly publisher is now under the rules of the Thor Power Tool Decision, and must pay inventory taxes. Had this attack on P&R not been reversed (which it was), I doubt if they could have lasted until 1990. Many Christian publishers have already had to shut down. At the same time as this, however, pornography is more and more rampant in our society. Christians definitely need to recapture the City of Books.

The second half of the story deals not with conquest but with occupation — faithful occupation. Caleb had given Achsah, and through her, Othniel, a south land, which would not have been very well watered. Achsah asks her father for water, so that the land would be fruitful, and Caleb gives it to her. Water is important in Scripture, in that the Garden of Eden was watered by springs, which flowed together into the river of Eden. Here we see the Edenic principle coming to the forefront, as it does so often in the Bible. The family property of Achsah and Othniel becomes a miniature Garden of Eden, fruitful and well watered. Such is the promise to every faithful man and wife. Such also is the promise for the Bride of Christ, for we may go to our Heavenly Father and ask for whatever we need to carry out the wonderful tasks He has given us.

The gift of springs of water, making the ground fruitful, is specifically called a blessing. Blessings are not only of the invisible, moral sort; they are also physical, such things as make for a good, productive, Godly life.

Human life is created to image the life of God (Gen. 1:26f.). Thus, we should not be surprised to see some very general, relatively more vague, images of the gospel in the stories recounted in the Old Testament. When a father sets a task for a son, or gives a gift to a daughter, this images the way God has acted toward His Son, and toward His daughter (the Church). While it would be pressing matters to insist on a full-blown typology here, there is certainly some imaging going on in this story. Caleb wins Achsah by destroying the giants, just as Christ won the Church. The Father gives the bride to the faithful Groom. Finally, the bride (Church) asks for water (the Spirit), and this additional blessing is given as well (Pentecost).

Blessings for the Kenites

16. And the sons of the Kenite, Moses' father-in-law, went
up from the City of Palm Trees [Jericho] with the sons of Judah,
to the wilderness of Judah which is in the south of Arad; and
they went and lived with the people.

The Kenites were part of the Midianites, descendants of
Abraham (Gen. 25:2). Moses had married into a Kenite tribe,
one presided over by Jethro. (Taking wives from outside Israel is
condemned when it involves idolatry, but when the woman con-
verts it is a form of evangelism, picturing the incorporation of
the gentiles into the Bride. We shall see this again when we get to
Samson. In this case, Jethro was a faithful worshipper of the
God of Abraham already, so no conversion was needed.)

Moses had persuaded part of Jethro's family to go to the
land of milk and honey with Israel (Num. 10:29-32). Since
Moses was of the tribe of Levi, and Levi had no inheritance in
Canaan, it was necessary for the Kenites to associate with
another tribe. They chose to associate with the royal tribe,
Judah. They broke camp at Jericho (the City of Palm Trees, 2
Chron. 28:15), and moved into Judahite territory, and lived with
the people of God there.

Here is a miniature picture of salvation. Those outside Israel
can either join with God's people and be saved, or war with
God's people and be destroyed.

Hormah

17. Then Judah went with Simeon his brother, and they
struck the Canaanites living in Zephath, and utterly destroyed it.
So the name of the city was called Hormah.

Now we see Judah making good her bargain with Simeon.
The destruction of Canaanite Zephath was total, so that the
place was called Hormah. This is not the only "Hormah," for we
read in Numbers 21:1-3 of a place that was also "devoted to
destruction," and as a result was called Hormah.

Hormah means "placed under the ban, totally destroyed."
To be placed under the ban is to be devoted to death. Just as the
Nazirite was devoted to God in life (for instance, Samson,
Samuel), so the banned person or city was devoted wholly to

God in death. To put under the ban means to curse and to devote to total destruction.

The preeminent example of a city devoted to total destruction is Jericho, the story of which is recorded in Joshua 6:15-19. Everything living was to be killed, all the treasures brought to the house of God, and the city was to be burned with fire. No personal booty was allowed.

More light is shed on this matter in Deuteronomy 13:12-18. The apostate city is to be banned, and "then you shall gather all its booty into the middle of its open square and burn the city and all its booty with fire as a *whole burnt sacrifice* to the LORD your God; and it shall be a ruin forever. It shall never be rebuilt" (v. 16).

From this we learn that it was God's fire, lit by Himself from heaven (Lev. 9:24; 2 Chron. 7:1), kept burning perpetually on the altar, which was used to ignite the city placed under the ban. (See also Gen. 22:6 and 1 Ki. 18:38.) The fact that God starts His fire shows that the sacrifice is *His* sacrifice, the sacrifice that He Himself provides to propitiate His own fiery wrath. Man has no hand in it, and only an ordained priest may handle it. Man is impotent in his salvation, so that man cannot even light the sacrificial fire. If he dares to do so, God destroys him (Lev. 10:1-2).

All men stand on God's altar. Those who accept God's Substitute, the very Lamb of God, Jesus Christ, can step off the altar and escape the fire. Jesus takes the fire for them. He becomes the whole burnt sacrifice. Those who refuse the Substitute, however, are left on the altar, and are burnt up by the fire of God. (See Gen. 19:24; Rev. 18:8; Rev. 20:14f.; and for further study, Heb. 12:29; Ex. 3:2-5; Heb. 12:18; Num. 11:1-3; Num. 16:35; Num. 21:6; Gen. 3:25; 2 Pet. 3:9-12; Rev. 8:3-5).

Thus, the destruction of Hormah was a priestly act, issuing from the flaming swords of the cherubic (priestly) guardians of the land, a revelation of God's direct fiery judgment against the wicked. Not every city was to be destroyed in this fashion, but certain ones were, as types of the wrath of God. This horrible judgment, introduced here at the beginning of Judges, comes again in Judges 20:40, when it is an apostate Israelite city that is burnt up as a sacrifice to God.

As mentioned above, here we see Simeon reversing his sin of Genesis 34. There he inverted his priestly calling, bringing judgment against those who had converted to the faith. Here he exercises his calling properly.

Summary

We have now reached the end of the section that details Judah's initial faithfulness. It would be good here to draw together some conclusions, before proceeding further. First, we see three fundamental ways in which God deals with His enemies. They are dispossession (driving the Canaanites out), retribution (perfect justice, an eye for an eye), and utter sacrificial destruction (seen at Hormah).

Second, we see a series of types or pictures of what it means to conquer Canaan. Since the great commission tells the Church today to "disciple all nations," we can learn lessons from this. Each of the conquests is a picture of some central aspect of wickedness that must be vanquished. Each conquest shows us what Christ (the royal Person, pictured by the royal tribe) has already done for us, and what we are to do in applying His work to our world:

Simeon—Christ invites those under the curse to join with Him, and find salvation. That is our task as well, for we also face world rulers, apostate churches (false Jerusalems), and giants.

Bezek—Christ destroyed the Prince of this World, and so do we (Rom. 16:20). He measured out perfect justice, and so must we.

Jerusalem—Christ destroyed the Old Jerusalem in 70 A.D., and established the New Jerusalem, His Church. It is our task to hold it.

Hill country, south country, lowland—Christ conquered the whole world, and now we must apply that conquest everywhere.

Hebron (Kiriath-Arba)—Christ conquered the giants, and in union with Him, no giants can stand against us. He has given us sanctuary in Him, and we must offer sanctuary to all men.

Debir (Kiriath-Sepher)—Christ cast down all philosophies and imaginations against Him, and replaced them with His Word, the true foundation of civilization; and this is our task as well.

Achsah—Christ has given his Bride a good land. We should

entreat the Father for the water (of the Spirit) needed to make it fruitful.

Kenites — Christ invites all men to join His New Israel, and that evangelistic task is ours as well.

Hormah — Christ has utterly destroyed His enemies for all time, by the application of Divine fire. The tongues of fire on Pentecost show us that it is the preaching of the gospel which applies that fire to the world today, burning away the chaff and purifying the gold.

The Response of Israel: Judah's Progressive Failure (1:18-21)

Philistines

18. And Judah took Gaza with its territory, and Ashkelon with its territory, and Ekron with its territory.

That's wonderful, but there were five Philistine cities. How about Gath and Ashdod? Joshua 15:47 makes it plain that all five of the Philistine cities were part of Judah's inheritance, but only three are listed here.

At this point, then, the story of Judah's conquests takes a subtle turn. Heretofore we have seen nothing but victories, together with a hint of the restoration of Edenic conditions among the faithful. Now, however, we begin to detect signs of failure.

Iron Chariots

19. Now the LORD was with Judah, and they took possession of the hill country; but they could not dispossess the inhabitants of the valley because they had iron chariots.

Chariots could not function in the hills, so Judah did not have to fight them there. Where the iron chariots could function, however, Judah did not succeed. In fact, all the places listed in Judges 1 are mountain places. God, however, did not limit Judah only to mountainous regions; in 1:2, God had given all the land into her hand. Moreover, as Judges 4 and 5 will show, God is fully capable of dealing with iron chariots. Thus, the problem was not the iron chariots. The problem was faith, or rather the lack of it.

In order to drive this point home, the narrator says, "Now the LORD was with Judah . . . ; *but.* . . ." God was willing, but man was faithless.

The plains were in the center of the land of promise. The continuing strength of the Canaanites here effectively divided Judah and Simeon from the rest of the tribes. Over the centuries, this isolation brought about cultural division, and caused more and more trouble until finally the two kingdoms split from one another. Thus do minor compromises grow into major troubles.

Jerusalem Lost

20. Then they gave Hebron to Caleb, as Moses had spoken; and he drove out from there the three sons of Anak.
21. But the sons of Benjamin did not drive out the Jebusites who lived in Jerusalem; so the Jebusites have lived with the sons of Benjamin in Jerusalem to this day.

These two verses are also designed as contrasts. The aged but faithful Caleb drove out the giants from Hebron, but the Benjamites did not drive the normal-sized Jebusites from Jerusalem, even after Judah had conquered it for them. Unbelievers continued to live in the holy city.

Faithlessness was the reason. This was a bad start for Benjamin, and their moral situation was to worsen until God saw fit virtually to liquidate them (Judges 19, 20).

(The phrase "to this day" indicates that Judges was composed before David conquered Jerusalem, and corroborates my thesis that Samuel most likely wrote the book.)

In summary, Judah started well, but failed to follow through. They compromised. All the same, as before we do have pictures of Christ in this passage as well:

Philistines — Christ destroyed "all five" Philistine cities, five being the number of preeminence and power.[1] This is pictured more fully by Samson later on, and the Samson story answers to the failure of Judah here in Judges 1.

---

1. On the number five, see my book, *The Law of the Covenant: An Exposition of Exodus 21–23* (Tyler, TX: Institute for Christian Economics, 1984), Appendix G, "Four and Five-fold Restitution;" and see discussion below on Judges 1:27.

High ground — Christ took the hill country, but also the lowlands as well. He conquered the whole world.

Iron chariots — Iron is a token of power, and Christ was able to break the yoke of iron that sin had put on His people. The story of Deborah in Judges 4 and 5 answers the failure of Judah here, and pictures the work of Christ in this regard.

Hebron and the Giants — mentioned here again. See the discussion above.

Jerusalem — mentioned here again. See the discussion above.

The narrative now changes focus to the tribes of Joseph.

The Response of Israel:
Joseph's Initial Faithfulness (1:22-26)

From Luz to Bethel

22. Likewise the house of Joseph went up against Bethel, and the LORD was with them.

23. And the house of Joseph spied out Bethel. Now the name of the city was formerly Luz.

24. And the spies saw a man coming out of the city, and they said to him, "Please show us the entrance to the city and we will treat you kindly."

25. So he showed them the entrance to the city, and they struck the city with the edge of the sword, but they let the man and all his family go free.

26. And the man went into the land of the Hittites and built a city and named it Luz, which is its name to this day.

Ordinarily the firstborn of the house receives both the rule over his brethren and a double portion of the inheritance. Jacob divided these two blessings, giving rulership to Judah, and the double portion to Joseph, so that the tribe of Joseph became two tribes, Ephraim and Manasseh (Gen. 48). Ordinarily Scripture refers to the tribe of Ephraim or the tribe of Manasseh. It is unusual to refer, as here, to the "house of Joseph." In this context, the initially faithful actions of the Joseph tribes are said to be the acts of Joseph, while the later failures of these tribes are said to be the acts of Manasseh and Ephraim.

Since the Joseph tribes received half of the blessings that come to the firstborn, they had a place of preeminence next to Judah. In time, Ephraim, which was ascendent over Manasseh

(Gen. 48:17ff.), came to be envious of Judah's royal preeminence. The conflict between Ephraim and Judah runs all throughout Israelite history, but we see it beginning in the book of Judges.

Beth-El means "house of God," and it was the place where God appeared to Jacob, and revealed to him Jesus Christ, the True Ladder that reaches up to heaven (Gen. 11:1-9; 28:10-22; John 1:51). Jacob had built an altar there, and had made Bethel his place of worship (Gen. 35:3ff.). Later on, the Tabernacle seems to have been placed at Bethel, at least some of the time (Jud. 20:18, 26; 1 Sam. 10:3).

In the conquest of Bethel, the Josephites used the same technique that had been used in the conquest of Jericho, in getting assistance from someone in the city. This man was surely glad to help, since the reputation of Israel must have been fearful by this time, and this was the only possibility he could have seen for saving himself. The fact that he left the land and built another city called Luz shows his desire to perpetuate the culture of Canaan, though in another place. The Cainitic culture of spiritual Babylon continued elsewhere, though driven out of God's land.

This event shows the provisional character of the Old Covenant. The victory was limited to a specific geographical area (the land of Canaan). Nonetheless, the victory of Joseph was real, in that Luz was no longer located close to Bethel, and God's people could pursue His designs in peace, undisturbed. By way of contrast, however, the New Covenant entails the conquest of the whole world, so that there is to be no place left for pagans to flee to. Every Luz is to be made a Bethel by the gospel.

When Jacob spent the night in the field outside Luz, God appeared to him, and Jacob realized that since God was there, it was the gate of heaven. Jacob stood outside the city, all alone, and pronounced that it would be called Bethel (Gen. 28:19). It was an absurd thing to do, humanly speaking. For centuries it continued to be called Luz. Here, however, Jacob's prophetic claim, made in faith, is brought to pass.

The Response of Israel:
Joseph's Progressive Failure (1:27-29)

Manasseh and Ephraim

27. But Manasseh did not take possession of Bethshean and its villages, or Taanach and its villages, or the inhabitants of Dor

and its villages, or the inhabitants of Ibleam and its villages, or the inhabitants of Megiddo and its villages; so the Canaanites persisted in living in that land.

28. And it came about when Israel became strong, that they put the Canaanites to forced labor, but they did not drive them out completely.

29. Neither did Ephraim drive out the Canaanites who were living in Gezer; so the Canaanites lived in Gezer among them.

When the house of Joseph is shown as unfaithful, they are called by the tribal names Manasseh and Ephraim. Five cities are listed as not conquered by Manasseh. Three of these towns (Taanach, Megiddo, and Dor) are named in Joshua 12, among the 31 cities there listed which precede all the other lists in Joshua, and which form the key to the whole system of the land. Four of them are listed in 1 Kings 4:11f., when Solomon strengthened the land, showing their strategic importance.

The number five in the Bible is a number of strength. It is used as the key to military formations, so that when Israel came out of Egypt, the text literally says that they marched as an army, five abreast (Ex. 13:18; and see Josh. 1:14; 4:12; Jud. 7:11; Num. 32:17). A study of the description of the Tabernacle in Exodus 25–40 shows that the number five occurs repeatedly in its dimensions, perhaps showing symbolically the army of God gathered around His throne. There are five fingers on the human hand, fingers with which to grasp. Thus, the fact that five cities are listed here is designed to show us that the Canaanites maintained a power, a grasp upon the land. They were not shaken loose.

Similarly, Ephraim did not drive out all the Canaanites from its territory. Indeed, the Canaanites were not cleaned out of Gezer until the reign of Solomon (1 Ki. 9:15-17). Gezer dominated part of the central plain, and so again the fact that it was not conquered resulted in an isolation of the southern from the northern tribes. Judges 1:19 presents this as partly Judah's fault, and here we see Ephraim also to blame.

The first degree of compromise is seen here, in that the Canaanites lived among the Israelites. During those times when Israel was strong, she reduced the Canaanites to slaves, but still did not obey God and drive them out. Moreover, such enslavement was usually by treaty or covenant. Such treaties, which establish a master-slave relationship between nations, are sometimes called "suzerainty treaties." However they are termed, Israel had been forbidden to enter into any treaties or covenants with the Canaanites (Ex. 23:32). Thus, what we have here is almost certainly not only a failure to follow out God's commands, but a direct violation of them.

The Response of Israel: The Other Tribes' Progressive Failure (1:30-36)

The First Degree of Compromise

30. Zebulun did not drive out the inhabitants of Kitron, or the inhabitants of Nahalol; so the Canaanites lived among them and became subject to forced labor.

The first degree of failure is for Canaanites to continue to live among the Israelites. We have already seen this in the case of Manasseh and Ephraim. Here it is noted of Zebulun as well.

This section, concerning the rest of the tribes, deals with Zebulun, Asher, Naphtali, and Dan. The first three tribes are the northernmost. Perhaps they are selected to show that the failure of Israel to follow through was comprehensive, stretching throughout the land.

Another aspect is that Joseph and Benjamin, the sons of Rachel, have already been mentioned. So have Judah and Simeon, sons of Leah. To round out the family, we have Zebulun (son of Leah's old age), Asher (son of Zilpah), and Naphtali and Dan (sons of Bilhah). Thus the descendants of all four wives are mentioned.

The Second Degree of Compromise

31. Asher did not drive out the inhabitants of Acco, or the inhabitants of Sidon, or of Ahlab, or of Achzib, or of Helbah, or of Aphik, or of Rehob.

32. So the Asherites lived among the Canaanites, the inhabitants of the land; for they did not drive them out.

33. Naphtali did not drive out the inhabitants of Beth-Shemesh, or the inhabitants of Beth-Anath, but lived among the Canaanites, the inhabitants of the land; and the inhabitants of Beth-Shemesh and Beth-Anath became forced labor for them.

The second degree of compromise is for the children of Israel to dwell among the Canaanites. Here apparently it is the Canaanites who predominate, even though they sometimes were reduced to forced labor.

Seven cities are listed that Asher did not conquer. Things are getting worse, for only five were listed for Manasseh. As five is the number of strength, so seven is the number of fulness. Apparently it can be said that Asher failed rather completely.

The same second degree of failure is noted regarding Naphtali, and two cities are singled out for especial mention. *Beth-Shemesh* means "House of the Sun God, Shemesh," and *Beth-Anath* means "House of the Fertility Goddess, Anath." In other words, these two cities were centers of the idolatrous cults of the Canaanites. God had specifically told Israel to "tear down the altars" of the Canaanites (Ex. 34:13). So far from this command's being obeyed, the Israelites dwelt among these idolatrous centers!

The Third Degree of Compromise

34. Then the Amorites pressed the sons of Dan into the hill country, for they did not allow them to come down to the valley;

35. Yet the Amorites persisted in living in Mount Heres, in Aijalon and in Shaalbim; but when the hand of the house of Joseph grew strong, they became forced labor.

36. And the border of the Amorites ran from the ascent of Akrabbim, from Sela and upward.

The third degree of compromise is marked for the tribe of Dan. Instead of Israel's driving out the Canaanites, here we see the Canaanites driving out the children of God. Judges 18 records the migration of the Danites, and shows the religious apostasy that underlay their inability to conquer the land God gave them. Because it is the design to the author to show how things are getting worse and worse, not only here in this section but also in the book of Judges as a whole, he postpones the story of the Danite migration until the end of the book, where it forms the first of the two appendices.

We read concerning Judah that they conquered the hill country, but could not take the plains (v. 19). Here we see, far worse, that Dan could not take all the hill country either. In verse 35, it is sad and striking to note that the Canaanites (Amorites) persisted in the region of Aijalon and Mount Heres ("Mountain of the Sun"), for this was where Joshua had defeated them and the sun had been made to stand still (Josh. 10:12). Indeed, it is where Joshua was buried (Jud. 2:9). What an appalling situation, that the Canaanites should recapture these great memorial sites! What a sad contrast with the former victory at this location!

Since Dan left this area, it came under the domination of Ephraim. When Ephraim became strong, and faithful (so that he is called "Joseph" here), he acquired some degree of domination over the Amorites.

Finally, in verse 36, we come to the appalling climax of the second section of this narrative, the response of man. We are told that the Amorites had a border. That is, they were so strong that they had a defined territory which was their own. They were not just hiding out in Israelite territory; they had their own land, and their own recognized border!

Summary

As we look at this section concerning Joseph and the other tribes, we can also see pictures of Christ, though generally in reverse.

Luz—It surely is Christ who conquered the pagan world of Luz, and turned it into a House of God (Beth-El).

The five cities Manasseh failed to conquer—Christ did break the five-fold power of the world, and in that these cities formed part of the key to the whole land, we see now that Christ has taken all the key places of the whole world.

Forced labor—Eventually all unconverted men will bow the knee, and do forced service to Christ the King forever.

"Did not drive them out completely"—Not yet, but on the final day Christ will drive them into hell forever.

The seven cities Asher failed to conquer—Christ has completely (*seven*-ly) conquered the world.

Beth-Shemesh and Beth-Anath—Christ has destroyed in principle all centers of idolatry, casting down all principalities and powers. As the book of Judges develops it, Deborah will be God's true Anath, and Samson will be God's true Shemesh, replacing the Canaanite counterfeits.

Dan's retreat into the hill country—While the Church may

be forced to retreat occasionally, yet in Christ her victory over all the world is secure, and she will always sally forth to greater victories in Him.

The border of the Amorites—In the New Covenant, the heathen have no more borders. The gospel invades everywhere.

The Evaluation of the Lord (2:1-5)

1. Now the angel of the LORD came up from Gilgal to Bochim. And He said, "I brought you up out of Egypt and led you into the land which I have sworn to your father; and I said, 'I will never break My covenant with you,

2. " 'And as for you, you shall make no covenant with the inhabitants of this land; you shall tear down their altars.' But you have not hearkened to My voice. What is this you have done?

3. "Therefore I also said, 'I will not drive them out before you; but they shall become *as thorns* in your sides, and their gods shall be a snare to you.' "

4. And it came about when the angel of the LORD spoke these words to all the sons of Israel, that the people lifted up their voices and wept.

5. So they named that place Bochim [Weepers]; and there they sacrificed to the LORD.

I don't care very much for clever alliterations in sermons, so I titled this chapter "Conquest, Compromise, Judgment, and Restoration." We are at the point of judgment and restoration. If you like alliterations, you might call this last section "Confrontation and Cure (or Re-Constitution, Re-Conversion, Re-Construction, Re-Creation)." This first section of Judges is a small version of the basic pattern discussed in the Introduction to this study: creation, fall and decline, judgment, and re-creation.

It is the Angel of the LORD who brings the Word of Evaluation to Israel. The reason for this is established in Exodus 23:20-23, for it was the Angel specifically Who was charged with bringing the people into the promised land; it was the Angel specifically Who was to be obeyed; it was the Angel specifically Who was to be feared; it was the Angel specifically Who would go before Israel to destroy their adversaries; and it was the Angel specifically Who stood as Captain of the LORD's host (Josh. 5:13ff.). Now we see, in terms of this, that as Exodus 23:21 had foretold it is the Angel specifically Who will pass judgment against sinful Israel.

It is clear that this Angel is God Himself, since He has the power to forgive sins, which is God's alone (Mark 2:7) and since He has the very name of God upon Him (Ex. 23:21, and compare Josh. 5:15 with 6:2.) Since no man has seen God (the Father) at any time, it being the Son Who has revealed Him (John 1:18), it is clear that the visible Angel is the Son of God Himself, the preincarnate Jesus Christ. It is He Who brings the judgment to Israel, just as He will on the final day.

When it says that the Angel came from Gilgal to Bochim, we are to understand that it is the Tabernacle which has been moved. Gilgal was where the Covenant with God had been renewed when Israel entered the land (Josh. 4, 5). Israel had started out well at Gilgal (which means "rolling-rolling" and refers to the rolling off of the foreskins in circumcision, sign of Israel's consecration to the LORD). Gilgal is a long way off, Spiritually, from Bochim, which means "weepers." We don't know where Bochim is, and it may be another name for Shechem or Bethel. At any rate, the fact that they sacrificed to the LORD at Bochim shows that the Tabernacle had relocated there (Jud. 2:5). In the wilderness, God had indicated where the Tabernacle was to be located by moving, in the pillar of cloud, to a new location. This was doubtless the case in this instance as well.

The LORD reminds them that He delivered them from Egypt; (so surely He could have destroyed the Canaanites, had they trusted Him). He reminds them that He had made good on His promise to the Patriarchs, in bringing them into the promised land (so surely He was willing to finish the job and destroy the Canaanites, had they trusted Him). He reminds them that He had sworn never to break His covenant with them (so surely He was ready to deliver Canaan into their hand, had they not broken their part of the covenant).

Their part of the covenant levied two rather simple demands on them. First, they were to make no covenants or treaties with the Canaanites by reducing them to slavery or by marrying them. Second, they were not to permit the Canaanite altars to remain standing.

The Word of the LORD then directly indicts them: You have not obeyed Me. They were guilty of keeping Canaanites around as slaves (covenants), and of not destroying all the altars (Beth-Shemesh, Beth-Anath). Then comes the question from the

LORD: What have you done? God always treats men as responsible, and His questions are designed to provoke self-examination ("Adam, where art thou?" "Simon Peter, lovest thou Me?"). Thus it is here: What have you done? Think about it. Meditate upon it. And repent.

Now the LORD passes judgment (verse 3), in strict accord with His threat articulated twice already (in Num. 33:55 and Josh. 23:13f.). The judgment is in line with the two indictments. First, since the Canaanites are still in the land, "they will be in your sides" (literally; the "as thorns" is added by the translators to bring out the sense). This first judgment has a number of ramifications. As the translators note, the Canaanites will be thorns in their sides. But also, since Eve came from Adam's side, the prediction is that Israel will intermarry with the Canaanites, which will lead to further woes. We can also imagine them walking side by side with Israel, tripping them up. Oxen are yoked side by side, so that for the Canaanites to be in the side of Israel implies that they were now "unequally yoked together with unbelievers" (2 Cor. 6:14).

Second, since the altars are still in the land, "their gods will be a snare to you." A snare lies on the ground, waiting to catch a bird or small animal. If a man steps into a snare, he receives a wound in the foot. The imagery here, thus, refers us to Genesis 3:15, where the enemy is said to have his head crushed, while the righteous receive wounds in the foot. Specific instances of foot wounds are not found in Judges (though Jud. 5:31 alludes to Gen. 32:31, and Jacob's limp), but the crushing of the serpent's head is a major theme in the book (see the Introduction for more on this).

The snares will trip them up. Later on, in Judges 3:2, we see that, as always, there is mercy mixed with this judgment; but here the judgment is expressed as total. It is tripping that must drive Israel, in desperation, to its knees.

These two sins and judgments (idolatry and adulterous covenanting) form a theme in Judges. They recur as the core description of Israel's sin in Judges 3:6. The two appendices to Judges explore each in depth. The first appendix deals with the Levites' failure to protect Israel from idolatry, and the consequences of this. The second appendix deals with the Levites' failure to protect Israel from adultery, and the consequences of this. Also, the snare of idolatry is particularly explored in the history of Gideon, which opens with Baal worship and closes with Ephod worship. And the snare of adultery is, of course, explored in the second part of the history of Samson.

Thus, the book of Judges explores the reality of sin in two of its aspects (not two sins, but two aspects of sin itself). First, making covenant with the Canaanites is associated with spiritual adultery. The image is that of the Canaanites being in their sides. This is in the kingly area, where Adam needs a helper meet for him, but the Canaanites are no proper helpmeets for these new Adams in their new garden. Second, not removing the altars is associated with idolatry. The image is that of the Canaanites being a snare. This is in the priestly area, where Adam needs to reject the serpent who attacks his foot. The Canaanites are like a serpent in the path.[2]

Total judgment is what we find here. The LORD does not soften the judgment at all. Yet, total judgment is what makes total grace possible, and we see in Israel the proper two-fold response of repentance and faith (verses 4 and 5). Repentance and faith are really one action having two aspects: a turning from and a turning to. Israel wept, and even named the location of their tears *Bochim,* "weepers." Here is repentance. Here is a permanent memorial to their sin, and to their repentance.

Then, we are told, they sacrificed to the LORD. Here is faith. On the altar they expressed their confession that they deserved the death penalty for their sins, that they deserved to be bound on the altar of God and burned up under His fiery wrath. But they also confessed their trust in God by sacrificing a substitute (according to the law of Leviticus 4:13ff.), which would take upon itself the wrath they deserved. Such a confession is a sweet savor in the nostrils of the LORD. For the Christian, this comes in the weekly Supper of the Lord, for "if we judge ourselves, we should not be judged" (1 Cor. 11:31).

There is grace for sinners. Despite their sins and failings, God's people have an altar of mercy and forgiveness to which they can repair. God's final Word to His covenant people is always "yes."

---

2. On Adam's kingly and priestly work, and the origin of these images, see my essay, "Rebellion, Tyranny, and Dominion in the Book of Genesis," in Gary North, ed., *Tactics of Christian Resistance* (Tyler, TX: Geneva Ministries, 1983).

2

SPIRALS OF CHASTISEMENT
(Judges 2:6 - 3:6)

This second introduction to Judges is thematic rather than narrative in character. Here again we can see the three-fold pattern, although the command/promise of the Lord is presupposed:

I. The Command/Promise of the Lord (Deuteronomy 6:4-9, 20-25)

II. The Response of Israel (Judges 2:6-13)
  A. The Failure of the First Generation (2:6-10)
  B. The Failure of Later Generations (2:11-13)

III. The Evaluation of the Lord (2:14 - 3:6)
  A. The Slavery-Deliverance Cycle (2:14-19)
  B. Turning Sins into Scourges (2:20 - 3:6)

The Command/Promise of the Lord
(Deuteronomy 6:4-9, 20-25)

The basic failure of the Israelites, as set forth in this passage, was this: They did not pass on to their children a sense of loyalty to the Lord. Since this was the fundamental command/promise that they violated, we should have it before us before we look at the passage itself. First of all, then, from Deuteronomy 6:

4. Hear, O Israel! The LORD is our God; the LORD is one!
5. And you shall love the LORD your God with all your heart and with all your soul and with all your might.
6. And these words, which I am commanding you today, shall be on your heart;
7. And you shall teach them diligently to your sons and shall talk of them when you sit in your house and when you walk by the way and when you lie down and when you rise up.
8. And you shall bind them as a sign on your hand and they

shall be as frontlet bands on your forehead [between your eyes].
9. And you shall write them on the doorposts of your house
and on your gates.

In this passage, God first identifies Himself as the only God,
and as YHWH, the Covenant King of Israel (v. 4). Then the
people are commanded to cleave unto God with all their being,
practising His presence moment by moment, day by day (v. 5).
God's Law is to be written on their hearts, by their meditating
on it constantly (v. 6). Note that the writing of the Law on the
heart is not a magical act that happens once at the point of salvation, but is something that increases in depth and breadth as
time goes along. Moreover, note that the Law written on the
heart is not a distinctive New Covenant blessing (Jer. 31:33). We
should say that what was fully and definitively done in the New
Covenant was also provisionally and partially done in the Old.

What is important for the book of Judges comes to us in
verse 7. God tells the people to teach the Law to their children,
by constant iteration and reiteration. In this way, the Law
would come to be written on the hearts of the children. Since the
Law is a transcript of the holy character of God, teaching the
Law is equivalent to teaching about God. It is God Who was to
be known by all. Teaching the children the Law was not to be a
school of Pharisaical legalism, but of evangelical submission to
a personal King and Father.

The children were to be taught that whatever is done by the
hand, and whatever is thought by the mind, is to be governed by
the Word of God (v. 8; contrast Rev. 13:16). Moreover, not only
personal morality, but also the doorposts of the house (family
morality) and the gates of the city (political life) were to be governed by God's holy Laws (v. 9)

20. When your son asks you in time to come, saying, "What
do the testimonies and the statutes and the judgments mean
which the LORD commanded you?"
21. Then you shall say to your son, "We were slaves to
Pharaoh in Egypt; and the LORD brought us from Egypt with a
mighty hand.
22. "Moreover, the LORD showed great and distressing signs
and wonders before our eyes against Egypt, Pharaoh, and all his
household;
23. "And He brought us out from there in order to bring us

in, to give us the land which He had sworn to our fathers.

24. "So the LORD commanded us to observe all these statutes, to fear the LORD our God for our good always and for our survival, as even today.

25. "And it will be righteousness for us if we guard, observing all this commandment before the LORD our God, just as He commanded us."

Here again the thought concerns what and how to teach the children (v. 20). At this point, however, the subject matter is not the content of the Law itself (the character of God), but rather the reason why the Law was given (the actions of God in history).

Phase one of God's mighty acts: He brought us out of Egypt. The children are especially to be taught about God's mighty signs and wonders, so that they will know Him to be a God of almighty power (so that they will not fear iron chariots). Phase two of God's mighty acts: He brought us in to the promised land, and gave us His Law as a rule of life. The children must understand that deliverance from Egypt was not by their own law-keeping, but by God's powerful action on their behalf. The Law was given *after* salvation as a rule of life. Nevertheless, keeping the Law is all-important, for it shows whether or not we fear (are afraid of and revere) God. The Law is given for our own good and for our survival (vv. 21-24).

In light of this, there is a temporal righteousness that comes to the believer who keeps God's Law. The language here is interesting. Adam was told to guard the Garden (Gen. 2:15, "keep" is "guard"). Adam failed to do so, and was cast out, and new guardians were appointed (Gen. 3:24). Here, as the people are restored to a kind of Edenic garden (Canaan, a land flowing with milk and honey), they are again told to "guard." The means of proper guarding, of proper stewardship, is by observing all God's commandments. (This interpretation is based on a literal reading of the Hebrew of v. 25. If we take it idiomatically, we get "and it will be righteousness for us if we are careful to observe all this commandment. . . ." The thought is more general, but does not conflict with the notion of guarding the new garden.)

So, the children must know two things: the Lord, and what

the Lord has done. If the children know these things, they will get to stay in the new garden. If they forget them, they eventually will be cast out. How did Israel keep these commandments?

The Response of Israel
(Judges 2:6-13)

6. When Joshua had dismissed the people, the sons of Israel went each to his inheritance to possess the land.

7. And the people served the LORD all the days of Joshua, and all the days of the elders who survived Joshua, who had seen all the great work of the LORD, which He had done for Israel.

8. Then Joshua the son of Nun, the servant of the LORD, died at the age of 110.

9. And they buried him in the territory of his inheritance in Timnath-Heres, in the hill country of Ephraim, north of Mount Gaash.

Joshua's dismissal of the people is recorded in Joshua 24. The people went to possess their inheritances. This hints at part of the reason why the land was not cleared of Canaanites: Israel settled down too soon and too much. It is a temptation to settle down and enjoy the fruits of victory before the victory is fully accomplished. The land was *essentially* but not *thoroughly* conquered. This temptation was not unique to ancient Israel. Christianity captured the Roman Empire essentially but not thoroughly. The Reformation captured Northern Europe essentially but not thoroughly. God does promise peace and prosperity as the fruit of victory, but only when the victory is thorough. It is dangerous to settle down too soon and too much. The war is real, and it is never really over. Eternal vigilance is the price of holiness. (Does this mean we may never settle down? No, only that we must be careful not to settle down too much, or too soon.)

Those who had seen God's miraculous works were faithful to the Covenant, in essence. We have seen that they were not thoroughly faithful in conquering the land, and we shall see in verse 10 that they were not thoroughly faithful in transmitting the faith to their children; but they were essentially faithful, and God is gracious often to count the will for the deed. The wording of verse 7 is also found in Joshua 24:13, with one exception. Here God's work is specifically called a "great" work, in order to highlight their failure to tell their children of it.

Joshua's death at 110 is noted, and then his place of burial. Both of these things had a significance to the people of that day, which is not immediately clear to us. That God gave Joshua 110 years of life would have caused the ancient Israelite scholar to meditate on the possible significance of the number 110. That is because the faithful Israelite scholar did not believe that God wasted His breath giving out mere information. Every detail is important. But, what could the number 110 mean, in this context?

Moses had lived 120 years (Dt. 34:7), and 12 is the number of the Covenant (12 tribes, 12 apostles, etc.). Eleven is the number reached by subtracting one from 12, and this is significant in Scripture. Thus, after Judas's treason and death, there were only eleven apostles. In line with this, the last story in the book of Judges shows the virtual obliteration of one of the twelve tribes, because of treason; and the next to the last story shows the apostasy of Dan, which eventually was blotted out from among the tribes (cf. Rev. 7:4ff.). Possibly, Joshua's death at 110 shows the void left when Moses, the greatest leader of all, died.

Also, Samson was betrayed for 1100 pieces of silver, and Micah betrayed the covenant for 1100 pieces of silver (Jud. 16:5; 18:2). Possibly, then, the use of the number 110 in connection with Joshua means this: The great work that Joshua did (110) was undone by betrayals (1100). So great was Joshua's work that it took ten times (1100) as much to undo it, as to perform it in the first place (110). Later in Scripture, eleven is used for the number of the destruction of the Covenant (Jer. 39:2), and Ezekiel picks this up to say that just as Jerusalem had been destroyed in the eleventh year, so also would be Tyre (Ezk. 26:1) and Egypt (Ezk. 30:20; 31:1). (See also Matthew 20:6, 9.)

So, drawing it together, we may say that possibly Joshua's death at 110 stood as a memorial to Israel, a threat that if they were not faithful, their number would be diminished, and they would lose their covenant status, just as Joshua had warned them in Joshua 23 and 24.

Similarly, Joshua's burial site was a memorial. It was at a place called in Joshua 24:30 Timnath-Serah, "Portion of Abundance," but here called Timnath-Heres, the "Portion of the Sun." This highlights the greatest and most miraculous work of

God during the Conquest: His making the sun stand still in the
heavens. This is particularly noted here in Judges 2:9 to point up
the greatness of the works God had done. Surely parents would
tell their children about it.

The Failure of the First Generation

10. And all that generation also were gathered to their fathers; and there arose another generation after them who did not
know the LORD, nor yet the work which He had done for Israel.

The sad sequel, however, is that they did not. The first generation failed to teach their children about God. The children
grew up ignorant of the two things specified in Deuteronomy 6.
They did not know the Lord, and they did not know His works
on behalf of Israel. What does this mean?

In the first place, it means that the older generation was too
busy doing what they supposed to be God's will, with the result
that their children were not taught. How often is this the case!
Scripture makes it plain that there is no more important task
any man or woman has than teaching his or her children about
the Lord. The very last verses of the Old Testament tell us that
the whole purpose of the Messiah's work can be summed up as
restoring family life under God. Satan loves to see Christians
who think that the Kingdom cannot wait, and they they must be
busy. Satan has time (he thinks); and he is willing to wait, in the
confidence that the next generation will be his. The older generation worked hard to occupy that part of the land they had conquered, but all their labors came to naught because they did not
train their children, and the land was conquered by enemies.

This sad story happens over and over in the book of Judges.
Israel's national disasters were a direct result of family disasters,
parents who did not understand God's priorities. Busy-busy
Christians and their rebellious children: a story common to all
ages of the Church. And is this now why so many preacher's kids
and missionary's kids turn out bad? And how often is this simply
the result of parental egotism? "I'm important and my work is
important, and I don't have time for my children." Parents with
such attitudes will pay dearly in old age, and so will society.

In the second place, it means that the children did not understand the reality of the war between God's people and God's

enemies. God's mighty works of war in the past, had they been taught them properly, would have taught them how desperate the situation really was. They would have known that God means business, and that He kills the wicked. They would have known that the Canaanites and the other nations round about hated them, and that peace was impossible. They would have known about the viciousness of Pharaoh, and of the Amalekites. They would have known of the seductiveness of the apostate Midianites, and of the craftiness of the Gibeonites. They would have remembered that Ammon and Moab refused them food (Dt. 23:3f., and cf. Ruth 1:1). They would have been on their guard against the enemy. Also, knowing that God had killed an entire generation of their forefathers in the wilderness, they would have been on their guard to stay close to the Lord. (For another slant on this, see Neh. 8:17 with Lev. 23:43. The Feast of Tabernacles, a week-long picnic encamped around God's Tabernacle, was designed to teach the children about the deliverance, but they never kept it after Joshua died.)

But they did not know these things. Rather, they grew up at ease, never being impressed with the seriousness of it all. It was easy to compromise, and to play around with Baal and Ashteroth. God seemed far away, and His mighty works seemed almost mythical, indeed primitive!, compared with the sophisticated new views propounded on all sides.

At this point, we must ask a further question, the answer to which is absolutely crucial to an understanding of the theology of the book of Judges. If the children grow up bad, what does this say about the relationship between the father and the mother? It is bad marriages that lead to bad children, as a rule. To understand the Biblical position on this, we have to go back to the first human marriage, that of Adam and Eve.

Adam had three "priestly" tasks to perform with Eve. He was to guard her, he was to give her food, and he was to instruct her. We see him failing at all three. He stands by and lets her do all the talking with the serpent (Gen. 3:6, "with her"). He takes food from her hand. He does not protect her. Now, in Christ we see the reverse of this: He protects the Bride, He gives food to the Bride from the Tree of Life, and He instructs the Bride.

These are the priestly tasks, and they are the duties of a man to his wife. Now, in Israel, the Levites were called to stand as priests for the Lord. In other words, they represented the Heavenly Bridegroom to the Bride. Leviticus 10:10, 11 says that the priests were supposed "to make a distinction between the holy and the profane, and between the unclean and the clean," which is their guarding or protecting work, and "to teach the sons of Israel all the statutes which the LORD has spoken to them through Moses," which is their instructing work (and they also managed the sacrifices, their feeding work). Similarly, Malachi 2:7 says, "the lips of a priest should preserve [guard] knowledge, and men should seek the law from his mouth, for he is the messenger [angel] of the LORD of hosts." Malachi goes on to condemn the Levites for being faithless to their wives, which is a sign of their faithlessness to Israel (2:10-16). The Levites had been given this special privilege, of being the husbands of Israel, because of their zeal to destroy the golden calf (Ex. 32:28f.; Dt. 33:8ff.).

What we find in Judges, especially in the appendix, is the failure of the Levites to act as proper husbands to Israel. They failed to teach and thus failed to guard. As a result, they left the Bride of the Lord exposed to danger. We are told by the New Testament that Eve was deceived, but that Adam was the one primarily guilty in the Fall of Man (2 Cor. 11:3; 1 Tim. 2:14). Thus, the primary blame falls on the husband when the wife sins. The Spiritual harlotry of Israel, the Bride, was due in large part to the failure of the Levites, representing the Groom, to guard her by means of sound instruction. The True Husband (the Lord) was not visible, and was soon forgotten, with the result that the lonely Bride went sinfully searching for an adulterous substitute. Wicked as her actions were, the primary blame lay on the Levites.

Baal means "lord, husband," and the temptation to Baalism is nothing more nor less than spiritual adultery. Moreover, the sin of Israel consisted in substituting the false marriage of Baal and Asherah for the true marriage of the Lord with His people, as we shall see.

The central section of Judges shows the nation drifting into Baalistic kingship. Since the Lord is not being made manifest as King, the Bride seeks another King/Husband. The reason for this is hinted at throughout the middle part of Judges (the various stories), but is not made directly clear until the appendices, which show the failure of the Levites as the primary cause for the apostasies. The reason the middle sections do not call particular attention to this underlying reason is that the Bride must also bear the blame for spiritual adultery. Just because the Levites were failing was no excuse for whoring after the gods of the nations, or erecting false ephods (Jud. 8:27), or setting up a mere man as king. At any rate, this explains why the book of Judges is written as it is, with two stories out of chronological order at the end. Actually, both of the appendices happened very early in the history of the period, and this fact also serves to show what the basic underlying problem was.

The coming of the Holy Spirit in power is the great gift of the New Covenant. The Holy Spirit acts to keep Christians aware of their Lord in a much more dynamic fashion than was the case under the Old Covenant. Christians can still fall away, but they now have even less excuse. Still, in a secondary way the officers of the Church stand as symbols for the Groom, and if the Church is weak, they must bear most of the blame. As always, judgment begins at the house of God.

The Failure of the Later Generations

11. Then the sons of Israel did evil in the sight of the LORD, and served the Baals.

12. And they forsook the LORD, the God of their fathers, who had brought them out of the land of Egypt, and followed other gods from among the gods of the peoples who were around them, and bowed themselves down to them; thus they provoked the LORD to anger.

13. So they forsook the LORD and served Baal and Ashteroth.

We notice that their sin was in the *sight* of God. They may have thought that God was far away, but He was near, and He saw it all. Moreover, in Genesis 1 we find repeatedly that God "*saw* that it was good." Such sight entails evaluation, and so it is here.

Again we are reminded of what God has done for them. The reason is that there is a general principle in Scripture: Your deliverer is your ruler, your lawgiver. As Zacharias said, Christ came "to grant us that we, being delivered from the hand of our enemies, might serve Him without fear" (Lk. 1:74). Thus, the text calls attention to God's delivering them from Egypt, in order to highlight the fact that they did not serve Him.

The essence of their apostasy is here mentioned. Baal was the male and Ashteroth the female principle in nature, according to the Canaanite religion. Worshipping Baal ties in with the sin of idolatry primarily, while worshipping Ashteroth (through sexual debauchery) ties in with the sin of covenant adultery. Here again are the twin aspects of sin as the theology of the book of Judges sets it out.

Baalism was the secular humanism of the ancient world. Since the battle in the days of the Judges was against this ancient form of humanism, we should take a few pages to set out in brief what it entailed.

Baalism: Ancient Humanism

We often distance our culture from that of the Canaanites, thinking that since modern man does not literally bow down to idols, he must be somewhat better off. Let the reader, however, consider whether he as a Christian ever literally bows down to his God. How many Protestant churches that have kneelers has the reader ever been in? Do Protestants show their respect for the King of kings by at least standing for prayer, or do they pray sitting down, a posture nowhere encountered in Scripture for prayer? If modern Christians have no more respect for their God than to address Him sitting down, why should we expect the modern Baalists to bow down to Nature? Ancient man bowed before his god, whether it was Nature (Baalism) or the Creator (YHWH). Modern man does not bow before his god, whether Nature (humanism) or the Creator (Christ).

Similarly, for ancient man, the heart of religious exercise was adoration, worship, prostration, sacrament (a fellowship meal with the god). This was true of Israel before the Lord, and of the Canaanites before Baal. And this is the Biblical view of worship: Preaching/proclamation is the Word from God, which leads to a response of adoration, prostration, sacrament. The modern Christian, however, sees the heart of worship as entertainment (from a choir and an entertaining preacher) or as philosophical meditation (from a scholarly preacher). The sermon, instead of leading into worship, has become itself the climax of worship. And, just as the modern Christian view of worship is not much more than studying doctrine, so the modern humanist worships his god in the same way. We don't see humanists bowing down to their gods, but we do see them studying them, lecturing about them, writing books about them. And we don't see Christians bowing down to the Lord either, but we do see them studying Him, preaching about Him, and writing books about Him.

Thus, there is indeed a big difference between ancient religions and modern ones. Ancient man *primarily* worshipped his gods, while modern man *primarily* studies his. This is true both of pagans and of conservative, orthodox Christians.

Once we understand this, however, we can see that the opposition between the Truth and the Lie is the same now as it was then. Ancient pagans worshipped Nature, while modern pagans philosophize about Nature. The belief is the same, however: the belief that Nature is self-creating. Similarly, ancient believers worshipped the Creator, while modern Christians tend mainly to philosophize about Him, but the belief is the same.

So, what was Baalism? In essence it was the ascription of power to Nature: The universe has within itself the force of life. The world as we know it is the result of the union of the ultimate male and female principles of the universe, which may be called Baal and Ashteroth (or Astartes). (A similar goddess is Asherah, mistranslated as "groves" in the King James Version. The difference between the two goddesses is technical, and both were expressions of the same religious principle.) Canaanite philosophers believed, of course, that these ultimate forces were impersonal, and that their union was not sexual; but the common people preferred to think of the matter mythically. The sun god copulated with the original mud of the world, and the animals and man resulted. How does such a myth differ from a more sophisticated expression of the same principle, such as can be found in any 20th century high school science textbook? Once, we are told, there was a vast primordeal sea. Then one day, sparked by sunlight, an organic molecule appeared, which evolved to become our present world. A "male" principle, sunlight, inseminates a "female" principle, the primordeal sea, and life is born.

The Baal-Ashteroth religion understandably was intimately concerned with fertility. The Creator God of the Bible had promised fertility to Israel if they were faithful to Him (Dt. 7:13-14), but what He demanded was moral loyalty, including especially sexual chastity (monogamy). The religion of Baalism, however, advocated exactly the opposite method of getting fertility. Chaotic sexual orgies would stimulate Nature (Baal and Ashteroth), and fertility would be the result (human, animal, and crop fertility). The true religion of Israel said that fertility was obtained by submitting to the Creator, while Baalism said that fertility was obtained by stimulating Nature. Thus, in true religion, man is the servant/slave of God, in submission to Him; while in Baalism, man is the lord of his god (Nature) who needs to be stimulated by him.

Nature religion is a religion of stimulation. Man has to stimulate Nature in order to get results. Like the Baal priests of the ancient world, he may engage in sexual orgies, or cut himself with knives (1 Kings 18:28), in order to arouse the sleeping god. This is also the philosophy of the modern world. Stimulating nature is not seen (as in Christian faith) simply as a form of technological dominion. It is also seen as a way of salvation, so that modern medical scientists believe they will solve the problem of disease by learning how to control nature, and modern philosophers believe that controlling nature will permit man to control evolution and advance humanity, while modern revolutionaries from Marx to Marcuse believe that simply stimulating society through the imposition of social chaos will automatically lead to a better world.

For the Christian, however, the problems of disease and social inequities are solved by submission to God and His law. Medicine is not wrong, but it can only help a little bit. Disease will not go away until God is pleased with humanity (Dt. 7:15). The same is true for other areas. Thus, Christian faith is a religion primarily of submission, not of stimulation. For the Christian to get himself all worked up (through "speaking in tongues" or some other means) avails absolutely nothing in the sight of God.

Thus, the heart of ancient Baalism was secular humanism. Secular humanism says that the universe is self-creating, so that Nature is ultimate (this being the "secular" aspect). Secular humanism also teaches that man is the lord of Nature, and that man must rule over (stimulate) Nature (this being the "humanism" aspect). There used to be such a thing as "Christian humanism," which taught that man was lord of nature, but only in submission to God. This is the true doctrine, although the term "humanism" has come to be offensive to Christians, so we no longer speak of "Christian humanism."

So, for the ancient Baalist to bow before his idol was not an act of submission, but an act of stimulation. What he believed was the same thing modern secular humanists believe: that man is the lord of Nature, and that there is no Creator God to whom man is responsible.

Now of course, the Israelite children did not deny the existence of the Lord altogether. He had His place as well, perhaps as the superintendent of the whole overall process. Israelite thinkers began to look at Genesis 1 with new eyes. What did this passage mean to express, they might ask, in its poetic framework? Surely it is not to be taken literally. We should realize that God is at work *through* evolution (that is, through Baal and Ashteroth). God gave to Nature certain intrinsic powers, and these powers are evolving and developing. Nature is a real, though lesser, power. We must respect Nature. Look at all the bounties Nature has given us. The Canaanites have understood this better than we have, although they do not see clearly that God is at work in Nature as well. The Canaanites are, on the whole, not very sophisticated about it — sacrificing children to stimulate Nature, for instance — although there is more to be said for the Canaanite philosophers. We shouldn't stop our ears to what these people are saying to us. Remember: We are to spoil the Egyptians of their goods, and surely Canaanite science and philosophy are part of the spoils.

So they doubtless thought. Baalism was evolution, the belief that Nature was the author of all life. Israel was sucked into theistic evolution first, and then later on into full Baalism. (By the way, spoiling the Egyptians means taking their fruits, not their philosophical roots.)

The details of the Baal cult are not of much importance to us now. It is the underlying philosophy of Baalism which is regnant in American education and life today, and which is taught in the science departments of almost all Christian colleges today, and not just in science departments either. Scripture teaches that God sustains life directly, not indirectly. There is no such thing

as Nature. God has not given any inherent power of develop-
ment to the universe as such. God created the universe and all
life by immediate *actions,* not by mediate *processes.* When God
withdraws His Breath (which is the Holy Spirit, the Lord and
Giver of life), death follows immediately (Gen. 7:22). The idea
that God wound up the universe and then let it run its course, so
that there is such a thing as Nature which has an intrinsic power,
is Deism, not Christianity. Theistic evolution is Deism, not
Christianity. To the extent to which the processes of Nature
replace the acts of God in any system, to ʾᵃat extent the system
has become Baalistic.

The Evaluation of the Lord (2:14 - 3:6)

The Lord's judgments against Israel are set out in two sections, both beginning with the phrase "And the anger of the
LORD burned against Israel" (2:14, 20), a frightening statement
if there ever was one. The first section explains the principle of
the slavery-deliverance cycle, while the second section explains
why the nations were allowed to remain in the land.

The Slavery-Deliverance Cycle

14. And the anger of the LORD burned against Israel, and He
gave them into the hands of plunderers who plundered them;
and He sold them into the hands of their enemies round about,
so that they could no longer stand before their enemies.

15. Wherever they went, the hand of the LORD was against
them for evil, as the LORD had spoken and as the LORD had
sworn to them, so that they were severely distressed.

16. Then the LORD raised up judges, and they delivered them
from the hands of those who plundered them.

17. And yet they did not listen to their judges, for they
played the harlot after other gods and bowed themselves down
to them. They turned aside quickly from the way in which their
fathers had walked in obeying the commandments of the LORD;
they did not do as their fathers.

18. And when the LORD raised up judges for them, the LORD
was with the judge and delivered them from the hand of their
enemies all the days of the judge; for the LORD was moved to
pity by their groaning because of those who oppressed and
afflicted them.

19. But it came about when the judge died, that they would turn back and act more corruptly than their fathers, in following other gods to serve them and bow down to them; they did not abandon their practices or their stubborn ways.

This passage deals with basic principles, which God used not only in dealing with Israel but also in dealing with His people of all ages. As a chastisement for their wickedness, God *sold* them (v. 14) into the hands of their enemies. God had delivered them from bondage in Egypt, but now He sells them back into bondage. A return to slavery is in view. The passage emphasizes that it is God Who is actively at work chastising His people, and strong language is used: "wherever they went, the hand of the LORD was against them for evil" (v. 15). But at the same time, it is stressed (v. 16) that it was also the LORD Who raised up the judges, who *saved* them. The word "saved" in Hebrew is *yasha'*, from which we get Joshua and also Jesus. It basically means "to put into a large, open place," which is what Joshua had originally done, and which is what each new Joshua (each judge) would do.

These deliverances by God did not have the desired effect of changing the culture. Such is the depravity of the human heart that "they turned aside *quickly*" from the Lord, and "played the harlot after other gods" (v. 17). The promise of the New Covenant is that such declensions will not occur as often, and that the Church will respond more favorably to God's deliverance in Jesus Christ (it being a greater deliverance; cf. Jer. 31:31-33). God has given greater Power (of the Holy Spirit) to the post-Pentecostal Church. Indeed, after the Exile, which was the low point of universal Church history (Is. 54:7-10), the children of God were much more faithful than they had been before. We never hear of Baalism again; rather, the problem becomes a loyalty to the Law divorced from the Person of God, a perverse loyalty called Pharisaism which made obedience the way of eternal salvation instead of a response to it. But we should note that by New Testament times, the Synagogue-Church had spread all throughout the Roman Empire and the Persian as well, an outflow of evangelism which was not characteristic of pre-exilic Israel. The people did respond to Ezra, Nehemiah, Zechariah, and Haggai; as their fathers had not responded to Elijah and

Isaiah and Jeremiah.

The prophecies of the Old Testament, and of Romans 11, indicate that the Church will gradually go from strength to strength, until all the world has been permeated with gospel influences. Thus, the history of steadily worsening apostasy and declension seen in the book of Judges must be understood in terms of the history of redemption (as we set it out in the Introduction), and we are today not living at the same stage of history as they were. There is a decline and there is an expansion, and we are living in the age of expansion (Matt. 28:18-20).

Nevertheless, the treachery of the human heart is a constant factor in all ages. Even though the Spirit has been given in greater measure to the Church, it remains a fact that all Christians tend to "turn quickly out of the way," and ignore the mighty acts God has wrought on their behalf. Moreover, the fact of a general forward motion to history and a general expansion of the gospel does not eliminate times of setback and apostasy. Surely the 20th century is a time of great apostasy in the Western world, and, just as surely, the sad history of the Judges sheds light on our sorry condition.

We are told (v. 18) that the Lord was with the judge, and that is was the Lord Who, through the judge, saved Israel. This is important, for it shows that the judges are pictures of Jesus Christ, Who is the Lord. When we look at the salvific actions of the judges (not at their sins), we must see the Lord there also; and where we see the Lord, we see Christ. The judges are types of Christ not only because their actions symbolize His, and not only in that they were anointed by the Spirit (making them "messiahs" — anointed ones), but also and especially because Christ was there with them directing and controlling their actions. We must see Him at work in this book of Judges. (More about the nature of these judges in chapter 3 of this study.)

The principle of progressive declension is articulated once again in verse 19. They not only turned away quickly (v. 17), but they acted *more corruptly* than their forefathers.

What this passage points to in a way of principle is this. Culture is an effect, a product, of religion. Those who serve the Lord will develop a Christian (Godly) culture, with the Christian benefits of liberty, mutual respect, and peace. Service to other gods likewise produces cultures that are in line with those gods, with the dubious "benefits" of statism, degradation, and war.

Israel had become enslaved to the Canaanite gods; it was therefore logical and necessary that they also become enslaved to the Canaanite culture. In effect God said, "So you like the gods of Ammon? Well then, you're going to just love being under Ammonite culture! Oh, you don't like being in bondage to Ammon? You'd like to have Me as your God once again? Wonderful, I'll send a judge, who will have My Son as his Captain, and set you free from Ammon." Yet, in a few years God would be saying this: "So you like the gods of Philistia? Well, I gather then that you will be extremely happy under Philistine culture!" And so it would go.

God's judgments are never arbitrary. God chastises and curses people by giving them what they want. Israel wanted Baalism as a philosophy, so God gave them into the hands of Baalistic civilizations. Since they were slaves of the gods of these cultures, it was only proper that they should be slaves of the cultures themselves as well.

The so-called Theology of Liberation, as articulated through the World Council of Churches, has called for "salvation in four dimensions." They are correct in seeing that salvation is comprehensive, and incorporates every dimension of life. They are dead wrong, however, in thinking that the political aspect of the gospel can precede the Spiritual essence of the gospel. Salvation is indeed total and comprehensive, but there is an order to it. Culture follows from, arises from, and is dependent upon faith. Spiritual loyalty to God, in faith, must precede and be the ground of all cultural change. It not only must be, it inevitably will be. The gospel has inevitable consequences, and so does Baalism.

In the way of principle we must also note that this passage says nothing about Israel's crying to the Lord for relief or for salvation. We read that they were "severely distressed" (v. 15) and that "the LORD was moved to pity by their groaning," but not that they cried out to the Lord for deliverance. Judges 3:9 shows that they did indeed cry out to God, but this is not mentioned here in 2:14-19. Rather, it is the sovereign love of God that is at the forefront of consideration. God pursues them in His love, though they spurn Him and play the harlot after other gods. In their distress, it is God Who sovereignly revives them. Throughout this paragraph we must see God actively at work: God angry, God selling them into slavery, God moved to pity, God raising up judges, God being with the judge.

Turning Sins into Scourges

20. So the anger of the LORD burned against Israel, and He said, "Because this nation has transgressed My covenant which I commanded their fathers, and has not listened to My voice,

21. "I also will no longer drive out before them any of the nations which Joshua left when he died,

22. "In order to test Israel by them, whether they will keep the way of the LORD to walk in it as their fathers kept [guarded], or not."

23. So the LORD allowed those nations to remain, not driving them out quickly; and He did not give them into the hand of Joshua.

Here we see that God knew all along that Israel would not be completely faithful, so He did not give all the nations into Joshua's hand, so as to test the next generation. Sure enough, the next generation failed the test, as we saw in the preceding chapter of this study. So God pronounced His judgment: He would let the nations remain as a continual test of Israel's faith.

Now this may seem strange and contradictory. God had told them to eliminate these nations. That was His revealed will. Now, however, His will is for them to remain. The way to understand this is to relate it to the principle we discussed above, that God's judgments are never arbitrary, but He makes the punishment fit the crime. Where there is compromise with sin, the very sin becomes the means God uses to chastise His children. Our sins become our scourges. "God doth of our pleasant vices make instruments to scourge us,"—*King Lear,* Shakespeare. The compromise with sin was the failure to drive out the Canaanites, so the scourge for sin was the continued presence of the Canaanites.

3:1. Now these are the nations which the LORD left, to test Israel by them (all who had not known any of the wars of Canaan;

2. Only in order [Solely for the purpose] that the generations

of the sons of Israel might know war, to teach them; only those who had not known it previously):

3. The five lords of the Philistines and all the Canaanites and the Sidonians and the Hivites who lived in Mount Lebanon, from Mount Baal-Hermon as far as Lebo-Hamath [the entrance of Hamath].

4. And they were for testing Israel, to find out if they would hearken to the commandments of the LORD, which He had commanded their fathers by the hand of Moses.

Here we are told (v. 2) that the *sole* reason why the Canaanites were left in the land was so that Israel might learn how to make war. This again seems to contradict something else in the passage, the clear statement of 2:22 and 3:1 that the purpose was to test Israel's faith. The way to reconcile this apparent contradiction is to examine what is meant by training Israel in the ways of war.

In the first place, Israel had to learn *that* there was a war, and that peace and compromise with Canaanites was impossible. In the second place, Israel had to learn *how* to fight the wars of the Lord. This does not mean military tactics, though such are not completely excluded, but rather means prayer and faith. The wars of the Lord are fought by faith and prayer.

As far as military tactics are concerned, Scripture is often not very helpful. The majority of Israel's battles were won on the basis of miracle. What military tactics can be learned from marching around Jericho seven times, or from the sun's standing still in the sky? Of course, there are some ordinary battles in Scripture, and there is always something to be learned from the study of any battle; but it is not tactics and strategy that are foremost in the picture here. Indeed, by forbidding the king to multiply horses to himself (Dt. 17:16), God indicated that Israel was not to have a standing war machine.

When Israel came out of Egypt, they were attacked by Amalek. This famous battle, recorded in Exodus 17:8-13, was fought by faith and prayer. As long as Moses' hands were upraised in prayer, Israel prevailed. When Moses grew weary, Aaron and Hur supported his hands. The upraised hands expressed dependence on God. Israel was taught that war could be fought and won only in wholehearted trust and dependence on God. And so we can see that testing Israel's faith and teaching

Israel war are the same thing. The issue of history is always the war of God and His people versus Satan and his, and that war is only properly and effectively prosecuted in an attitude of faith and prayer, dependence on God.

In the light of this, we may say that faith entails an attitude of warfare (hatred) against sin and evil, in dependence upon the grace of God. Unfortunately, in much of modern Christendom these two things are separated. Many Christians who are actively fighting secular humanism, communism, and other Canaanite tribes, are doing so by political activism not grounded in prayer and faith. On the other hand, many modern Christians are not involved in the war at all, and their dependence upon God is a hollow and unreal thing. God calls us to war in dependence upon Him. Such is true faith.

Thus, the testing of faith is linked to the testing of obedience. Faith without works is dead. Faith, warfare, obedience — these are inseparable in the life of the child of God.

> 5. And the sons of Israel lived among the Canaanites, the Hittites, the Amorites, the Perizzites, the Hivites, and the Jebusites;
> 6. And they took their daughters for themselves as wives, and gave their own daughters to their sons, and served their gods.

Here we see again (v. 6) the two-fold sin of Israel: idolatry and covenant inter-marriage. The failure of family life comes to its climax here, where we are told that the Israelites inter-married with the Canaanites. Inter-marriage with non-Christians is one of the most destructive of all sins. It is placed here with idolatry as the summation of Israel's apostasy. Inter-marriage *guarantees* the failure of the next generation.

Conclusion

We may make three applications from this second introductory section to Judges. First, it is apparent from this passage, as from so many in Scripture, that pluralism is a great evil in God's sight. Pluralism is the belief that many different faiths should be tolerated in society, as if society were religiously neutral. Since we are not omniscient, we should indeed tolerate different

Christian churches, such as confess the Trinity and the in-fallibility of Scripture. God, however, will be against us if we tolerate anti-Christian cults in our midst. The Bible teaches that such cults may pursue their beliefs unmolested only so long as they do not attempt to proselytize for their anti-Christian beliefs (see for instance Deuteronomy 13).

This is not just some "Old Testament" notion. The great commission precisely commands us to work to "disciple the na-tions," and we are not at liberty to restrict such discipleship only to the level of the personal or the familial. Society as a whole should be discipled also. Throughout all the ages of the Church, the Christian faith has held that society must be publicly and openly Christian, that the laws of the land must be in accord with Biblical principles, and that paganism must not be permit-ted openly in the marketplace (though it may continue quietly in private).

This Biblical principle was compromised sorely in the 19th century, and seems to have been given up by most churches in the 20th. Surely this is the same compromise with Baalism that brought God's judgment against Israel of old. It will just as surely bring God's judgment against America today. We Chris-tians are finding our dominion greatly restricted today because our forefathers compromised with the Baalistic philosophy of pluralism. The enemy knows that there is a war on, and he is closing Christian schools as fast as they open in some parts of America. For too long Christians have advocated a total toler-ance and pluralism. We are now experiencing a rise of child por-nography, human sacrifice, and cannibalism in America. Pluralism is a dead end, and brings the judgment of God. There can be no compromise. The war is to the death. (See Psalm 139:19-22.)

The sword in this war is the declaration of the Word of God. This makes it all the more monstrous when preachers are declar-ing pluralism as the Christian view. By doing so, they throw away the one great power for change they possess: the preached Word. Christians do not war to take over society by the sword; rather, it is the preaching of the intolerant, fiery holiness of God, and of salvation in Christ alone, followed by a life of obe-dience, which is the sword of the Spirit in this war. Let us not blunt the Sword.

A second application from this passage is that God shakes up compromisers by means of war and enslavement. With America today as far gone as it is, and with the Church as compromised as it is, we may reasonably expect war and enslavement to be brought to our shores. What right have we to think that it cannot happen here? If the U.S.S.R. tomorrow issued an ultimatum, how likely is it that our humanistic leaders would have the backbone to resist? If Scripture has any relevance to us today at all, we surely may expect war and conquest, unless we repent.

Third, and finally, we see from this passage that personal declension and compromise is the root of social problems, especially as that personal declension comes to expression in the family. Only through prayer, active declaration of the Word of God, and rebuilding family life can we have any hope of restoring our society and culture. Christian involvement in politics is important, but it will be little more than a holding action unless the Church and the families of America are rebuilt according to the Word of God.

3

OTHNIEL: BABYLON ANTICIPATED
(Judges 3:7-11)

What were the judges? They were civil rulers and deliverers of Israel. God is concerned with all of human life and society. It is false to try to limit His interest only to the institutional Church, though as the sacramental body of Jesus Christ, the Church is the foremost earthly "institution." The judges show us God delivering His people from His and their enemies, in particular in social and political situations. According to Scripture, the civil magistrate bears the sword of iron (as distinct from the Sword of the Scriptures) as a threat to evildoers. A magistrate is a minister of God, no less than a Church officer is, but the magistrate is a minister of God's vengeance, while the elder is a minister of redemption. (See Romans 13.)

The judges were civil magistrates. Their normal work was to act as magistrates for Israel, settling disputes (Ex. 18:21ff.). Their special work was to act as avengers for Israel, destroying the enemies of God. This is still the duty of the magistrate today: to settle disputes in court and to prosecute defensive warfare against aggressors. The book of Judges focuses in on the exceptional work of vengeance and deliverance, because this is what is important for the purpose of revealing and foreshadowing the redemptive work of Christ.

In Scripture there are two offices or official works to which a man may be called beyond his normal capacities as worker, husband, and father. These two offices are those associated with redemption and vengeance. Those called to these offices are ordained for the purpose. Ordination is by the Holy Spirit, as represented by oil. In the Old Testament, the Levites and the kings (the house of David) were ordained regularly by oil, as a rite installing them in their official duties. We do not find such ritual anointing in the case of the judges, however; rather, they

47

were anointed directly by the Spirit.

This does not mean they were not elected officials. E. C. Wines has provided a good commentary on this point: "Four stages may be noted in the proceedings relating to Jephthah; — the preliminary discussion, the nomination, the presentation to the people, and the installation (Judges 10:17, 18 and 11:1-11). The enemy was encamped in Gilead. At this point, the people and their rulers, assembled in convention on the plain, said to one another, 'Who shall be our chief, to lead us against the foe?' This was the discussion, in which every citizen seems to have had the right to participate. In the exceedingly brief history of the affair, it is not expressly stated, but it is necessarily implied, that Jephthah, of Gilead, a man of distinguished military genius and reputation, was nominated by the voice of the assembly. But this able captain had been some years before driven out from his native city. It was necessary to soothe his irritated spirit. To this end the elders went in person to seek him, laid before him the urgent necessities of the state, softened his anger by promises of preferment, and brought him to Mizpeh. Here, manifestly, they made a formal presentation of him to the people, for it is added, 'the people made him head and captain over them.' That is, they completed the election by giving him their suffrages, recognizing him as their leader, and installing him in his office. Here, then, we have, 1. The free discussion of the people in a popular assembly concerning the selection of a leader; 2. The nomination of Jephthah by the meeting to be chief; 3. The elders' presentation of him to the people for their suffrages; and 4. His inauguration as prince and leader of Israel. It is to the analysis of such incidental relations as this scattered here and there through the history, that, in default of a more exact account of the primitive order of things, we are compelled to resort, in our study of the Hebrew constitution, for much of the information, which it would be gratifying to find in a more detailed and systematic form."[1]

Thus, the judges were not self-appointed men, but were leaders recognized by the people. This is obvious even if Wines's analysis be not convincing in its every detail. There was a regu-

---

1. E. C. Wines, *The Hebrew Republic* (originally published as *Commentary on the Laws of the Ancient Hebrews,* vol. 2; reprint, Uxbridge, MA: American Presbyterian Press, n.d.), p. 110f.

lar way to *appoint* judges, then, even if there was no *anointing* with oil involved.

Wines enumerates the political characteristics of the judgeship system in Israel as follows:[2]

1. "The Hebrew judges held their office for life." This was true of Moses and of Joshua, and is presupposed throughout the book of Judges.

2. "The office was not hereditary. Moses took no steps to perpetuate this magistracy in his family, or to leave it as an hereditary honor to his posterity." We may note that when Samuel tried to set his sons up as judges, it did not work out, and the people demanded a king.

3. "The chief magistracy of Israel was elective. The oracle, the high priest, and all the congregation, are distinctly recorded to have concurred in the elevation of Joshua to this office (Num. 27:18-23). Jephthah was chosen to the chief magistracy by the popular voice. Samuel was elected regent in a general assembly of Israel (1 Sam. 7:5-8)." There is nothing to indicate the contrary in the case of any other of the judges.

4. "The authority of these regents extended to affairs of war and peace." These were their special and general works.

5. "A contumacious resistance of the lawful authority and orders of the Hebrew judges, was treason." See Joshua 1:18 and Deuteronomy 17:12. This is important is evaluating Jephthah's response to the rebellion of Ephraim in Judges 12.

6. "The authority of the Israelitish regents was not unlimited and despotic. It was tempered and restrained by the oracle. This is distinctly affirmed, in the history of the appointment of Joshua to the chief magistracy, as the successor of Moses (Num. 27:21). It is there said, that he should stand before Eleazar the priest, who should ask counsel for him, after the judgment of urim before the Lord." In Christian lands, this means that the state should consult the Church in matters where the Church has competency.

"The power of the Hebrew chief magistrates was further limited by that of the senate and congregation." They were not bound to consult with the body of elders on every point, but we see that "in important emergencies, they summoned a general

---

2. *Ibid.*, pp. 148ff.

assembly of the rulers, to ask their advice and consent. This we find to have been repeatedly done by Moses, Joshua, and Samuel."

"Still another limitation to the authority of the Hebrew judges was in the law itself. Their power could not be stretched beyond its legal bounds."

Wines sums it all up this way: "No salary was attached to the chief magistracy in the Hebrew government. No revenues were appropriated to the judges, except, perhaps, a larger share of the spoils taken in war, and the presents spontaneously made to them as testimonials of respect (Jud. 8:24; 1 Sam.9:7; 10:27). No tribute was raised for them. They had no outward badges of dignity. [This may be a bit extreme on Wines's part, since there probably was some type of robe of office, but Wines is certainly right in what follows.] They did not wear the diadem. They were not surrounded by a crowd of satellites. They were not invested with the sovereign power. They could issue orders; but they could not enact laws. They had not the right of appointing officers, except perhaps in the army. They had no power to lay new burdens upon the people in the form of taxes. They were ministers of justice, protectors of law, defenders of religion, and avengers of crime; particularly the crime of idolatry. But their power was constitutional, not arbitrary. It was kept within due bounds by the barriers of law, the decisions of the oracle, and the advice and consent of the senate and commons of Israel. They were without show, without pomp, without retinue, without equipage; plain republican magistrates." While Wines may go a bit too far in rejecting all outward symbols of office, since these were common and expected in this period of history, in the main he is clearly correct. As we shall see, the history of the period of Judges shows the regents of Israel gradually aggrandizing to themselves more and more of the trappings of power. This will be our main focus of attention in chapter 9 of this study.

Kings and judges are shepherds. The central section of Judges, at which we have now arrived, is concerned with this. Priests, prophets, ministers, Levites—these are guardians. The two appendices of Judges deal with Levites, and their failure to guard Israel properly. The point of the appendices (Judges 17–21) is to show that the failure of these moral guardians was the basic underlying cause of all the moral problems discussed in the preceding chapters (Judges 3-16). Thus, the ultimate guardians of society are the officers of the Church. Theirs is the powerful, positive work of instruction and worship (Ex. 18:19-20), which must underlie the negative, vengeance work of the judge (Ex. 18:21ff.). The guardian's role is to *prevent* evil; the judge's role is to *deliver* from evil, once it has been allowed in.

(We should add that one often hears of the three "offices" of prophet, priest, and king. While there are indeed three separate *functions,* Scripture knows of only two *offices.*)

Messiahs: Anointed Ones

The charismatic anointing of the judges is referred to in the following places, and with the following effects:

3:10	Othniel	Enabled to judge Israel; that is, settle disputes and wage war.
6:34	Gideon	Enabled to wage war.
11:29	Jephthah	Enabled to wage war.
14:6	Samson	Enabled to kill a lion barehanded.
14:19	Samson	Enabled to kill thirty men.
15:14	Samson	Enabled to break his bonds and kill 1000 men with a jawbone.

It is sometimes argued that there is something important about the inclusion or omission of this reference to Spiritual anointing in the cases of the various judges. We believe that there is something important about the *inclusion* in each instance, as we shall attempt to eludicate in the various passages as we come to them. But we believe that the *absence* of this notice is not significant. All of the judges had this anointing, or they would not have been judges.

The point of the argument is that some commentators object to the actions taken by Ehud, for example, in deceiving Eglon, so they note that the phrase "the Spirit of the LORD came upon him" is lacking in the text of the story of Ehud. This, however, is a specious and self-defeating argument, for the phrase occurs in the story of Jephthah immediately before the story of Jephthah's rash vow. The occurrence of the phrase in connection with the short story of Othniel, the *first* judge, is sufficient to cover all of the judges.

A similar argument is found in some commentators to the effect that certain judges are omitted from the list of the faithful in Hebrews 11:32. There are a lot of other people omitted from this list, however, such as Hezekiah, Josiah, and Zerubbabel. Also, those included in the list number Jephthah and Samson, surely not perfect men. The omission of Ehud, Jael, Shamgar, Ruth, etc. only shows that their histories are not quite as strikingly relevant to the essential point of Hebrews 11. The omission says nothing about the rightness or wrongness of Ehud's deception. If Ehud's deception caused him to be omitted from Hebrews 11, why is Rahab included?

The anointing of civil leaders with the Spirit is first seen in Numbers 11:24-29. The seventy elders were civil leaders; the religious guardians were the Levites. Civil magistrates need the Spirit no less than Church elders. There was a time in the Christian past when civil authorities were anointed by the Church. Even today, though it does not mean much, prayers are offered when a new magistrate takes office.

Moreover, we must keep in mind that God is a Unity, One and Three. We cannot have a partial relationship with God, as if we could experience only one of His attributes or one of His graces without experiencing the rest. If the judges partook of the Holy Spirit, as they indeed did, then they partook of all of His graces, not just of certain select ones. Scripture expects us to keep this in mind. The graces of the Spirit are enumerated in Isaiah 11:2 as wisdom, understanding, counsel, strength, knowledge, and fear of the Lord. To say that Samson, for instance, partook of the Spirit of strength, but not of the Spirit of wisdom and of the fear of the Lord, is absurd. Samson's failures were real, and they are recorded for our instruction; but these failures were not the *characteristic* expression of Samson's life. The characteristic expression of his life is found in the fact that the Spirit of the Lord came upon him, and thus he partook of the qualities listed in Isaiah 11:2. Samson's sins were the exceptions, not the rule.

This anointing with the Spirit shows us that the judges are symbols or types of Christ, Who is the final Judge (Luke 4:18; John 3:34). The narrative histories of the judges are not just inspiring stories of how God saved His people in times past, though they are that; these stories are also *freighted with sym-*

bolic weight which makes them typical of God's continuing war against Satan, and of Christ's victory in particular. It is in this sense that the pregnant term *yasha'*, "savior," can be used of them. The book of Judges repeatedly calls the judges "deliverers, saviors," and speaks of their work as "deliverance, salvation," all translations of *yasha'* in its various forms. (As mentioned in chapter 2 of this study, *yasha'* is the foundation for the names Joshua and Jesus.) We should not limit this only to "political salvation" (though it includes that), for it is a fuller, Spiritual as well as cultural deliverance that is in view. Apart from Spiritual repentance and conversion, there would never have been any of the deliverances recorded in the book of Judges.

The judges were, in the ordinary way of life, civil rulers; but in Scripture, as their work is recorded for our profit, they are spoken of as anointed ones—in Hebrew, *messiahs*—and as saviors. Thus, the book of Judges tells us something about the normal work of the civil magistrate in a Christian society, but it also tells us something about the special work of Christ, the final Messiah or Anointed One, the greater Joshua or Savior.

With these introductory remarks in view, let us now turn to the story of Othniel, the first judge.

Othniel

3:7. And the sons of Israel did what was evil in the sight of the LORD, and forgot the LORD their God, and served the Baals and the Asherahs.

8. Then the anger of the LORD was kindled against Israel, so that He sold them into the hands of Cushan-Rishathaim king of Aram-Naharaim; and the sons of Israel served Cushan-Rishathaim eight years.

9. And when the sons of Israel cried to the LORD, the LORD raised up a deliverer (*yasha'*) for the sons of Israel to deliver (*yasha'*) them: Othniel the son of Kenaz, Caleb's younger brother.

10. And the Spirit of the LORD came upon him, and he judged Israel. When he went out to war, the LORD gave Cushan-Rishathaim king of Aram-Naharaim into his hand, so that he prevailed over Cushan-Rishathaim.

11. Then then land had rest forty years. And Othniel the son of Kenaz died.

After the elders who survived Joshua died, the people began to worship the Baals (local varieties of Baalism) and the Asherahs.

Asherah was a slightly different goddess from Ashteroth, but both were expressions of the Canaanite Venus goddess. This idolatry provoked the Lord to anger, and He *sold* them into slavery, back into Egyptian-type bondage.

Cushan-Rishathaim means "The Cushite of Double Wickedness." He ruled over Aram-Naharaim, which means "Syria of the Two Rivers," in English versions usually translated Mesopotamia. The Hebrew is slightly humorous, as can be seen—after all, "The Cushite of Double Wickedness" was probably not this king's real name—but there is more than humor. These words use the rare Hebrew dual form. The ending *-aim* is neither singular nor plural, but dual, expressing two-fold. This points to the idea that this bondage was doubly severe.

They weren't sold south this time, but north. Mesopotamia is the land of Babylon and of Assyria. Scripture calls attention to the place Cushan came from, the place of Babylon. At the end of the Israelite monarchy, when God finally judged His people in a definitive way, it was the northern peoples of Assyria and then of Babylon whom He used for that purpose. We must see that the *first* oppressing power brought against sinful Israel was from the same place. God here issues a warning, and hints at the future, for the bondage that Israel eventually experienced in Assyria and Babylon was doubly as severe as what they had experienced in Egypt. (This idea is carried further by Jeremiah 50:21, where Babylon is called Merath*aim*, "Double Wickedness.")

This prophetic interpretation is reinforced when we recall that Abraham had been called out of Babylon (Ur of the Chaldees) to begin with. Babel had been erected so that the people could make a name for themselves (Gen. 11:4), but God promised to give a name to Abram (Gen. 12:2). Joshua had called this to their attention in Joshua 24:2. From all this, it should have been clear to them that if they rejected the Lord, they would wind up back under Babylonian rule. If God had threatened to take them back into Egypt, He would have been threatening to undo the Mosaic deliverance, but they could still have had confidence in the Abrahamic promises. By threatening to take them back under Babylon, however, God threatened to remove everything from them, even the Abrahamic blessings. The first exodus, the exodus of Abram out of Ur, would be reversed, and there would be nothing left. Such was the threat. (When it finally came to pass, at the exile, we find that the grace and love of God is so great that He did not cast them off totally after all.)

They were oppressed eight years. The number eight in Scripture frequently points to new beginnings. Man's sin defiled his first week, but God grants him a new opportunity on the eighth day (the day circumcision was performed, and day of Christ's resurrection).[3] Possibly the deliverance in the eighth year here was designed to show that God was giving Israel a second chance. (By the way, it is not possible to construct a strict chronology for the book of Judges, since various judges ruled locally, and their rules overlapped. Totalling up all the numbers gives us too many years, well more than the 480 years permitted by the statement of 1 Kings 6:1. This makes it all the more likely that the numbers in Judges, in addition to being historically accurate, have theological significance.)

The deliverer God raised up was Othniel. The meaning of his name is not absolutely known, but probably "God is Powerful" or "Lion of God" is correct. Regardless of the literal meaning of his name, Othniel certainly was a lion of the Tribe of Judah. He was not, however, a descendant of Judah, but a converted Kenizzite, as we have seen in our comments on Judges 1:11-15. Since most of the tribe of Judah were bastards, at this time none were eligible for public office in Israel. (We shall return to this matter later in this commentary.) In his victory over this proto-Babylon, we can see a foreshadowing of the Greater Othniel, Who destroyed the ultimate Babylon in Revelation 19:11-16.

Babylon is still with us today, in Washington, D.C., as well as in the Kremlin. Those who reject the salvation offered by the Greater Othniel will wind up in slavery to some modern Doubly-Wicked bureaucrat or commissar.

After the oppression, there were forty years of peace. Whether Othniel lived to judge this entire period we are not told. We ought probably to envision the normal process of judging according to the pattern given by Jethro in Exodus 18. Most civil judgments would be rendered by local elders over tens,

---

3. I have discussed this at greater length in my book, *The Law of the Covenant: An Exposition of Exodus 21–23* (Tyler, TX: Institute for Christian Economics, 1984), p. 164.

fifties, hundreds, and thousands, while "the difficult disputes they would bring to Moses" (Ex. 18:26). The heir of Moses was Joshua, and of Joshua were the judges, and of the judges were the kings. Only really tough cases were brought before this final court (see 1 Kings 3:16-28).

Othniel probably died long before these forty years were up, since he was doubtless an old man by the time he was called to battle. But he left a good legacy, for forty is the number of a generation. He raised up his generation well, and it was not until another generation came along that the land fell into apostasy and judgment once again.

4

EHUD: SODOM AND AMALEK RESURGENT
(Judges 3:12-31)

The liturgical structure (that is, God's Word and man's response) of Judges 3:12-31 is as follows:

1. God's command: be faithful
2. Man's response: disobedience
3. God's evaluation: Judgment — Moab invasion (Implied Command: repent and be delivered)
4. Man's response: repentance
5. God's evaluation: Blessing — Ehud raised up (Implied Command: obey the judge)
6. Man's response: submission to Ehud
7. God's evaluation: Blessing — deliverance and 80 years of peace.

The following is an outline of events:

I. Enslavement (Judges 3:12-14)
II. Definitive Deliverance: The Savior crushes the Leader of the Enemies (3:15-26)
III. Full Deliverance: The People follow the Savior and destroy the Enemies (3:16-29)
IV. Peace (3:30)
V. Appendix: Shamgar and the Philistines (3:31)

Enslavement

3:12. Now the sons of Israel again did evil in the sight of the LORD. So the LORD strengthened Eglon the king of Moab against Israel, because they had done evil in the sight of the LORD.

13. And he gathered to himself the sons of Ammon and Amalek; and he went and smote Israel, and they possessed the City of Palm Trees.

14. And the sons of Israel served Eglon the king of Moab eighteen years.

Each of the enemies mentioned here is significant. The leader against Israel was Moab, and to him was joined his cousin Ammon. Moab and Ammon were descendants of Lot by incestuous breeding with his daughters. The daughters learned such morality from their lives in Sodom and Gomorrah, and Moab and Ammon are, in Scripture, seen as historical extensions of Sodom and Gomorrah (Gen. 19). When we read of Moab and Ammon in Scripture, we must see behind them the perversity and cruelty of Sodom and Gomorrah (see Zeph. 2:8-10). By selling Israel into their hands, God was not only saying, "This is what you deserve," but also "This is what you are like; this is the kind of culture you properly are placed in." The fat, gluttonous Eglon is a picture of a Sodomite king.

Also joined with them were the Amalekites. Amalek was, according to Numbers 24:20, the first of the nations of the world. They were, moreover, the fiercest foe of Israel, and the enemy that Israel had defeated first (Ex. 17:8-13). How humiliating to be under the thumb of Amalek after having defeated them once already! Amalek was an exceptionally cruel and vicious opponent. The reference to Amalek's cutting off Israel's "tails" in Deuteronomy 25:18 may be read to mean either that Amalek attacked the stragglers at the rear or "tail" of the Israelite march, or that Amalek poked fun at circumcision by castrating the men they killed. However we translate the Hebrew, it is clear that Amalek was a monstrous enemy. God regarded them as such, vowing to war against them forever (Dt. 25:19; Ex. 17:16).

More irony appears from the place Eglon made his headquarters: Jericho, the City of Palm Trees. This was the first place Israel conquered in Canaan, and it was wholly dedicated to the Lord by being burned with sacrificial fire. Now it had fallen into the hands of the enemy, again a pointed goad in Israel's side, to show them what they had become. (For a picture of God's true City of Palm Trees, see Ezekiel 41:18-26.)

Finally, the oppression lasted eighteen years. Ten is the number for totality, plus a full week of seven, until we come to the eighth year, the year of deliverance. This is an increase in judgment over what had gone before.

H. C. Hoeksema comments: "But if these eighteen years reveal that the chastisements of the Lord increase in severity as the sin is repeated, they also show that there was need of a very severe oppression. Was it not true that as soon as the people would cry to the God of their fathers in true repentance, He would deliver them? The situation was thus, then, that it required eighteen years of oppression for the children of Israel to learn their lesson. For a long time apparently they simply submitted to the inevitable. They did not turn to Jehovah in repentance; they did not turn from the service of the gods of the nations. They continued to make friends with the nations in whose midst they dwelled. They persisted in giving their daughters in marriage to the nations of the kingdom of darkness. Hence, it required some time to make Israel listen. Meanwhile the oppression became heavier, no doubt, as the years went by. It must have been when finally the burden became unbearable that they cried to the God of the covenant for help and salvation. It was then, and not before, that Jehovah sent deliverance. Before this, salvation could not be sent, for the simple reason that the lesson had to be learned by the people. How could Jehovah deliver them as long as they served Baalim and Ashteroth and forgot the Lord their God? Would they not acknowledge these idol gods for the deliverance which Jehovah had wrought, and would they not continue to amalgamate with the nations round about them? But this might not be. The people had to learn war. They had to be taught to change their attitude over against the nations with whom they made friends. They had to be taught to fight against the kingdom of darkness. The purpose of the oppression, therefore, was not reached before Israel understood that the alliance with the kingdom of darkness was only to their hurt, before they learned to hate the power of heathendom as it oppressed them, before they became able to distinguish between the gods of the nations and the God of Israel, before they turned from the gods that afford no help and in faith and repentance turned to their God, in order that He might save them."[1]

It had been the faith of Abraham that had saved Lot from

---

1. H. C. Hoeksema, *Era of the Judges* (Grandville, Michigan: Theological School of the Protestant Reformed Churches, 1981), pp. 67f.

Sodom, but the people lacked that faith, so they were back in Sodom. It had been the prayers of Moses that had saved Israel from Amalek, but the people lacked those prayers, so they were oppressed again by Amalek. It had been the convictions of Joshua that had destroyed Jericho, but the people lacked those convictions, so Jericho had been recaptured by the enemy, and resettled. In all this we must remember what verse 12 says: It was the Lord who strengthened Eglon, raising him up to chastise Israel. As always, it is not the visible enemy with whom we have to do, but rather with the Lord. When He is pleased with us, the enemy will vanish.

The Savior and His Methods

15. But when the sons of Israel cried to the LORD, the LORD raised up a deliverer (*yasha‘*) for them, Ehud the son of Gera, the Benjamite, a left-handed man. And the sons of Israel sent tribute by his hand to Eglon the king of Moab.
16. And Ehud made himself a sword which had two edges, a cubit in length; and he bound it on his right thigh under his cloak.
17. And he presented the tribute to Eglon king of Moab. Now Eglon was a very fat man.
18. And it came about when he had finished presenting the tribute, that he sent away the people who had carried the tribute.
19. But he himself turned back from the idols which were at Gilgal, and said, "I have a secret message for you, O king." And he said, "Keep silence." And all who attended him left him.

Ehud, whose name possibly means "Strong," was the savior. He was of the tribe of Benjamin. When Rachel gave birth to Benjamin, as she died she named him Ben-Oni, "Son of My Sorrow" (Gen. 35:18). Jacob changed his name to Ben-Jamin, "Son of the Right Hand." In Hebrew this is a pun, for it can mean either "I come from my father's right hand, the hand of authority and rulership," or "I am right-handed." Benjamin, however, seems to have been left-handed, for we find that left-handedness became a characteristic of his descendants (Jud. 20:16).

Ehud is a true Benjamite. He is left-handed, and though his life commences in the sorrow of persecution, he is elevated to the right hand in becoming a ruler. In this he portrays Christ, the True Benjamite. Our Lord was the Man of Sorrows (Is.

53:3), but His "name" was changed when He was elevated to the right hand of the Father (Acts 7:56), the seat of rule and authority. (See Micah 5:2-3 for a prophetic commentary on this.)

Ehud was well thought of already. The tribute money was sent by his hand to the oppressing ruler, Eglon. Indeed, Eglon held Ehud in such esteem as to grant him a private conference later on. This would have been possible only if Ehud had already been a leader in Israel.

Ehud's two-edged sword is noted here. The sword had no crosspiece, for it sank completely into Eglon. It was apparently the length of a short cubit, from elbow to knuckles. Ehud bound it on his right thigh, so that it would be available to his left hand. The sword is specifically noted as two-edged, calling to mind Christ's two-edged sword, the Word of God (Ps. 45:3; Eph. 6:17; Heb. 4:12; Rev. 19:15).

After presenting the tribute, Ehud and his men retired, and separated at the "graven stones" at Gilgal. These might refer to idols set up by Eglon at that historic site, in which case they doubtless galled and goaded Ehud into action; or the reference might be to the memorial stones set up by Joshua (Josh. 4:1-8, 20), which would also have called his purpose to his mind. While it is not actually forbidden by Scripture, it is unlikely that Joshua's memorial stones would have been graven, on analogy with Exodus 20:4 and 25. Thus, I think it most likely that Moab had defiled Gilgal with idols.

Ehud left a force of men there, and returned to Eglon's abode. Gilgal was between Jericho and the Jordan, and Eglon's army would have to retreat toward the Jordan, passing by the trap set for them at Gilgal. There is also a snapshot of redemption here, in that the Lord's army was told to wait while the Lord's anointed messiah struck the definitive blow. Christ strikes the killing blow against Satan, and then His army moves in to mop up Satan's fleeing army.

Ehud asked for a private conference, saying that he had a secret message for Eglon. That he was granted it again shows his position as a magistrate in Israel. He announced that he had a message for the king, one so important that it could only be delivered in secret. This message was the Word of God, in its negative aspect of judgment, though Eglon did not know it then. The king ordered all his retainers to keep silence, that is, to be quiet so that he could hear the message. This meant in effect that they would have to leave him, since their very presence constituted "noise" which interfered with the secrecy of the message.

The Savior Crushes the Head of the Enemy

20. And Ehud came to him while he was sitting alone in his cool roof chamber. And Ehud said, "I have a message from God for you." And he arose from his seat.

21. And Ehud stretched out his left hand, took the sword from his right thigh, and thrust it into his belly.

22. The handle also went in after the blade, and the fat closed over the blade, for he did not draw the sword out of his belly; and the refuse came out.

23. Then Ehud went out into the vestibule and shut the doors of the roof chamber behind him, and locked them.

24. When he had gone out, his servants came and looked, and behold, the doors of the roof chamber were locked; and they said, "He is only covering his feet [having a bowel movement] in the cool room."

25. And they waited until they became ashamed; but behold, he did not open the doors of the roof chamber. Therefore they took the key and opened them, and behold, their master had fallen to the earth dead.

Eglon received Ehud in a room on the roof, doubtless having lots of windows so that the cool breeze could blow through. Ehud deceived Eglon by leading him to think that he had a verbal message from God for him, whereas in reality the message was the judgment of cold iron. Ehud used the word "God," not the term YHWH, LORD, for Eglon did not respect the Lord of Israel, but he would respect the unspecified "God." At the mention of a message from God, Eglon stood up in respect, showing more respect for his pagan conception of divinity than most Christians show for the true God. (By the way, historically the congregation has stood during the actual reading of the Bible, the message of God, in worship.)

So standing, his great belly was exposed, and Ehud reached out his left hand to draw the knife from his right thigh. Eglon might have suspected something if Ehud had stretched forth his right hand and reached to his left thigh, for this would have constituted a reasonable threat: All men carried swords on their left thighs. But Eglon suspected nothing, it seems, because Ehud was left-handed. In many cultures of the world, left-handedness is regarded as bad, and left-handed children are forced to become right-handed as they grow up. Israel was more enlightened than to practise such a stupid and superstitious custom, but is it entirely possible that the pagan Eglon was from a culture that suppressed left-handedness. He may never have encountered a left-handed adult.

The sword sank fully into Eglon's flesh, indicating just how fat he really was. The fat closed completely over the blade, so that the sword disappeared from view. Later on, when the servants of Eglon peered through the windows or latticework of the roof chamber, they saw him sitting on the floor, where he had fallen, and did not see a sword sticking out of him. Ehud did not have to try to sneak a bloody sword out of the house. Eglon's fat was used by God to buy Ehud time to escape and raise his army. The symbol of Moab's power (Eglon's sheer size) was used against them in their destruction. Here we see God's ironic humor, as he uses the works of men against them.

God used something else as well. The last part of verse 22 says that "it" came out. Commentators have sometimes debated the question, but there is no doubt as to what "it" was. In death, the muscles of the colon relax, and sometimes excrement issues from the body. According to verse 24, Eglon's courtiers thought that he was "covering his feet in the cool room." The expression "covering the feet" is used for private acts in Scripture. Here it clearly refers to a bowel movement. They could only have thought this if they had smelled the odor. Eglon was a *very* fat man (v. 17). His excrement would therefore have been copious, poorly digested, and very noisome. God used this stench to buy Ehud time to escape.

In all of this we see God using the sins of men against them. Eglon's foul manner of life, his gluttony, and his idolatry (standing up at the mention of what he assumed was his own false god), all were used against him in the end. God always makes the punishment fit the crime, and the criminal; and God often does so humorously (see Ps. 2:4).

Eglon means "calf." Matthew Henry comments that "he fell like a fatted calf, by the knife, an acceptable sacrifice to divine justice." Henry is correct, for as we have seen in connection with Judges 1:17, those who do not have Christ as their Substitute Sacrifice must themselves become an acceptable sacrifice. The two-edged sword, the sword of God's divine Word and of His judgment, slew Eglon.

It is sometimes objected against Ehud that he engaged in deception and assassination to further God's purposes. Some commentators believe that Ehud did right, but that he had a special warrant for doing so. Against both of these views we must maintain that Scripture nowhere rules against deception in warfare. We shall have more to say on this matter when we get to Judges 4:18, but suffice it to note that Eglon had no business on Israelite soil. He was an invader, and doubtless had taken many lives. David refused to touch the Lord's anointed (1 Sam. 24:6; 26:9, 11, 16; 2 Sam. 1:14ff.), and it is true that the ruler of any country is anointed by God (Rom. 13:1-5) in a sense; but it is also true that Eglon was not anointed king or judge in Israel. He was an invader, a conqueror, and he had no business being where he was; and so he forfeited peace. Ehud was making war, as God was teaching His people to do (Jud. 3:2), and in wartime killing, assassination, and deception are proper, assuming the war itself is a just and holy war. What Ehud did was proper in terms of wartime ethics. Moreover, as we have noted, Ehud was not a private vigilante, but an Israelite magistrate, already recognized as such. Thus, it was proper for him to spearhead a war against the enemy.

Ehud's position is also seen in that he locked the doors. This was done for practical reasons, obviously, but it also has theological overtones. It is the keys of the kingdom that are given into the hands of God's officers (Matt. 16:19), and it is ultimately Christ Himself Who opens and Who locks (Rev. 3:7). In the Old Testament, the elders sat in the gates, as guardians of the doors of the city (compare the cherubim, Gen. 3:24). When Ehud locked the door, he exercised the power of the keys, closing the gate between God's people and His enemies.

When they saw that the roof chamber was locked, the servants drew the conclusion, based on the smell, that Eglon was "covering his feet." This same expression is used in 1 Samuel 24:3 to refer to bowel movements. In Deuteronomy 23:12-14, God directed His army to place a latrine outside the camp, and

not to place it inside. Outside the camp is the place of uncleanness (Dt. 23:10) and inside the camp is the place of cleanness (v.
11). It is true, of course, that such a law as this has an hygienic
benefit, but the specific reason given in the actual text of Scripture is this: "Since the LORD your God walks in the midst of
your camp to deliver you and to defeat your enemies before
you, therefore your camp must be holy; and He must not see the
nakedness of anything among you lest He turn away from you"
(v. 14). Excrement in the camp is the equivalent of exposing nakedness, which is forbidden in the Levitical code (Lev. 18:6ff.).

Nakedness is associated with shame. Genesis 2:25 calls attention to the fact that Adam and Eve were naked and not ashamed.
When they sinned, they sewed fig leaves to cover the shame of
their nakedness, which was localized at their loins (Gen. 3:7).
The sacrament of circumcision, performed on the loins of the
male, is said to roll away shame (Josh. 5:9; see also Micah 1:11).

Man's sense of shame is psychologically localized in terms of
his "private parts," his genitals and bowels, in terms of sex and
excretion. Thus, both activities are performed in private, and
exposed public toilets, such as are common in men's locker
rooms, are initially humiliating to the men who must use them.
(In the light of Scripture, such arrangements must be condemned as perverse, a hangover of Greek homosexual views of
athletics and physical education.) Thus, these two activities were
normally referred to in Israelite society under a figure of speech.
The private parts of the human anatomy, below the waist, were
called "feet," and covering or uncovering the "feet" referred to
covering or exposing nakedness. (See Ruth 3:4, 7-9; 2 Kings
18:27; Is. 36:12; Ezk. 16:25, in Hebrew or in marginal English
renderings; "urine" is literally "water of the feet.")

"Uncovering the feet" refers to sexual relations, in that the
man and the woman are properly naked to each other, and
wrapped in one garment (Ruth 3:4, 9). "Covering the feet"
refers to the covering of an act of shame or nakedness, and thus
to excretion. Covering their "feet" is exactly what Adam and
Eve did when they felt shame. Eglon's servants assumed that he
was "covering" his shame in the roof chamber, but God did not
permit Eglon's shame to be covered, and exposed it for all the
world to see and laugh at.

Scripture nowhere explicitly says so, but my own belief is

that before the Fall, excrement did not give off a noisome stench, and thus was not putrid, foul, dead, and unclean. It is possible that the bad smell is a byproduct of imperfect digestion, itself a result of the Fall. Uncleanness in the Law is associated with death. Unclean means "dirty," and to understand the religious meaning of this, we need only remember that the soil was cursed under the Old Covenant, and that the curse was death (Gen. 3:17, 19). The serpent travels in the environment of curse, and eats the curse to himself (Gen. 3:14). Anything rotting on the ground is returning to dust, and thus is dirty and unclean—thus contact with any kind of dead body caused uncleanness (Leviticus 11; Numbers 19). Excrement, rotting on the ground, is thus tied with dead things, and thus it has the smell of death. Because of this complex of associations, designed by God, excrement is ceremonially unclean, and must be kept out of the place where God dwells, outside the camp. Eglon wallowing in his own filth is like the serpent crawling in the cursed soil. Finally, we may contrast the stench of Eglon's cool room with the perfumed incense of the house of God (Ex. 30:7).[2]

By calling attention to Eglon's excrement, Scripture notes that the man was ceremonially unclean, outside the camp. His nakedness was exposed. His servants were covered with *shame* (v. 25, in Hebrew) when they realized that something was wrong. Meanwhile, Ehud went back to Gilgal (v. 26), where the shame or reproach of Egypt had been rolled away from Israel (Josh. 5:9). Eglon was ashamed in his death, but Ehud was not ashamed of the gospel (Rom. 1:16). (I should note that the Hebrew word used in Joshua 5:9 is the word for reproach, not for shame; but these two things are inseparable, and virtually synonymous, as in Isaiah 47:2, 3, where the Hebrew word for reproach is actually translated "shame," and associated with nakedness.) It was Jesus Christ Who, on the cross, had His nakedness exposed as our Substitute, so that we might be clothed and unashamed.

Having crushed the (political) head of the enemy, the savior now summons his army, and leads them to victory against the remainder of the enemy's forces.

---

2. In the New Covenant, the curse on the ground is removed by Christ's having taken all curse upon Himself.

The Savior Leads His Army to Victory

26. Now Ehud escaped while they were delaying, and he passed by the idols and escaped to Seirah.

27. And it came about when he had arrived, that he blew the horn in the hill country of Ephraim; and the sons of Israel went down with him from the hill country, and he was in front of them.

28. And he said to them, "Pursue, for the LORD has given your enemies the Moabites into your hands." So they went down after him and seized the fords of the Jordan opposite Moab, and did not allow anyone to cross.

29. And they struck down at that time about 10,000 Moabites, all robust and valiant men; and no one escaped.

30. So Moab was subdued that day under the hand of Israel. And the land was undisturbed for eighty years.

Ehud did have time to escape. First he went to Gilgal, the place where shame was removed, to rally the detachment he had left there. Then he went north, and backtracked somewhat to rally his forces in Ephraim. As the Israelite forces swept down out of the hills, Ehud was in front of them. They joined their fellows at Gilgal and took possession of the crossing place of the Jordan. The Moabites, in disarray at the death of their leader, and a long way from home, began a hurried retreat toward the Jordan. All were slain by Ehud's men.

The Jordan was the boundary into the Promised Land. It was the place of transition from death to life, the place (later on) of baptism and judgment. For Israel, the judgment had been unto life, because circumcision was a bloody sacrifice that took away their sin. There was a hill of foreskins by the gateway into Canaan (Josh. 5:3). This formed a bloody "pillar" like a gate post, which corresponded to the blood on the doorposts of the houses in Egypt at Passover. God spared them when He saw the blood. But for Moab, there was no slain lamb's blood on the doorpost, and no hill of foreskins at the gate. Thus, for them the place of judgment was a place of destruction. (This theme of the Jordan as a place of judgment recurs twice again, in Judges 7:24 and 12:5.)

Numerologically, the 10,000 slain represents a total and complete victory, ten being the number of totality. Just as Moab had oppressed Israel totally and fully (10 + 7), as we saw above, so Moab was totally and completely defeated. God had ordered that Amalek be completely obliterated (Ex. 17:14-16; Dt. 25:19), and so every neo-Sodomite and Amalekite warrior was faithfully destroyed by Ehud. This faithful "response of man" led to eighty years of blessing as "God's evaluation."

Ehud himself killed the enemy leader; Ehud's men killed the enemy's troops. Thus it is with Christ also. He has dealt with Satan, and we are called to deal with Satan's legions. Revelation 19:11-16 pictures the Greater Ehud as He leads His army to victory by the use of the proclamation of the Word, the two-edged sword that comes from His mouth.

God's people emerged to rule over their enemies. They had driven back the opposition, and the land rested eighty years, two generations. This indicates that Ehud and his generation must have been quite faithful in teaching the Truth to their children, for it was not until the third generation that God again chastised His people.

Finally, we must see that it was the Lord Who raised up the enemy (v. 12); it was the Lord Who raised up the savior (v. 15); and it was the Lord Who gave the victory (v. 28). We must ever see the Lord at work in Scripture.

Shamgar: The Surprise Judge

31. And after him came Shamgar the son of Anath, who struck down six hundred Philistines with an oxgoad; and he also saved (*yasha'*) Israel.

Shamgar is not an Israelite word, so it is possible, yea likely, that he was a convert to Israel's God and cause. He is said to be the son of Anath, meaning either that he came from an environment of Anath-worship, or that his father's name was Anath, the same as that of the fertility goddess mentioned in Judges 1:33. In either case this again makes it likely that Shamgar was a convert.

He lived in the southern part of Israel, where the Philistines were. Thus, he was an heir to Ehud, working during the eighty year period mentioned in v. 30. He probably labored toward the end of that period, since he was a contemporary of Deborah (Jud. 5:6). Under his Spiritual guidance, the southern part of

Israel was at peace from oppression for a long time, and the wars of Deborah and of Gideon were fought against invaders in the far north. The very silence of Scripture concerning the fate of Judah, Simeon, and Benjamin during this period speaks eloquently of Shamgar's effectiveness as a Spiritual leader, and as a warrior.

Shamgar's name may possibly mean "one who flees." This certainly makes sense in view of his method of fighting. Over the years he clocked up 600 dead Philistines, using a surprise weapon, an oxgoad. These were about eight feet long, two inches thick at one end and sharpened to a point at the other. No one would expect this simple farmer, driving his oxen along the road, to turn suddenly and lay low the troublesome Philistines watching him. With such an eight foot long spear, no one could get close to Shamgar when he fought.

Shamgar's weapon was not a weapon at all, but an implement of work. The contrast between a work-oriented culture and a conquest-oriented culture runs throughout the Scripture. The Bible guarantees that the "carpenters" will eventually overcome the "horns," those who work will overcome those who live by force and power (Zech. 1:18-21). We shall see several times in Judges the theme of implements of work destroying those who live by implements of war (for instance, Jael's tent peg, and the upper millstone that killed Abimelech).

The gospel is the greatest example of humor in history. The essence of humor is surprise, the twist of a phrase, the unexpected happening that changes everything. It was at history's darkest hour, on the cross, when surprise! Satan was defeated and our salvation accomplished. "He that sits in the heavens laughs," we are told (Ps. 2:4). The book of Judges is a book of humor. The death of Eglon, in its every aspect, is a belly full of laughs for the righteous Christian.

Thus it is here also. Shamgar was a big surprise to his Philistine opponents. They did not expect a Canaanite to be a loyal defender, yea judge, in Israel. Nor did they expect this simple farmer to spear them. Surprise, Philistines!

The number six is the number of humanity in sin, cast out of Eden, failing to come to the sabbath of seven, doomed to labor in slavery forever. The number five is usually associated with the Philistines, because of the pentapolis (five cities); but here the number arrived at (by Divine superintendence) is six, to show that the work of the judge is to destroy the old Adam, in order to give salvation. It is Christ, the Greater Shamgar, who destroys the sinful "six" of Adamic humanity, and raises His people into the "seven" of fulfillment and sabbath rest.

We are told that Shamgar "saved" Israel (*yasha'* again). This means that he gave Israel living space by driving away the enemy. Living space meant that southern Israel could pursue God's work of dressing and guarding the Garden in peace. Cultural advance was possible.

Things were not so well in the north, however. Zebulon and Naphtali were always under the threat of enemy invasion. They were effectively "Finlandized" for much of history, so that they were a people who walked and dwelt in darkness (Is. 9:1, 2). Jabin was oppressing them even as Shamgar worked in the south, and the judgess Deborah had had to leave her home in Issachar (Jud. 5:15) and move to the middle (hill) country of Ephraim. These people in the north, however, were about to see a great light (Is. 9:2), the deliverer Barak, whose name means "lightning."

5

DEBORAH: A MOTHER FOR ISRAEL
(Judges 4)

The liturgical structure of the events of Judges 4 and 5 is this:

1. God's command: be faithful
2. Man's response: disobedience
3. God's evaluation: Judgment — Canaanite invasion

4. (Implied Command: repent and be delivered)
5. Man's response: repentance
6. God's evaluation: Blessing — Deborah raised up

7. God's command to Barak: lead the army
8. Barak's response: not unless Deborah goes along
9. God's evaluation: a woman will get the glory

10. God's command to Israel: follow Barak and Deborah
11. Israel's response: some tribes come, and some do not
12. God's evaluation: the song of Deborah

The following is an outline of the text:

I. Enslavement (Judges 4:1-3)

II. God's command/promise (4:4-7)

III. Man's response (4:8-24)
    A. Barak's response and God's evaluation (4:8-9)
    B. Israel's response (4:10-16)
    C. Jael's response (4:17-22)
    D. Continuing response (4:23-24)

IV. God's evaluation (Judges 5)
    A. Stanza 1: The Situation (5:2-11)
    B. Stanza 2: The Battle (5:12-22)
    C. Stanza 3: The Aftermath (5:23-31)

Canaan Resurgent

4:1. Then the sons of Israel again did evil in the sight of the
LORD, after Ehud died.

2. And the LORD sold them into the hand of Jabin king of
Canaan, who reigned in Hazor; and the commander of his army
was Sisera, who lived in Harosheth-Hagoyim [Harosheth of the
Gentiles].

3. And the sons of Israel cried to the LORD; for he had nine
hundred iron chariots, and he oppressed the sons of Israel
severely for twenty years.

Each enemy is significant: Babylon, Amalek, Sodom, and
now the Canaanites. Here the Lord delivers Israel (*selling* them,
the language of enslavement) into the hand of Jabin, king of
Canaan. Irony of ironies! The Canaanites, who had been
defeated once, now rule Israel. Those who were under the curse
as "slaves of slaves" now rule over the righteous, the proper
rulers of the world (Gen. 9:25ff.).

"Jabin" is to Canaan what "Pharaoh" is to Egypt, a name
carried by all the rulers. He reigned in Hazor. Under Joshua, an
earlier Jabin had been liquidated (Josh. 11:1-15). The defeat of
the king of Canaan had been the climax of the conquest of Canaan. Thus, Jabin's city of Hazor had been totally devoted to
the Lord, just as the first city conquered had been (11:11ff.). The
conquest of the land, from Jericho to Hazor, had been
bracketed by "hormahs," cities totally devoted to God by means
of sacrificial fire. Hazor and Jabin had been the *head* of the Canaanite city-states (11:10), and so the capital city was devoted to
the Lord for destruction. Here is the theme of the crushing of
the head (political) of the serpent. Finally, we note from this
first conquest that iron chariots had not stopped Joshua (11:4ff.;
compare Jud. 1:19), and that the victory took place in connection with water: "So Joshua and all the people of war with him
came upon them suddenly by the waters of Merom, and
attacked them" (11:7), a clue to the means God would use to
deliver Israel from Jabin a second time.

Now Hazor had been rebuilt, and a new Jabin was on the
throne. The Israelites in the north had been asleep, and the
enemy had refortified himself. Each of the stories in Judges has
a particular meaning, and this one no less. To understand this

story fully, we have to bear in mind that Canaan is a type or symbol of the whole world, as well as of the Garden of Eden. The New Testament equivalent of the conquest of Canaan is the conquest of the whole earth by and for Christ (Matt. 28:18-20). Thus, in a figure, Jabin is king of the world. He has usurped Adam's place as ruler of the Garden, of Canaan, of the whole world. Jabin and his military commander thus are types or symbols of Satan, usurper of this world's throne.

If Jabin is king, then Sisera is his right hand. The text mainly focuses on the destruction of Sisera; little is said about Jabin. Why is this? The answer is that just as Christ, the Son, is the right hand of the Father, so Sisera is the right hand of the king. The right hand acts for the supreme commander, the king. By focusing on the defeat of Sisera by Deborah, Jael, and Barak, the text calls attention to the war of the seeds: the right hand and seed of the Lord versus the right hand and "seed" of Jabin. And of course, preeminent in this section is the Mother, the bride of the Lord who raises up the seed, and the mother of Sisera who raised him up. This explains why the text focuses almost exclusively on the destruction of Sisera, and not on Jabin.

Harosheth-Hagoyim means "Harosheth of the Gentiles," and is the same place, roughly, as "Galilee of the Gentiles" of later times. This is important, for it keys this story in to the prophecy of Isaiah 9:1ff. and its fulfillment in Matthew 4:12ff. The story of Deborah and Barak is linked with the story of Gideon in Psalm 83 and in Isaiah 9:1ff., for both histories are concerned with Zebulon and Naphtali, and take place in the north, in Galilee. Let us be aware, then, at the outset that these two histories will be freighted with symbolic overtones that point to Christ and His work.

Sisera had 900 chariots. We saw in Judges 1:19 that Israel had failed the test of faith when opposed by iron chariots. God is now ready to show that He is fully capable of eliminating such. Twice the passage gives the number of chariots as 900 (here and in 4:13). The significance of the number eludes us, however, since the number nine does not have any established meaning in Scripture. Ten is the number of totality, and 900 includes 10×10, just as the period of oppression is $10 + 10$, signifying the severity of the bondage.

Why the nine, though? It might be thought that nine tribes were affected, but Judges 5:14-18 lists ten different groups. Possibly nine is used to indicate that man's forces are never totally adequate (that is, 900, not 1000). Possibly nine is used because Jabin/Hazor had already been conquered once and devoted to the Lord (Josh. 11). That which is devoted to the Lord is a tithe, one tenth. Thus, maybe the reason Sisera only had 900 chariots is that the Lord had already taken His tithe in the days of Joshua. The definitive blow had already been struck, and what was left was a mopping up exercise.

We note, finally, that verse 3 calls the oppression "severe," language used of the Egyptian bondage (Ex. 1:13-14).

The Mother of Israel

4. Now Deborah, a woman, a prophetess, the wife of Lappidoth, was judging Israel at that time.
5. And shè used to sit [or dwell] under the Palm Tree of Deborah between Ramah and Bethel in the hill country of Ephraim; and the sons of Israel came up to her for judgment.

We are so used to thinking of the enmity between the Seed and the Serpent, that we tend to forget the first part of Genesis 3:15: "And I will put enmity between you and the woman." Satan not only attacks the seed throughout Scripture, he also attacks the woman (note especially Gen. 12, 20, 26). Preeminently the hatred of the woman for the snake is seen, however, when the snake attacks her child, the seed. It is the mother who, to protect the seed, wars most fiercely against the serpent. In her song, Deborah identifies herself as the mother of Israel, and contrasts herself with the mother of Sisera (Jud. 5:7, 28). This contrast lies at the heart of the meaning of this story.

Deborah, as the aged mother in Israel, has raised up a righteous generation, led by Barak. Sisera's mother has also raised up a seed. It is now time for the seed of the woman (Deborah's Barak) to crush the seed of the serpent (Sisera). In the background stand the two mothers.

Humanity was created to symbolize, to image, God (Gen. 1:26). There are some parallels between the woman as God's image, and the Holy Spirit. The woman is taken from the side of man (Gen. 2:21), just as the Spirit, the Paraclete, comes from

the side of the Word (John 14:16, 26). Just as the woman glorifies her husband, so the Spirit glorifies the Word (1 Cor. 11:7;
John 16:14).

But there is another dimension to this as well. It is the Spirit
Who hovers over the Church, and identifies with the Bride so as
to make her fit. We say, rightly, that the Church is the mother of
believers, but that motherhood is a direct result of the work of
the Spirit. We may also say, then, that the Spirit is the mother of
believers.

Deborah's work of raising up a godly generation is thus
analogous to the work of the Spirit and of the Church in raising
up a godly culture. Godly magistrates, such as Barak, are sons
of the Church, of the Spirit. In an age of anarchy such as ours,
Deborah's role as mother to her generation has a lot to say to us
about the present duty of the Church.

Deborah means "Bee," and one wit has remarked that she
had honey for her friends and a stinger for her enemies. (These
images are indeed used in Scripture, as in Ps. 19:10; Ps. 119:103;
Prov. 16:24; Prov. 24:13-14, where honey is associated with the
wisdom of the Word; and in 1 Cor. 15:55f.; Rev. 9:1-10, where
stinging is associated with judgment.)

Deborah was from Issachar (Jud. 5:15), but had moved to
Ephraim, somewhat to the south, in the center of Israel. This
may have been for some reason connected with her husband's
work, or it may have been the result of Jabin's oppression. The
latter is far more likely, since to move to Ephraim meant that
Lappidoth had to abandon his family property.

The place where Deborah lived, or more likely where she
held court, was known as the Palm Tree of Deborah. The Bible
has a lot to say about trees, and we cannot go into it in depth
here. Suffice it to say that trees produce leaves, which are seen as
medicinal (healing), and fruit, for food (Rev. 22:2; Psalm 1). The
trunk of the tree, stretching from earth up to a leafy crown,
easily signifies a ladder stretching from earth up to the glory
cloud of God's heaven (compare Gen. 28:12-17, and the fact that
Deborah was judging near Bethel, where this vision of a ladder
had occurred). At the foot of the ladder/tree is the gate of
heaven, and the gates were where judgments were rendered by
the judges and elders of Israel, for we always read of the elders
sitting in the gates. (I recently saw the film *El Cid*, made in the

early 1960s. As presented in the film, the throne of the king of Spain had behind it a large frescoed tree. Apparently the association of trees with thrones of judgment was not uncommon in the Western world either.)

Important people are frequently seen sitting under trees in Scripture, and indeed the Tabernacle, the central manifestation of the gate of heaven, was pitched under a great tree (Josh. 24:26). Palm trees in particular are used to represent the righteous (Ps. 92:12). As they picture God's people arrayed in His presence, they are found all over the walls of the Temple (1 Kings 6:29-35; Ezk. 40:16 - 41:26). Finally, it is the bride who is compared to a palm tree in Canticles 7:7-8.

Thus, the palm tree is a fitting symbol for Deborah herself. She constituted a gate to heaven for her people, rendering judgments for them, and raising up a godly generation. As a picture of the True Judge, she provided leaves for healing, the fruit of the Word for eating, and shade for protection.

We have mentioned that Bethel, the house of God, was the place where God's ladder had touched earth in Jacob's vision. It remains to note that the other place mentioned in connection with Deborah is also important. Ramah is between Bethel and Bethlehem-Ephratha. It was while making a journey from Bethel to Ephrath that Rachel died giving birth to Benjamin (Gen. 35:16), and Jeremiah 31:15 identifies the place of her death as Ramah. The death of Rachel in childbirth is the climactic fulfillment in Genesis of the prophetic judgment levied against the woman in Genesis 3:16: "I will greatly multiply your pain in childbearing; in pain you shall bring forth children." When Rachel names her son Ben-Oni, "Son of Sorrow," she is confessing her faith and her acceptance of the conditions of Genesis 3:16. The mother suffers to bring forth the child, but her sorrow is turned to joy when he turns out to be the deliverer.

Rachel died and did not get to see Benjamin grow up. Deborah, however, lived to see the triumph of her sons and daughters. That greater Deborah, Mary (whose name means "Bitter"), lived to see her son, Jesus, triumph over all humanity's enemies. (Notice that the praise heaped upon Jael, Deborah's twin in helping protect the seed, is applied to Mary in the New Testament: Jud. 5:24; Luke 1:28.)

Bethel, the place of the Church, the Mother of Israel; and

Ramah, the place of the mother who suffers to give birth to the righteous — these are the places associated with Deborah, and serve to point up the meaning of her story.

We note that the sons of Israel came "up" to her for judgment. The court of God is almost always placed on high ground in Scripture, as can be seen from Mt. Sinai and Mt. Zion, as well as many other locations. We ascend into the hill of the Lord (Ps. 24:3; 15:1), to receive a blessing from the Lord (Ps. 24:5). Thus, Deborah held God's court in a high place.

This brings us to the thorny question of explaining (or explaining away, as the case may be) how a woman might judge and rule over Israel. The text is quite specific about this. The New American Standard Bible says for verse 4, "Now Deborah, a prophetess, the wife of Lappidoth, was judging Israel at that time," but the Hebrew text literally says, "Now Deborah, a *woman*, a *prophetess,* the *wife* of Lappidoth. . . ." The emphasis is on the fact that we have a female judge here.

An investigation of the Biblical material reveals that there are judgesses and queens in the Bible, and though there are not many, nobody seems to be surprised about it. There are also prophetesses, and again though they are few, nobody seems to be amazed at it. But there are no priestesses. The reason for this is found (as usual) in Genesis 2 and 3.

The woman was made to be a helper to the man in his work. That work was the work of dressing the garden, understanding it, ruling over it, seen first of all in the naming of the animals (Gen. 2:15-20). Man's second work was to guard (in English Bibles, "keep") the garden (Gen. 2:15). The woman at his side was part of what he was supposed to guard; indeed, the woman is a kind of symbol for the garden as a whole, as the analogies in Canticles make clear. When Satan attacked, however, the man failed to guard his wife (though he was standing next to her during the whole conversation — Gen. 3:6, "with her"), and thus failed to guard the garden (Gen. 3:1-6). As a result, man was cast out as guardian, and angels took his place (Gen. 3:24).

Guarding is man's priestly task, as shepherding is his kingly task. It is precisely because it is the bride who must be guarded, that the woman cannot be a priest. She is not the priest; rather, she is what the priest (imaging the Divine Bridegroom) guards and protects. Thus, the woman may not take up a leading liturgical role in worship, for she cannot represent the Groom to the Bride (1 Cor. 14:34).

In the Bible, sexuality goes all the way down. The woman is made distinct from the man, altogether. Thus, there are not female prophets in the Bible, but rather there are prophetesses; there are not female deacons, but there are deaconesses (a separate group); there are not female judges, but there are judgesses. The male prophet and the male king both stand as representives of the Groom to the Bride. The female prophetess and queen cannot take that position, but stand *within the Bride* as counsellors. Since all humanity are feminine before God, as the Bride, there is nothing wrong with a queen or prophetess giving direction to men. The one thing that is excluded is the central liturgical function of imaging the Groom.

Thus, there is nothing wrong with women as rulers in any area of life except the Church. And there is nothing wrong with women as teachers in any area of life, including informal teaching in the Church. Women may teach men in Sunday School, but they may not assume the liturgical/symbolic role of leader in formal worship, in the presence of the sacrament, before the throne of God.[1]

Now, obviously any type of ruling function involves guarding. In a general way, women partake of the priesthood of all believers. Since the woman is the helper of the man, she helps him guard; but she does not guard herself, for that is his job. The woman's guardianship comes to expression not as she guards the Bride (which is nonsense), but as she guards her children. The priestly task of the woman as guardian is seen as she assists the Father in guarding the Seed. Thus, she may serve at the doorway of the Tabernacle (Ex. 38:8; especially since doors are associated with birth; we shall take this up in detail when we get to the story of Jephthah and his daughter). Thus, the names of the Queen mothers of the kings of Judah are given for every single king but one, in either Kings or Chronicles (mostly in

---

1. At various places, Paul forbids women to teach or exercise authority over men. The context each time, however, indicates that he is speaking of public worship, or a central ecclesiastical function. If we try to expand this principle into other spheres of life, we run into the problem that the Bible itself allows for prophetesses, showing that women may indeed teach men in more "informal" settings.

Kings). The importance of the mother in guarding and raising the seed cannot be overestimated.

Deborah is an archetype of this. She serves at the doorway of the Tabernacle. She is a "priestess" in the sense that she guards the children, but she knows that she cannot guard the Church, the Bride. Thus, when the child grows up, she seeks to transfer guardianship to a true male priest, Barak, who as we shall see was a Levite.

Barak, the Lightning Bolt

6. Now she sent and summoned Barak the son of Abinoam from Kedesh-Naphtali, and said to him, "Behold, the LORD, the God of Israel, has commanded, 'Go and march to Mount Tabor, and take with you ten thousand men from the sons of Naphtali and from the sons of Zebulun.

7. " 'And I will draw out to you Sisera, the commander of Jabin's army, with his chariots and his multitude to the river Kishon; and I will give them into your hand.' "

Barak means "Lightning," and Abinoam means "My father is delightful." This family was from Kedesh-Naphtali. Kedesh means "sanctuary," and Kedesh-Naphtali was a city of refuge in Naphtali, and thus a Levitical city (Josh. 20:7; 21:32). Barak was a Levite, thus a priest of some sort. This fact has a number of implications.

First, it means that Barak was one of the appointed guardians of Israel. Deborah's attempt to transfer leadership to him is the woman's attempt to yield guardianship to her now-grown son. Barak's refusal to assume this role leads to a minor judgment against him. The failure of the Levite to act as priest-guardian becomes a major theme in Judges 17 - 21.

Second, it means that this is *holy* war. The Levites, who were in charge of the special execution of God's wrath against the sacrificial substitutes, here are put in charge of executing God's wrath against those who are themselves sacrifices.

Third, as we shall see in verse 10, the nature of the battle involved the extension of God's sanctuary over all His people, with the result that His enemies were repulsed. Barak, as a sanctuary guardian, signifies this as he leads the army.

Barak's Response and God's Evaluation

8. Then Barak said to her, "If you will go with me, then I will go; but if you will not go with me, I will not go."

9a. And she said, "I will surely go with you; nevertheless the honor shall not be yours on the journey that you are about to take, for the LORD will sell Sisera into the hands of a woman."

Barak had the Word of God, the word of Command/Promise. After years under Deborah's tutelage (as prophetess and mother of Israel), he should have known to trust it. Barak might have said, "I'm rather nervous about going out there alone. Would you come with me? I have the promise, but I should like the presence of the Spirit with me as well. Since the Spirit is with you, Deborah, would you consider going with me?" This would have been a reasonable request. God never gives His children a promise/command without also giving His presence to help us fulfill it.

But that is not what Barak said. He said, "If you will not go with me, I will not go." This is not a statement of faith, not a request, but an attempt to put a condition on God. "It's hard to walk by faith. I demand a little sight as well." Barak was not a coward, as verse 14 shows (he led the army into battle); rather, he had faith, but weak faith.

Well, since Barak has sinned, I suppose that we should expect some strong rebuke, and a demand that Barak weep buckets of tears, etc. That is what some forms of popular piety would require here. Note, however, that the Lord's rebuke, delivered through His prophetess, is mild. The punishment fits the crime, indeed, but this one lapse of faith is not turned into an occasion for maximum punishment. In this we see the gentleness of the Lord, in dealing with our frailties. Let Church leaders take note of it.

The honor would go to a woman. This prophecy is fulfilled in Judges 5:6, "In the days of Jael, the highways were deserted." It might have read, "In the days of Barak," but Barak forfeited the right to this honor, the honor of having his name sung at the watering places of Israel (5:11). The days were not the days of Barak, but the days of Jael.

This is clearly a humiliation, to some degree, for Barak. It is the man who should lead, and the woman who should be right next to him as a "helper" (Gen. 2:18). It was not humiliating for Barak, as a child in Israel, to submit to the guardianship of Deborah, the mother of Israel. Now, however, Barak is grown. Like Adam, he is supposed to take up a role as guardian of the Bride/Garden. Though his faith is real, it is also weak, and so Barak receives the humiliation of having a woman do his job.

This gives us the principle that when the man defaults, the woman may step in to do the job. This is true in every area of life except, as we have noted, the central core area of liturgy, where it requires a man to signify the Groom to the Bride. This is one of the things going on in the story of Deborah. Because the men were children, God raised up a mother for them. Even when the men were grown, they still did not want to take up their God-ordained role, so God let a woman do the man's task.

Thus, we have two different, but overlapping principles. The first is that the woman may rule as a mother, even in the larger sense of a mother to society at large. The second is that the woman, as vice president, may rule when the men have defaulted. Both principles are valid, but it is the first principle that has power. The mother raises up a son, who turns around and saves her, as Jesus did Mary (Luke 1:47; 1 Tim. 2:15).

Israel's Response

9b. Then Deborah arose and went with Barak to Kedesh.

10. And Barak called Zebulun and Naphtali together to Kedesh, and 10,000 men went up at his feet. Deborah also went up with him.

11. Now Heber the Kenite had separated himself from the Kenites, from the sons of Hobab the brother-in-law of Moses, and had pitched his tent as far away as the oak in Zaanannim, which is near Kedesh.

12. Then they told Sisera that Barak the son of Abinoam had gone up to Mount Tabor.

13. And Sisera called together all his chariots, 900 iron chariots, and all the people who were with him, from Harosheth-Hagoyim to the river Kishon.

14. And Deborah said to Barak, "Arise! For this is the day in which the LORD has given Sisera into your hands; behold, the LORD has gone out before you." So Barak went down from Mount Tabor with 10,000 men following him.

15. And the LORD routed Sisera and all his chariots and all his army, with the edge of the sword before Barak; and Sisera alighted from his chariot and fled away on foot.

16. But Barak pursued the chariots and the army as far as Harosheth-Hagoyim, and all the army of Sisera fell by the edge of the sword; not even one was left.

The people gathered at Kedesh-Naphtali, a sanctuary city, or city of refuge. These were cities that provided temporary refuge or protection (priestly covering) for people suspected of crimes of violence (Num. 35). The priests of the cities guarded those who appealed to them for protection. This was a sign of the Levitical guardianship of the whole land.

In Genesis 12:7, 8, and 13:18, we see Abram building altars in the land. These were sanctuaries, places of refuge in God. Just as Abram set up three sanctuaries, so Israel was to have three cities of refuge (Dt. 19:1-3). The place where Abram settled down, Hebron, later became one of the sanctuary cities of Israel (Josh. 21:13). When Lot was captured (Gen. 14), Abram took his men, left Hebron, defeated Lot's captors, and restored Lot. In this we see the priest of God temporarily extending the sanctuary all the way across the length of the land in order to give refuge to Lot. In order to give sanctuary to Lot, Abram had to destroy his captors.

That is exactly what is happening here. Barak, the sanctuary priest, leads an army of Nazirites (see comments on 5:2, p. 93 below) to cleanse and purge the land (see comments on 5:21, p. 103 below). The whole holy land is cleansed, and becomes again a fit sanctuary.

Zebulun and Naphtali are the only tribes mentioned here and in verse 7, and are singled out for special mention in 5:18. Other tribes joined in the war, but apparently it primarily concerned these two northern tribes. What we read in this story fulfills the prophecy of Genesis 49:21 concerning Naphtali: "Naphtali is a doe let loose, He gives beautiful words." The doe is the swift female deer, and a picture of Barak's swift attack under Deborah's female leadership. The beautiful words point to Deborah's ministry in general, and to her song in particular.

Ten thousand men went with him. Ten being the number of totality, this represents the total power of God. Also, ten thousand is a myriad, and is frequently found in connection with the hosts of God (Dan. 7:10; Heb. 12:22; Rev. 5:11; and especially Jude 14, where Enoch prophesied that God's army was a perfect myriad in number).

Notice is made here of Heber the Kenite. This man had apostatized from Israel, rejecting the grace shown to his ancestors who, as we have seen, joined themselves to the tribe of Judah (1:16). We find in verse 17 that he had formed an alliance with Jabin. What is of interest here is the reference to the oak tree in connection with his tent. Jael, as a twin of Deborah, is another woman who has to step in and help because the men are in sin (in this case her husband). Like Deborah, her dwelling is pictured in association with a tree, in this case the oak, under which Abraham also dwelt (Gen. 13:18, etc.). Unlike Sapphira, who went along with the sins of her husband Ananias, Jael is going to make her own independent judgment in favor of the Lord and His cause.

From verse 14 we see that Deborah had to take charge of the situation, and determine the moment to begin the battle. Here we see Barak defaulting again. At the same time, Hebrews 11 views Barak as a hero of the faith. Hoeksema's comments on this are worth reproducing here: ". . . In spite of all the odds that were against him, he nevertheless did not refuse to obey the word of God, but went to Mount Tabor to deliver Israel. From a mere human point of view, it must be noted that to gather Israel on Tabor at this time over against the enemy was sheer folly. In the first place, let us notice that he was to gather but ten thousand men of Israel behind him. . . . Ten thousand men surely is not a large army. Besides, we may assume that these men were but poorly prepared from a military point of view. If we take into account the words of Deborah that there was no spear or shield seen among the forty thousand in Israel, we may surmise that Sisera had taken care to deprive Israel of almost every means of defense or attack. The men behind Barak were not used to the battle, but were accustomed to endure oppression; and they had even been afraid to show themselves on the highways for fear of the enemy. With these ten thousand men he was to go to Mount Tabor. Tabor was an isolated, conical shaped mountain at the northeastern corner of the plain of Esdraelon, rising to a height of about two thousand feet above sea level. It has been pointed out that Mount Tabor makes a strong position for defense against an enemy in the valley. This is undoubtedly true. But what must be remembered in this connection is that Barak with his ten thousand men ascending to the top of Tabor put everything at stake. From Mount Tabor there was no escape. Once on the mountain, Barak and his men had no choice. They had to meet the enemy. They had to fight and gain the victory, or die. On the other hand, there was the enemy. They were undoubtedly strong in number, for Deborah speaks of them as a multitude. Secondly, the men of Sisera were veterans in battle, used to victory. Finally, they were well armed and equipped with nine hundred chariots of iron. The two forces therefore could stand no comparison. From a mere human point of view it was impossible to expect that Barak would gain the victory. How he would defeat the enemy was a thing not to be seen. There was but one power that could sustain Barak, but one strength in which he could proceed to Tabor: It was the strength of faith in the name and the word of Jehovah. Jehovah had spoken, and Jehovah would win the battle."[2]

The Lord went before the army. It was really His battle; men's actions come afterward simply to mop up. Barak led the human army. We see here what is pictured in fullest form in Revelation 19:11-16, the Greater Barak leading His army to victory. Barak responded to the Word from Deborah with unmixed faith this time, and every single soldier in Sisera's army was slain. A total victory, picturing the final victory of Christ and His saints over all enemies. (After all, this is the famous battle of Megiddo, Jud. 5:19, which is the type of the great Battle of Ar-Megiddon.)

The Lord destroyed Sisera's army. We are not told how here, because the focus is on the fact of the victory itself. The Song of Deborah explains that God brought a rainstorm that turned the plains into mud, and grounded the chariots. Here the focus is on the simple fact that God can stop chariots any time He pleases. Sisera had to run away on foot. Now the contest was more nearly "equal."

Jael's Response

17. Now Sisera fled away on foot to the tent of Jael the wife of Heber the Kenite, for there was peace between Jabin the king

---

2. Hoeksema, *Era of the Judges*, p. 88.

of Hazor and the house of Heber the Kenite.

18. And Jael went out to meet Sisera, and said to him, "Turn aside, my master, turn aside to me. Do not be afraid." And he turned aside to her into the tent, and she covered him with a rug [blanket].

19. And he said to her, "Please give me a little water to drink, for I am thirsty." So she opened a container of milk and gave him a drink; then she covered him.

20. And he said to her, "Stand in the doorway of the tent, and it shall be if anyone comes and inquires of you, and says, 'Is there anyone here?' that you shall say, 'No.' "

21. But Jael, Heber's wife, took a tent peg and placed a hammer in her hand, and went secretly to him and drove the peg into his temple, and it went through into the ground; for he was sound asleep and exhausted. So he died.

22. And behold, as Barak pursued Sisera, Jael came out to meet him and said to him, "Come, and I will show you the man whom you are seeking." And he entered with her, and behold Sisera was lying dead with the tent peg in his temple.

Sisera came to the tents of Heber, and went to that particular tent which housed Jael, Heber's wife. (Jael in Hebrew is not composed of the words *Jah* and *El,* but is a word meaning "mountain goat.") Heber was at peace with Jabin, so that there was some kind of treaty between them. When Jael slew Sisera, she violated that treaty, and acted in disobedience to her husband. Sisera would not normally have dared to approach a woman's tent, since to the ancient mind there was a parallel between the house and the human body (see for instance Eccl. 12). To go into the tent of another man's wife was the same thing as adultery. Practically speaking, there was no other reason why a man would go into a woman's tent. Thus, Jael had to come out and invite him in, deceiving him with the words "fear not." What Jael was saying, in effect, was that in view of the extraordinary circumstances, her husband would understand why she was giving refuge to another man in her tent, and normal social conventions could be set aside.

Symbolically, however, Sisera's invasion of Jael's tent points to the rape of Israel by Jabin's army. This is a theme that is picked up in Judges 5:30, where one of the goals of Sisera's war is said to be the capture of Israelite women. The enmity between

Satan and the woman takes the form that Satan wants to possess the bride, and raise up his own wicked seed through her (as in Gen. 12, 20, and 26). Thus, it is fitting that here the woman crushes the serpent's head.

Sisera was thirsty, and asked for water. She gave him milk, or as Judges 5:25 indicates, a kind of buttermilk or yogurt. This would make him sleepier than mere water would have. It is also, again, an essentially womanly act to give milk. Just as Deborah had fed Israel with the milk of her words for years, so Jael gives milk to Sisera; but that milk which strengthens the righteous is poison to the wicked (compare 1 Cor. 11:30 and 2 Cor. 2:16).

So convincing was her deception that Sisera asked a further favor of her, that she misdirect anyone looking for him. He wanted her to act as his guardian. This request builds the humor of the situation: He was asking Israel's guardian to guard him. He did not in the least anticipate what was about to happen to him.

Once Sisera was sound asleep, Jael drove a tent peg through his head. Her faith in God calmed her nerves for this frighteningly gruesome task. It was the woman's job to set up tents, and she would have known how to drive a tent peg from years of experience. Christ has crushed Satan's head definitively, in His victory on the cross. Christ's people are called to join with Him in this victory, and the promise is that we too shall crush Satan's head, in union with Christ (Rom. 16:20). We who live after the cross reflect the work of Christ, but those who lived before the cross anticipated His work. Jael, then, is a prophetic picture of Christ, the ultimate Seed of the Woman.

Barak was pursuing Sisera, intending to kill him, when Jael beckoned him to come and see her work. Thus was Barak brought face to face with the fulfillment of Deborah's prophecy.

Commentators have not been very nice to Jael. Most seem to be squeamish about some aspect of what she did, some criticizing her betrayal of the "laws of hospitality," other lighting on her out-and-out deception and lie to Sisera, "fear not." Most give her credit, like Rahab, for having identified with the cause of Israel, but all seem to feel that somehow she should have done something other than what she did.

What are the charges against Jael? We may list them as follows:

1. Disobedience to her husband, in breaking his treaty with Jabin, 4:17.
2. Breaking the treaty her household had with Jabin, 4:17.
3. Actively going out of her way to deceive Sisera, 4:18.
4. Lying to Sisera, saying "fear not," when he had, in fact, much to fear, 4:18.
5. Violating the laws or rules of hospitality, 4:18-21.
6. Murder, 4:21.

Now, what is God's evaluation of Jael? It is given in Judges 5:24-27, and includes the phrase, "Most blessed of women is Jael." This the language used of the virgin Mary in Luke 1:28, "Blessed are you among women." The parallel is certainly significant, and indicates a rather high evaluation of Jael on God's part.

Looking further, we find that Judges 5:25 calls specific attention to Jael's initial *hospitality* as part of her *deception:* "He asked for water, and she gave him milk; in a magnificent bowl she brought him curds." Approval of her actions in these areas is clear. Approval of her act of "murder" is clear from the celebration of it in Judges 5:26-27.

Some of the commentators are, however, not daunted by this. The Song of Deborah, they tell us, while infallibly recorded in Scripture, still reflects the primitive morality of these barbaric times, and is not to be taken as God's Word of evaluation. This subterfuge is, however, impossible to accept, because Judges 4:4 positively identifies Deborah as a prophetess. Chapter 5 is clearly a prophetic oracle; it reads like many passages in Isaiah and Jeremiah. All through the Song of Deborah judgments are rendered, as we shall see. Thus, we cannot escape the clear approval of God for Jael's actions.

Obviously, Jael's critics are off in their understanding of God's moral standards. To help us think clearly about this, let us take the charges against Jael in order. First, she is charged with disobeying her husband. Is it ever right for a wife to disobey her *lord* (1 Pet. 3:6)? Certainly it is on some occasions, for every Christian woman must put God before her own husband and family. The point is clearly made by Jesus in Matthew 10:34-37 and Luke 14:26, where we are told that a person's enemies will be those of his (or her) own household, and that we must be ready to "hate" our dearest kin for the kingdom's sake.

The background of this command is Exodus 32:26-29 and Deuteronomy 33:8-9: The people had rebelled against God, and He called for faithful men to execute His judgments. The Levites stepped forward to do so, and we are told that they did not spare even the members of their own families, so consumed were they with God's holiness and justice. From all this it is plain that when a husband becomes an enemy of God, the wife must side with God and become an enemy of her husband. For the most part she will continue to love her husband and submit to him, but in a crisis, such as Jael faced, she must side with God.

Second, Jael is charged with breaking a treaty. All men at the point of birth have, so to speak, a peace treaty with Satan. Conversion to Christ necessarily involves breaking this treaty and going to war against Satan. Jael broke the treaty with the Satanic Jabin because she converted to the side of the Lord. There is no middle ground — either we are for the Lord or we are against Him.

Third, Jael is charged with active deception. Rahab lied to the men of Jericho when they came to her door. In a sense her deception was passive; Rahab did not go out of her way to deceive the Jerichoites. We must note, however, that Rahab's action did not take place in a time of open war, on a battlefield. Jael's did. It was an open, killing battle, and Jael, a member of God's army, used as a military tactic a deception of the enemy. Scripture commends her for it. Deception is often used on a battleground to lure the enemy within range of a hidden striking force.

Fourth, Jael is charged with lying. Some commentators think that it is all right to conceal the truth, but no verbal lie ought ever to pass our lips. This distinction will not stand up, however, because deception is deception, whether verbal or nonverbal. God Himself lies to people when they rebel against Him, in order to lure them to their destruction. See for example 1 Kings 22:19-23, where God deliberately lied to Ahab to lure him to his doom. We might also take note of 1 Samuel 16:1-2, where God put the lie into Samuel's mouth, so that Saul would not kill him. Also, God expresses His approval of Rahab's lie in James 2:25: Rahab's true faith was shown by her *good* works, "when she received the messengers and set them out by *another* way."

Another way? A way other than what? Rahab sent the spies out by a way other than what she told the men of Jericho. She is expressly commended for her lie. Rahab had changed sides in the war of God against sinful humanity (humanism), and in a time of active hostility, she deceived the enemy by her words.

There is another observation on lying that we should make. Lying is primarily a woman's tool. Faced with the tyrant, the woman is not in a position to fight, but she can lie and deceive. I have explored this at length elsewhere,[3] but here I can call attention to the following women who used lying to deceive tyrants bent on evil: Sarah (Gen. 12, 20), Rebekah (Gen. 26, 27), the Hebrew Midwives (Ex. 1), and Jael. According to Genesis 3:15, Satan attacks the woman as well as the seed. Since Satan made his initial assault on the woman by means of a lie (Gen. 3:1-5), it is fitting that the woman defeat him by means of a lie, according to the principle "eye for eye, tooth for tooth" — lie for lie. It is the Satanic, humanistic tyrant in whose face these women told their brazen lies, and God blessed them each time for it (see the blessings in Gen. 12:16-17; 20:7, 14ff.; 26:12ff.; Ex. 1:20; Matt. 1:5; Jud. 5:24).

Fifth, Jael is charged with violating the laws or conventions of hospitality. Hospitality is important in Scripture, and it is clear enough that normally we are not to murder our guests! The New Testament, however, makes it clear that we do not show hospitality to the enemies of God (2 John 10). God comes first, hospitality second.

Sixth, Jael is charged with murder. In reply we simply point out that killing in wartime or on a battlefield is not murder.

As the war of humanistic Satanism against Christianity grows more and more severe in our day, especially in the attacks on Christian schools, serious Christians need to consider ways to deceive the enemy. Vigilante-style lynchings, assassinations, and murders are not permitted in the Bible; killing, such as Ehud's and Jael's, is permissible in time of war, but not in vigilante form. On the other hand, deception and lying are authorized in Scripture any time God's kingdom is under attack. The Protestant Reformers travelled throughout Europe under

---

3. See my essay, "Rebellion, Tyranny, and Resistance in the Book of Genesis," in Gary North, ed., *Tactics of Christian Resistance* (Tyler, TX: Geneva Ministries, 1983).

false names and with faked papers. They were not the first or the last Christian preachers to deceive tyrants, either. If we have to deceive and lie to bureaucrats in order to keep our churches and schools running, we must do so freely and with relish, enjoying the opportunity to fight for the Lord.

Summary and Conclusion

23. So God subdued on that day Jabin the king of Canaan before the sons of Israel.

24. And the hand of the sons of Israel pressed heavier and heavier upon Jabin the king of Canaan, until they had cut off Jabin the king of Canaan.

It was God Who did the work. We must always give Him the credit. He is our Deliverer.

It took a while, but Jabin and his culture were destroyed. This verse points forward into the future, for as a matter of fact the Canaanites did continue to live in the land of God, though they never again rose up against Israel as they did under Jabin. Zechariah 14:21 points to the time when all Canaanites will finally be gone from the land, the house of God.

The Hebrew verb translated "cut off" is the word used for making a covenant and for cutting off the foreskin in circumcision. Circumcision is a picture of castration, just as baptism by sprinkling is a picture of drowning. The righteous are circumcised/sprinkled; the wicked are castrated/drowned (see Gal. 5:12). As we noted above, Satan/Sisera's design was to capture the bride and use her to raise up his own seed. Thus it is theologically fitting that the verb used to describe his destruction is the verb that is used for castration.[4]

The evaluation of the Lord is the Song of Deborah, which we analyze in the next chapter of this study.

---

4. I have discussed circumcision at length in my book, *The Law of the Covenant; An Exposition of Exodus 21-23* (Tyler, TX: Institute for Christian Economics, 1984), pp. 78ff.; 243ff. A particularly graphic use of "cut off" is Psalm 58:7, where it refers to arrows which have the heads cut off the ends; the parallel to castration is obvious.

6

THE SONG OF DEBORAH
(Judges 5)

5:1 Then Deborah and Barak the son of Abinoam sang on that day, saying:

The verb "sang" is feminine singular, indicating that it was Deborah who wrote and sang the song. Apparently, then, Barak accompanied her with a musical instrument (remember, he was a Levite; see 1 Chron. 23:3-5). The song is authored by God's prophetess, and is God's evaluation.

The Song of Deborah sounds gory to the ears of those not prepared to hear it. Deborah delights in describing the victory over her Lord's enemies, and their total destruction. Part of her delight is not immediately obvious to us, however. One of the aspects of the Song is that it pokes fun at the religion of Baalism. This active ridicule of the religion of the Canaanites is part of the fun, the Divine humor of redemption. For instance, Baal was supposed to be the god of the storm, but it turns out that the Lord is the true ruler of the storm, and uses the storm to destroy Baal's followers, under the leadership of a man named "Lightning Bolt" (Barak).

All pagan religion is a cheap and perverted copy of the truth. The triune God of Scripture is the true Lord of the storm; Baal is but a twisted copy. Some commentators have thought that Deborah is "drawing on Canaanite mythical elements in order to praise the Lord." This is not the case. Rather, Deborah praises the Lord for what He truly is. There is no mythology here. But we can properly say that the selection of material in the Song is designed to contrast God and Baal, and heap ridicule on Baalism. Deborah does have an eye on certain Baalist conceptions, which she ridicules. We shall note this as we go through the Song.

In Canaanite mythology, one of Baal's wives (or consorts) is Anath. Anath is the bloody goddess. Because of her fierce love for Baal, she delights to drown Baal's enemies in blood. There is a parallel between some of the Anath poems and the Song of Deborah, and the reason for it is that Deborah presents herself (and thus, the Church) as the true Bride of the Lord, and she shows the Bride rejoicing in the bloody destruction of the Lord's enemies. Anath is, then, but a cheap and perverted copy of the true Bride.[1]

Scholars have often divided the Song of Deborah into three stanzas, but have not always agreed on where the divisions should be placed. There may be better ways to do it, but what seems best to me, and most useful, is the following:

> Stanza 1 (vv. 2-11): Introduction: the Situation
> Stanza 2 (vv. 12-22): The Hosts of the Lord and the Battle
> Stanza 3 (vv. 23-31): The Aftermath

The reader will notice that I have had the Song typeset in such a way as to bring out the Hebrew parallelism in the text. Usually in Hebrew poetry the same thing is said two times. This is in order to form a testimony of two witnesses to the Word of God, and is also for liturgical reasons. When used liturgically, the leader in worship says the first phrase, speaking the Word of the Lord as His representative (which is why he must be a man), and the congregation responds with the second phrase, the response of humanity (the Bride).

For the most part the phrases in the Song of Deborah are very short, creating a rhythmic atmosphere of sharpness and exuberance when read out loud.[2]

---

1. An in-depth discussion of the Anath theme in the Song of Deborah is provided by Stephen G. Dempster, "Mythology and History in the Song of Deborah," *Westminster Theological Journal* 41 (Fall, 1978): 33-53.

2. The translation used here is for the most part the New American Standard Version, though I have made a few modifications at certain points in order to make clear my own understanding of the Hebrew original. There are a number of mistakes in the King James Version, by the way. The translators of the KJV did the best they could with the knowledge at their disposal, but since that time there has been some progress in the study of Semitic languages, and certain obscure phrases in the Song can be given better translations.

Stanza 1

This section begins with Deborah's praising the Lord because the people were willing to volunteer and fight. This was a confirmation of her own ministry. She next addresses the kings of the nations, informing them that the Lord is the true God of the storm, as shown by the storm at Mount Sinai. Then she describes the situation in Israel: The people had lost control of the highways, because they had chosen new gods and the Lord had chastised them; but God had raised up a mother in Israel, and the people had repented. They had volunteered to destroy the enemy, and this is the occasion for this Song, which will be sung at all the watering places in Israel.

> 2. That long locks of hair hung loose in Israel,
>   That the people volunteered,
>   Bless the LORD!

This is a literal translation. The reference is to the Nazirite vow, the details of which are found in Numbers 6, and we shall take up those details when we get to Samson. All of Israel were a nation of priests, and it is the priests who prosecute holy war. God Himself had established a parallel between the war camp and the Tabernacle, both holy places, as can be seen in Deuteronomy 23:9-14 (discussed on pages 64ff.) and from the fact that the number five (the number of military organization) is so prominent in the architectural design of the house of God. Just as the people were to avoid sexual relations in the special presence of the true Divine Husband of Israel (Ex. 19:15), so they were to avoid sexual relations during holy war (2 Sam. 11:11). During holy war, the men took the Nazirite vow not to drink wine or eat grapes or raisins, sacrificing the legitimate pleasures of common life in order to make time for a temporary special task. They also vowed to let their hair grow long. This long hair, a sign of glory and strength, was then dedicated to the Lord at the end of the vow.

Normally the text of Scripture does not call special attention to the wartime Nazirite vow. Here in Judges 5:2 attention is directed to it because of the priestly nature of the entire narrative (the battle was led by a Levite; it involved an extension of sanctuary; etc.).

3a. Hear, O kings;
    Give ear, O rulers!
3b. I—to the LORD, I will sing,
    I will sing praise to the LORD, the God of Israel.
4a. LORD, when Thou didst go out from Seir,
    When Thou didst march from the field of Edom,
4b. The earth quaked, the heavens also dripped,
    Even the clouds dripped water.
 5. The mountains quaked [flowed] at the presence of the LORD,
    This Sinai, at the presence of the LORD, the God of Israel.

The victory at Megiddo was public. Deborah calls upon the kings of neighboring areas to take note of it, and of the God of Israel, Who clearly is superior to all the neighboring false gods. God's public deeds in history should occasion men to fear. If you are thinking about attacking Israel (or Christ's Church), think twice, lest you provoke Omnipotence.

Since the Baals were supposed to be lords of the storm, Deborah calls attention to the fact that the true Master of the storm is the Lord. The first pair of lines in verse 4 reminds us of the covenant God made with Israel at Mount Sinai. As Israel came from Egypt to Sinai, they faced Edom and Mt. Seir. As God's glory cloud arose over Sinai, it appeared to be marching from Edom. In other words, God marched from the promised land, where He had been preparing a place for them, through Edom, to meet them at Sinai.

Let's imagine the scene. We are standing at the foot of the huge Mount Sinai, but we don't dare touch it lest we die. We are looking toward the promised land, and a huge, black storm cloud is moving rapidly from that land, through Edom, towards us. Within that cloud is the chariot-throne of the God of all creation, guarded by four cherubim with flaming swords (Ezk. 1). We see these flaming swords as flashes of lightning. The sound gets louder and louder, like the sound of a vast trumpet announcing judgment day, until we think we shall become deaf. As the cloud reaches Sinai and covers it, it looks as if the mountain is erupting like a volcano, and is covered with fire. The mountain quakes violently. And then, God speaks the Ten Commandments in a Voice so loud, so powerful, and so overwhelming that we join with all the people in begging Moses to act as a mediator on our behalf (Ex. 19:10–20:21).

Verse 4b tells us of the great rainstorm that accompanied God's presence at Sinai. The comparison is important, for God brought a rainstorm to destroy Sisera. In other words, the same God Who made covenant with Israel at Sinai is keeping covenant with them still at Megiddo.

Verses 4b and 5 remind us of the quaking of the ground at Mount Sinai, which caused the mountains to flow with rockslides (or perhaps verse 5 is a reference to water flowing down the mountainside). The earth itself trembles when God approaches. (Do we?) Deborah repeats the phrase "the LORD, the God of Israel." What other god brings such a response in the earth and sky? Take heed, O kings! Your storm-god Baal is no match for the Lord God of hosts, the God of Israel!

6a. In the days of Shamgar the son of Anath,
In the days of Jael,
6b. The highways were deserted [had ceased],
And travelers [walkers] went by roundabout [twisted] ways.
7a. The peasantry ceased, [or, Iron implements ceased]
They ceased in Israel.
7b. Until I, Deborah, arose,
Until I arose, a mother in Israel.
8a. New gods were chosen;
Then war was in the gates.
8b. Not a shield or a spear was seen
Among forty thousand in Israel.

While Shamgar judged in the south, Deborah judged in the north. As noted in the preceding chapter of this study, these might have been the days of Barak, but Barak lost honor to Jael because of his weak faith. The explicit reference to Shamgar as "son of Anath" is probably important. Anath has not been able to hold her followers; they are converting to the Lord. Indeed, Anath as a warrior goddess and bride of Baal, is no match for Deborah and Jael who are part of the Bride of the Lord.

The highways were captured by the Canaanites. The people had to go by twisted, crooked "Indian paths" through the forests of the mountains. This ties in to the theme of sanctuary, for God had said, "You shall prepare the roads for yourself, and divide into three parts the territory of your land, which the LORD your God will give you as a possession, and it shall be for

every manslayer to flee there" (Dt. 19:3). There was no effective
sanctuary without clear, open, and kept up roadways. If God's
sanctuary protection is to be restored to His people, then the
guardian priests will have to clear the roads. This is Barak's
priestly work, and the work of an army of Nazirites.

Verse 7a includes a Hebrew word that occurs nowhere else
in the Old Testament except in verse 11b. Scholars have guessed
that it may mean "villagers, peasants," but recently it has been
suggested that it refers to iron.[3] I am in no position to decide
this question, though I lean towards the "iron" translation as
more attractive. At any rate, I shall comment on the text both
ways.

Assuming verse 7a refers to the peasantry, we see an example
of the principle that the overall cultural effect of the loss of
special sanctuary is the loss of general sanctuary as well. The
peasantry who lived in the countryside were the prey of the Canaanites. Massive state taxation was killing agriculture, and
people were leaving their lands; and of course, peasant girls and
wives were continual prey. Once the highways to the special
sanctuaries were restored, however, the peasantry would be
safe. And so it is that when the special sanctuary of the Church
is unprotected, then society at large is unprotected; but when
the highway to the Church is rebuilt, then God extends general
sanctuary over all of life. Judgment and restoration begin at the
house of God.

Assuming verse 7a refers to iron, we have here an indication
that Sisera and the Canaanites had carefully removed all tools
and weapons of iron from Israel. This is reiterated in verse 8b.
Since Israel lacks iron, God must act as Iron on her behalf, as
verse 11b indicates.

Verse 7b tells us that Deborah's purpose was to be a mother
in Israel. We have discussed that at length, but there is one more
point to be made. A mother implies a new birth, and clearly
what Israel needed was repentance and a new birth.

Verse 8a is interesting, because the two phrases do not seem
to be parallel, yet they are. If men rebel against the Lord and
choose new gods, then it will naturally follow that there will be

---

3. Giovanni Garbini, "*Parzon* 'Iron' in the Song of Deborah?" *Journal of
Semitic Studies* 23 (1978): 23f.

war in the gates. And accordingly, before there can be peace through victory, there must be repentance and a return to the "old" God, the true God of Israel, the God Who marched from Seir (v. 4). Since the people had chosen the gods of the Canaanites, God put them under the culture of the Canaanites.

Verse 8b tells us that although the men of Israel did have a few weapons (which they used in this battle), yet they dared not let them be seen. The tyrant's eyes were everywhere. Just as modern Baalists want gun registration laws (instead of laws punishing criminals), the ancient Baalists had shield control laws, and spear registration laws.

I interpret the number 40,000 to be four times 10,000. As noted in the previous chapter, a myriad is the number of the Lord's host. Four is the number of the land, with its four corners. Thus, 40,000 is a number representing the Lord's host as guardians of the whole land.

> 9. My heart is [goes out] to the commanders of Israel,
>   The volunteers among the people;
>   Bless the LORD!
> 10. You who ride on white donkeys, you who sit on carpets,
>   And you who travel on the road—sing! [or, consider this:]
> 11a. The voice of the minstrels at the watering places,
>   There they shall recount the righteous deeds of the LORD,
> 11b. The righteous deeds of His peasantry in Israel. [or, The
>   righteous acts of His iron in Israel.]
>   Then the people of the LORD went down to the gates.

All the various classes of Israelite society volunteered to fight, and all are exhorted to sing the Song of Deborah. (Is it ever sung in your church?) Verse 9 points out that both leaders and people volunteered.

Verse 10 refers to the two classes as they travel on the (newly-restored) highways. The wealthy would ride on white donkeys or sit on fine rugs (in a carriage, perhaps, or on a donkey), while the poorer members of society would walk. Both groups are called upon to do something. The most likely translation is "sing," though the word may mean "consider." If they are being told to sing, then we find that all are to join in the Song of Deborah. Those who fight for God, also sing to Him. If the proper meaning is "consider," then both groups are being told to consider the fact that Deborah's song will be sung at all the watering places in Israel, as praise to the Lord.

The first phrase of verse 11 is obscure, and literally says "At the voice/sound of *those who divide* at the watering places." Some have thought that the dividing spoken of is the dividing of flocks, but most likely it refers to the dividing of strings on stringed instruments (that is, pressing the string into the board at various places to produce various pitches, like a guitar). Most scholars now agree that this is a reference to minstrel singers.

The Song of Deborah will be sung in all these places. This will be a great embarrassment to certain people, as we shall see. It will also be a humorous way of ridiculing Baalism. Singing is a very "conservative" thing. People don't like to learn new songs, and feel good about the "good old songs." Songs, thus, have a way of sealing, protecting, or guarding a culture. Luther once said that he did not care so much who wrote the theologies, as long as he could write the hymns. Deborah's task, as the mother of Israel, was to protect her children from Baalism. By creating a song that ridicules Baalism while simultaneously praising the Lord, she was engaged in a very important priestly work. Those who sang the Song of Deborah would be less likely to lapse back into Baalism.

Water is a token of life in Scripture, though in great quantity it is also a sign of death. Just as Eden was well watered, so God promises to give water to His people. This was made clear over and over during the wilderness wanderings, where so many of the conflicts had to do with water. When Jabin ruled the land, Israel was cut off from the wells; but now that the Lord has defeated Jabin, the watering places are restored.

If we take verse 11b to refer to peasantry, we have the notion that Barak's was a peasant army. A peasant army defeated Sisera's professionals! On the other hand, if we take verse 11b as referring to iron, then the idea is that God's miracle is His "iron." The Canaanites had sought an iron monopoly, as the Philistines also did later on (1 Sam. 13:19-21). They made a big mistake, because they did not reckon with the True Iron of Israel, their Secret Weapon—the Lord of Hosts!

Finally, the last phrase in verse 11 completes the thought begun in verse 8. Those who faced war in the gates now come out of hiding and go down to the gates of their towns to face the enemy. A strengthened, reborn Israel is now ready to fight and destroy the enemies of God.

Stanza 2

Stanza 2 gives a list of the tribes who came to fight, and those who did not. Deborah praises one group, and ridicules the other. The battle is then described.

In addition to parallelism, one of the fundamental literary forms in the Bible is what is called chiasm. Chiastic structure takes the form A-B-A or A-B-B-A, as opposed to normal parallelism which has the form A-A-B-B or A-B-A-B. It is easiest to see what chiastic structure is by taking an example. Deborah's ridicule of Reuben has a chiastic structure:

A = v. 15b: Among the divisions of Reuben . . .
  B = v. 16a: Why did you sit among the sheepfolds . . .
A' = v. 16b: Among the divisions of Reuben . . .

There is a larger chiasm in most of this stanza as a whole, which we can outline as follows:

A. Barak takes captive his captives (12b)
  B. The righteous come to fight (13)
    C. Praise for the tribes who fought (14-15a)
      D. Ridicule for the tribes who stayed away (15b-17)
    C′. Praise for the tribes who fought (18)
  B′. The wicked come to fight (19)
A′. God destroys the wicked (20-22)

12a. Awake, awake, Deborah;
     Awake, awake, sing a song!
12b. Arise, Barak;
     And take captive your captives, O son of Abinoam.

Deborah encourages herself to sing. In the lips of others, this is an exhortation to the Church to sing the song of God's victory.

Deborah encourages Barak to lead his captives captive. This is a curious exhortation, since there were no captives (4:16)! The same language is, however, used of the Lord in Psalm 68:18 and of Christ in Ephesians 4:8. In principle, then, we are exhorting the Greater Barak to bare His arm and fight His victories.

13. Then the remnant of the nobles came down;
    The people of the LORD came down to me as warriors.
14a. From Ephraim those whose root is in Amalek;
    Following you, Benjamin, with your peoples.
14b. From Machir commanders came down,
    And from Zebulun those who wield the pen of the scribe.
15a. And my princes of Issachar were with Deborah; as was
    Issachar, so was Barak;
    Into the valley they rushed at his feet.
15b. Among the divisions of Reuben
    Great resolves of heart.
16a. Why did you sit among the sheepfolds [or saddlebags],
    To hear the pipings for the flocks?
16b. Among the divisions of Reuben
    Great searchings of heart!
17a. Gilead remained across the Jordan;
    And why did Dan stay in ships?
17b. Asher sat by the seashore,
    And remained by its landings.
18. Zebulun was a people who despised their lives even to death,
    And Naphtali also, on the high places of the field.

Both nobles and commoners came to fight (v. 13). Now we have a list of those who fought. First is Ephraim. The association of Ephraim with the area formerly inhabited by Amalek is unclear, though this might be a figure of speech for fierce warriors. There is no supporting evidence for such a conjecture, however. Maybe it points to the fact that God's people were once His enemies, though now converted by grace. Seedy origins are no reason not to join the Lord's army.

Benjamin, tiny as a result of the war recorded in Judges 19–21, came along with Ephraim as part of their force. Being small is no reason not to join the Lord's army.

That part of Manasseh located on the Mediterranean side of the Jordan river is meant by "Machir." They contributed commanders. This was an important battle for them, because Taanach and Megiddo (v. 19) were part of the territory they had failed to conquer in Judges 1:27.

Zebulun contributed some scribes, in addition to soldiers. These scribes enrolled the men, and collected the required atonement money (Ex. 30:12ff.). Every time the army of the Lord was mustered, the men paid each a half shekel of silver to atone for the blood spilled in war, which money went to the upkeep of the Tabernacle.[4]

Issachar was Deborah's tribe, as verse 15 makes clear ("*my princes*"). They were right there with Deborah, and with Barak. As Barak led the attack, they were right behind him. They followed the Lord's anointed ones.

Now Deborah begins pointedly, and even sarcastically, to ridicule the tribes who did not come to fight. Reuben, the first-born of Jacob, should have had the preeminence, but because he was unstable as water, doubleminded, he lost his birthright (Gen. 49:3-4). Reuben's magnanimous resolutions became empty deliberations. The first couplet and the third are identical, save that the resolves of Reuben have disintegrated into searchings. They could not be stirred from lethargy. Brave talk, when not followed up with brave deeds, makes a man an object of scorn. The other tribes who failed to show up at least did not make bold promises of support.

Gilead is trans-Jordanic Manasseh and Gad. They, with Dan and Asher, were in the vicinity and should have showed concern, but they were too busy with their day-to-day affairs to be bothered with exterminating Canaanites. The Canaanite domination did not bother them very much, since they were not peasants; so they did not come to help. Their coldness and compromise is stingingly recorded for all time.

Judah and Simeon are not included in this roll call because they dwelt so far in the south that their participation was not expected. Also, they were busy, under Shamgar, with Philistines. Levi is also not included, since it was not a political tribe but was scattered throughout Israel; though of course, Barak was a Levite.

Then Deborah returns to heap especial praise on the two tribes who did the most: Zebulun and Naphtali.

19a. The kings came and fought;
     Then fought the kings of Canaan
19b. At Taanach near the waters of Megiddo;
     They took no plunder in silver.
20. The stars fought from heaven,

---

4. I have discussed this at length in my book, *The Law of the Covenant* (Tyler, TX: Institute for Christian Economics, 1984), pp. 225ff.

    From their courses they fought against Sisera.
21. The torrent of Kishon swept them away;
    The ancient torrent, the torrent Kishon.
    O my soul, march on with strength.
22. Then the horses' hoofs beat from the dashing,
    The dashing of his valiant steeds [mighty ones].

More description of the battle is given here than was given in Judges 4. The fact that the Canaanites took no spoil is picked up again in verses 28-30. It is included here as an ironic understatement: The Canaanites lost far more than booty. The location of the battle, as mentioned already, takes up from Manasseh's failure to clear out the Canaanites in Judges 1:27.

The concept of the stars fighting in heaven, and of the stars controlling the weather (bringing rain), was common in Baalism. Here Deborah asserts that the stars are part of God's heavenly host, and that their (angelic) control of the weather is for the good of Israel. Baalism is impotent. The notion that those who trust in the Baals have the stars and the weather on their side is a lie.

Stars in Scripture are associated with angels (Job 38:7, Is. 14:13; Rev. 12:4). Storms, at least special ones, are also associated with angels (Ezk. 1; 10; Ps. 18:9-12; 104:2-4; Ex. 19:16 with Heb. 2:2). Because of the influence of neo-Baalism (secular humanism) in our modern culture, we tend to think that God, when He made the world, installed certain "natural laws" or processes that work automatically and impersonally. This is a Deistic, not a Christian, view of the world. What we call natural or physical law is actually a rough approximate generalization about the ordinary activity of God in governing His creation. Matter, space, and time are created by God, and are ruled directly and actively by Him. His rule is called "law." God almost always causes things to be done the same way, according to covenant regularities (the Christian equivalent of natural laws), which covenant regularities were established in Genesis 8:22. Science and technology are possible because God does not change the rules, so man can confidently explore the world and learn to work it. Such confidence, though, is always a form of faith, faith either in Nature (Baal) and natural law, or faith in God and in the trustworthiness of His commitment to maintain covenant regularities.

The Kishon river flooded, swamping the chariots of Sisera. Thus, the Lord showed His power over the dreaded iron chariots. God used Baal's own weapons, weather and water, to destroy Baal's army. The Kishon was particularly appropriate for this work, since it is a very swiftly flowing river. The theme of the river purging the land has been seen once already in Judges (3:28), and will recur again (7:24; 12:5).

Why the Kishon is called an ancient torrent is not immediately clear. The reference, however, is almost certainly to the Flood and to the destruction of Pharaoh at the Red Sea. God has an ancient torrent that sweeps away His enemies. The sprinkling of water was used for the cleansing of the righteous, and floods of water to cleanse the land of the defilement of Canaanites. The Kishon was later used to sweep Baalists out of the land again, in 1 Kings 18:40, under Elijah's orders. Still later, Josiah pointedly destroyed Asherah idols at the Kishon.

Deborah interrupts the duple rhythm of her Song at this point to sing out, "O my soul, march on in strength." It is man's part to march for God, but it is God Who gives the strength (compare Ex. 15:2; Ps. 44:5).

The enemy tried to escape, either on foot or on horseback, cutting the horses free of the harnesses to the chariots. This attempt failed. The horses were trapped in the mud, and their thrashing hooves slew many Canaanite soldiers. The beautiful war machine, the valiant steeds (mighty ones), turned into a liability rather than an asset under the vengeful providence of the Omnipotent.

Stanza 3

The third stanza is the aftermath. It passes out curses and blessings, and closes with rejoicing at the destruction of the wicked. Meroz is cursed and Jael blessed. Deborah laughs at the grotesque death of Sisera, and at the coming sorrows of the evil anti-mother, the mother of Sisera.

23a. "Curse Meroz," said the angel of the LORD,
    "Utterly curse its inhabitants;
23b. "Because they did not come to the help of the LORD,
    "To the help of the LORD against the warriors."

Meroz must have been in the immediate area of the battle and feared reprisals should the Canaanites win. For their lack of faith and commitment they were cursed. We are not told if the Israelites destroyed the town, although the command probably implied such action. It is the angel of the Lord, the captain of the Lord's host, who gave this command. The curse on Meroz for its refusal to aid Israel was effective—no one today knows where Meroz was located! The curse on Meroz is to be contrasted with the following verse, which blesses Jael for her action in the same circumstances.

24. Most blessed of women is Jael, the wife of Heber the Kenite;
    Most blessed is she of women in the tent.
25a. He asked for water;
    She gave him milk.
25b. In a magnificent bowl,
    She brought him curds [buttermilk; yogurt].
26a. She reached out her hand for the tent peg,
    And her right hand for the workman's hammer.
26b. Then she struck Sisera, she smashed his head;
    And she shattered and pierced his temple.
27a. Between her feet he bowed, he fell, he lay.
    Between her feet he bowed, he fell.
27b. Where he bowed,
    There he fell devastated.

The picture given in Genesis 3:15 is of the serpent's head crushed by the foot of the seed. Thus, the attention called to Jael's feet again causes us to see the Messianic aspects of this event. Sisera's humiliation is stressed in his bowing at her feet. He was already asleep. We can only assume that in his death spasm his body curled up into a bowed position.

We mentioned in chapter 4 of this study that "feet" can refer to private parts, and in chapter 5 we showed how Sisera's entering Jael's tent also has sexual overtones. With this in mind, we are in a position to see an added dimension in these verses, which would not have been lost on the Song's original hearers. It is as if Sisera had been struck down in the process of trying to carry out a rape. In fact, the first phrase of verse 27a could be a graphic description of rape: "Between her feet he bowed, he fell, he lay." This is particularly evident in that the verb "lay" is the verb used for rape in Deuteronomy 22:23, 25, 28, and the verb "bow" is used for sexual relations in Job 31:10. For years, Canaanite men had been raping Hebrew women in just this fashion. This time, however, the man is unsuccessful.

Cutting off (castrating; see p. 90 above) the Canaanites in the process of attempted rape is, in fact, exactly what did happen in a wider sense, as the next verses of the Song indicate. The serpent seeks to rape the Bride in order to raise up his own ungodly seed, but the serpent's head is crushed, and he dies "between her feet."

28a. Out of the window she looked and lamented,
　　　The mother of Sisera through the lattice,
28b. "Why does his chariot delay in coming?
　　　"Why do the steps [hoofbeats] of his chariots tarry?"
29. Her wise princesses would answer her,
　　　Indeed, she repeats the words to herself:
30a. "Are they not finding, are they not dividing the spoil?
　　　"A womb, two wombs for every warrior?
30b. "To Sisera a spoil of dyed work,
　　　"A spoil of dyed work embroidered?"
30c. Dyed work of double embroidery
　　　On the necks of the spoil!

The mother of Israel now speaks of the mother of Sisera. She is pictured as waiting for her son's return. Why the delay? She is comforted by the thought that Sisera must have taken great spoil, and it will take him time to collect it all. The men will have taken girls for themselves. This carries forward the idea of rape alluded to in the preceding verses. The term translated "damsel, maiden" in most Bibles actually means "womb." She refers to the girls using coarse soldier talk that views women only in terms of their genitals. But more than that, it is always the goal of the serpent to possess the bride in order to raise up his own godless seed through her. Satan wants the wombs, as we have noted earlier.

We might start to sympathize with Sisera's mother. She held him in her arms as a baby and played with him as a child—naturally she is worried about him. But if we think that way, we lose God's perspective. The Bible will not permit it. We are jarred to reality by the coarse language of verse 30. To give it a modern translation we would have to find crude language that would give an equivalent effect — language that is still regarded as "unprintable," at least in Bible commentaries, so I shall have to leave it to the reader's imagination to come up with something equivalent to what Deborah, under Divine inspiration, puts in the mouth of the anti-mother of the anti-Christ. Her serving women say this to her, and "indeed she repeats the words to herself." We begin to realize that the reason why Sisera was such a vicious enemy of God's people, and such a cruel man, was that he had such a mother! The hand that rocks the cradle rules the world, for good or for evil — that is the whole point of Judges 4 and 5. Let us not, then, sympathize with her!

Then she thinks about the beautiful cloths of embroidery that her son will bring home to her. Here the irony of the poem becomes very heavy. She is looking for dyed cloth. Unknown to her, Sisera is lying dead with his doubly embroidered garment dyed with his own blood. Deborah interjects her own comment at the end of verse 30 (thus I take the Hebrew), that Sisera himself is the spoil. He and his army are the captives taken captive by Barak.

Deborah delights in the misery of the enemy mother, whose savage expectations will not be realized. This "vindictive gloating," as one commentator calls it, is part of the inspired Word of God. (We may note that gloating and rejoicing are the same thing, the only difference being whether or not you sympathize with the person doing it.) If the reader is troubled by it, the reader must change his or her own mind, for the Bible is not going to change. We may call attention here to Proverbs 1:20-31, where Wisdom, clearly the pre-incarnate Christ though pictured in feminine language (Prov. 8:22-31), warns the scoffers not to scorn the Truth. Those who scoff at God "will eat of the fruit of their own way" (Prov. 1:31). On the day of judgment, God will scoff at them (Prov. 1:26-27).

With this understanding, we may consider Deborah's attitude toward the mother of Sisera. The Canaanite mother was gloating (rejoicing) in the anticipation of the destruction of God's people. Those who scoff will be scoffed at; those who gloat will be gloated over. In terms of this principle, Deborah rejoices in the humiliation of her womanly adversary. The age of grace had come to an end for the army of Sisera.

It may help the reader to bear in mind what is said in Ecclesiastes 3:8, "A time to love, and a time to hate; a time for war, and a time for peace." We do not live in a static, changeless condition. There are appropriate ways to think and feel about various situations and conditions of life. There are times to hate: "Do I not hate those who hate Thee, O Lord? And do I not loathe those who rise up against Thee? I hate them with the utmost hatred; they have become my enemies" (Ps. 139:21-22). We may well rejoice when the rapists, and the Hitlers, Stalins, and Idi Amins of this world are dead. Until they die, we extend the gospel to them, thereby loving God's and our enemies. Once they are dead, however, let us rejoice in their destruction!

> 31. Thus let all Thine enemies perish, O Lord;
>   But let those who love Him be like the rising of the sun in
>   its might. [End of the Song.]
>   And the land was undisturbed for forty years.

The final prayer is addressed to God: In this manner let all Your enemies perish. In what manner? By having their heads crushed. All the enemies of God are arrayed under Satan's banner, and they are all to receive the same curse as was placed on him in Genesis 3:15. A man might live with a bruised heel, or a crushed hand, but not with a crushed head. Total elimination is prayed for here.

Even as God's enemies are being destroyed, God's people will rise in history, in glory and power, just as the sunrise. Deborah refers here to Genesis 32:31, where the sun rose as Jacob crossed into the holy land, after wrestling with God all night. Deborah prays that all Israel will be like their father, able to wrestle with man and with God, and prevail. Her prayer receives an immediate fulfillment in the next story in Judges, where Gideon, after finding the strength to pursue the enemy all night (Jud. 8:4), returns from battle at the rising of the sun (8:13, literal translation). A further fulfillment is in Samson, whose name means "Sun." All this is fulfilled fully in Revelation 1:16, where the face of Christ is seen as "like the sun shining in its strength."

Summary and Conclusions

The Song of Deborah is built upon contrasts. There are, obviously, the two mothers, and the two seeds raised up by them.

This contrast has been developed already.

Second, there are the two storms, one at Sinai, the other at Megiddo. Yet, we ought not to see these as two disparate events. God's fierce storm rages throughout all history, ever destroying His enemies, as seen in Revelation 16:12-19. In Revelation 16:18 the storm at Ar-Mageddon that destroys Babylon is described in language taken directly from Exodus 19:16-18. This great storm of history did not destroy God's people at Sinai because they were under the blood of the Passover Lamb. This same storm bypasses God's people at the battle of Megiddo, because the people were with Barak the Levite in the sanctuary of Kedesh-Naphtali. But as for the enemies of God, Sisera and his army, the great storm of God destroys them.

In this great storm it is Christ Himself, the Greater Barak, who is the Lightning Bolt. Lightning is God's sword to render judgment on His enemies (Dt. 32:41). It is seen within His glory cloud (Ezk. 1:4, 13, 14). Lightning bolts are His arrows (Ps. 18:14; Zech. 9:14). When Christ comes in judgment, it will be "just as the lightning comes from the east and flashes to the west" (Matt. 42:27).

God's great storm of judgment rages throughout all history. Either we are safe in the sanctuary with Christ, or we are outside, exposed to His wrath.

Connected to the great storm of history is the great flood of history. That ancient torrent was created in Genesis 1:2, and out of it came the dry land (Gen. 1:9). When man's sin reached a climax, the ancient torrent washed clean the land of the whole earth in the Flood. The ancient torrent withdrew to let Israel pass at the Red Sea and again at the Jordan, but swept away Pharaoh and his chariots. Take your children to the ocean, and show them the hungry sea seeking to devour the land, but being restrained, as Job 38:8, 11 teaches. It is the grace of God that keeps us safe; it is Christ Who still calms the sea. Those who are sprinkled with the waters of baptism will not be drowned in the ancient torrent. Ultimately the ancient torrent flows from God Himself, and signifies His judgment, for the voice of the Lord is as the voice of many waters (Ezk. 1:24; 43:2; Rev. 1:15; 19:6).

Third, there are two responses to the call. We are not surprised to read a rollcall of the faithful tribes who came to fight with Barak against Sisera. Praise for good works comes easy (or should, anyway). What is harder to swallow is the open ridicule of the tribes who did not come to fight. Year after year, these tribes heard this ridicule at all the watering places of Israel. How embarrassed the compromising tribes must have been when they heard the Song of Deborah!

On the day of judgment, Christ will judge His people, and the judgment will be thorough and specific. But the Song of Deborah does not come at the end of history. Perhaps we need a list of so-called evangelical leaders who refuse to stand up and be counted in the abortion battle. Perhaps they should be subjected to sustained public ridicule. When Rev. Everett Sileven was languishing in the Cass County jail in Nebraska, because he would not permit the pagan state to license his church school, many pastors from around America came to march and to protest, or supported him in other ways. Many more could not be bothered. Others hung back until they saw which way the wind was blowing. Maybe some day we'll be singing the Song of Sileven, in which he will list those who came, and those who refused to come.

While we as Christians must not be a people characterized by personal vengeance and bile, yet we ought not to shy away from frank and truthful dealings either. Compromisers ought to be exposed, for the good of the Church.

Finally, there are two responses to opportunity. Deborah's Song is clearly a song of judgment and evaluation. Meroz was in the area of the battle, and as an Israelite city should have taken the opportunity to assist God's people in the fray (much as so-called Reformed and evangelical churches in Nebraska should have assisted Sileven). For their dalliance and refusal to help, they were cursed. (This theme recurs in Judges 8:4-9). On the other hand, Jael, who was not a member of Israel directly at all, though her forefathers had joined themselves to Israel, and who moreover was by treaty joined to the camp of the enemy—this Jael took the opportunity to ally herself with the Lord and strike for Him. For this bold deed she is praised above all women, even above Deborah herself.

In the crisis, hearts are revealed. Let us pray that we will prove to be faithful Jaels, not faithless Merozes, when that day comes.

7

GIDEON: GOD'S WAR AGAINST BAAL
(Judges 6:1 - 8:28)

The story of Gideon and of his son, Abimelech, is not easy to divide up into sections. There are several apparent concerns in the text, which are woven together in such a way as to overlap. The larger concerns include these:

1. Judgment for sin, oppression by Midian, Amalek, and Ishmael, and deliverance.
2. God's maturation of Gideon's faith.
3. Israel's drift toward a Baalistic, statist order.
4. Judgment for sin, oppression from within the nation, and deliverance.
5. The LORD's war against Baal.

There are two periods of oppression, the first under Midian, and the second under the false king Abimelech.

Rather than give a list of all the interactions between God and man in Judges 6–9, it is simpler to summarize by noting that God judges Israel for her sin in Judges 6, Israel begins to repent, and God raises up a deliverer. God interacts with Gideon in a series of command/promises, to which Gideon responds each time in faith. After the battle, Gideon passes a whole series of judgments (evaluations) from the Lord: against the heads of the enemy army, against two Israelite towns, and against the tribe of Ephraim. Gideon's final command, speaking for the Lord, is that their king is God, not a man. In his old age, however, Gideon begins to be unfaithful to this rule, and since Israel lusts for a king, God gives them one. Even though nothing is said about human repentance, God eventually does deliver Israel from Abimelech, this time without a human deliverer. Rather, God simply lets the evil destroy each other.

The following is an outline of the text:

I. Judgment for Sin (Judges 6:1-10)
   A. The Oppressor (6:1-6)
   B. God's Judgment (6:7-10)

II. God raises up a Deliverer, and grants Deliverance (6:11-7:23)
   A. Stage 1: God Restores Fellowship with Gideon, and
      with His People in Union with Gideon (6:11-24)
      1. God's Loving Initiative (6:11)
      2. The Promise of Presence (6:12-13)
      3. The Promise of Strength (6:14-15)
      4. The Promise of Victory (6:16)
      5. The Sign of Restored Communion (6:17-21)
      6. The Promise of Peace (6:22-24)
   B. Stage 2: Cleansing Begins at Home (6:25-32)
      1. God Attacks Baal (6:25-27)
      2. Gideon Vindicated (6:28-32)
   C. Stage 3: The Messiah Anointed (6:33-35)
   D. Stage 4: Baal Refuted (6:36-40)
   E. Stage 5: Holy War Fought by Faith Alone (7:1-8)
      1. The First Sorting (7:1-3)
      2. The Second Sorting (7:4-8)
   F. Stage 6: Reassurance Before Battle (7:9-14)
      1. God's Gracious Initiative (7:9-11)
      2. God's Wrathful Initiative (7:12-14)
   G. Stage 7: The Battle is the Lord's (7:15-23)
      1. Preparations (7:15-18)
      2. Psychological Operations (7:19-23)

III. Evaluations: The Rendering of Judgments (7;24 - 8:21)
   A. Oreb and Zeeb (7:24-25)
   B. Ephraim: The Vainglorious (8:1-3)
   C. Succoth and Penuel: The Faithless (8:4-9, 14-17)
   D. Midian, Amalek, and Ishmael (8:10-13)
   E. Zebah and Zalmunna (8:18-21)

IV. The Oppression of Humanistic Kingship (8:22 - 9:57)
   A. The Desire for a Humanistic King (8:22-23)
   B. The Drift toward a Humanistic King (8:24-35)
      1. Gideon's Ephod (8:24-28)
      2. Gideon's Polygamy (8:29-32)
      3. Israel's Ingratitude (8:33-35)
   C. The Enthronement of a Humanistic King (9:1-6)
      1. Abimelech's Argument (9:1-3)
      2. Baal's Counterattack against the Lord (9:4-6)

D. The Doom of Humanistic Kingship (9:7-57)
  1. Prophesied (9:7-21)
    a. The Place (9:7)
    b. The Parable (9:8-15)
    c. The Application (9:16-21)
  2. Implemented (9:22-55)
    a. Growing Discontent (9:23-25)
    b. From Bad to Worse (9:26-29)
    c. The Self-Destruction of the Wicked (9:30-57)
      (1) Gaal (9:30-41)
      (2) Shechem (9:42-45)
      (3) Baal (9:46-49)
      (4) Abimelech (9:50-55)
  3. Summary and Conclusion (9:56-57)

Part and parcel of Baalism, and of all non-Christian philosophy, is statism, the absolute rule of man over other men by means of force. As we saw in chapter 2 of this study, the essence of Baalism as a philosophy is the belief that Nature is ultimate, and that man is the stimulator and thus the ruler of Nature. This also means that man is the stimulator and ruler of other men, since they are part of Nature. The story of Gideon and Abimelech shows the connection between Baalism and statism, a theme that begins here and is carried forward throughout the rest of the book of Judges.

God's Judgment

6:1. Then the sons of Israel did what was evil in the sight of the LORD; and the LORD gave them into the hands of Midian seven years.

2. And the hand of Midian prevailed against Israel. Because of Midian the sons of Israel made for themselves the dens which were in the mountains and the caves and the strongholds.

3. For it was when Israel had sown, that the Midianites would come up with the Amalekites and the sons of the east and go up against them.

4. So they would camp against them and destroy the produce of the earth as far as Gaza, and leave no sustenance in Israel as well as no sheep, ox, or donkey.

5. For they would come up with their livestock and their tents, they would come in like locusts for number, both they and their camels were innumerable; and they came into the land to devastate it.

6. So Israel was brought very low because of Midian, and
the sons of Israel cried to the LORD.

God now begins to lose patience with Israel. That their sin
centrally involved Baalism is made clear from Judges 6:25, as we
shall see. So provoked was the Lord by this recurring apostasy,
that He did not sell them into bondage this time; instead, He
gave them away. They were under incredibly severe oppression
for seven years, the number of fulness, implying that there was
no sabbath for them during this time (even as there had been no
sabbath for them in Egypt). As before, the deliverance in the
eighth year (Jud. 6:33) is a sign of new birth, or a new week for
humanity.

The severity of the oppression is noted in terms of several
factors. The first is that the Israelites made caves (still visible in
the time of the writer) in which to hide. Man is made of dust,
and the curse is for him to return to dust from which he came.
To hide underground is always a sign of being under the curse in
Scripture, as in the case of Lot, who dwelt in a cave after leaving
Sodom, and who there sired two of the great enemies of Israel:
Moab and Ammon. Later it will be the enemies who will hide in
the caves.

Second, each year for seven years (until the eighth year of
deliverance) the enemy would sweep into the land with an army
vast as locusts (135,000 men, Jud. 8:10). Like locusts they would
strip the land bare of vegetation, as well as of livestock. Verse
four identifies the area of oppression as the northern part of
Israel. Apparently the Midianites did not want to challenge the
Philistines in the south.

Third, the presence of the cruel Amalekites among the oppressors indicates the severity of the oppression.

The leaders of the enemy were Midianites, apostate descendants of Abraham (Gen. 25:2). These Midianites had attacked
Israel during the wilderness wanderings (Num. 22–25, 31). On
the advice of Balaam, the Midianites had sent their women into
the Israelite camp to seduce Israel to sin, so that the Lord would
be against Israel. Israel was delivered when Phineas took a spear
and skewered a fornicating couple. Gideon will be a second
Phineas. Also joined with Midian were the "sons of the east," a
phrase that refers to Ishmaelites (Jud. 8:24) and other descen-

dants of Abraham (Gen. 25:6, 18).

These people were nomads, scavengers of the earth. They had no culture and no home, but wandered from place to place, robbing and pillaging. They had rejected the cultural mandate of Genesis 1:26-28 and 2:15, and they were under the curse of Cain, living in a land of wanderings (Gen. 4:16). Now the nomads oppress the dominion men.

> 7. Now it came about when the sons of Israel cried to the LORD on account of Midian,
> 8. That the LORD sent a prophet to the sons of Israel, and he said to them, "Thus says the LORD, the God of Israel, 'It was I who brought you up from Egypt, and brought you out from the house of slaves.
> 9. " 'And I delivered you from the hands of the Egyptians and from the hands of all your oppressors, and dispossessed them before you and gave you their land,
> 10. " 'And I said to you, "I am the LORD your God; you shall not fear the gods of the Amorites in whose land you live." But you have not hearkened to My voice.' "

There is no instant deliverance this time, when they cry for salvation. God is angry enough to make them wait. Indeed, rather than comfort them immediately, He sends a prophet to charge them with sin. A prophet is a mediator, one who speaks on behalf of two parties. Primarily prophets are seen speaking on behalf of God to man, though they sometimes speak for man to God (see Gen. 20:7, and the whole ministry of Moses as go-between in Ex. 19–35). The use of prophets is a sign of God's grace, since to speak with God face to face is terrifying, and even destructive (Ex. 20:19; 33:20). Thus, even in judgment there is grace, for every judgment gives an opportunity to repent.

There is no separate "office" of prophet in the Bible. God raised up prophets from time to time to speak His word and to act as reconcilers. Usually, however, it was the Levites who acted the role of prophet, since communicating truth from the Groom to the Bride was part of the Levitical role. Indeed, the Levites were the "messengers" (in Hebrew, "angels") for the Lord (Mal. 2:7). Possibly, then, this prophet was a Levite, and so here we see the Levites doing their job. On the other hand, possibly even at this early date God was raising up prophets because the Levites were failing to do their job. My own inclination, given the theology of Judges as a whole, is to see this prophet as raised up because of the failure of the Levites, but we cannot say for certain.

Every historical judgment includes grace, except the judgment of personal death. This is because there is always a chance to repent — until the last judgment. The fact that God brings judgment, and says so, is wholly of grace. After all, at this very time (as always) the Chinese people were being oppressed, but God did not (to our knowledge) send a prophet to explain judgment to them; thus, they were not given opportunity to repent.

The prophet here utters what scholars call "the covenant lawsuit." The people had broken the covenant, and so they are charged in God's court. God reminds them that He had delivered them from Egypt. This fact is reiterated, to show that God is *able* to save and protect Israel, thus demonstrating that their present low estate has come about because God has brought it to pass by removing His protection of them.

There is a principle in Scripture: The one who delivers us gains the right to rule us by virtue of the deliverance (see Luke 1:71-75). Israel had forgotten this fact, and they continue to forget it even after the victory is won (Jud. 8:22). God asserts this principle here in Judges 6:10. He had saved them, therefore He ruled them. He had told them not to worship Baal, the god of the Amorites, but they had disobeyed Him. This makes it clear, again, that the basic problem is not oppression, but Baalism.

God Restores Fellowship

11. Then the angel of the LORD came and sat under the oak that was in Ophrah, which belonged to Joash the Abiezrite as his son Gideon was beating out wheat in the winepress in order to save it from the Midianites.

12. And the angel of the LORD appeared to him and said to him, "The LORD is with you, O valiant warrior."

13. Then Gideon said to Him, "Oh my lord [master], if the LORD is with us, why then has all this happened to us? And where are all His miracles which our fathers told us about, saying, 'Did not the LORD bring us up from Egypt?' But now the LORD has abandoned us and given us into the hand of Midian."

14. And the LORD looked upon him and said, "Go in this your strength and deliver (*yasha'*) Israel from the hand of Midian. Have I not sent you?"

15. And he said to him, "O lord [master], with what shall I deliver (*yasha'*) Israel? Behold, my family is the least in Manasseh, and I am the youngest in my father's house."

16. But the LORD said to him, "Surely I will be with you, and you shall smite Midian as one man."

Right away we have to mark that God takes the initiative in restoring fellowship with Israel. God's initiative is one of the major themes in the Gideon story. It is the angel of the Lord Who comes to the foot of the tree, once again a symbol of the place where God meets man, the foot of the "ladder to heaven," to initiate conversation with Gideon. We are reminded that this Angel is the Captain of the Lord's host (Josh. 5:14), and He comes to marshal Gideon to the fray.

Gideon was threshing in the winepress, out of sight below ground, rather than in the mill, so as to avoid notice from the Midianites. Later it will be Midianites who will hide in winepresses. The reference to wheat and wine is significant in the Bible. Wine and bread are the food of kings (Gen. 40). To honor Abram as true king of Canaan, Melchizedek gave him bread and wine (Gen. 14:18). The picture of Gideon threshing out wheat in a winepress is a sign to Israel of how he would serve them, and the good things that would come from him. The New Testament fulfillment of this theme should be obvious: It is Christ, the Greater Melchizedek, who gives to His people the food of kings.

Here at this early stage, Gideon is seen preparing the food of kings. Like Jesus Christ, he will rule by being a servant (treating others as kings), rather than by lording it over the people (Mark 10:42-45). Later, at the end of his life, Gideon will fall from this noble beginning.

Threshing is also a frequent sign in the Bible of the historical process of judgment and winnowing. In Luke 3:17 John the Baptist says that Christ will thresh the world, separating wheat from chaff. God had been threshing Israel with judgments because of her Baal worship. If Gideon is God's servant, he will also thresh Israel. In fact, the first thing God tells him to do is thresh his father's household. (In connection with this theme, it is interesting to note by the way that the Temple was built on a threshing floor, a sign of how God's kingdom is built, 2 Sam. 24:18ff.)

God opens the conversation with a striking promise, the promise of His presence. This is the basic promise of the Covenant: Immanuel, God with us. Because God is with him, Gideon will be a valiant warrior.

Gideon's response shows true faith. He judges himself, and confesses that the disasters that have befallen Israel are really from the Lord, not from the human enemy. At one level, he is patently contradicting the word of the Angel: the Lord clearly is *not* with us. On the contrary, the Lord is against us. While this might be an expression of rebellion, in Gideon's mouth it is not. He agrees almost word for word with what God has already said, referring to the deliverance from Egypt and to God's giving (not selling this time) them into the hand of Midian. It is a confession of sin. Gideon has judged himself, and so he will not be judged (1 Cor. 11:31), and on that basis communion with God can be restored.

Upon his confession of sin, the Lord "turns toward" him (v. 14), indicating restoration of true fellowship. The Lord gives him a second promise and this time also a command. This is the promise of strength. What is "this your strength?" It is the same as Deborah's strength (5:21), the presence and promise of the Lord: "Have not *I* sent you?"

Gideon responds with humility. He is the youngest son of Joash, and the family of Joash is least in Manasseh, and after all Manasseh is one of the inferior tribes compared with Ephraim (Gen. 48) and Judah. Gideon is a most unlikely candidate for this task. It will be necessary for God to build up his faith. We must remember that God is teaching His people how to make war (Jud. 3:2), and that holy war is fought by faith. The emphasis in this section of Judges is precisely that: warring by faith. Gideon and Israel had to learn that no matter how weak they were, God could still destroy the enemy, when they looked to Him in faith. There is much here for the weak Church at the end of the 20th century to learn from.

Gideon, in fact, was no raw youth, but middle-aged. He had a teen-aged son (Jud. 8:20). In a society that venerated age and wisdom, however, he was still a relatively young man. He shows the proper humility and consciousness of his youth, something very rare in the American Church today.

There are two important Biblical themes that come up here. The first is the theme of the son replacing and redeeming the father. Jesus is the Son of Man, which simply means the Son of Adam. Adam, the father, rebelled against God and fell into sin. Jesus the son replaces him, becoming the Second Adam, and also redeems those who fell in Adam. This theme is present here in the Gideon story, since Gideon's father Joash was a Baal worshipper, but Gideon's faithfulness saves him.

The second theme is that of the younger son. Jesus is the Younger Brother who replaces the firstborn Adam. Throughout the book of Genesis, we always see the firstborn son falling into sin and being rejected (Cain, Ishmael, Esau, the older sons of Jacob, and even Manasseh), but we also see the younger son rise up and deliver the older brothers (especially in the story of Joseph). To take one more example, David was the youngest son of Jesse (1 Sam. 16:11).

The temptation that comes to the youth is to think more of himself than he ought, so that he rises up and seizes power prematurely. This was the sin of Ham.[1] Gideon's humility marks him as a faithful youth, who should mature into a wise old man.

The Lord rewards this humility with yet a third promise, the promise of victory (v. 16). Because God is with him, his victory over Midian will be total.

This conversation reminds us of another conversation between God and a humble man, indeed the meekest man of the Old Covenant (Num. 12:3). And like Moses in Exodus 3 and 4, Gideon asks for a sign.

17. So he said to Him, "If now I have found favor in Thy sight, then show me a sign that it is Thou who speakest with me.

18. "Please do not depart from here, until I come back to Thee, and bring out my offering and lay it before Thee." And He said, "I will remain until you return."

19. Then Gideon went in and prepared a kid and unleavened bread from an ephah of flour; he put the meat in a basket and he

---

1. I have dealt with this at length in my essay, "Rebellion, Tyranny, and Dominion in the Book of Genesis," in Gary North, ed., *Tactics of Christian Resistance* (Tyler, TX: Geneva Ministries, 1983).

put the broth in a pot, and brought them out to Him under the oak, and presented them.

20. And the angel of God said to him, "Take the meat and the unleavened bread and lay them on this rock, and pour out the broth." And he did so.

21. Then the angel of the LORD put out the end of the staff that was in his hand and touched the meat and the unleavened bread; and the fire sprang up from the rock and consumed the meat and the unleavened bread. Then the angel of the LORD vanished from his sight.

22. When Gideon saw that he was the angel of the LORD, Gideon said, "Alas, O Master LORD! For now I have seen the angel of the LORD face to face."

23. And the LORD said to him, "Peace to you, do not fear; you shall not die.

24. Then Gideon built an altar there to the LORD and named it The LORD is Peace. To this day it is still in Ophrah of the Abiezrites.

God graciously consents to Gideon's request, for it was made not in unbelief, but in weak faith. "Lord, I believe; help me in my unbelief!" was his prayer (see Mark 9:24). It is not a bare sign Gideon wants. We do not enjoy a meal if someone we intensely dislike is present with us. In the Orient, the meal is eaten only with family and friends. To share salt and a meal with someone is to enter a covenant of communion with them. This is part of the meaning of the Lord's Supper. Gideon knows that if God has restored fellowship with His people, then He will share a meal with them.

An ephah of flour is no little amount, for an ephah was a vessel large enough to hold a person (Zech. 5:7). Gideon made a lot of bread. Considering that bread was hard to come by, in that one could not make much flour threshing in a winepress, Gideon's gift was quite generous. God will consume all of it in fire, and this will be somewhat of a test for Gideon's faith. It was unleavened, the bread of the Exodus. Just as the old leaven of Egypt was not brought to the land of God, but new leaven was found there, so Gideon refuses to use the old sinful leaven, looking to God to insert a new leaven of the Spirit into the dough of humanity.[2]

---

2. On leaven, see the discussion in my book *The Law of the Covenant*, pp. 186ff.

He also prepared a kid. This was also a generous sacrifice. A whole kid would be valuable enough under ordinary circumstances, but after seven years of Midianite pillage, after they had left "no sustenance in Israel as well as no sheep, ox, or donkey," we can well imagine that a kid would be precious indeed. The kid is a young goat, and just as all the sacrificial animals symbolize humanity in its various aspects, the kid is especially connected to youth. Thus, it is fitting that it was a kid that Gideon offered.[3]

The meal had three parts: drink (broth), bread, and meat. This corresponds to the Peace Sacrifice of the Mosaic Law. To understand fully what happens here in the story of Gideon, we must have some understanding of the Peace Sacrifice. In the Peace Sacrifice a meal was shared among the offerer, the officiating priest, and the Lord. Some of the characteristics of this meal were as follows:

1. The offerer eats part of the sacrifice (Lev. 7:15-17).
2. Some of the meat is given to the Lord, Who gives it back to the priest to eat (Lev. 7:28-34; 10:14f.; 21:22).
3. The fat and certain organs are burnt up, turned into smoke, as food for the Lord (Lev. 3:11, 16; 22:25).
4. The unleavened bread is burnt up as food for the Lord, while leavened bread is eaten by offerer and priest (Lev. 7:11-14).
5. Wine is poured out for God to drink, while the participants also drink wine (Num. 15:1-10).
6. Some examples of Peace Sacrifices are found in Genesis 18:1-8, Genesis 31:54, Exodus 18:12, and Exodus 24:1-11. Passover is a variant of the Peace Sacrifice.

The unhewn rock formed a temporary altar (Ex. 20:25), and at the Lord's command Gideon poured out the broth for the Lord to drink. Then the Lord touched the bread and meat with his rod, which speaks of judgment, and all went up in flames. God showed thereby that He was willing to eat a meal with His people once again. Communion was restored.

God had told Moses, "You cannot see My face, for no man can see Me and live" (Ex. 33:20). Gideon, realizing fully now just Whom he has been conversing with, is struck with fear for

---

3. *Ibid.,* pp. 190ff., 272ff.

his life. God reassures him, promising him peace. This indicates fully that what we have here was a variant of the Peace Sacrifice (Divinely adjusted to the circumstances). Gideon will not die, for the consumption of the meat on the altar was his substitute. (The Peace Sacrifice is, after all, a sacrifice as well as a meal.) The promise of peace means that God is finished warring against Israel.

When Phineas smote the Midianites, God rewarded him, saying "Behold, I give him My covenant of peace" (Num. 25:12). Gideon, called to war against Midian resurgent, is given the promise of Phineas. He must be a new Phineas, consumed with zeal for the Lord's honor.

As a memorial, Gideon built a memorial-altar. It was visible for generations, a reminder of God's judgment and God's peace. In the New Covenant, the Lord's Supper is our memorial-altar, our reminder of God's judgment and peace through Jesus Christ.

Gideon had used a vast amount of grain (an ephah), and it was now all gone, consumed in the fire. He had slaughtered a whole precious kid. In a time when Israel was near starvation, brought "very low" (Jud. 6:6), this "holy waste" surely would seem to make matters worse. Next God will tell Gideon to kill one of the few bulls left in the land! Deliverance would have to come soon, and Gideon was put in a position of having to trust the Lord for it.

Baal Destroyed

Before the invaders can be cleared away, Israel must repent and turn from Baalism. Thus, the first battle is against Baal. The Lord initiates the battle.

25. Now the same night it came about that the LORD said to him, "Take your father's bull, even the second bull seven years old, and pull down the altar of Baal which belongs to your father, and cut down the Asherah that is beside it;
26. And build an altar to the LORD your God on the top of this stronghold in an orderly manner, and take the second bull and offer a burnt offering with the wood of the Asherah which you shall cut down."
27. Then Gideon took ten men of his servants and did as the

LORD had spoken to him; and it came about, because he was too afraid of his father's household and the men of the city to do it by day, that he did it by night.

Here again, every detail God sees fit to include in the text is important. It is important that Gideon use the second bull. It is important that the bull be seven years old. It is important that the altar be built on the stronghold. It is important that the same bull that tears down the altar of Baal be sacrificed to the Lord. If these details were not important, they would not be included. We are not doing justice to the sacred text of God's Word unless we at least try to understand how all this fits together.

God's command came at night. We have already mentioned the sunrise theme in Scripture in our comments on Judges 5:31. God's appearances at night are tokens that glory is coming. Even in creation, there was evening first and then morning; but in the world under sin, night signifies the darkness of sin's dominion. God's revelations in the Old Covenant frequently came at night (Gen. 15, for instance). Indeed, Zechariah 1 through 6 are a series of visions that grow darker and then brighter as the night passes toward morning. And of course, Nicodemus came to see the Sun of Righteousness at night (John 3; Mal. 4:2). After Gideon's victory, the sun rises upon him (Judges 8:13).

God's command came the same night as He appeared to Gideon. When fellowship with God is restored, reformation must begin immediately, and it begins at home and in the home town. God launches a direct assault against Baal. Baal's altar and the carved pillar of his wife Asherah must be wrecked, and God's altar must be put in their place. Gideon's household had to change sides in the great war of history. The fact that the altar of Baal belonged to Joash indicates that Gideon had been brought up in a Baal-worshipping household, though doubtless the Lord was given some lip-service as well. The change of allegiance had to be public, and God's altar was to be built high up on the stronghold, where all could see it as a public confession of faith.

Joash and his people had sought fertility and prosperity for their land by worshipping fertility gods and goddesses. The result had been virtual starvation. If they return to the Lord, the true Giver of life, fertility, and prosperity, things will change.

The NASV does not have the sense of the Hebrew here, for it indicates that two bulls were to be used. Rather, it was the "second" bull that did all the work. The second or younger bull points to the theme of the replacement of the firstborn. The fact that the bull was seven years old ties to the oppression of Midian, which had lasted seven years, corresponding to seven years of apostasy for Israel. The Levitical law required that a national sin be atoned for by a bull (Lev. 4:13-21). The seven years of this bull atoned for the full week of Israel's sin. It cancelled out the defiled first week, and made possible the resurrection of the eighth day, and a new week in righteousness for humanity, led by the Son, the Younger Brother.

The bull that destroys Baal is the same as the bull that is sacrificed, for both actions picture Christ, whose death destroyed Satan forever. This was a Whole Burnt Sacrifice, signifying total judgment and devotion to destruction.

Gideon obeyed God. Because of fear, he did it at night. (Also, if he had done it in broad daylight, he probably would have been stopped.) He got a total complement of ten men to help him, but a secret shared by ten men is no secret, and so the town found out that Gideon was the one who tore down the altar of their beloved Baal.

28. When the men of the city arose early in the morning, behold, the altar of Baal was torn down, and the Asherah which was beside it was cut down, and the second bull was offered on the altar which had been built.

29. And they said to one another, "Who did this thing?" And when they searched about and inquired, they said, "Gideon the son of Joash did this thing."

30. Then the men of the city said to Joash, "Bring out your son, that he may die, for he has torn down the altar of Baal, and indeed, he has cut down the Asherah which was beside it."

31. But Joash said to all who stood against him, "Will you contend for Baal, or will you deliver (*yasha'*) him? Whoever will contend for him shall be put to death by morning. If he is a god, let him contend for himself, because someone has torn down his altar."

32. Therefore on that day he named him Jerubbaal, that is to say, "Let Baal contend against him," because he tore down his altar.

The glorious sunrise revealed redemption accomplished, and the resurrection of true religion. This was not met with joy by all, however.

Surprisingly, Joash follows the lead of his son. This in itself is a remarkable thing, showing the active grace of God. The men want to put Gideon to death, but Joash reminds them that Baal supposedly is a god, and should be able to take care of himself. This seems to be the meaning of verse 31, which is difficult to translate. The middle sentence of that verse, which the NASV renders, "whoever will contend for him shall be put to death," might also read as if Joash is addressing those who are contending for Baal, thus, "He (you) who would contend for Baal, let him (Gideon) be put to death by morning." I offer the following paraphrase of the whole verse: Joash said to all who stood against him, "Does Baal need *you* (emphatic) to plead for him? Does Baal need *you* to deliver him? Listen to me, those of you who want to contend for Baal. Let him, the one who has attacked Baal, be found dead by tomorrow morning. Give Baal 24 hours to avenge himself. If Baal is a god, let him fight for himself, since someone has torn down his altar." Of course, the impotent Baal was unable to get revenge on Gideon. God protected Gideon. Baal's revenge would come much later (Jud. 9:4-5).

Jerubbaal means "Let Baal Contend." Its use as Gideon's nickname was a constant reminder to everyone that Gideon was a Baal Fighter. Gideon was marching on, and let Baal stop him if he can! Thus, Gideon was the Baal Fighter, and in this study we shall use that English phrase to translate the challenging sense of "Jerubbaal." Before any of us weak Gideons can be effective for God, we must fight our own Baals, and tear down our own altars. And before the Christian community can make a mark against humanistic America, our families and communities must tear down the modern altars of Baal.

We see God continuing to encourage Gideon's weak faith. What an encouragement to see his father Joash, an old Baal follower, coming around to the side of the Lord! God makes Gideon's fearful yet faithful action gloriously successful.

The Messiah Anointed

33. Then all the Midianites and the Amalekites and the sons of the east assembled themselves; and they crossed over and camped in the valley of Jezreel.

34. So the Spirit of the LORD clothed Gideon; and he blew a trumpet, and the Abiezrites were called together to follow him.

35. And he sent messengers throughout Manasseh, and they also were called together to follow him; and he sent messengers to Asher, Zebulun, and Naphtali, and they came up to meet him.

It is now that time of the year when the three nomadic tribes come into Israel to devastate the land. Just as they arrive, God strikes.

The Spirit is imparted to Gideon. This anointing makes him a Messiah, an anointed one. The fulness of this is seen at the anointing of Christ at His baptism. ("Christ" is Greek for the Hebrew term "Messiah.") Though all the judges were anointed, there is a specific reason why attention is called to the time and place of the anointing of some. I believe that the reason attention is called to it in the case of Gideon has to do with the typology of this story. God has now finished doing the primary work needed for man's redemption. That primary work entails sacrifice for sin and the definitive destruction of the enemy. After God does His part, man steps in to do his, which involves mopping up the enemies of God and growing in renewed righteousness. The Spirit is given after the primary work of redemption is accomplished. This sequence finds its fulfillment in the New Testament, when it is after Christ has accomplished eternal salvation through His sacrifice and destruction of Satan, that the Spirit is poured out at Pentecost to empower the Church for growth and for the mopping up work.

It is most important to see this. The first and preeminent thing the Church must do is not defeat her enemies, but break the idols at her heart. When Baal is gone, and the altar of the Lord is renewed, the enemies will fall rapidly enough. At this point, with the destruction of Baal, the battle is really already over. All that is left is a cleaning up exercise. Though Gideon does not realize it, the hardest part is already past.

The anointing of the Spirit here is literally a "clothing." When the Spirit comes upon a man, He flows down over him as his garment, like the anointing oil that symbolized Him during the Old Covenant (see Ps. 133 for a picture of this). The result is that the man is re-created after the image of God by the work of the Spirit. Gideon is such a new man.

We may return at this point to the theme of the youth. God had permitted the sins of man's youth to ripen to full maturity before the Flood, but after the Flood He promised never again to permit the sins of youth to mature (Gen. 8:21). God promised to intervene in the life of man, so that the youth is either cut off or redeemed before he comes to full age. The theme of the cutting off of the youth comes to full expression in the Servant Song of Isaiah 53:8. It is because Christ was cut off in youth (a mere 33 years of age, and childless), that we can be saved in the midst of our lives, before our sin comes to full fruition. Gideon's salvation as a youth, and his investiture with the Spirit, point to this.

The blowing of the trumpet was the way Israel was summoned. Gideon may have trembled as he blew it (or had a bugler blow it). Who would come to the side of the least of the least of the least? Who indeed! The first to rally to his side were the Abiezrites, his own home town! All those men who had seen little Gideon as a child, now followed him as their leader. This required a monumental work of grace, for it is a proverb that a prophet is not without honor, save in his own home town, as even Jesus learned (Matt. 13:54-58). What a tremendous encouragement this must have been for Gideon, to see his father and uncles, older brothers and cousins, all taking his orders willingly. God continues to build his faith: All things are possible with Him.

Others also came. The tribe of Manasseh, Gideon's tribe, and also Asher, Zebulun, and Naphtali. All were moved by the Spirit to hearken to the call. The tribe of Ephraim was also in this area, though a little to the south. Ephraim always lorded it over Manasseh, and tried to lord it over all the rest of the tribes as well. Gideon was reluctant to call them, lest his bothering them make them angry. He preferred to leave them alone. They were an ill-tempered bunch.

Baalism Refuted

36. Then Gideon said to God, "If Thou wilt deliver (*yasha'*) Israel by my hand, as Thou hast spoken,

37. "Behold, I will put a fleece of wool on the threshing floor. If there is dew on the fleece only, and it is dry on all the ground, then I will know that Thou wilt deliver (*yasha'*) Israel by my hand, as Thou hast spoken."

38. And it was so. When he arose early the next morning and squeezed the fleece, he drained the dew from the fleece, a bowl full of water.

39. Then Gideon said to God, "Do not let Thine anger burn against me that I may speak once more; please let me make a test once more with the fleece, let it now be dry only on the fleece, and let there be dew on all the ground."

40. And God did so that night; for it was dry only on the fleece, and dew was on all the ground.

This passage has occasioned a good deal of speculation regarding its prophetic meaning. The dew on the fleece but not on the ground is supposed to portray the Old Covenant, Israel being the fleece and the nations being the ground. The reversal is supposed to portray the New Covenant, God favoring the nations with His life-giving water, but Israel dried up. While such an interpretation might have something to say for itself in some contexts, there simply is nothing in the story of Gideon whatever even to hint that future relations among God, Israel, and the nations are in view.

What is very much in view is the distinction between the Lord and Baalism. The religion of the Bible is a religion-philosophy that ascribes all events to personal actions on the part of personal, accountable agents (God, angels, and men), as we have seen. The eternally active Triune God brings all things to pass through His eternal activity, not through the establishment of impersonal processes. Baalism, on the other hand, is a religion-philosophy that ascribes all events to impersonal processes on the part of impersonal forces, which may be mythologized as gods and goddesses.

Gideon had been raised in Baalism. Joash had taught him doubtless that God created the world, but that Nature ran it. Nature (Baal) was a process, so miracles were by definition impossible. What are miracles? The Deistic view of miracle sees it as a disruption of the processes of nature that God established at the creation. A proper Christian view of miracle sees it as God's acting in a way different from the way He usually acts. God does not "set aside the physical laws" in miracles, for there are no such laws or processes to set aside. The importance of miracles in Scripture is that they pointedly demonstrate that God is the eternally active God, and that the universe is not a self-sustaining process. Miracles refute Baalism, whether Pantheistic (the universe as self-originating) or Deistic (God created it, and left it to run itself).

Now, sophisticated Baalism has an answer for us. "Obviously," they say, "the universe is not *all* process. There would be no progress or even change if there were not also such a thing as *chance*. What you call a 'miracle' we explain in terms of chance, the principle of contingency. Chance may reverse gravity on some occasion, maybe. Chance may make a fleece dry while the ground is covered with dew. To do justice to us Baalists, you need to put process together with chance. Impersonal process plus impersonal chance equals the real world."

But God's miracles also answer this sophisticated Baalism as well. Miracles do *not* happen randomly, but purposefully. Miracles, whether performed by God or by demons (Ex. 7:11f., 22; 8:7), do not happen just at random; they are caused by persons. To put it another way, the *timing* of the miracle refutes the Baalistic philosophy of chance, while the *action* of the miracle refutes the Baalistic philosophy of process. Because the Christian God is a Person, the miracle is personal, and thus has a purpose and a timing that no philosophy of chance and process can account for.

This is seen especially in that the God of the Bible predicts in advance what His miracles will be. (Note particularly the ten plagues upon Egypt.) There is no way a philosophy of chance can have predictions, since how can you predict a specific chance event? Predictions are only possible in a context of regularity or normalcy. We can predict that the sun will rise tomorrow because it always does. The Baalist can make the same prediction, because of his philosophy of process. But the striking thing about the God of Scripture is that He predicts the exceptions, the miracles. This is something utterly outside the philosophy of Baalism, and utterly outside the capacity of the human.[4]

After the first test, Gideon realized that perhaps the fleece had simply absorbed all the dew because the fleece was naturally more absorbent. A second, more clearly miraculous, test was necessary. God also granted this miracle.

Thus, the meaning of the story of Gideon and the fleece is this: God is not Baal; God is not limited as is Baal; God is sovereign over Baal. God did not rebuke Gideon for asking for a sign, but graciously gave him the signs he needed.

Now, this does not mean that God will answer every request for a miraculous sign. There are two reasons why we should not look for signs. First of all, miraculous signs were given to help the faith of people before the Bible was completed. Now that the Bible is complete, and that the Spirit has been poured out in His fulness, our faith should be able to stand squarely on the Word of God alone, without any miracle other than His special presence in the sacrament. Second, miracles are given, as in this case, to help the faith of the very weak. Missionaries going into new places often report miracles, but these same miracles are not seen in places where the gospel has begun to do its work in society. This is the way God acts, and we must understand it and conform to Him. God does not want people *depending* on miracles, but on His Word; and so God acts to bring His people up to maturity, so that they will not always be looking for miracles.

We have been speaking of *sign* miracles. At the same time, we tend to place too little confidence in the eternally active, loving, Fatherly God. Our modern philosophy of process makes us hesitant about taking matters of our daily life to God in prayer. It is as easy for God to keep my car running as it is for Him to let it run down. When we see that God is active in everything, our dependence on Him should greatly increase. While we

---

4. It might be thought that when the Baalists sought to get fire from heaven, in 1 Kings 18, they were seeking a miracle. Actually, however, they were engaging in an act of stimulating Baal (Nature). Within their system of belief, this was not a miracle, but a "scientific" way of manipulating forces to achieve a desired result. The same thing is true of "Indian rain dances." It is *within* the overall philosophy of process that these stimulations take place. (They don't work, of course.)

should not look for miracles in the sense of signs (the Bible is our *sign,* telling us how to live), we should be looking all the time to the eternally active God to bring things to pass. There is much that we should be asking for, except that our Baalistic philosophy of process causes us to think that it is no use asking for it. We should take everything to God in prayer.

There are things in our lives that we have gotten used to, and we think "Well, that's just the way things are." In reality, however, these things we have gotten used to are the way God is doing things, and God can do things differently if He wants to. There would probably be a great deal less chronic sickness among us if we would stop treating sickness as a process and start treating it as the action of God, correctable by Him. 2 Chronicles 16:12 condemns Asa for looking solely to the physicians rather than to God for healing. James 5:14-15 tells us the primary thing we should do in the case of sickness (without despising the ministries of Luke the physician).

Baalism is rampant in America today, in the classroom, in science, in social science (how to manipulate people by manipulating processes), on the right (cycles of civilization), on the left (irresistible force of dialectical materialism), etc. We as Christians must keep reminding ourselves that God is a Person, our relationship with Him is personal, He is personally interested in every atom of the universe, He governs all things by His personal actions, we are surrounded by angels, we can ask and He will answer.

When God performs these miracles, exactly according to what had been agreed upon beforehand, Gideon knows that God will deliver Israel. Gideon knows that God is *able* to do a miraculous event (deliver Israel by the hand of Gideon), and Gideon knows that God is *willing* to do it, because God has foretold it.

Beyond this anti-Baalist philosophy of miracle, is there any symbolic meaning to the dew on the fleece? Possibly, though we cannot be certain. Two possibilities present themselves, in view of the fact that dew is a frequent symbol for blessing in the Bible (Gen. 27:28; Dt. 33:13, 28). First, it may be that the fleece represents Israel. Thus, when God blesses Israel, God dries up the nations round about, and they are unable to threaten her. On the other hand, when God dries up Israel because of her sins, God blesses the nations round about so that they are able to attack and punish Israel. The problem with this interpretation is that it goes contrary to the sequence. We should expect a dry fleece followed by a wet one, if the fleece represents Israel.

A second symbolic interpretation takes note of the connection of the threshing floor with the sanctuary of God. In this case, the fleece signifies God's sacrifice, and the threshing floor signifies Israel. Israel is dry, bereft of blessing. God's blessing does, however, rest on His holy Lamb. As a result of the work of the Lamb, which wrings Him out, blessing is spread to Israel, the threshing floor. This interpretation does better justice to all the facts, in that it takes into account the specific details of the threshing floor and the wringing of the fleece. Yes, God will deliver Israel, and blessing will come to the threshing floor, but not because the threshing floor deserves it. Rather, it is because of the sacrifice (wringing) of the fleece (the Lamb of God) that blessing can be given to the threshing floor (Israel).

By Faith Alone

As we discussed in chapter 2 of this study, holy war must be fought by faith alone. To make this clear, God commanded Gideon to give his army some curious tests.

> 7:1 Then Jerubbaal (that is, Gideon) and all the people who were with him, rose early and camped beside the Spring of Harod; and the camp of Midian was on the north side of him, but the hill of Moreh in the valley.
>
> 2. And the LORD said to Gideon, "The people who are with you are too many for Me to give Midian into their hands, lest Israel glorify itself against Me saying, 'My own hand has delivered (*yasha‘*) me.'
>
> 3. "Now therefore come, proclaim in the hearing of the people saying, 'Whoever is afraid and trembling, let him return and depart from Mount Gilead.' " So 22,000 people returned, but 10,000 remained.
>
> 4. Then the LORD said to Gideon, "The people are still too many; bring them down to the water and I will test them for you there. Therefore it shall be that he of whom I say to you, 'This one shall go with you,' he shall go with you; but everyone of whom I say to you, 'This one shall not go with you,' he shall not go."

5. So he brought the people down to the water. And the LORD said to Gideon, "You shall separate everyone who laps the water with his tongue, as a dog laps, as well as everyone who kneels to drink."

6. Now the number of those who lapped, putting their hand to their mouth, was 300 men; but all the rest of the people kneeled to drink water.

7. And the LORD said to Gideon, "I will deliver (*yasha'*) you with the 300 men who lapped and will give the Midianites into your hands; so let all the other people go, each man to his place."

8. So the 300 men took the people provisions and their trumpets into their hands. And he sent all the other men of Israel, each to his tent, but retained the 300 men; and the camp of Midian was below him in the valley.

Gideon is called Jerubbaal, the Baal-Fighter. He is going to war against Baal, in the confidence God had given him the night before. They rose early, with the sun. The rising of the sun is a picture in Judges of the strength of God's righteous people.

Deuteronomy 20:8 commands that when the army is summoned, those who are fearful should be sent home. The Lord reminds Gideon to implement this law now. Holy war cannot be fought except by men of faith, who have confidence in the Lord and are consequently basically unafraid. Moreover, the Lord is showing Israel that ultimately He alone is the Deliverer; they have no active part except to mop up after the battle has definitively been won. Twenty-two thousand men departed, and thus the place came to be called the Spring of Harod ("Fearful, Trembling").

In the second test, it was those who were singleminded who were chosen. Lapping as a dog laps is explained in verse 6 as taking water in the palm and bringing it to the mouth. They used their hands the way a dog uses its tongue to scoop up water. These men were so conscious of the holy war that they did not kneel down to drink, but remained standing and alert. They were wholly consecrated to their task, singleminded. God's wars can only be fought by such men.

Gideon's band numbered 300; the enemy 135,000. This is a ratio of 450:1, in favor of the enemy. Not good odds, humanly speaking. God's plan, as revealed in verse 18 and following, required each of the 300 men to have his own torch, trumpet, and jar, so that these had to be collected from the provisions of the larger camp. The rest of the men returned to their tents. They would be summoned for the mopping up operation, after the first blow had been struck.

Reassurance before Battle

9. Now the same night it came about that the LORD said to him, "Arise, go down against the camp, for I have given it into your hands.

10. "But if you are afraid to go down, go with Purah your servant down to the camp,

11. "And you will hear what they say; and afterward your hands will be strengthened that you may go down against the camp." So he went with Purah his servant down to the outposts of the army that was in the camp.

12. Now the Midianites and the Amalekites and all the sons of the east were lying in the valley as numerous as locusts; and their camels were without number, as numerous as the sand on the seashore.

13. When Gideon came, behold, a man was relating a dream to his friend. And he said, "Behold, I dreamt a dream; and behold, a loaf of barley bread was tumbling into the camp of Midian, and it came to The Tent and struck it so that it fell flat, and turned it upside down so that the tent lay flat."

14. And his friend answered and said, "This is nothing less than the sword of Gideon the son of Joash, a man of Israel; God has given Midian and all the camp into his hand."

15a. And it came about when Gideon heard the account of the dream and its interpretation, that he bowed in worship.

If God left us to ourselves, we would never turn to Him (John 6:44). God loves His people, despite their sin and rebellion, and He ever takes the initiative to bring them back to Himself. It was God Who sent the prophet to call Israel's attention to their sins (Jud. 6:8). It was God Who took the initiative in calling Gideon to be the savior (6:11). It was God Who took the initiative in attacking Baal (6:25). It was God Who sent the Spirit to clothe Gideon (6:34). It was God Who created Gideon's band of 300 guerillas (7:2, 4). Now it is God Who comes to Gideon to encourage him before the battle. This is the love of God, dealing gently with his immature child.

God suggests to Gideon that he go to the Midianite camp, and take another man along for moral support, to see how God has prepared the way for their victory.

Verse 12 piles up imagery to impress on our minds just how awesome was the host of God's enemies. Surely this vast sea of trained warriors knows no fear! It is Gideon who must be afraid.

The barley loaf was the bread of the poor in Israel. As a result of seven years of invasions, all Israel was poor. The invaders took all the wheat, leaving only barley for the Israelites to eat. The loaf of barley bread, then, clearly symbolizes Israel. (And see Lev. 23:10f. + John 20:22, and Lev. 23:15-18 + Acts 2; and 1 Cor. 10:17.) It is a round loaf, which rolls aggressively into the camp of Midian. This symbolizes the fact that Israel will launch the attack.

The tent symbolizes the Midianite host. The fact that it is *the* tent rather than *a* tent that is spoken of indicates that it is the commander's headquarters that is in view. This tent is struck by the Israelite barley loaf, and turned completely upside down. It is hard to imagine a tent's being turned completely upside down, but in a dream anything can happen. This clearly means that the fortunes of the Midianites will be inverted, reversed. The tent lies flat, abandoned.

The interpretation of the dream, however, is what is most amazing. Instantly the friend of the dreamer jumps to the conclusion that the dream refers to Gideon. Amazing! Who would have thought that these Midianites had ever even *heard* of Gideon, let alone know his father's name? Even more, they obviously are terrified of Gideon! How could this have come about?

It could only have come about through God's interference and initiative. Here we see the other side of God's gracious initiatives to Israel and Gideon. Here we see God's wrathful initiative against His enemies, as He acts to strike terror into their hearts. Gideon and Israel are being delivered from fear, while Midian is being delivered unto fear. The army of Midian has heard reports about Gideon, a mysterious man who has suddenly arisen out of nowhere and who has organized an army overnight. They respond to this news with an irrational dread. After all, humanly speaking they have no real cause for alarm: No matter who this Gideon is, he could not possibly defeat 135,000 men. God, however, is at work.

What an encouragement this is to Gideon! The enemy knows his name, the name of God's anointed messiah, and is terrified of it! They know that God is with Gideon, and against them. Gideon bows in worship.

Preparations for Battle

15b. He returned to the camp of Israel and said, "Arise, for the LORD has given the camp of Midian into your hands."

16. And he divided the 300 men into three heads [companies], and he put trumpets and empty pitchers into the hands of all of them, with torches inside the pitchers.

17. And he said to them, "Look at me, and do likewise. And behold, when I come to the outskirts of the camp, it shall come about that just as I do, so you shall do.

18. "When I and all who are with me blow the trumpet, then you also blow the trumpets all around the camp, and say, "For the LORD and for Gideon.' "

Gideon realizes that the prediction means that the Lord has given His enemies into Israel's hands. He divides his 300 men into three companies, three "heads." These heads of Israel will crush the heads of the enemy. These three companies will go to three places around the camp. Each man has a trumpet slung at his waist. Each man carries an earthenware jar in his right hand and a burning torch, inserted into the jar, in his left hand.

They are told to imitate Gideon. We need to see Gideon here as the messiah, the anointed deliverer of Israel. Just as we are to imitate Jesus Christ, the ultimate Messiah, they were to imitate Gideon, doing as he did. The words they were to shout into the camp were significant. It is not self-centered vainglory that caused Gideon to order that his own name be shouted along with that of the Lord. Rather, Gideon knew from the dream that his own name was a terror to the Midianites. Thus, it was tactically important to use it. Moreover, again we must remember that Gideon was the messiah at this point in history. Thus, we may paraphrase the shout: "For the LORD and for His Messiah." Surely that is what Christians of all ages have shouted into the sleeping camps of the enemy.

Psychological Warfare

19. So Gideon and the hundred men who were with him came to the outskirts of the camp at the beginning of the middle watch, when they had just posted the watch; and they blew the trumpets and smashed the pitchers that were in their hands.

20. When the three heads [companies] blew the trumpets and broke the pitchers, they held the torches in their left hands and the trumpets in their right hands for blowing, and cried, "A sword for the LORD and for Gideon!"

21. And each stood in his place around the camp; and all the army ran, crying out as they fled.

22. And when they blew 300 trumpets, the LORD set the sword of one against another even throughout the whole army; and the army fled as far as Beth-Shittah toward Zererah, as far as the edge of Abel-Meholah, by Tabbath.

Students of military tactics in the twentieth century know that Gideon's actions are discussed in manuals describing psychological operations in guerilla warfare.[5] Humanly speaking, the battle was won based solely on psyops. The following components of the operation should be appreciated:

1. It was the earlier part of the night, the beginning of the middle watch. We sleep more soundly during the first part of the night than during the early hours of the morning. The Midianite host, when it awoke, would be highly disoriented.

2. The watch had just been posted. These men, coming from the lights of the camp, would not have had their eyes fully adjusted to the dark environment of the watch area. They would not have been able to tell anything about the situation, except to see 300 torches and hear 300 trumpets, which had to mean that there were 300 *armies* or companies just beyond the perimeter.

3. The men returning from the first watch were moving about the camp, finding their tents. As men awoke from deep sleep, hearing the shouting and the trumpets, they knew they were under attack. Looking about, they saw armed men moving about the camp, going into tents. They did not realize that these

---

5. Paul M. A. Linebarger, a devout Christian expert in psychological warfare, is the source of this, entering it into the literature. See his *Psychological Warfare* (New York: Duell, Sloan and Pearce, 1954 [reprint Arno Press]).

were their own comrades, returning from watch. Thus, they attacked each other.

4. The trumpets and noise and fire would stampede the camels, causing havoc and killing men.

5. The name of Gideon would strike fear into the hearts of all who had heard of him.

All the same, we must not speak humanly about this operation. What we read is what Israel also saw at the Red Sea, "Stand fast and behold the deliverance of the LORD which He will accomplish for you today" (Ex. 14:13ff.). It was the Lord Who gave this plan to Gideon, and it was the Lord Who made it work. It was His psychological operation.

The elements employed show that this was a human imaging of the coming of God's glory cloud. The glory cloud is the environment around God's chariot throne, and consists of His host. We get to see into that cloud in the book of Revelation. When the cloud appears, it is regularly accompanied by such phenomena as light (lightning flashing), trumpet sounds, and the shouts of a multitude. All these elements are here present, and indicate that this human army is imaging the host of the Lord.[6]

First they set down the jars and blew the trumpets. Then, shattering the jars, they raised the torches in their left hands, and kept blowing the trumpets and shouting "A *sword* for the LORD and for His Messiah." The elements of this action are not unique. On the contrary, the components of this action are found at other places in God's plan of history as well. What we need to do is identify the principles at work in this attack, and see how these principles continue to operate throughout history. This is not "spiritualizing," for we are not saying that there is no literal meaning to the events, but we are dealing with the underlying principles. What we have here is nothing less than a picture of the gospel.

What do we see? A sleeping world is shattered by a trumpet of judgment, a shining light, and the proclamation of a specific message about a sword, God, and the Messiah.

1. The sleeping world is a common enough image in Scrip-

---

6. On the glory cloud and the phenomena which attend it, see Meredith G. Kline, *Images of the Spirit* (Grand Rapids: Baker, 1980), especially chapter 4.

ture. (See, for instance, 1 Thess. 5:5-8.) The camp of God's enemies is asleep to the real issues of life. Their cultures are stagnant, with no social or scientific progress. Into these stagnant, sleeping cultures comes the gospel, which shakes them up, causing discord. (Compare Matt. 10:34-36 and Luke 12:51-53.)

2. The trumpet is the herald of judgment. The trumpet announced the judgment of Jericho (Josh. 6:20) and will announce all judgments of God (Rev. 8:2). It is a message of judgment that is thrown into the camp of the ungodly.

3. The light is the witness of Truth (John 3:19; 1 John 1:5-7; 2:9-10; etc.). It is the light of Truth that is shone into the camp of the wicked, but men love darkness more than light. Light blinds them, and it also shows up their sins and filth.

4. The sword is the proclamation of the Word, and especially of the gospel: The Lord and His Messiah (Is. 11:4; 2 Thess. 2:8; Heb. 4:12; Rev. 19:15). The proclamation of the Word throws the sleeping camp of the wicked into consternation.

All we have to do is stand fast and preach the full gospel of judgment and salvation, and God will destroy the enemy, by causing the enemy to self-destruct. The self-destructive character of evil men is represented here, as the enemy kills itself off, but since this is the theme of the entire ninth chapter of Judges, we shall postpone discussion of it until we get there.

This accomplished victory is the final stage of the upbuilding of Gideon's faith. Now all Israel fall in line behind him, to mop up what is left of the enemy as they flee. The theology here is the same as we have already seen in Judges: The first and definitive blow is struck by God Himself, and then the armies of the righteous are called in to finish mopping up the remnants of the enemy. We confess that Christ Jesus has won the definitive victory, and now we as His Church follow Him, privileged to put down all His enemies on the earth.

Judgment: Oreb and Zeeb

24. And Gideon sent messengers throughout all the hill country of Ephraim saying, "Come down to meet Midian and take the waters before them, as far as Beth-Barah and the Jordan." So all the men of Ephraim were summoned, and they took the waters as far as Beth-Barah and the Jordan.

25. And they captured the two leaders of Midian, Oreb and

Zeeb, and they killed Oreb at the Rock of Oreb, and they killed
Zeeb at the Wine Press of Zeeb, while they pursued Midian; and
they brought the heads of Oreb and Zeeb to Gideon from across
the Jordan.

Once the battle was clearly won, Gideon summoned
Ephraim, that proud and surly tribe. These stationed themselves
along the Jordan and slew every Midianite who tried to cross.
(See my comments on Judges 3:28.) This was near Beth-Barah,
which apparently means "House of the Ford," and is referred to
in John 1:28 as the place where John was baptizing; that is, a
place of judgment, either unto life or unto death.[7]

The Ephraimites captured and killed Oreb and Zeeb, the
commanders of the Midianite army. Oreb means "Raven" and
Zeeb means "Wolf," both beasts that indicate the character of
the Midianite enemy. The places where they were killed became
landmarks. The Rock of Oreb reminds us of the rocks in which
the Israelites had been hiding (Jud. 6:2). Now the enemy tries to
hide in a rock, to escape their doom (compare Rev. 6:15). God's
holy humor is full of irony.

The Wine Press of Zeeb reminds us of Gideon's threshing in
the wine press (6:11). Gideon had been hiding from the Midianites; now the Midianite leader is hiding from him (and compare Is. 63:1-6). This type of irony is deliberate in Scripture, and
serves to encourage the saints.

To bring out the theology of the crushing of Satan's head,
the text calls attention to the fact that the heads of Oreb and
Zeeb were cut off, and brought as trophies to Gideon.

Judgment: Ephraim

8:1. Then the men of Ephraim said to him, "What is this
thing you have done to us, not calling us when you went to fight
against Midian?" And they contended with him vigorously.

2. But he said to them, "What have I done now in comparison with you? Is not the gleaning of Ephraim better than the
vintage of Abiezer?

3. "God has given the leaders of Midian, Oreb and Zeeb,

---

7. Some versions of the Greek NT say "Bethany" in John 1:28. This would
be the same place, though there is no particular reason not to stick with the
traditional reading, which is "Betha-Barah."

into your hands; and what was I able to do in comparison with you?" Then their anger [spirit] toward him subsided when he said this thing.

Ephraim took no joy in the Lord's victory. Their only concern was with their own glory. They were furious not to have been included in the glories of battle, and they were contending vigorously with the Lord's anointed messiah.

Gideon, however, decided that a soft answer could turn away their wrath (Prov. 15:1; Rom. 12:10; Phil. 2:3). He compares the leftovers of Ephraim's grape harvest, the gleanings, with the choicest vintage of Abiezer's. Ephraim's leftovers are better than Abiezer's vintage. In saying this, he is comparing the two battles. Abiezer's vintage is the battle of 300 against 135,000, while Ephraim's gleanings is the battle at the crossing of the Jordan.

Ephraim's gleanings were superior, he asserts, because they killed the commanders, Oreb and Zeeb. Note, though, that Gideon does given them a mild rebuke: "*God* has given the leaders . . . into your hands."

Pacified, Ephraim left off threatening the Lord's messiah. Ephraim did not learn their lesson, however, and their attitude worsened. Later on, Jephthah would treat them differently when they threatened him, and they would receive what they deserved for their sin (Jud. 12:1-6).

Was Gideon right to deal so mildly with Ephraim? I believe so. This was no time for a church fight. The enemy was fleeing, and this was the opportunity to destroy him. It is often better to keep the peace of the Church by a show of humility, rather than to try and force our brethren into a spiritual state they have not yet attained.

Traitors: Succoth and Penuel

4. Then Gideon and the 300 men who were with him came to the Jordan and crossed over, weary yet pursuing.

5. And he said to the men of Succoth, "Please give loaves of bread to the people who are following me, for they are weary, and I am pursuing Zebah and Zalmunna, the kings of Midian."

6. And the leaders of Succoth said, "Is the palm of Zebah and Zalmunna already in your hands, that we should give bread

to your army?"

7. And Gideon said, "Just for that, when the LORD has given Zebah and Zalmunna into my hand, then I will thrash your flesh with the thorns of the wilderness and with briers."

8. And he went up from there to Penuel, and spoke similarly to them; and the men of Penuel answered him just as the men of Succoth had answered.

9. So he spoke also to the men of Penuel, saying, "When I return safely, I will tear down this tower."

While the larger army was mopping up at the crossing of the Jordan, Gideon's guerilla band was in hot pursuit of the kings of Midian and their remaining 15,000 men. We invite the reader to meditate on what it means that they were "weary, yet pursuing." There surely is a lesson here for each of us.

Having had no chance to eat, though they could drink at the Jordan, Gideon asked for bread; not meat, just bread. Deuteronomy 23:3-4 tells us that God had cursed Moab and Ammon because they did not give bread to hungry Israel as they came out of Egypt. Jesus makes the same point in Matthew 25:34-40. It is important to realize that Midian was often allied with Moab and Ammon, as in the story of Balaam and Phineas, which is in the background of the story of Gideon (Num. 22-25; Dt. 23:4).

Thus, when Succoth refused to help God's people, they were identifying themselves with the Moabites, Ammonites, and Midianites. Indeed, they were bold to say so: They wanted to take no risks with the Midianite kings still on the loose. They had no faith or trust in God. Spiritually they were Midianites, and deserved to be treated as such. Like good liberals, they wanted to have peace by having detente with the enemy.

The expression "is the palm . . . already in your hands?" refers to the practice of chopping off the hands of the enemy. It was the "hand" of Midian that oppressed Israel (Jud. 6:1, etc.), and to symbolize victory, the hand of the enemy leader would be cut off his corpse. Just as in death his head would be cut off (as we have seen), so also his hand would be cut off, that he might no longer bear a sword against God and His people.

Part of the irony here is the names God gives to the leaders of Midian. Zebah means "Victim," and Zalmunna means "Shade Denied," that is, "Protection Denied." These were probably not their real names! The writer has given them these ridiculous names in order to make the point that God had already appointed them to destruction. By using such names in this paragraph, the writer highlights the faithlessness of Succoth and Penuel.

Gideon is confident that the Lord will give the victory. By saying so, he rebukes Succoth for their lack of faith. Succoth has chosen to identify itself with these nomads, who live under the curse of Genesis 4:16, roaming the wilderness outside Eden. Thus, the fitting punishment for them is to be scourged with thorns, which grow abundantly in the wilderness, and which speak of the curse (Gen. 3:18; Matt. 27:29). They did not trust in Christ's substitutionary crown of thorns, so they got the thorns for themselves. They wanted the curse, so they got the curse.

Penuel was a fortress city, and they relied on their strong tower to save them (1 Kings 12:25). They were not putting their faith and trust in the Lord, Who should have been their Mighty Fortress (Ps. 46), but in their own man-made tower. Like good conservatives, they trusted in their defensive armaments rather than in the Lord. Gideon promises to return, and tear down their tower.

Judgment: Midian, Amalek, and Ishmael

10. Now Zebah and Zalmunna were in Karkor, and their armies with them, about 15,000 men, all who were left of the entire army of the sons of the east; for the fallen were 120,000 men who drew the sword.

11. And Gideon went up by the Way of Those Who Live in Tents [the Route of the Nomads] on the east of Nobah and Jogbehah, and smote the camp, when the camp was unsuspecting.

12. When Zebah and Zalmunna fled, he pursued them and captured the two kings of Midian, Zebah and Zalmunna, and routed the whole army.

13. Then Gideon the son of Joash returned from the battle by the ascent of Heres [at the rising of the sun].

The tribes of Israel had already destroyed a significant 120,000 men, twelve being the number of Israel. Only 15,000 were left.

When they reached Karkor, the remnant of the Midianite

army, consisting mainly of sons of the east, Ishmaelites, stopped their flight for rest. Surely they were far enough away to be safe from immediate attack. Bone weary, they rested. Unbeknownst to them, Gideon was coming around them by way of a caravan route. The Manassehite town of Nobah and the Gadite town of Jogbehah supported him. Geographical study shows that he went all the way around the camp to the other side, and attacked during the night from the east, the quarter they would least have expected an attack to come from.

Gideon returned from the battle at the ascent of the sun, as the sun was rising. (This is what "ascent of heres" means.) We are reminded of Deborah's prayer that God's people would be like the rising of the sun in their strength. Gideon has fought all night, run all day, and fought all night a second time: Surely Deborah's prayer has been answered!

This was at or near Penuel, which is Peniel, where Jacob wrestled all night and crossed the river at the rising of the sun (Gen. 35:22-32). This is important background for the story of Gideon, for Jacob's wrestling with God had a particular meaning. God was not angry with Jacob, for Jacob had been "perfect" from his youth, and indeed had been regenerate in the womb (Gen. 25:22, 27 — "peaceful" is literally "perfect" as in Gen. 17:1 and Job 1:1.). When he was attacked, Jacob could not know who it was who fought with him. Was it Laban? Was it Esau? These had been God's and Jacob's enemies, with whom he had wrestled in faith for many years. Then it turned out that it was God who was wrestling with Jacob. The meaning was this: All these years, it was God Who had raised up these enemies. They had not been raised up to punish Jacob for sins, but to train him for maturity. Like a father getting down on the floor to wrestle with his son, so the Lord had wrestled with Jacob for years, in order to train him for maturity. The theme of God maturing a man through stages of conflict is also at the heart of the history of Gideon. It was a sign to Israel that God had not forsaken them, but was training them unto maturity.

Judgment: Succoth and Penuel

14. And he captured a youth of the men of Succoth and questioned him. Then the youth wrote down for him the princes of Succoth and its elders, 77 men.

15. And he came to the men of Succoth and said, "Behold Zebah and Zalmunna, concerning whom you taunted me, saying 'Is the palm of Zebah and Zalmunna already in your hand, that we should give bread to your men who are weary?' "

16. And he took the elders of the city, and thorns of the wilderness and briers, and he made the men of Succoth acquainted with them!

17. And he tore down the tower of Penuel and killed the men of the city.

Gideon's method of attacking Succoth reminds us of the way Jericho was spied out, and also of Luz (Jud. 1:24). Now it is an Israelite town that is treated as an enemy. The full complement of the city's rulers, 77 men, were scourged with thorns. They would not "know" the Lord, so they were made to "know" the curse, firsthand!

Gideon not only tore down Penuel's tower, but he killed the men (leaders probably) of that city. Why he was harder on Penuel than on Succoth we do not know. He had his reasons, and since he is not condemned, we trust they were good ones. Perhaps it was because Penuel's sin of trusting in their own tower was more serious than Succoth's.

Both Succoth and Penuel were cities in Gad. Gad had failed to support Deborah (Jud. 5:17), and apparently was pretty weak spiritually. All was not lost, however, for the Gadite town of Jogbehah supported Gideon (Jud. 8:11).

Why did Gideon punish Succoth and Penuel when he did nothing of the sort to Ephraim? The difference is all important. Ephraim was *selfish,* and this is a sin; but Ephraim did fight on the Lord's side. Ephraim is in the position of a genuine Christian who has a habitual sin; he needed a rebuke, not full judgment. Ephraim was in sin, not in open apostasy. Time would tell which way he would go. Paul was able to rejoice when the gospel was preached by contentious men (Phil. 1:15-19). Paul knew that God would eventually deal with them. Jephthah would deal with Ephraim by and by.

Succoth and Penuel, on the other hand, were *faithless,* and this is apostasy. They did not fight on the Lord's side, and since neutrality is impossible, they were against the Lord. They were God's enemies, and they were treated as such.

Judgment: Zebah and Zalmunna

18. Then he said to Zebah and Zalmunna, "What kind of men were they whom you killed at Tabor?" And they said, "They were like you, each one like the form of the sons of a king."

19. And he said, "They were my brothers, the sons of my mother. As the LORD lives, if only you had let them live, I would not kill you."

20. So he said to Jether his first-born, "Rise, kill them." But the youth did not draw his sword, for he was afraid, because he was still a youth.

21. Then Zebah and Zalmunna said, "Rise up yourself, and fall on us; for as the man, so is his strength." So Gideon arose and killed Zebah and Zalmunna, and took the crescent ornaments which were on their camels' necks.

What happens here is ambiguous. Possibly Gideon does nothing wrong here, but more likely this paragraph indicates a lapse of true obedience. Let us look at the problem.

Israel's wars were supposed to be holy wars, against God's enemies. Deuteronomy 20:13 specifies that all the men of the enemy are to be killed. Now, however, suddenly it seems as if Gideon is treating it as a personal matter. There is nothing wrong with his asking about his brothers, but there seems to be something wrong indeed with the statement, "if only you had let them live, I would not kill you."

Before condemning Gideon, let us try to put the best possible construction on his action. Possibly he already knew the answer to his question. Thus, possibly the entire conversation was designed to make a symbolic or theological point: "As the anointed one of Israel, it is my task to be the blood avenger for my brethren. What you have done to Israel as a whole, you have done in particular to my own brethren; and what I do to you to avenge the blood of my brethren, is what God does to you to avenge all His children. If you had left my family alone, you would also have left all God's family alone. But when you attacked my family, that is part and parcel of attacking God's family, because as the anointed one, I am closely identified with the Lord as His agent. Thus, my personal vengeance is also the Lord's vengeance." If we put this positive construction on it, we see that Gideon's avenging his family is parallel to Christ's avenging His saints.

Still, it seems as if we are straining at a gnat and swallowing a camel to take such an interpretation. It seems more likely to me that Gideon's failures begin here, failures that will become more manifest in the next paragraph.

Assuming that Gideon is deflected from his holy purpose, we see him also make a stupid move. He wants his teenaged son, Jether, to slay Zebah and Zalmunna. This would have been humiliating to the two kings, to have been slain by a raw youth, but it also indicates again that Gideon is making this a family matter. Do we see just a hint of dynastic thinking here? Jether, however, is too young and timid to do it. Gideon might have remembered that a few months before, he himself had been a timid "youth," yet now he expects his own son, twenty years younger then he, to perform a very scary act: killing these two powerful and frightening kings. Gideon does not show, in dealing with his son, the kind of grace that God showed in dealing with him.

God causes Gideon's personal vengeance to fall flat. When men depart from the Lord's ways, they begin to make stupid moves. Gideon is put in the humiliating position of receiving good advice from the enemy. Be an example to your son, they say, for "as the man, so is his strength," that is, his son. (The first-born son is considered the first of a man's strength, Gen. 49:3; Dt. 21:17; Ps. 78:51.)

Gideon's taking the spoils from the two kings is in accordance with Deuteronomy 20:14.

Kingship Rejected, but Foundations Undermined

22. Then the men of Israel said to Gideon, "Rule over us, both you and your son, also your son's son, for you have delivered (*yasha'*) us from the hand of Midian."

23. But Gideon said to them, "I will not rule over you, nor shall my son rule over you; the LORD shall rule over you."

24. Yet Gideon said to them, "I would make a request of you, that each of you give me an earring [or, nose-ring] from his spoil." (For they had gold earrings, because they were Ishmaelites.)

24. And they said, "We will surely give them." So they spread out a garment, and every one of them threw an earring

there from his spoil.

26. And the weight of the gold earrings that he requested was 1700 shekels of gold, besides the crescent ornaments and the pendants and the purple robes which were on the kings of Midian, and besides the neck bands that were on their camels' necks.

27. And Gideon made it into an ephod, and placed it in his city, Ophrah, and all Israel played the harlot with it there, so that it became a snare to Gideon and his household.

28. So Midian was subdued before the sons of Israel, and they did not lift up their heads any more. And the land was undisturbed for 40 years in the days of Gideon.

The men of Israel do not look with the eyes of faith, and thus fail to see that it is the Lord Who delivered them, and it is the Lord Who should rule them. Moreover, they want Gideon to establish a dynasty. Thus, it is clearly their desire to establish some form of humanistic kingship that will be perpetual. They do not want Gideon merely for a judge. They want a king on a throne with a dynasty. They are putting their trust for safety and security not in the Lord but in the principle of a centralized state.

Gideon seems to take the Lord's rebuke (assuming our interpretation of verses 18-21 is correct), for he rejects the crown offered to him, and also rejects the notion of a dynasty. Note that in verse 22 we find explicitly stated the principle that the savior is the lord. Those who separate Christ as Savior from Christ as Lord are completely out of line from Scripture at this point. Gideon's reply is sound: The Lord saved you, so the Lord must be your king.

This verse initiates the theme of humanistic kingship, which will dominate the next chapter and the two appendices at the end of Judges. What happens next is a small picture of the larger problem discussed in Judges 17-21. Gideon does well to reject human kingship, but his next action undermines the whole social order, and makes humanistic statism inevitable. When men are religiously faithful, then the Lord truly is king, and even if we have a human king (such as David) it is no threat to liberty. But when men depart from the Lord, then they will have humanistic statist rulers soon enough. So it was in the time of the judges, and so it is today. The appendices to Judges show that it was the religious failure of the Levites that undermined the Israelite social order and led to oppression and statism. The same point is made here.

Gideon was from a poor family, and thus the spoils of war were attractive to him. There is nothing wrong with taking the spoils of war, as delineated in Deuteronomy 20:14. If the people wanted to thank Gideon, they were entitled to give him gifts.

Gideon asked for one ring from each man. These were almost certainly earrings, because it was women who wore nose-rings in the ancient world. The Ishmaelite men wore earrings, but the Israelites did not. When they came out of Egypt the Israelites had contributed their earrings to make a golden calf (Ex. 32:2-4). They had "played the harlot" with it, and had been punished by God for their idolatry. As a result, when they repented they forswore the wearing of earrings and like ornaments (Ex. 33:4-6). Thus, the earrings of the spoils were of no use to anyone as earrings; they would have to be made over into something else.

Israel had spoiled not only the gold of Egypt, but also the philosophy of Egypt. The Bible emphasizes the goodness of taking over spoils from the pagans, but warns against taking their philosophy. It is easy for Christians to fall on either side of this matter. Some are too ready to adopt the thinking of the world. Others, in reacting against vain philosophies, reject the good things of the Lord along with them. The Biblical position is to take the goods of paganism, and build God's tabernacle out of them, not a golden calf.

Gideon used this gold, and the other spoils given to him, to make an ephod. We are told that all Israel "played the harlot" with it in Ophrah, where Gideon placed it. The parallel between this incident and that of the golden calf must not be missed. As Gideon drifts into a *de facto* though not *de jure* (in fact, though not in law) humanistic kingship, the golden calf type of image worship also creeps into society. Later on, the blatantly Baalistic humanistic king, Jeroboam I, would openly reintroduce golden calf worship (1 Kings 12:28-29). Jeroboam I put one of his golden calves at Dan, which had for a long time been a center of ephod worship (Jud. 17-18).

Thus, there is a complex of connections, or principles, at work here. When men are not satisfied with God and His worship, they begin to set up their own ways of doing things. In the area of politics, this means a humanistic, centralized power state. In the area of worship, this means a magical, image-centered, emotional, sensual worship. In the case of Jeroboam I, there was a deliberate attempt to revive a superstitious and statist form of society. Jeroboam named his sons Nadab and Abihu (1 Kings 14:1, 20), which had been the names of Aaron's apostate sons (Lev. 10:1-2). Jeroboam was saying, in effect, that Aaron and Moses had deflected Israel from the true worship of God, and that he was going back and restoring the original purity of the Church by reintroducing calf worship.

In the case of Gideon, of course, there was no such deliberate intent. Gideon doubtless reasoned somewhat as follows:

1. God has dealt with me specially, and commanded me to build Him an altar at Abiezer. He even commanded me to offer sacrifice (Jud. 6:26).

2. The ephod at the tabernacle sanctuary is a long way off. If I am going to judge Israel, I need to have some contact with God, to get answers from Him. It will be more convenient if I have my own ephod here at Ophrah.

3. Also, having this ephod here will serve to unify the people.

Now these seem to be good reasons. We don't know exactly how the ephod worked. It was a garment worn by the high priest, which had a breastplate covered with twelve stones, one for each tribe, and which as a pouch contained the urim and thummim. These apparently were two stones, probably flat, that were tossed to the ground and that gave yes and no answers (Ex. 28:6-35; 1 Sam. 23:6-12). Such a device would be useful to a judge.

It was not a wise move, however, because:

1. God had not commanded Gideon to do this.

2. This ephod would not unify all Israel, but would create two centers of religious oracle.

3. Most significantly, the ephod would be separated from the whole tabernacle system as a unit. Exodus 28:1-35 makes it clear that the ephod was a unique part of the clothing of the high priest. No one else was to have such clothing; it was holy (set apart). Numbers 27:21 makes it clear that it was only at the high priest's ephod that any question was to be asked. It was

because Aaron and the ephod were in God's presence continually (Ex. 28:30) and because Aaron (the high priest) represented Christ the Mediator, that the ephod would not degenerate into a merely superstitious oracle, like the oracle at Delphi. By wrenching the ephod out of its God-centered setting, Gideon set the stage for just such superstitious behavior, which soon developed.

A similar thing can happen in the Church today. When men take only part of the Scriptures, or some part of the truth, and harp on it alone, soon they fall into a snare. Those who never study the Old Testament, and only use the New Testament, soon wind up bringing in humanistic philosophies to fill in the vacuum. After all, the Old Testament is the platform on which the New is erected. If we strip away the platform, we shall soon have to find another. Similarly, it is possible for a church to prize its creed or confession so much that it pretty well ignores all the rest of the truth found in Scripture. When that happens, soon humanism creeps in to fill the void. Or a preacher may only preach on certain topics, leaving his congregation open to influences in all other areas. That is why Paul the Apostle was so careful to preach the whole counsel of God (Acts 20:27). We are indeed "New Testament" believers, and our creeds and confessions are of real value, but they must not become ephods separated from the Bible as a whole.

The ephod at Ophrah came to be regarded as a magical answer box, and people looked to it rather than to the Levites and the Lord for answers. Even Gideon lost sight of the personal character of God, and came to regard the ephod with superstitious awe. It corrupted him, his family, and the community. As Gideon lost sight of the personal rule of God the Lord, he lost sight of Who Israel's true King really was, and picked up more and more of the characteristics of an oriental, humanistic king.

The ephod at Ophrah, not surrounded by the rest of God's typical ordinances, was rapidly absorbed into the prevailing Canaanite, Baalistic philosophy. It became a stimulus to Baalism, not a safeguard against it.

Israel "played the harlot" with the ephod. It was the Lord Who was their husband and king. It was His Word they were to listen to, as brought by the Levites and the High Priest and through the true ephod (Lev. 10:10, 11; Num. 27:21). By hearkening to another ephod, they were committing spiritual adultery against their Lord.

Despite his flaws, however, Gideon apparently judged Israel with a good deal of wisdom, and the land had peace for a generation (40 years), until he died. We must remember that Scripture mentions Gideon's flaws because Scripture is teaching us about humanistic statism, and Scripture is leading up to the story of Abimelech. What Scripture does not bother to remind us of, because we should know it, is that as a judge Gideon was especially empowered by the Holy Spirit of God. For the most part, he was a good man.

The next verse (Jud. 8:29) should, to be consistent, say something like this: "Now after the death of Gideon, the sons of Israel again did what was evil in the sight of the LORD, and the LORD gave them into the hands of some enemy." But this is not what we find. Instead, the story of Gideon is extended one more generation, showing the consequences of this drift toward statism. Indeed, Israel was sold into bondage—to enemies from within!

8

ABIMELECH: ISRAEL'S FIRST KING
(Judges 8:29 - 9:57)

There are three overarching concerns of the book of Judges that are particularly dealt with in this section, though they run throughout much of the whole book. First, there is the theme of God versus Baal. We have seen that the whole story of Gideon is permeated by this concern. The battle against Midian is secondary compared with the war against Baal, for the war against Baal is a war for purity within Israel itself. Gideon, having launched an attack on Baal within his own household, is known as Jerub-Baal, the Baal Fighter. The sign of the fleece confirmed God's power over Baal, and the falsity of Baalism. In the section we come to now, we see Israel drifting back into Baalism. Indeed, their response to Gideon's victory already showed that they did not understand the genius of God's way of life, and still clung to Baalistic political ideas. Baal strikes back at Jerubbaal the Baal Fighter by killing all his sons, but God destroys Baal in the end. This is one motif in this section.

The second motif is that of the self-destructiveness of evil. It is self defeating to fight against God, of course; but this chapter brings out a principle that can also be seen in Judges 7:22. Each evil man wants to play God (Gen. 3:5), and to play God means to rule everyone else. Since each man wants to be king, self-destructive warfare is inevitable in any humanistic, Satanistic culture. It is, then, the essence of Baalism to be self-destructive. This is clearly one of the principal themes of this section, since it is the whole point of the prophecy of Jotham.

The third motif concerns the theme of enslavement into bondage. Over and over in the book of Judges we see God selling Israel back into slavery to some alien power, because Israel had lusted after the gods of that alien power. This time the alien power is themselves. Israel is sold into bondage to Israel. The

153

peculiar form of Baalism mentioned here is "Baal-Berith," the
Baal of the Covenant. Here we see a mixture of true religion, the
Covenant that God made with His people, with the false idolatry of Baalism. This is a peculiarly Israelite form of Baalism,
and so God sells His people into bondage to a segment of Israelite society that epitomizes this half-breed religion. God delivers
Israel this time not by raising up a judge, but by removing His
restraining arm and letting evil self-destruct.

Gideon's Polygamy

8:29. Then Jerubbaal the son of Joash went and lived in his
own house.

30. Now Gideon had 70 sons who came from his loins, for
he had many wives.

31. And his concubine who was in Shechem also bore him a
son, and he appointed his name Abimelech [My Father is King].

32. And Gideon the son of Joash died at a ripe old age and
was buried in the tomb of his father Joash, in Ophrah of the
Abiezrites.

Gideon is called Jerubbaal in verse 29, because he did not
live in a palace but in his own house, thus eschewing the Baalistic tendency to become a statist king. At this point, Gideon
was acting as a Baal Fighter.

The name Gideon is used in verse 30, because here we see the
"natural man" in him acting up. The Biblical position is always
monogamy, because man is to image God in his life, being the
very image of God by creation. The Lord is monogamous; His
bride is the Church, and He has no other. If a man does not
stick with one wife, he does not properly image the Lord in his
life. Since the essence of ethics is human conformity to the very
character of God, any failure to image forth that character is
sin.

Polygamy is forbidden in Leviticus 18:18, which says "You
shall not marry a woman in addition to her sister, to be a rival
while she is alive, to uncover her nakedness." If Jacob was out
of line marrying two sisters, then surely so also would any other
Israelite. Moreover, any second wife would be a rival (1 Sam. 1),
and any second marriage would expose the first to shame (uncover nakedness) because it would advertise to the world that

the first wife was not satisfactory. Thus, Leviticus 18:18 clearly outlawed all polygamy in Israel.

Moreover, polygamy is particularly forbidden to kings and rulers (Dt. 17:17). This is partly because they are more susceptible to the temptation, since they can afford it. It is also because the many wives usually meant foreign alliances, which were forbidden.

This is the command of God. The response of Gideon is disobedience. The evaluation of God brings judgment against the house of Gideon. By setting up a false ephod Gideon brought Israel into spiritual adultery. By committing polygamy, Gideon acted out in life the principle he had established by setting up a second ephod.

Gideon's many wives show the drift toward humanistic kingship in him. He is aggrandizing himself. Moreover, the text pointedly notes that he had 70 sons. We have seen, in our comments on Judges 1:7, that the number 70 connotes the nations of the world. The fact that Gideon had 70 sons hints darkly at some type of aspiration toward rule and dynasty, a fact that Abimilech will be able to capitalize on when he sends a warning to the men of Shechem. The number 70 makes us uneasy. What is going on? We do not know for sure.

But verse 31 presents an even sadder situation. The concubine wife is not really a harlot, but rather a wife who remains in her father's house instead of coming to live with her husband. The husband visits her from time to time, but the children of the marriage are brought up in the wife's home. We see this again in Judges 15:1. Such an arrangement is a violation of Genesis 2:24, and is sinful.

It is even worse when we realize that the woman is probably a Canaanite. The argument of Judges 9:28 makes no sense unless there were still a lot of Canaanites living in Shechem, and the wife's relatives in Judges 9:1-4 demonstrate their identity with Baal. Jotham calls her a slave girl in Judges 9:18, which again points to her status as a Canaanite (Jud. 1:28). Here we see a fulfillment of the warning in Judges 3:6, that the Israelites would marry such Canaanites as were not exterminated. It is pretty clear from the passage as a whole that Abimelech is a halfbreed.

The saddest thing of all, however, is the name Gideon (not

called Jerubbaal here!) gave to his son: Abimelech. It means "My Father is King." If the boy's mother had been the one to give him this name, it would be understandable. That Gideon gave it shows that his heart had been ensnared to some degree by the desire to rule over men as a potentate. The ephod had snared him, and now humanistic kingship had snared him. No father can harbor such desires without his sons picking it up, and Abimelech acts out in life what his father had only dreamt of in his weaker moments. (We see the same principle in the life of David. David's several wives become Solomon's multitude. David's taking of Bathsheba becomes Amnon's rape of Tamar. Like father, like son.)

As a "youth" Gideon had been presented to us as one who provided the food of kings, bread and wine, to God's people. He was a true servant, a man of real humility, oriented toward serving others and ruling them in that fashion. Now, however, he has forgotten this to an extent, and has begun to lord it over other men to some degree, however slight. Such is the tendency of the human heart. Let each of us pray that if God gives us dominion, we will not lose our servant hearts.

Still, the phrase "Gideon the son of Joash died at a ripe old age" indicates that he received the blessing of the Lord, despite his sins and failings. This is encouragement to us. Gideon was blessed not because he was a perfect man, but because Christ was the perfect Man in his place.

Israel's Ingratitude

33. Then it came about, as soon as Gideon was dead, that the sons of Israel again played the harlot with the Baals, and made Baal-Berith [The Baal of the Covenant] their god.

34. Thus the sons of Israel did not remember the LORD their God, who had delivered them from the hands of all their enemies on every side;

35. Nor did they show kindness to the household of Jerubbaal (Gideon), in accord with all the good that he had done to Israel.

Despite his flaws, Gideon must have restrained Baalism effectively. After his death, Israel went a-whoring after Baal again, openly. Baal-Berith, the Baal of the Covenant, was a syncretistic (combination) god composed of elements from Baalism and the true faith. Its champion will prove to be the halfbreed Abimelech. Its center will be the mixed town of Shechem. Syncretism, mixtures of faiths, will be a concern of Judges 9. A modern example of Baal-Berith religion is Mormonism. The essence of the Mormon religion is fertility cult belief, with all humanity descended from Mr. and Mrs. God, and multiple marriages (to bring forth many spirit children) the goal. Yet, this modern Baalistic cult uses the language of the Bible, speaks of Christ, the ten commandments, and so forth.

Israel forsook the Lord and His anointed one, whose name was Baal Fighter. Being Baal worshippers, they did not like a family of Baal Fighters. This is why the name Jerubbaal is used in verse 35. Instead of selling them into the hands of a foreign power, the Lord gave them over to Abimelech. The story of his disastrous three-year rule over Israel is the "oppression" that corresponds to the invasions described in the other stories in Judges. They were worshipping a half-breed god, so the Lord gave them into the hands of a half-breed man. They wanted a humanistic king, so they got one. As always, God punished His people by giving them what they wanted.

The King Enthroned—on Human Sacrifices

9:1. And Abimelech the son of Jerubbaal went to Shechem to his mother's brothers, and spoke to them and to the whole clan of the household of his mother's father, saying,

2. "Speak now in the hearing of all the leaders [baals] of Shechem, 'Which is better for you, that 70 men, all sons of Jerubbaal, rule over you, or that one man rule over you? Also, remember that I am your bone and your flesh.' "

3. And his mother's brethren spoke all these words on his behalf in the hearing of all the leaders of Shechem; and their hearts inclined after Abimelech, for they said, "He is our brother."

Abimelech spoke to his mother's relatives, and they spoke on his behalf to the rulers of Shechem. The rulers are called "baals," or lords. This is not an uncommon designation for leaders and prominent men in Scripture, and usually it is neutral in connotation. In Judges, however, it is not neutral. Except for three scattered appearances, its usage is limited to this chapter, and it appears thirteen times here. The rest of the book of Judges uses the words such as men, princes, elders, and judges to denote leaders of a city. The point is, then, that in Shechem we have a lingering outpost of Canaanite culture, baalistic in character. The leaders, followers of the idol Baal, are called "baals."

In the light of this it is even more important to note that Abimelech refers to his father not as "Gideon" but as "Jerubbaal," the Baal Fighter. He suggests that the Shechemites must choose between him and the seventy sons of Jerubbaal the Baal Fighter. As recorded in verse 2, he presents four arguments, subtly:

1. "Centralized rule by one man is preferable to decentralized rule by seventy men." The true Godly system is one God, but many diversified human rulers. The pagan system is one statist rule, but as many idols and gods as you wish.

2. "Jerubbaal's seventy sons will become rulers." There is no hard evidence that they had such aspirations, but Abimelech suggests they do.

3. "You Shechemites are worshippers of Baal-Berith. Do you want a family of Baal Fighters ruling over you?"

4. "I, on the other hand, am from your hometown. I am related to you by blood. I understand and sympathize with your situation. I am a worshipper of Baal-Berith just as you are." And from what we can see in verse 3, it was this last argument that was most effective.

4. And they gave him 70 pieces of silver from the house of Baal-Berith with which Abimelech hired worthless and reckless fellows, and they followed him.

5. Then he went to his father's house at Ophrah, and killed his brothers the sons of Jerubbaal, 70 men, on one stone. But Jotham the youngest son of Jerubbaal was left, for he hid himself.

6. And all the men of Shechem and all Beth-Millo assembled together, and they went and made Abimelech king, by the oak of the pillar which was in Shechem.

The destruction of the house of Gideon (Jerubbaal) was financed by the temple of Baal-Berith. Thus, we must see this as an action in the continuing war between the Lord and Baal, between the Trinity and Satan. As we shall see, the temple of Baal-Berith eventually financed its own destruction at the hands of its own people.

The fact that the seventy sons were still at Ophrah argues against their having much aspiration for rule. On the other hand, they might still have been in mourning over the death of their father. The most significant matter in this verse is the statement that all the men were killed "on one stone." The fact that they were all carefully slain on one stone indicates that they were regarded as human sacrifices to Baal. Just as Jerubbaal had torn down the altar of Baal and reestablished the worship of the Lord by sacrificing a bull to Him (Jud. 6:25-27), so sacrifice to Baal is reestablished by the sacrifice of the seventy sons of Jerubbaal.

The matter of human sacrifice should be remarked on, if only briefly. According to Genesis 4:1-10 and Hebrews 12:24, the blood of Abel was a human sacrifice. God had revealed to the family of Adam that all men were under a penalty of death, and that only the death of an acceptable substitute could atone, cover, for that death penalty. Both Cain and Abel knew this. Abel brought an acceptable substitute. By so doing, he acknowledged that he was a sinner, that his sin needed to be purged, expiated, out of the world. By so doing, he also acknowledged that he was under the wrath of God and that God's wrath needed to be appeased, turned away, propitiated. When the Cherubim used their flaming sword to ignite Abel's sacrifice, which had been brought to the gate of Eden on the east side (this is the configuration of the Tabernacle later on, and we read it back into the situation in Genesis 4), Abel and Cain knew that God had respect for Abel *and* for his sacrifice.

For Cain and for his offering, however, God had no respect. No fire from God consumed it. Cain had brought of the work of his hands. He was trying to bribe God into giving him good things. His view of an offering was that it was a gift to God. He sought to stimulate God, as would the Baalists of a later day. He did not see himself under the death penalty. He did not see the need for a substitute. He wanted to make a deal with God. He was angry when God did not accept his gift. He was humiliated in front of his younger brother. As far as Cain was concerned, all Abel had done was bring a gift from his own labor, just as Cain had done. Cain refused to realize that if Abel had been the tiller of the ground, he would have purchased a lamb and would not have brought vegetation as a bribe to God.

God graciously came to Cain and reminded him to do well, that is, to offer an acceptable substitute. Sin was crouching at Cain's door, and Christ was knocking at his door also (Rev. 3:20). Cain needed to beware of his own heart; but God encouraged him that with grace, Cain could become an overcomer (Rev. 3:21) and master this sin. Cain told Abel what God had said, and Abel doubtless encouraged Cain to hearken to the Lord's words. This was more humiliation than Cain could stand, and he slew Abel.

Is this murder or human sacrifice? We may argue that all murder is an attack on the image of God in man, and thus an attempt to kill God. We may also argue that all murder is an expression of wrath, and the desire to propitiate oneself, and so all murder has a sacrificial element. We may argue that murder, sacrifice, and the death penalty are ultimately inseparable, for all involve the taking of human life in order to propitiate someone's wrath, either the wrath of man or the wrath of God. Here, however, we do not need to argue so generally or theologically. The text itself says that Abel's blood cried from the ground (Gen. 4:10), and Hebrews 12:24 expressly ties this crying to the crying of the blood of Christ Jesus. Christ's blood cries for the redemption of His people, while Abel's blood cries for vengeance. Crying blood, however, is inevitably sacrificial blood in some sense.

Why does Cain kill Abel? Is the response commensurate with the stimulus? Satan had said that man would be like God (Gen. 3:5). Cain is an unregenerate man, and is trying to be like God. He believes that his wrath must be propitiated, appeased, satisfied. He wants to see the problems and disorders of his own little world purged out, expiated. Cain does not see himself as the problem. It is clearly Abel who is the problem. God favors Abel, and Cain will not admit that there is a legitimate reason why God favors Abel. In Cain's little world there is a distracting, evil thing that must be purged out, expiated: Abel. Cain finds that he is angry, wrathful, and that his wrath is directed against the One Who has offended him. Cain is god! and his wrath must be satisfied, appeased, propitiated. His wrath is directed against the Lord and against His servant Abel. Abel is God's favorite, so it will hurt God if Cain kills Abel. Besides, Abel has also offended Cain, by being so pious.

Expiation, propitiation — these are theological terms that have to do with the sacrificial atonement for sin. Cain's action is clearly sacrificial, even though he may not consciously have conceived of it as such. God treats it as sacrificial. Let us note that Cain goes out and builds a city, a culture, based on his misdeed. It is a culture that has at its heart not the substitutionary death of Christ, but the murder of man to propitiate the wrath of man. *All humanistic societies are built on the sacrificial murder of man.* The continual murder of millions of innocent people was the foundation of National Socialism in Germany and is the foundation of International Socialism in China and the U.S.S.R. (For a description, see the three volumes of *The GULAG Archipelago* by Aleksandr Solzhenitsyn.) And we are not saying too much to point out the millions of aborted babies that seem to be the chief product of our humanistic American society.

We shall return to the theme of human sacrifice as the foundation of human society when we get to Jephthah. For now, the curious reader might consider 1 King 16:34, where a ritual human sacrifice seems to be the foundation of the rebuilding of Jericho. And is it not Jesus Christ, sacrificed and resurrected, Who is the foundation stone and cornerstone of the Church, the New Jerusalem?

Abimelech's rule in Shechem, and the restored Canaanite culture of Shechem, are based on the human sacrifice of the seventy sons of Jerubbaal the Baal Fighter. We shall see that Abimelech is definitely a man of wrath who must propitiate his wrath whenever it is aroused. This is not his last act of human sacrifice.

The place where Abimelech was made king is important. According to Joshua 24:1, 24-26, this pillar was a monument erected by Joshua as a memorial stone to remind the people of their covenant with the Lord. It was to remind them that the Lord was their King. Now, in a tremendous act of perversion, the Lord is explicitly rejected at this very spot, and a murderous humanistic king enthroned. Here in a capsule we see the apostasy of Israel. To get the full weight of it, read Joshua 24 all the way through, and then consider what is done here.

Also, the Tabernacle of the Lord had formerly been pitched next to this oak and pillar (Josh. 24:26). Unquestionably this site is now the location of the house of Baal-Berith (Jud. 9:4). Again we see the substitution that has been made.

Why did God allow Gideon's 70 sons to be killed? Because they had sinned against Him. They died as a result of their father's sin, for there would have been no Abimelech had Gideon lived faithfully with one wife, and no tendency toward kingship if Gideon had effectively cut it off; but they died, as well, as a result of their own sins, for Judges 8:27 says that Gideon's ephod became a snare to himself "and his household." The 70 sons were compromised, just as Gideon was. They had fallen, along with their father. This fits the basic Biblical pattern we set out in the introduction to this study: re-creation, then fall, decline, and judgment. The re-creation was the victory of Gideon over Baalism in his house and the consequent cleansing of the land, reestablishing Eden. The fall was the creation of the false ephod. The punishment for man's fall is death, and so it came to pass here.

Yet, these 70 sons were doubtless much better men than their half-brother Abimelech. Had they lived, and exercised influence, things would have been better for Israel. All Israel, however, had fallen into sin. Thus, the deaths of the 70 sons were, in the providence of God, part of His judgment against Israel. God gave Israel over into the hands of the worst of the lot.

Jotham is here called the "youngest" of Gideon's sons. This connects with the theme established in Genesis of the younger brother replacing and redeeming the older brother, the second Adam replacing and redeeming the first Adam. Here it is not redemption but vengeance that is in view. By pronouncing this curse, Jotham avenges his other brothers. Throughout the Old Testament, the fathers and older brothers sin and die, and younger sons rise to replace them. All of this points to Christ, the Redeemer and Avenger of His "older brothers," those dead in Adam.

The sins of Gideon and his sons brought this judgment upon them, but the one who slew the sons was not acting as God's avenger, and thus was himself judged. This same pattern is seen when God brings in the enemy to punish His people, and then turns around and punishes the enemy because they had a wicked attitude about it (cf. Dan. 9:27, and the whole prophecy of Habakkuk).

The Doom of Humanistic Statism Prophesied

7. Now when they told Jotham, he went and stood on the top of Mount Gerizim, and lifted his voice and called out. Thus he said to them, "Listen to me, O men of Shechem, that God may listen to you.

Mount Gerizim is expressly mentioned as the place where Jotham stood to pronounce God's judgment. Shechem was located in the valley between Mounts Gerizim and Ebal. When the people came into the land, and had made the initial conquest, they divided into two groups and stood on these two mountains, to affirm the blessings and curses of the Covenant. These are recorded in Deuteronomy 27:11-16, and the curses concern secret sins that would not likely be found out by the magistrate. Those whom the magistrate does not curse on God's behalf, are to be cursed directly by God Himself. The fulfillment of this command is recorded in Joshua 8:30-35. It is because Shechem was located between these two mountains that it was convenient for the Tabernacle to be kept there for a time.

Thus, it was at the traditional site for blessings and curses that Jotham pronounced the curse of Shechem and Abimelech. Mount Gerizim was actually the mount of blessing, while Ebal was the mount of curses. This may be important in showing that the blessings of Gerizim are turned into curses for covenant breakers like the Shechemites. Or it may simply mean that Jotham could get a better hearing from Gerizim than he could have from Ebal.

By standing on Gerizim, Jotham invokes the ancient curse of God against the Shechemites. They have broken the covenant with the Lord. Now may the curses of the covenant come upon them, as their ancestors had vowed.

8. "Once the trees went forth to anoint a king over them, and they said to the olive tree, 'Reign over us!'
9. "But the olive tree said to them, 'Shall I leave my fatness with which by me God and men are honored, and go to wave

over the trees?'

    10. "Then the trees said to the fig tree, 'You come, reign over us!'

    11. "But the fig tree said to them, 'Shall I leave my sweetness and my good fruit, and go to wave over the trees?'

    12. "Then the trees said to the vine, 'You come, reign over us!'

    13. "But the vine said to them, 'Shall I leave my new wine, which cheers God and men, and go to wave over the trees?'

    14. "Finally all the trees said to the bramble, 'You come, reign over us!'

    15. "And the bramble said to the trees, 'If in truth you are anointing me king over you, come and take refuge in my shade; but if not, may fire come out from the bramble and consume the cedars of Lebanon.'

    The trees' desire for a king parallels, of course, Israel's desire for the same. The trees have a King, their Creator. They no more need a bureaucrat as king than do men. The three wise trees see this. Each has its work to do. Each is productive in the free market. Each gets joy from its work. None is interested in giving up the joys of work for the privilege of "waving over the trees," a sarcastic reference to the stupid pleasures of lording it over others in the mere exercise of visible power.

    These three trees are associated with Israel throughout Scripture. They signify the Godly man or woman who is fulfilling his or her tasks under God. A Godly society is made up of hard working people who are fulfilling the cultural mandate of Genesis 1:26-28; 2:15. Because the majority of people are engaged in productive work, capital expands, and a good life comes to everyone. The olive tree produces oil, which is used in anointing men to office, honoring both them and the God Whom they represent. The vine produces wine, which gives pleasure to the hearts of men, and also to God when poured out as libations and food for Him. The fig produces sweet fruit. Each takes pleasure, and a certain proper pride and joy, in fulfilling its appointed task. Each sees itself as serving "God and man," God first, and then man. In this, they are unlike fallen man, and unlike Abimelech.

    The bramble does not produce good things for life. The bramble is a thorny plant (Ps. 58:9), and thus an emblem of the curse on the ground (Gen. 3:18; Matt. 27:29). The bramble is not a productive member of the economy. It grows along the ground, and the demand that all the other trees take shelter in its shade is, thus, ridiculous. It is a demand that all society be reduced to the lowest common denominator. In order to outshine the vine, fig, and olive, the bramble must reduce them to a position lower then himself. This will result, of course, in their becoming unproductive, since they dare not outshine the bramble, and the bramble produces nothing!

Thus we see that the bramble is not oriented toward productive work. Rather, he is oriented toward tyrannical rule. He represents the ungodly man who builds up a society based on taking what other people have labored to produce. His is a socialistic society, based on massive confiscation of the wealth of other people, their hard earned savings and capital. His is an imperialistic society, based on the conquest of weaker people and of their production. His is a slave society, based on the forced labor of other people. The bramble society is indeed the society of the curse.

True to his unregenerate nature, the bramble is a man of wrath. If things don't go his way, he intends for fire to consume those who obstruct his plans. Brush fires, spreading along the dried runners of brambles, were sometimes a real threat to trees, and Jotham's parable builds on this fact. The bramble is so brazen as to threaten even the mightiest of trees, the cedars of Lebanon.

If the bramble had never been made king, he would not have been in a position to enforce his threats. Having made him king, however, the trees must hearken to his vicious threats, for they have delivered to him the power to enforce his vengeful will.

The point of the parable is that good men do not desire to lord it over others. Good men are happy being productive for God and for their fellowmen. They realize that the road to greatness is the way of the servant, as their Lord taught (Mark 10:42-45). The only kind of men who desire political authority for its own sake are bramble men—unproductive men who seek to attain fame and fortune by taking it from others who are productive.

The political inactivity of Christians and of their sometime fellow travellers, the conservatives, in our modern society is partly explained by this parable. Christians are oriented toward serving God and man through work in the marketplace. Their satisfaction comes through productivity. They believe that the solution for modern social problems is faith in God and hard, productive work. Unfortunately, most modern men look to the state, to the bramble, for answers.

Those who greatly desire to be kings are usually the least qualified for the post. Far wiser government generally comes from those who only reluctantly shoulder the heavy burdens of office. The good wise trees were reluctant; the bramble was anxious to rule.

16. "Now therefore, if you have dealt in truth and integrity in making Abimelech king, and if you have dealt well with Jerubbaal and his house, and if you have dealt with him as he deserved [according to the dealings of his hands]—

17. "For my father fought for you and risked his life and delivered you from the hand of Midian;

18. "But you have risen against my father's house today and have killed his sons, 70 men, on one stone, and have made Abimelech, the son of his maidservant, king over the men of Shechem, because he is your brother—

19. "If then you have dealt in truth and integrity with Jerubbaal and his house this day, rejoice in Abimelech, and let him also rejoice in you.

20. "But if not, let fire come out from Abimelech and consume the men of Shechem and Beth-Millo; and let fire come out from the men of Shechem and from Beth-Millo, and consume Abimelech."

21. Then Jotham escaped and fled, and went to Beer and remained there because of Abimelech his brother.

Jotham reminds the men of Shechem that Gideon had fought for them in years past. He also reminds them of their slaughter of Gideon's seventy sons; not everyone in earshot may have been apprised of this gory deed. He tells them that if this was a good thing to do, they should be happy. God will vindicate their deed, if it was good. We are doubtless supposed to compare this with Joash's speech about Baal in Judges 6:31. Unlike the impotent Baal, the Lord God of Israel will prove completely able to wreak vengeance upon His enemies.

And since their deeds were clearly evil, that is what they can expect. Fire will come from the bramble (Abimelech) and devour his kingdom. Then Jotham adds a second thought: Fire will come from the Shechemites and devour Abimelech. They are not productive trees—they also are brambles.

The wrath of the two brambles, Abimelech and the Shechemites, will mutually destroy one another. Like the Gingham Dog and the Calico Cat, they will fight all night, and in the morning no one will find them, because they will have devoured one another. Evil is self-destructive. Each man wants to play god, and each man seeks to murder those who thwart his plans. Each wants to have his own wrath propitiated, by sacrificing the troublemaker. Each wants to expiate the problem out of the situation, and it is always the other guy who is the problem.

Because of this fact, the brambles cannot win in history. Eventually they destroy each other. This same point is made in Zechariah 1:18-21. The four horns represent the bramble-powers of the world. Horns represent power and dominion, whether on the four corners of God's altar, or on the helmets of Vikings. The bramble horns acquire wealth not by work, but by taking what they want through force or taxation.

The carpenters, smiths, or craftsmen represent God's people. They just quietly go about their business of laboring in the garden of God, working to produce good things, being thrifty, helping their neighbors, and so on. One would think that such hard working people will always be a prey to the tyrants of this world; but no! Scripture says that the craftsmen will overcome the horns! A civilization based on hard work and capital accumulation will eventually overcome a civilization based on theft, rapine, and violence. This is due in part to the fact that God will give power to His own (Zech. 4:6: "Not by might, nor by power, but by My Spirit, says the Lord"). It is also due to the self-destructiveness of evil.

The destruction of evil culture is seen in Zechariah 14:12-15. Evil civilizations are destroyed in four complementary ways:

1. They rot away due to their own inner corruption and will to death, v. 12 (compare Prov. 8:36).

2. They are destroyed by mutual hate and strife, v. 13 (the theme of Judges 9).

3. They are conquered by the militant kingdom of God, by the preaching of the gospel, v. 14 (compare 2 Cor. 10:4).

4. They are destroyed by the decapitalization of their resources, v. 15. The wicked abuse what they have and waste and consume their own resources.

For these reasons, the wicked cannot continue to rule the world indefinitely. If the Lord tarries, the victory of the Kingdom is inevitable (Matt. 13:31-33).

A Short Reign

22. Now Abimelech ruled over Israel three years.

23. Then God sent an evil spirit between Abimelech and the men of Shechem; and the men of Shechem dealt treacherously with Abimelech,

24. In order that the violence done to the seventy sons of Jerubbaal might come, and their blood might be laid on Abimelech their brother, who killed them, and on the men of Shechem, who strengthened his hands to kill his brothers.

25. And the men of Shechem set men in ambush against him on the tops of the mountains, and they robbed all who might pass by them along the road; and it was told to Abimelech.

Evil men will be at one another's throats soon enough, but God in His graciousness to His own people accelerates the drift toward mutual hate and strife. The bramble men began to war against each other after a mere three years. Theologically, the three-day or three-year period signifies the world under the curse before the resurrection of Christ on the third day inaugurates the day of righteousness. Practically, it is also true that the popularity of bramble kings does not last long. Bramble men always grow to hate their bramble leaders.

We might add here that the mutual hate, strife, and suspicion among evil men is a fact that eliminates many of the conspiracy theories popular in conservative and in some Christian circles. It is utterly impossible to think that evil men, each seeking to be god, could cooperate for decades, yea centuries! in a long-term plot to overcome the world. What is perceived as a conspiracy is in fact *sin*. Sin always leads in the same basic direction, and evil men are thus always trying the same things over and over again. Conspiracy theories usually are a species of *selective depravity,* which blames some group of people for the problems of the world. Christianity affirms *universal depravity,* and exonerates no group from blame. There are indeed conspiracies in history, more than most of us will ever know much about. Conspiracies are not, however, the problem. Sin is the problem. If men worshipped God and lived right, there would be no one to listen to the siren songs of the bramble conspiracies of this age.

We may remind the reader that God's pitting these bramble men against each other merely continues the policy He used in Judges 7:19-22. The reason for God's direct action is given. He, the great Avenger of Blood (Ps. 18:47), is avenging the deaths of the seventy sons of Jerubbaal.

It should not surprise us that God is able to send an "evil" spirit. All angels, including evil ones, are at God's command. God normally does not permit Satan to have his way, but God does send evil spirits when it suits His purposes, as Job 1 and 2 illustrate. We also see this in 1 Kings 22:18-23. God can raise up the Assyrians to do His work of judgment, and they are happy to do it, but God still judges them for their evil hearts and actions. So it is also with the fallen angels. It is false to think that Satan has some independent realm from which he makes war on God. That is a Manichaean, and heretical, viewpoint. From the Biblical point of view, Satan is a fallen member of God's court. His doom is sure, but he is still under God's command. Satan can only act against God's people with God's permission. Satan delights to do evil, and God uses thus uses him to punish His people from time to time; but Satan has no realm of independent action. When Satan oppresses God's people, it is with His permission, and all for our good.

The Shechemites decided to get rid of Abimelech. They set an ambush for him, but he found out about it. Also, they became highway robbers, showing that they were indeed bramble men themselves. This constant highway robbery brought Abimelech's rule into disrepute, and would embarrass him.

From Bad to Worse

26. Now Gaal the son of Ebed came with his brothers, and crossed over into Shechem; and the men of Shechem put their trust in him.

27. And they went out into the field and gathered of their vineyards and trod them, and held a festival; and they went into

the house of their god, and ate and drank and cursed Abimelech.

28. Then Gaal the son of Ebed said, "Who is Abimelech, and who is Shechem, that we should serve him? Is he not the son of Jerubbaal [the Baal Fighter]? And is Zebul not his lieutenant? Serve the men of Hamor the father of Shechem; but why should we serve him?

29. "And who will give this people into my hand? Then I would remove Abimelech!" And he said to Abimelech, "Increase your army, and come out."

Abimelech was a halfbreed, and his religion was a halfbreed religion combining symbols of the true faith with the philosophy of Baalism to form the religion of Baal-Berith, the Baal of the Covenant. The man who now appears on the scene is a full-blooded Canaanite, who advocates returning to whole-hearted Baalism and rejecting all Israelite influence. The English versions call him Gaal the son of Ebed, but "ebed" is simply the Hebrew word for "slave." Gaal means "Loathsome" in Hebrew. It may have meant something else in the original Canaanite tongue, or it may be a name affixed to him by the writer of this passage. Just as God gives His people new names for the better, so He can give His enemies new names for the worse. At any rate, it is clear that Loathsome Slave-son is no good whatsoever, and that he is a full Canaanite (slave).

Gaal's "brothers" came with him. This would include relatives, and probably his whole motorcycle gang of followers. He was already a big man, and the Shechemites turned to him to deliver them from their wonderful, marvelous king, Abimelech.

Some type of harvest festival, a perversion of the Feast of Tabernacles, is going on. It is held in the temple of Baal-Berith. This is the same place where the Shechemites had originally covenanted with Abimelech. Now they covenant with Loathsome in the same place.

Gaal uses the very same argument against Abimelech that Abimelech had used against his seventy brothers. He notes that Abimelech is the son of Gideon Baal Fighter. He encourages Shechem to cast out all remnants of Israelite culture and return wholly to the original Canaanite culture of the city. The city had been founded by Hamor, who named it for his son Shechem (Gen. 34:2). Abimelech was king over "Israel" (v. 22), though this probably only really means the area around Shechem. Zebul was his vassal in charge in Shechem. To paraphrase verse 28, which is somewhat obscure: Then Gaal the son of a Canaanite slave said: "Who is this Abimelech? Is he not the son of Jerubbaal, the Baal Fighter? Why should we Baalists serve him? And who is Shechem, that they should serve Zebul, Abimelech's lieutenant? The Shechemites should serve someone who stands in the honorable line of Hamor and Shechem, true Canaanites. Why should we serve Abimelech?"

Gaal boasts that if the people were under his authority, and would join the Hell's Angels under him, he would remove Abimelech. In the drunkenness of the feast (v. 27), he calls on Abimelech to come out and fight.

The Doom Implemented: Gaal

30. And when Zebul the ruler of the city heard the word of Gaal the son of Ebed, his anger burned.

31. And he sent messengers to Abimelech privately, saying, "Behold, Gaal the son of Ebed and his brothers have come to Shechem; and behold, they are stirring up the city against you.

32. "Now therefore, arise by night, you and the people who are with you, and lie in wait in the field.

33. "And it shall come about in the morning, as soon as the sun is up, that you shall rise early and rush upon the city; and behold, when he and the people who are with him come out against you, you shall do to them whatever you are able [what your hand finds to do]."

34. So Abimelech and all the people with him arose by night and lay in wait against Shechem in four heads [companies].

35. Now Gaal the son of Ebed went out and stood in the entrance of the city gate; and Abimelech and the people who were with him arose from the ambush.

36. And when Gaal saw the people, he said to Zebul, "Look, people are coming down from the tops of the mountains." But Zebul said to him, "You are seeing the shadow of the mountains as if they were men."

37. And Gaal spoke again and said, "Behold, people are coming down from the highest part of the land, and one head [company] comes by the way of The Diviner's Oak."

38. Then Zebul said to him, "Where is your mouth now, with which you said, 'Who is Abimelech that we should serve him?' Is this not the people whom you despised? Go out now and fight with them!"

39. So Gaal went out before the leaders of Shechem and fought with Abimelech.

40. And Abimelech chased him, and he fled before him; and many fell wounded up to the entrance of the gate.

41. Then Abimelech remained at Arumah, but Zebul drove out Gaal and his brothers so that they could not remain in Shechem.

Zebul found out about Gaal that very night. His advice was to strike immediately, before Gaal could create a large fighting force, and while Gaal and his followers were still hungover from their all-night drunk. Even though Abimelech is himself an evil man, we still see the Biblical way of thinking, which puts the victory at sunrise.

Abimelech divided his forces into four groups (with Zebul in the city making a fifth column!), four being the number of dominion over the land. Gaal's confusion of Abimelech with the mountain is a humorous twist on the common imagery of the ancient world, found also in Scripture, that pictures great nations as mountains (see for instance Zech. 4:7). The mountains were indeed falling on him. The Leather Jacket Boys were no match for the army of The Establishment. Gaal's bunch was not very brave, and many died trying to get back into the city (v. 40).

The Doom Implemented: Shechem

42. Now it came about the next day, that the people went out to the field, and it was told to Abimelech.

43. So he took the people and divided them into three heads [companies], and lay in wait in the field; when he looked and saw the people coming out from the city, he arose against them and smote them.

44. Then Abimelech and the company who was with him dashed forward and stood in the entrance of the city gate; the other two companies then dashed against all who were in the field and smote them.

45. And Abimelech fought against the city all that day, and he captured the city and killed the people who were in it; then he razed the city and sowed it with salt.

Abimelech is now a very angry man. His wrath must be satisfied! He will be avenged against all these people who have turned against him! He will kill them all! Thus the world will see what happens to those who dare to betray Abimelech the Great!

Abimelech divided his forces into three groups. Once the people had come out of the city to their labors, one company of men stationed itself at the city gate, so that no one could get back inside. The other two companies moved in against the people working in the field, probably from two directions in a pincers action, killing everyone in between. Then he entered the city, killed everyone in it, and sowed it with salt. Sowing with salt is an emblem of the curse, for it makes the ground completely barren (Dt. 29:23).

In his actions, Abimelech imitates (parodies) God, playing God as it were. As God's cherubim keep men from Eden, so Abimelech's men guard the gates and let no one run in. Just as a city that commits treason against the Lord is to be completely destroyed (hormah), so Abimelech completely destroys the city that betrays him.

The Doom Implemented: Baal

46. When all the leaders of the tower of Shechem heard of it, they entered the inner chamber of the House of El-Berith.

47. And it was told Abimelech that all the leaders of the tower of Shechem were gathered together.

48. So Abimelech went up to Mount Zalmon, he and all the people who were with him; and Abimelech took an axe in his hand and cut down a branch from the trees, and lifted it and laid it on his shoulder. Then he said to the people who were with him, "What you have seen me do, hurry and do like me."

49. And all the people also cut down each one his branch and followed Abimelech, and put them on the inner chamber and set the inner chamber on fire over those inside, so that all the men of the tower of Shechem also died, about a thousand men and women.

Ancient cities frequently had not only walls around them, but a second wall around the highest part of the city, called the citadel. Here was the central fortress, where the most important people might hold on longer. Apparently the temple of Baal-Berith was located in the strongest part of the citadel (tower) of Shechem.

The "baals" or lords of Shechem, who were associated with

the citadel, fled to the temple. The tower of Shechem reminds us of the tower of Babel, the seat of humanistic government, man's attempt to storm the gates of heaven and take God's throne for himself. Each little humanistic city-state had its own tower, or ziggurat, which was the seat of government. Now the leaders take refuge in the temple of their god. "El" means "god" just as "baal" means "husband, master." The word "el" particularly stresses the power of God, or god, depending on whom it is being used to refer to. Here Baal-Berith is sarcastically called El-Berith, to stress his impotence to defend his supporters.

And Baal does prove again his utter impotence to defend his people. These bramble men are destroyed by fire that comes from the bramble man, Abimelech, just as it was prophesied. Indeed, the use of branches to start the fire reminds us of the literal brambles of the parable. These were the leaders of the Shechemite kingdom — once again the heads are "crushed."

Notice again how Abimelech parodies the Lord's ways, this time imitating his father. "Watch me, and do as I do," he says (compare Jud. 7:17). The difference is that in all the battles fought by the righteous, the Lord is seen as going first, with the messiah right behind him, and the army third. (In Christ the Lord and the messiah are one and the same.) Here, Abimelech plays the role of the Lord. He is about to be rewarded for his blasphemy.

Perhaps what is most noteworthy here is that Baal's loyal follower, Abimelech, is the one who burns Baal's temple. The war of Baal against God ends with Baal's temple being destroyed by his own followers. Here again we see God's heavy irony, just as in the Song of Deborah. We are to laugh as we see the wicked, impenitent enemies of God destroying themselves. Evil men are self-destructive. So are evil religions.

This brings me to a final comment. Here we see clearly that the heart of pagan religion is not found in its gods, but in humanism. It is nothing to Abimelech to burn Baal's temple, because what is most important in Abimelech's religion is himself, not Baal. The gods only exist to serve men, and to scare them. If we get mad at the gods, we can burn their temples to teach them a lesson. This attitude seems strange to us, since we think that pagans view their gods the same way we Christians view ours. But that is not the case, as any reading of religious literature of the ancient world will show. In Baalism, it is ultimately man who is most important, not the gods.

The Doom Implemented: Abimelech

50. Then Abimelech went to Thebez, and he camped against Thebez and captured it.

51. But there was a strong tower in the center of the city, and all the men and women with all the leaders of the city fled there and shut themselves in; and they went up on the roof of the tower.

52. So Abimelech came to the tower and fought against it, and approached the entrance of the tower to burn it with fire.

53. But a certain woman threw an upper millstone on Abimelech's head, crushing his skull.

54. Then he called quickly to the young man, his armor bearer, and said to him, "Draw your sword and kill me, lest it be said of me, 'A woman slew him.' " So his young man pierced him through, and he died.

55. And when the men of Israel saw that Abimelech was dead, each departed to his place.

Continual sin destroys the mind of man, and Abimelech has now become a fool. His wrath knows no bounds. He is determined to destroy everything in his reach. If I can't have it, nobody can, is his attitude. So, he goes to fight Thebez. He tries the same tactic here as had worked at the temple of Baal, but this time he is killed. Even though he tries to die honorably, his humiliating death at the hands of a woman is enshrined in Scripture for all generations to laugh at (cp. Jud. 4:9).

Once again the head of the serpent is crushed. Once again it is a woman, the protectress of the covenant and the guardian of the seed, who crushes the head. Abimelech is thus equated with Sisera.

There is more, though. Stoning was the prescribed mode of capital punishment in the Old Testament. Abimelech is stoned to death, in fit recompense for the murder of his brothers. Just as he had slain them on one stone, so he is slain by one stone — eye for eye, tooth for tooth.

Finally we should note that this is no mere stone. The Holy Spirit takes the trouble to pen the fact that it was an upper millstone. To keep it from being stolen, this woman had removed the small upper millstone and carried it with her. In the providence of God, it is an *implement of work* that kills the man of blood. We are back, then, to the by now familiar distinction between good trees and brambles, between horns and carpenters. Ultimately, it is the craftsmen and the millers who will overcome the horns and bramble men.

Some readers may think we are drawing too much out of this verse (v. 53). But let the reader consider that the Spirit might just as easily have written, "But someone threw a stone and it hit Abimelech so that he was dying." That is not, however, what the Spirit chose to write. He calls our attention to the woman, to the millstone, to the crushing of the head. We therefore are obliged to take note of these details.

Conclusion

56. Thus God repaid the wickedness of Abimelech, which he had done to his father, in killing his seventy brothers.

57. Also God returned all the wickedness of the men of Shechem on their heads, and the curse of Jotham the son of Jerubbaal came to them.

These two verses make it plain that God was at work avenging the family of Gideon Baal Fighter against Abimelech and the men of Shechem, returning their wickedness upon their *heads*. Every single person involved in the crime was killed (9:43, 45, 49, 54). We may rejoice with trembling to see how God avenges the blood of His saints. God emerged victorious over Baal. Baal was destroyed by his own followers. The wicked destroyed themselves, and the children of Israel were able to go home and leave off this unnecessary and fratricidal war. The ambitions of men who would not leave their fellows alone to work out their own affairs under God were responsible for this bloodshed, though it was almost all their own blood that was shed. All this, however, blossomed from the seemingly minor compromises made by Gideon, the faithful warrior of God. Let each of us pray that we do not make similar compromises, for it is our children who will pay if we do.

9

THE MINOR JUDGES: DRIFTING
TOWARD HUMANISTIC KINGSHIP
(Judges 10:1-5; 12:8-15)

The Protestant Reformers were much taken with the book of Judges. In an age of mounting tyranny, the Reformers were confronted with an Italo-Papal absolutism that had restructured the Church in the image of the imperial state, and also with the increasingly absolutist claims of the various monarchs of northern Europe. The Reformers found in Judges ammunition against this trend. They found that Judges presented the underlying problem as moral and spiritual disloyalty to Christ, and so they stressed that unless the Levites (preachers) got busy and reformed the Church, social conditions would continue to go from bad to worse. Second, they found in Judges that the Bible was opposed to centralized statism. The ideal Christian republic was decentralized and localized — free men under the Law of God. The lust for political power was dangerous. And third, they found in Judges that God sometimes blesses resistance movements, when it is really the righteous who are throwing off the yoke of a genuine tyrant.

Martin Bucer, one of the most important of the Reformers and the key Reformer in Strassburg, preached through Judges early on. Curiously, Judges was one of the few books Calvin did not tackle, but the reason was that he thought Bucer had done such a fine job. Bucer's commentary on Judges was published in Calvin's Geneva in 1554, enabling Calvin to skip that book and press on to lecture through Deuteronomy (1555-56) and Samuel (1563). Calvin's own commitments to republican rule and limited government are strongly articulated in these two sets of sermons. Calvin's Deuteronomy sermons were put into English in 1685 and went through several editions, though neither his Samuel nor his Deuteronomy lectures are available in modern

English.[1]

Bucer spent the last few years of his life in England, where his republican views were favored by the Puritans. Meanwhile, Bucer's close friend Peter Martyr Vermigli had also lectured through Judges, and his lectures had been translated into English and published in 1564. These made quite an impact, and also constituted a strong attack on political absolutism. Richard Rogers's 1615 commentary on Judges notes especially Vermigli's work as its foundation.[2]

Thus, from Bucer and Calvin on the one hand, and from Vermigli on the other, a strong belief in limited government based on Divine law, already present in the British world, was reinforced. The Puritans readily received this heritage, and made the book of Judges their own in the years of the English Civil War. Later on, their descendants in America found in the thirteen Israelite republics a model for their own thirteen states, loosely united under one Constitution, but with no absolute king, and a strictly limited federal government.

A full study of the impact of the book of Judges on Protestant political thought needs to be written. I have been able only to sketch it here, as an introduction to this chapter on the minor judges.

Why mention Christian political thought here? Because to a great extent it pertains to the section of Judges that we now take up, which is chapters 10 through 12. The following is an outline of this section:

I. Minor Judges (10:1-5)
   A. Tola, not drifting toward monarchy (10:1-2)
   B. Jair, drifting toward monarchy (10:3-5)

II. The Sin of Israel and the Lord's Anger (10:6-16)
   A. Northern tribes sold to Ammon.
   B. Southern tribes sold to Philistia.

III. Jephthah and the Ammonites (10:17 - 11:40)
   A. Jephthah's halfbreed heritage (11:1-11)
   B. Jephthah's warning to Ammon (11:12-28)

---

1. Geneva Ministries, 708 Hamvasy Lane, Tyler, TX 75701, has reprinted some of the Deuteronomy sermons in modern English, however. A subscription to these is available for a contribution.
2. Available in reprint form from Banner of Truth Publications (1983).

    C. Jephthah's dynastic aspirations thwarted (11:29-40)

IV. Jephthah and the Ephraimites (12:1-7)

V. Minor Judges (12:8-15)
    A. Ibzan, drifting toward monarchy (12:8-10)
    B. Elon, not drifting (12:11-12)
    C. Abdon, drifting toward monarchy (12:13-15)

The trend toward monarchy, which began with Gideon, continues here. The story of Jephthah, which is the heart of this section, concerns the desire to set up a dynasty. It concerns, in a sense, the seed to come. Instead of awaiting God's time and God's Seed (Jesus Christ), Jephthah is interested in establishing a dynasty. How God (graciously) thwarts his aspirations is the central story in this section.

Bracketing this narrative at the beginning and at the end are brief notices concerning minor judges, whose names are not exactly household words. These men seem to have no importance whatsoever, and seem to be included simply out of a desire for completeness (or so that the total number of judges would be twelve, which it is). Actually, however, the theme of aggrandizement and of the tendency toward tyranny is what governs the arrangement of the text here.

It is not the case that every paragraph of Scripture can stand by itself with a clear, discernable message. Some parts of Scripture only make sense when taken with a larger section. Such is the case here. Taken one at a time, or even as a group, the stories of these minor judges seem to have little purpose, but taken in a larger context, these notices are meaningful. Let us take a look at each one, first, and then return to the larger context.

Tola

10:1 Now after Abimelech died, Tola the son of Puah, the son of Dodo, a man of Issachar, arose to save (*yasha‘*) Israel; and he lived in Shamir in the hill country of Ephraim.

2. And he judged Israel 23 years. Then he died and was buried in Shamir.

Tola means "worm," a strange name. But "tola" can also refer to the scarlet-colored cloth made from a dye created by crushing worms. Such would be a robe of honor, signifying the dignity of the office of Judge. Maybe it was not his true name, but one given him by the author in order to connect him to Jesus Christ, the Greater Tola (Ps. 22:6), the great Crushed Worm whose blood dyes our sinful robes white (Rev. 7:14). He and the other four minor judges worked in northern Israel. Nothing is said about Tola's wives or his children. This is important.

Jair

3. And after him, Jair the Gileadite arose, and judged Israel 22 years.

4. And he had 30 sons who rode on 30 donkeys, and they had 30 cities which are in the land of Gilead that are called the Towns of Jair to this day.

5. And Jair died and was buried in Kamon.

Jair judged in Gilead, across the Jordan, for 22 years. Jair means "splendid." This might be an honorable name, but we see something of self-aggrandizement in Mr. Splendid as well. We are told that he had 30 sons. Therefore, he had more than one wife. We are also told that he appointed his 30 sons over 30 cities, and that they rode honorably on 30 donkeys.[3] Jair, then, in contrast to Tola, is seen as moving in the direction of royal and dynastic privileges.

An earlier Jair had conquered the towns that were known as "towns of Jair" (Num. 32:41). According to 1 Chronicles 2:22, these only numbered 23. The later Jair expanded the Towns of Jair to 30, to accommodate his designs for his sons.

Jair was a judge. Therefore, the Spirit of God was with him, and he was undoubtedly a wise and Godly man for the most part. He had weaknesses, however, and he gave in to the pressures of the time, pressures toward an exalted, humanistic state.

Jephthah

Jephthah will command our attention in detail in the next two chapters of this study. Here we note that the men of Gilead offered some sort of crown to him, which he demanded in exchange for delivering them. Jephthah, as we shall see, intended

---

3. The horse was not used in Israel at this time. It was only later that Israelite rulers ventured to bring in the horse; cf. Dt. 17:16.

to build for himself a kingdom by symbolically sacrificing his firstborn at the threshhold of his own house. God thwarts his design by taking his firstborn to His own house. God's is the only kingdom that He tolerates to be built.

Ibzan

12:8. Now Ibzan of Bethlehem judged Israel after him [Jephthah].

9. And he had 30 sons, and 30 daughters whom he sent outside [gave away in marriage], and he brought 30 daughters from outside for his sons. And he judged Israel seven years.

10. Then Ibzan died and was buried in Bethlehem.

Ibzan was from the Bethlehem in Zebulun. If Bethlehem in Judah had been his home, the text would say so, or else say Bethlehem Ephratha. We are still among the northern judges here.

Ibzan had 60 children, therefore several wives. The text stresses his patriarchal dynasticism by mentioning the careful disposition of his daughters and the careful arranging of the marriages of his sons, each of which would have involved some sort of alliance.

Elon

11. Now Elon the Zebulunite judged Israel after him, and he judged Israel ten years.

12. Then Elon the Zebulunite died and was buried at Aijalon in the land of Zebulun.

Elon, whose name means "oak tree," stands out as a contrast between Ibzan and Abdon. Nothing is said about any 30 sons for Elon. He apparently resisted such temptations.

Abdon

13. Now Abdon the son of Hillel the Pirathonite judged Israel after him.

14. And he had 40 sons and 30 grandsons who rode on 70 donkeys; and he judged Israel eight years.

15. Then Abdon the son of Hillel the Pirathonite died and was buried at Pirathon in the land of Ephraim, in the hill country of the Amalekites.

Abdon must have been an old man when he became a judge, for he already had 40 sons and 30 grandsons (not nephews, as the AV has it). Abdon means "servant," but he obviously was not as much a servant as he should have been, because he also was a polygamist. He extended his dynastic activity to his grandsons, a progression beyond what we have already seen. The number 70 comes up here, as it did in connection with Gideon (Jud. 8:30). It brings us full circle in the treatment of the theme of the drift toward statism.

This is as good a place as any to comment on the death and burial notices given for the judges. Beginning with Gideon, we are told of the burial place for each of the judges, except Abimelech. Why does the text tell us that each judge died? Did we have any doubt about it? Obviously not. We have to look for a theological reason, and it is not far to find. By calling attention to the deaths of these judges, Scripture reminds us that the deliverances wrought by them were only temporary. Death still had the last word, and thus men were still not really delivered from the curse of original sin. This points to the need for a final Deliverer, who would save us from death itself. It points to the resurrection.

Why mention the burial sites? Because tombs were memorials. They were memorials that reminded people of the curse of death for sin, and they were memorials of the sure and certain hope of the coming Deliverer who would raise men from the dead. Thus, the Old Testament always pays attention to the burial sites of prominent persons. Where the text does not mention a burial place, as with Abimelech, this indicates by way of contrast that there was no memorial for him.[4] We shall note the peculiarities of Jephthah's burial when we come to it.

Summary

It is apparent from these notices that the last three judges were old men when they began to judge, and probably Tola and Jair were getting along in years also. In contrast to Gideon, these were important men in their communities, probably

---

4. That is, by way of contrast in this context. The context is the second half of Judges. Death and burial are not recorded for Ehud and Deborah, but that stands outside this context. It is beginning with Gideon that the text begins to call attention to burial sites.

known as wise and responsible citizens, and they were made judges as a result. It may be that they simply rose in rank from being elders over tens, to being elders over 50s, 100s, and 1000s until they became the judge of all Israel (Ex. 18:21ff.). Because they were elderly when they came to office, there is no particular message in the fact that they only judged for short periods of time.

The three polygamists, Jair, Ibzan, and Abdon, must have indulged this vice prior to becoming judges over all Israel, for Abdon (for instance) could not have produced 40 sons and 30 grandsons in eight years. What this indicates is that the leaders in Israel were drifting into a position of seeking special honors and privileges, and of viewing themselves as above certain provisions in the Law, particular the prohibition against polygamy. We see the trappings, the effects, the manifestations of kingship, but without the name of it. The powerful were beginning to act less like servants of the people and of the Lord, and more like an aristocracy. We may contrast Boaz, in Ruth 3 and 4, with this.

The following chart summarizes the message of the minor judges, when seen in the context of the drift toward humanistic kingship, which is one of the major themes of the second half of the Gideon story, and of Judges 10–12:

Gideon	70 sons		people sought to make him a king
Abimelech			made himself a king
Tola			contrast: no regal manifestations
Jair	30 sons	30 donkeys	put sons in charge of 30 cities
Jephthah			sought to establish dynasty
Ibzan	30 sons	30 daughters	sought to build up importance of family through alliances
Elon			contrast: no regal manifestations
Abdon	70 "sons"	70 donkeys	extended dynasty to grandsons

(The numbers 3 and 7 in Scripture, by the way, connote fulness and a sense of arrival, because the third day and the seventh day are arrival points in history; cf. Num. 19:12. Thus, there would have been a certain sense of satisfaction, a feeling of accomplishment, of having arrived, if a man had 30 sons, or even better if he had 70. Thus, the numerology of the passage reinforces its basic message. While this type of numerology seems strange to 20th century readers, it is only because they have not been educated in it. It was normal for ancient, medieval, and early modern writers to employ numerological structures, and the Bible is no exception to this.)

The social system given in Exodus 18 had two aspects. One was the ministry of the Levites. These were locally scattered throughout Israel, and basically were the pastors of the local churches. Their job was to train the people in the Law, so that they would mature in self-government. The other aspect was the system of judges and courts of appeals. There were judges over 10s, 50s, 100s, and 1000s, with a final court of appeal at the top of the system. The whole thrust of this system was localistic. Immediate, day to day decisions would be made by the local elders, the "elders of the gate," which were the elders over 10s sitting as a group. Only hard cases would be appealed up the line, and only the toughest of all would ever come to the judge of all Israel, at the top (for an example, see 1 Kings 3:16ff.). Thus, although there was a strong government over the whole nation in one sense (defiance of the judge resulted in the death penalty, Dt. 17:8ff.), yet this central government had next to nothing to do with the day to day affairs of the citizens. It only existed as a final court of appeals.

The tendency, however, is for sinful man to reverse this. Instead of local churches with courts of appeal, we get top heavy denominational structures that tend to invade and consume local ministries. Instead of local government, we get national government, universal conscription, and heavy national taxation. Instead of local police, locally accountable, we tend to get national police (not yet in America, though). This is because in Baalistic humanism it is man, not God, who is king.

Since God is omnipresent, He can manifest His rule in every place, and every place the same if the Levites (Church) are strong and teaching the same Law (Bible) in every place. God's omnipresence, manifest through the work of the Church, makes for a civilization that is fundamentally uniform throughout, without that uniformity's being imposed by tyranny, so that there is also rich diversity of local color.

When men want to play God, however, they can only impose their will over a large area by using implements of force and violence. To get a uniform culture, they have to impose it from above, and this works to nullify all local diversity. In a Biblical society, the larger government sets only general policy, and serves as a court of appeal; but in a humanistic state, the larger government sets all policy, specific as well as general, thus destroying local diversity, and there is no court of appeal because all local courts are manifestations of the central court.

The bottom line is that man was never created to be omnipresent. Men are by nature local; they can only be one place at a time, and they can only effectively govern a small number of things. A wise man can manage a court of appeals, for only a few things are appealed. No man, however, can rule all the details of a whole civilization. Whenever men try to do so, it is because they are usurping God's prerogatives, and they become tyrants.

Did Israel learn from Samuel's warning (assuming Samuel wrote Judges)? No, and Samuel reiterated the warning in capsule form in his sermon recorded in 1 Samuel 8. It is not wrong to be like the nations in having a king, but it is wrong to want a king who is like the kings of the nations. A king "like all the nations" would create a standing army and a forced draft; he would make himself rich by taking over large land holdings; he would take their daughters for his own purposes; he would confiscate their traditional family property; he would tax them heavily and take a tithe (making himself God); he would take their servants and their best animals; and finally he would make them all his slaves. This would all be done in the name of efficient central government.

This was the warning Israel refused to heed. This same warning was given us by our Puritan forefathers, who knew first hand what they were talking about. We have not heeded it either. If the book of Judges has a message for us it is this: When God is once again King in his Church, and the Levites are doing their job, and the people are obeying Him, then the tyrant will be gone. The first part of Judges shows that God can take care of foreign tyrants. The second part warns that we will also face internal tyrants as well.

10

JEPHTHAH: REACHING FOR THE CROWN
(Judges 10:6 - 11:40)

The liturgical order of Judges 10:6–12:7 is as follows:

1. God's judgment: Philistines and Ammon (10:6-9)
2. People's response: superficial repentance (10:10)
3. God's evaluation: no relief (10:11-14)
4. People's response: more sincere repentance (10:15-16)
5. God's response: deliverer raised up (10:17–11:3)

For the rest of the passage, God's commands are general laws that lie in the background:

Judges 11:

1. God's command: I am your King.
2. Israel and Jephthah's response: Jephthah will be king.
3. God's evaluation: Jephthah's plans destroyed.

Judges 12:

1. God's command: Submit to My anointed one.
2. Ephraim's response: Make war on the anointed one.
3. God's judgment: The anointed one destroys Ephraim's power.

We may outline the passage as follows:

I. God's Judgment (10:6-16)
    A. Sin and Judgment (10:6-9)
    B. God's anger (10:10-16)

II. The Deliverer Raised up (10:17–11:11)
    A. The Attitude of Gilead (10:17-18)

B. The Origin of Jephthah (11:1-3)
C. The Demands of Jephthah (11:4-11)

III. The Gospel Offered to Ammon (11:12-28)

IV. Jephthah's Plans Thwarted (11:29-40)
A. God Provokes a Vow (11:29-31)
B. God Defeats Ammon (11:32-33)
C. God Destroys Jephthah's Aspirations (11:34-40)

V. Ephraim's War against God (12:1-7)

God's Judgment

10:6. Then the sons of Israel again did evil in the sight of the LORD, and served
(1) the Baals
(2) and the Ashtaroth,
(3) the gods of Aram [Syria],
(4) the gods of Sidon,
(5) the gods of Moab,
(6) the gods of the sons of Ammon,
(7) and the gods of the Philistines;
thus they forsook the LORD and did not serve Him.
7. And the anger of the LORD burned against Israel, and He sold them into the hands of the Philistines, and into the hands of the sons of Ammon.
8. And they [Ammon] shattered and crushed the sons of Israel in that year; for eighteen years they afflicted all the sons of Israel who were beyond the Jordan which is in Gilead in the land of the Amorites.
9. And the sons of Ammon crossed the Jordan to fight also against Judah, Benjamin, and the house of Ephraim, so that Israel was greatly distressed.

This paragraph introduces a turning point in Judges. The people have apostatized before, and God has delivered them before. Now, however, they move into a seven-fold (complete) apostasy. Any god is preferable to the Lord. As a result, God hands Israel over to Ammon in the north and west, and to Philistia in the south. The rather grotesque histories of the last two judges deal with these two oppressions. Each story shows the inadequacy of man to be his own deliverer, even with the Lord's aid. In this way, each story points to Jesus Christ as the only final Deliverer.

We read the terrifying phrase "the anger of the LORD burned against Israel." So great was His anger that He permitted the Ammonites to "shatter" Israel. The word for shatter is used only one other time in the Bible, in Exodus 15:6 where it refers to God's shattering of the Egyptians!

> 10. Then the sons of Israel cried out to the LORD, saying, "We have sinned against Thee, for indeed, we have forsaken our God and served the Baals."
>
> 11. And the LORD said to the sons of Israel, "Is it not so that
>> (1) when the Egyptians,
>> (2) and when the Amorites,
>> (3) and when the sons of Ammon,
>> (4) and when the Philistines,
> 12. (5) and the Sidonians,
>> (6) and the Amalekites,
>> (7) and the Maunites
>
> oppressed you, and you cried out to Me, then I delivered (*yasha'*) you from their hands? [This is a literal translation, not the NASB, for verses 11 and 12.]
>
> 13. "Yet you have forsaken Me and served other gods; therefore I will deliver (*yasha'*) you no more.
>
> 14. "Go and cry out to the gods which you have chosen; let them deliver (*yasha'*) you in the time of your distress."

Here we have superficial repentance. The children of Israel have become experts at sinning and repenting. Like the followers of the modern cult leader R. B. Thieme, they have learned the "rebound technique": Just name your sin and God will automatically forgive it, just like that. God is an impersonal computer, it seems; type in the right message, and He will spit out forgiveness.

God rejects their "easy believism" theology. They find that He is a Person, and that He is offended. He calls attention to seven deliverances in the past, which they have respected by now going into seven-fold apostasy!

Egyptians	Exodus 1–14
Amorites	Numbers 21:21-35
Ammonites	Judges 3:13
Philistines	Judges 3:31
Sidonians	Judges 4–5
Amalekites	Judges 6:3 (Ex. 17:8-16; Jud. 3:13)
Maunites	Judges 6:2

From Judges 18:7 and 28 we learn that Sidon was overlord to the territory of Jabin, so that the deliverance from the Sidonians refers to the deliverance from Jabin. The Maunites are unknown, but scholars suggest that this refers to that group of apostate Midianites whom Gideon fought.

There is grace buried in this list, as in all God's chastisements of His people. He reminds them that He has delivered them from Ammon and Philistia before, thus encouraging them to know that He can do so again.

But God says, "I will save you no more." How can God change His mind? We have to understand that this is covenantal language. God told the Ninevites that He would destroy them in forty days, yet when they repented, God spared them, as the book of Jonah shows. God's threats and promises of wrath are always to be taken in a covenantal context of human sin, and God can and does "change His mind" when He grants repentance and salvation to men.

15. And the sons of Israel said to the LORD, "We have sinned; do to us whatever seems good to Thee; only please deliver us this day."
16. So they put away the foreign gods from among them, and served the LORD; and He could bear the misery of Israel no longer.

Israel's repentance was more genuine this time, but hardly thoroughgoing, as we have seen. The desire for a Statist rather than a Godly order remained. What is far more important is the statement in verse 16 that the Lord was vexed by the misery of Israel. God will deliver them this time, not because of their half-hearted repentance, but because He loves them in spite of their sins. The longsuffering of the Lord has not yet come to an end. God will raise up for them a deliverer, Jephthah, who will show them their own spiritual shortcomings by exemplifying them.

The Gileadites

17. Then the sons of Ammon were summoned, and they camped in Gilead. And the sons of Israel gathered together, and camped in Mizpah.
18. And the people, the leaders of Gilead, said to one

another, "Who is the man who will begin to fight against the sons of Ammon? He shall become head over all the inhabitants of Gilead."

Although Ammon had afflicted Israel for 18 years, some definitive move was now underfoot. As revealed in Judges 11:13, Ammon intended to take Israelite territory back wholly under its domain. Instead of depending wholly on the Lord, the Gileadites seek for a strong military leader, and they intend to make a deal with him. Up until now, each judge has been expressly raised up by the Lord for his task (3:9, 15; 4:4-6; 6:11-12). Up until now, the people have confessed that they deserved to be destroyed, and have cast themselves wholly on the Lord, and so He saved them. The Gileadites, however, are not relying wholly on the Lord. They put their faith in a deal they will make with some military deliverer. They will offer him the crown, if he saves them.

The Origin of Jephthah

Several problems confront us in the story of Jephthah. Did he really kill and burn up his daughter? Was he a man of real faith? Before looking at the text, I think it would be well to deal in general with these problems.

Some commentators assume that Jephthah had a real, but grossly ignorant faith. He lived in barbarous times, they say, and did not know any better than to try to make a deal with God, and to sacrifice his daughter. In fact, however, Jephthah is listed as a hero of faith, real true faith, in Hebrews 11:32. Even if he were not, the fact is that the book of Judges calls explicit attention to his anointing with the Spirit of God, and just before he makes his supposedly rash vow (Jud. 11:29). As we have seen (pp. 51ff. above), such an anointing implies all the graces of the Spirit, at least in some measure. There can be no doubt but that Jephthah knew the law of God, for his letter to the king of Ammon shows a thorough familiarity with the events recorded in Numbers. He was no ignorant man.

There can be no doubt but that Jephthah's daughter was not killed, but was devoted to perpetual virginity and service at the door of the Tabernacle. Bible commentators and opera writers have turned the story of Jephthah's daughter into a Greek tragedy more often than not; but they have been too much influenced by the story of Agamemnon and Iphigenia. We shall take up the argument in detail below.

Recognizing these facts, some other conservative commentators have argued that Jephthah did absolutely nothing wrong. He was a great hero of the faith. God provoked his vow, and his vow was good. There is nothing here to criticize.

I think that both sides have missed the overall theology of Judges, and of this section of Judges in particular. I have tried to lead into this story of Jephthah by making that overall theology clear, so that what Jephthah does will make sense. Yes, he was a real hero of the faith. Yes, God provoked his vow. But Jephthah had a weakness, and his weakness was the weakness of Israel as a whole. Israel thought that they needed a human king as deliverer, and Jephthah thought so too. Jephthah's flaw was his desire to start up a dynasty, doubtless for the good of Israel. The faithful Lord of Israel acted to prevent this, removing from Jephthah any possibility of stumbling, and teaching Israel a lesson.

As we shall see, Jephthah's vow was not rash. It was well thought out. He had something definite in mind, for a threshold sacrifice is connected to the establishment of a house or dynasty. God moved Jephthah to make this vow, because God wanted to make it clear that it was His house that was the true house of the King, and it was His house (the Tabernacle) that would be built (on the threshold sacrifice of the virginity of the women who ministered at its doorway). Thus the Lord reproved Jephthah and Israel for desiring a human king, and reminded them that He alone was their King, and that it was His house that had to be built up.

This may seem strange, but I believe it is because we are not used to thinking as people in ancient Israel thought. My task is to make this interpretation clear as we now turn to the text.

11:1. Now Jephthah the Gileadite was a mighty man of valor, but he was the son of a harlot. And Gilead begat Jephthah.

2. And Gilead's wife bore him sons; and when his wife's sons grew up, they drove Jephthah out and said to him, "You shall not have an inheritance in our father's house, for you are the son of another woman."

3. So Jephthah fled from his brothers and lived in the land of Tob [Good]; and worthless fellows [men without means; impoverished men] gathered themselves to Jephthah, and they went out with him.

It is unclear whether Jephthah knew his father or not. Verse 1 reads as if "Gilead" was his father, in the sense that any man in the region could have been his father. In verse 7 we find that it was all the men of Gilead who drove him out. Moreover, when Jephthah died (Jud. 12:7) it simply says that he was buried "in one of the cities of Gilead." We get the impression that this man had no home, no family, and that his burial place is as unspecific as his origin.

If this interpretation is correct, then the "wife of Gilead" in verse 2, and the brothers, simply refer to the legitimate women and sons in the district. Possibly, of course, by Divine providence Jephthah's father had the same name as the district, so that a pun is possible.

Since daughters of Israel would never have become harlots, this woman was not an Israelite. Jephthah was a half-breed, like Abimelech; but he was a regenerate half-breed. His father, Gilead (whether a particular man or just anybody living there), symbolizes Israel, and his mother symbolizes the spiritual whoredom of Israel. Jephthah is a product of this mixture. He represents and encapsulates the half-breed religion of his day; but unlike Abimelech, he is a picture of the Christian who has been influenced by the world, rather than a picture of the pagan who simply uses some Christian vocabulary.

Bastards could not be full citizens of Israel until the tenth generation (Dt. 23:2). The same thing was true of Ammonites (Dt. 23:3). God, in His holy humor, is secretly raising up an excluded man to destroy these excluded people.

It may seem cruel, this law; but its purpose is two-fold. First, it should make a man think twice before siring a bastard, to know that for ten generations these people will be excluded from full citizenship. Second, the law also excluded eunuchs (Dt. 23:1) because they had no stake in the future, and excluded bastards because they had no respect for the past. They inherited no responsibilities from the past. God does not want His nation governed by present-oriented people, but by those who have a respect for heritage and a concern for the future.

Judah was the royal tribe in Israel; yet most of Judah were bastards (Gen. 38). Thus, they had to wait ten generations before they could take up full citizenship in Israel, and thus it was ten generations before any Judahite could become king. The genealogy in Ruth 4:18-22 shows that David was ten generations away from his bastard ancestor. This fact shows one of the reasons why Israel was not to have a king during the period of the Judges. Only someone from Judah could be king, and virtually all of Judah was temporarily excluded. This fact shows the folly of what Jephthah tried to accomplish, though he doubtless would not have called himself "king," because of it. As a bastard he was not to be a full citizen, and certainly could not set up a dynasty. (The main reason, of course, that there was to be no human king at this time is that God wanted it thoroughly established that He was the True King before He allowed a human king to be set up as His viceroy.)

Abraham sent his other sons away from the area where Isaac dwelt, but he gave them gifts (Gen. 25:5, 6). There is no statement in the law that allows for a bastard to be driven from the house, and given nothing whatsoever. The action of Jephthah's brothers (literal or figurative) was thus cruel and wicked. God repays them for it. They humiliated Jephthah; they will be humiliated before Jephthah.

Nehemiah 5:13 shows that the word translated "worthless" in verse 3 really only means "impoverished." Like David later on, Jephthah gathers a band of impoverished men around him. Just as David became famous for raiding the enemies of Israel, so Jephthah acquires fame for striking at Ammon. There can be no doubt, given Jephthah's spiritual character, that his raids were conducted against the enemy. It is a work of God's grace that Jephthah is not bitter against Israel, but uses his skills to protect the people who had so mistreated him. This is because Jephthah's true loyalty is to the Lord.

Jephthah is said to have lived in the land of Tob. Tob means "good." While God punished and wasted His own land, He took care of His faithful man in another place, a good place. God takes care of His own.

The Demands of Jephthah

4. And it came about after a while that the sons of Ammon fought against Israel.

5. And it happened when the sons of Ammon fought against Israel that the elders of Gilead went to get Jephthah from the land of Tob.

6. And they said to Jephthah, "Come and be our chief that we may fight against the sons of Ammon."

7. Then Jephthah said to the elders of Gilead, "Did you not hate me and drive me from my father's house? So why have you come to me now when you are in trouble?"

8. And the elders of Gilead said to Jephthah, "For this reason we have now returned to you, that you may go with us and fight with the sons of Ammon and become head over all the inhabitants of Gilead."

9. So Jephthah said to the elders of Gilead, "If you take me back to fight against the sons of Ammon, and the LORD gives them up before me, will I become your head?"

10. And the elders of Gilead said to Jephthah, "The LORD is hearer between us; surely we will do according to your word."

11. Then Jephthah went with the elders of Gilead, and the people made him head and chief over them; and Jephthah spoke all his words before the LORD at Mizpah.

The elders of Gilead had said that whoever delivered them from Ammon would become their chief. This was according to the rule we have mentioned earlier: He who saves you becomes your ruler. This "rash vow," however, put the men of Gilead in an awkward position. It was, first, humiliating to have to offer this title to Jephthah; these elders had acquiesced when the brothers expelled Jephthah (or, if by "brothers" we are to understand all of Gilead, then they themselves expelled Jephthah, which is what verse 7 implies). Second, however, their vow now put them in a position of violating the law, for Jephthah, being a bastard, could not possibly become a ruler in Israel in any full and normal sense. The reason why there are no judges from the tribe of Judah during this period (curious, isn't it, that the royal tribe contributes no judges?) is that virtually the whole tribe were bastards, as mentioned before. Now, however, the Gileadites are forced to offer rule to a bastard. Jephthah does indeed become a judge, exceptional as this is. The bastard judge was a continuing sign to Israel of her spiritual condition — the best man available was not qualified for the job!

Jephthah's faith is seen in his expression that the Lord will be their Deliverer (v. 9). All the same, however, he chooses to ignore the law excluding bastards, and shows a desire to become some sort of king. The whole deal is ratified in the presence of the Lord, which probably means that the Ark of God was in the field at Mizpah (2 Sam. 11:11).

There is an ambiguity throughout the story of Jephthah, which causes some commentators to treat him too harshly and others to treat him too leniently. Jephthah was a mixture, as Israel was a mixture; and his actions were mixed as well.

The Gospel Offered to Ammon

12. Now Jephthah sent messengers to the king of the sons of Ammon, saying, "What is between you and me, that you have come to me to fight against my land?"

13. And the king of the sons of Ammon said to the messengers of Jephthah, "Because Israel took away my land when they came up from Egypt, from the Arnon as far as the Jabbok and the Jordan; therefore, return them peacably now."

The fact that Jephthah sends messengers to Ammon is a sign that he is primarily a man of peace, contrary to the assertions of some commentators who present him as a rash and violent man. Also, the fact that the message of the Word of God is sent to Ammon means that Jephthah is preaching the gospel to them. If Ammon will recognize that Israel is priest to the nations, and allow Israel to do her priestly work, then Ammon can be saved. Samson's offer of marriage to a Philistine girl is also a sign of the gospel offered to the gentiles, as we shall see, and this is a tie between the Jephthah and the Samson stories. Jephthah preached the Word to Ammon calling on them to repent of their actions against God's priestly nation. The opportunity to repent is provided before judgment falls.

Jephthah has entered into discussion, and has heard Ammon's claim, that Israel stole their land. He now refutes this claim with a series of arguments. (The fact that Jephthah refers to Israel as "my land" need not worry us. As the judge, he represented the Lord in warfare, and was identified with Him, so that in some sense Israel was Jephthah's land.)

14. But Jephthah sent messengers again to the king of the sons of Ammon,

15. And he said to him, "Thus says Jephthah, 'Israel did not take away the land of Moab, nor the land of the sons of Ammon.

16. " 'For when they came up from Egypt, and Israel went through the wilderness to the Red Sea and came to Kadesh,

17. " 'Then Israel sent messengers to the king of Edom, saying "Please let us pass through your land," but the king of Edom would not listen. And they also sent to the king of Moab, but he would not consent. So Israel remained at Kadesh.

18. " 'Then they went through the wilderness and around the land of Edom and the land of Moab, and came to the east side of the land of Moab, and they camped beyond the Arnon; but they did not enter the territory of Moab, but the Arnon is the border of Moab.

Jephthah's first argument is that Israel respected the borders of the relative nations Edom and Moab, and thus, by implication, Ammon. Israel had politely requested highway passage, and being denied it, they went around these nations.

19. " 'And Israel sent messengers to Sihon king of the Amorites, the king of Heshbon, and Israel said to him, "Please let us pass through your land to our place."

20. " 'But Sihon did not trust Israel to pass through his territory, so Sihon gathered all his people and camped in Jahaz, and fought with Israel.

21. " 'And the LORD, the God of Israel, gave Sihon and all his people into the hand of Israel, and they smote them; so Israel possessed all the land of the Amorites, the inhabitants of that country.

22. " 'So they possessed all the territory of the Amorites, from the Arnon as far as the Jabbok, and from the wilderness as far as the Jordan.

Jephthah's second argument is that Israel took the disputed territory from the Amorites, not from Ammon. (I can hear him say it, "We took it from the Amorites, not from the Ammonites, dummy. *Amor* not *Ammon!* Got it?") Moreover, Israel fought and conquered this territory because Sihon attacked them first. You are attacking us now, O Ammon; do you want to lose your territory too?

23. " 'Since now the LORD, the God of Israel, drove out the Amorites from before His people Israel, are you then to possess it?

Jephthah's third argument is that it was the Lord who gave this land from the Amorites to Israel.

24. " 'Do you not possess what Chemosh your god gives you to possess? So whatever the LORD our God has driven out before us, we will possess.

Jephthah's fourth argument is that Ammon should stick with what their false god has given them, and let Israel have what the Lord has given them. There are two problems here. First, Chemosh was the god of Moab, while Molech was the god of Ammon. Was Jephthah misinformed? Impossible. Was he being sarcastic, deliberately insulting? Possibly. Were the Ammonites, always close to the Moabites, in a temporary historical phase of worshipping the Moabite god? Possibly. There is no sure answer, though the third is most likely.

We are distressed to read this argument. Is Jephthah saying "live and let live"? Is he failing to call Ammon to repentance? Is he putting Chemosh on the same level as YHWH? "You have what Chemosh gives you, and we have what YHWH gives us." It certainly seems so, unless we go back and read Numbers 21. There we find that Sihon king of the Amorites had captured much of Moab and Ammon. When Israel destroyed Sihon, they liberated much of Moab and Ammon, and gave it back to them (Num. 21:29-30). So far from capturing Ammonite territory, then, it was Israel who gave them back their land!

But the real punch is that Chemosh had been utterly powerless to defend Ammon against Sihon. It was the Lord Who had defended Ammon, and Who had given them their land. Jephthah's message is indeed sarcastic then: "If you trust in Chemosh to give you land, guess how much you will have? But if you will take a look at history, you will see that the Lord is the only true God, and that He has given Israel this land. By the same token, though, if you will repent and trust the Lord, He will give you land as well." That is Jephthah's gospel message to Ammon.

25. " 'And now are you any better than Balak the son of Zippor, king of Moab? Did he ever strive with Israel, or did he ever fight against them?

Jephthah's fifth argument is a subtle (not so subtle, really) reminder that Israel had whipped the tar out of Moab back in the days of Balak (Num. 22-25, 31). Would Ammon like the same treatment?

26. " 'While Israel lived in Heshbon and its villages, and in Aroer and its villages, and in all the cities that are on the banks of the Arnon, 300 years, why did you not recover them within that time?

Jephthah's sixth argument is that 300 years have passed since Israel allegedly stole Ammonite land. They have lived in this place for centuries. Something should have been said about it before now!

27. " 'I therefore have not sinned against you, but you are doing me wrong by making war against me; may the LORD, The Judge, judge today between the sons of Israel and the sons of Ammon.' "
28. But the king of the sons of Ammon did not listen to the words which Jephthah sent him.

Jephthah closes by affirming that he is not the judge. It is not Jephthah with whom Ammon has to do. They are warring against The Judge, Who is YHWH, God of Israel. Jephthah's true faith is seen here, for he knows full well Who the real Judge of Israel is. Also, we see from this passage that Jephthah is fully acquainted with the book of Numbers. He knew the Bible well. He was not an ignorant man living in an ignorant age.

Ammon rejects the gospel, thus bringing judgment upon themselves, just as later on the Philistines will bring judgment on themselves by rejecting the marriage offer of Samson, the Mighty Bridegroom.

Jephthah's Vow and Victory

29. Now the Spirit of the LORD came upon Jephthah, so that he passed through Gilead and Manasseh, then he passed through Mizpah of Gilead, and from Mizpah of Gilead he went on to the

sons of Ammon.

30. And Jephthah made a vow to the LORD and said, "If Thou wilt indeed give the sons of Ammon into my hand,

31. "Then it shall be that whoever [not whatever] comes out of the doors of my house to meet me when I return in peace from the sons of Ammon, it shall be the LORD's and I will offer it up as a whole burnt sacrifice."

32. So Jephthah crossed over to the sons of Ammon to fight against them; and the LORD gave them into his hand.

33. And he struck them with a very great slaughter from Aroer to the entrance of Minnith, 20 cities, and as far as Abel-Keramin [the Plain of the Vineyards]. So the sons of Ammon were subdued before the sons of Israel.

The Spirit anoints Jephthah, empowering him for special service. Immediately Jephthah makes his "rash" vow. We have to see that the Spirit provokes him to this vow; and as we shall see, the vow was calculated, not rash.

There was nothing wrong with this vow. Jacob made a similar vow in Genesis 28:20, that if God would bring him back to the land of promise, he would give God a tithe of all he earned in the strange land. This is not a bargain with God. Rather, it is a confession that God is able to do the work, and a confession that man owes a debt of gratitude to God. The vow makes specific and concrete what will be done to pay that debt of gratitude.

Jephthah vows to offer as a whole burnt sacrifice whoever comes out of the doors of his house. We cannot read "whatever comes out," because the Hebrew original implies a person, and because practically speaking only a human being would be in the house. Cats and dogs may have been kept in the house in those days, but they were not acceptable as sacrifices. Sacrificial animals, such as oxen, sheep, and goats, were certainly not found in the house. Also, Jephthah says "comes out of the doors of my house *to meet me*," which can only refer to a human being. Thus, Jephthah expects one of his servants to meet him after the battle, and he intends to dedicate that person wholly to God's service.

The whole burnt sacrifice represents the consecration of the whole person to God, wholly dedicated to Him, as Paul says in Romans 12:1, "I urge you therefore, brethren, by the mercies of

God, to present your bodies a living and holy sacrifice, well-pleasing to God." Jephthah knew the Scriptures, as we have seen, and he was filled with the Spirit. It is utterly inconceivable that he would offer to kill a human being in exchange for a victory from God. Not only is this unthinkable in terms of the conscience of the believer, it is also the case that Jephthah knew that sinful man can never be a sacrifice acceptable to God. In fact, that is one of the primary reasons why there is no human sacrifice in Scripture except for the sacrifice of the one perfect human who ever lived, Jesus Christ. Moreover, just as the people prevented Saul from killing Jonathan (1 Sam. 14:45), so priests and people would not have stood idly by and allowed such an abomination as human sacrifice to take place. (And it would have been an abomination, not primarily because it would have been a murder, but first of all because a sinful human being is not an acceptable sacrifice to the Most Holy One.)

Rather, it is clear from the sequel that he had in mind some permanent service to God that would prevent the person from living a normal life. We find in Exodus 38:8 and 2 Samuel 22:2 that women did serve full time at the Tabernacle, and we know from Leviticus 27 that such vows of service were possible; there can be little doubt but that this was what Jephthah had in mind. We find women serving the Incarnate Tabernacle in Matthew 27:55-56 and Luke 8:2f., and we find women set aside on a special roll to serve in the New Testament Church (1 Tim. 5:1-16).

But why the first person who comes "out of the doors of my house"? There is a specific reason for this, and it tells us much of what Jephthah had in mind, and why he mourned when it turned out to be his only child who came out. The doors of the house in Scripture are symbols of birth. They correspond to the "doorway" on the woman's body, where the baby is born.

This association of doorways with birth is common in the Bible, but it may seem strange to us, so we should get some verses in mind before proceeding further. In Genesis 18:10, it is while standing in the doorway of her tent that Sarah hears she will have a child. In 1 Samuel 1:9, Hannah is standing in the doorway of the temple when she hears that she will have a child. In 2 Kings 4:15 the Shunamite woman is standing in a doorway when she is told that she will have a son. In a reverse twist, Eli hears that God will kill his sons from Samuel who is standing in the doorway of the Tabernacle (1 Sam. 3:15ff.), and Jeroboam's wife is crossing the threshold of a house both when she hears that her child will die (1 Kings 14:6ff.), and also when her child dies under God's judgment (1 Kings 14:17). Thus, rituals conducted at doorways are new-birth rituals. At the exodus, when Israel came out through the doorways bloodied with the passover lamb, they were experiencing a new birth. Similarly, Jesus calls Himself the Door, and says that those who go through Him find salvation and a new birth (John 10:9).

The first person to come through Jephthah's door after the battle, then, is a kind of firstborn of his house after the battle. Sacrificing that firstborn is a way of establishing his house. How do we know that? Because the firstborn is a symbol for the entire house. When God passed judgment at the exodus, He struck at the houses of Egypt and Israel by threatening the firstborn. Blood on the *house* covered for the *child*. The firstborn is the right hand of the father, his principal heir (getting the double portion), and the representative and spokesman for the family. The sacrifice of the firstborn, as a substitute for the family, was the salvation for the rest of the family.

Human sacrifice is, thus, demanded in the Bible, but human beings are defiled by sin and are unacceptable. Thus, the lamb of Passover substituted for the firstborn. All the same, God claimed the firstborn of Israel as His own from that day forth (Ex. 13:2, 12; Num. 8:17). When the firstborn failed to serve Him, by building a golden calf (Ex. 32), God substituted the Levites for them (Num. 8:16). Notice, however, that the Levites were not put to death, but served at the Tabernacle. This is exactly parallel with Jephthah's daughter.

The sacrifice of the firstborn is the foundation for the building of the house. Among the pagans, killing children at the doorway, and building the house on their graves, was not uncommon. We have a recorded instance of this in 1 Kings 16:34, where we find (on a proper reading) that Hiel killed his firstborn son when he laid the foundations for the rebuilding of Jericho. The death of the firstborn was designed to satisfy the wrath of God (or of the gods) and ensure peace to the city. We know that it is only the death of Jesus Christ, the Firstborn of the Father, that is an adequate foundation for the City of God, the New

Jerusalem. The Church is built upon His substitutionary death.

There is more to all this, however, having to do with the basic victory-housebuilding pattern in the Bible. First, a battle is fought against the enemy. After the enemy is defeated, the triumphant king returns and builds a house. The spoils of the enemy are used to build this house, but the death of the first-born is also required. The whole book of Exodus follows this outline. Egypt is defeated, and its spoils are used to build God's house, and we notice that abundant blood sacrifices are made in connection with the building of that house, in addition to the Passover sacrifice which underlay it all and which substituted for the death of the firstborn. Similarly, it is when David was finally completely victorious, so that "the LORD had given him rest on every side from all his enemies," that he moved to build the Temple (2 Sam. 7:1ff.). This, of course, reaches its fulfill-ment in the work of Christ, whose defeat of Satan was simultan-eously a foundation-sacrifice, resulting in the creation of His new house on Pentecost.

This is precisely the way Jephthah is thinking in this passage. He wants to establish his dynasty. He has won the victory, with God's help, and now he offers to sacrifice his firstborn, the first person "born" from the doorway of his house after the battle. He vows to sacrifice this person to the Lord, to perpetual Taber-nacle service, in exchange for the Lord's building of his house.

In itself this was not an unreasonable request. Notice in 2 Samuel 7 that David wants to build God's house, but God says that this must wait for Solomon. God goes on, however, to guarantee David a perpetual dynasty, to build David's house (2 Sam. 7:12ff.). Why didn't God do this for Jephthah? Because Jephthah was not the one God had in mind, and Jephthah should have known it. He was out on three counts. First, he was a bastard. Second, he was not of the tribe of Judah. Third, God had not chosen him to be a king, but to be a judge.

Thus, God acts to frustrate Jephthah's design. Yes, Jephthah will indeed consecrate to Tabernacle service the firstborn of his house, but it will be his only daughter, and that will end his dynastic aspirations.

(We might summarize here the parallels between Jephthah and David. Both were exiled. Both gathered impoverished men around them. Both harassed the enemy for years. Both defeated the enemy and delivered Israel. The women sang and danced for both. Both aspired to build a house, but David's motives were relatively more pure.)

Jephthah's Aspirations Thwarted

34. When Jephthah came to his house at Mizpah, behold, his daughter was coming out to meet him with tambourines and with dancing. Now she was his one and only child; besides her he had neither son nor daughter.

35. And it came about when he saw her, that he tore his clothes and said, "Alas, my daughter! You have brought me very low, and you are among those who trouble me; for I have given my word to the LORD, and I cannot take it back."

36. So she said to him, "My father, you have given your word to the LORD; do to me according to what has proceeded out of your mouth, since the LORD has avenged you of your enemies, the sons of Ammon."

37. And she said to her father, "Let this thing be done for me; let me alone two months, that I may walk about and go down on the mountains and weep because of my virginity, I and my companions."

38. Then he said, "Go." So he sent her away for two months; and she left with her companions, and wept on the mountains because of her virginity.

39. And it came about at the end of two months that she returned to her father, who did to her according to the vow which he had made; and she knew no man. Thus it became a custom in Israel,

40. That the daughters of Israel went annually to commemorate [talk with] the daughter of Jephthah the Gileadite four days in the year.

The story of Jephthah is probably the hardest to understand in the book of Judges. This is partly due to the prejudice of most commentators, who have confused the matter horribly by insisting that Jephthah killed his daughter. The main problem, however, comes from the fact that all the basic elements in this story presuppose that we are familiar with certain fundamental ways of thinking that were common in the ancient, medieval, and early modern world, but that are completely unknown today. We have already mentioned the victory-housebuilding pattern, the correspondence between doorways and birth, and the notion of the sacrifice of the firstborn as a foundation for the city. Now we come to several other strange notions, which we also find hard to understand, among them the idea of going up to the mountains to mourn, and especially the idea of virginity and the sacrifice of virginity. We shall have to try to understand these matters as best we can.

First, after the victory Jephthah's daughter came out to him dancing. It was customary for the women to dance after a great victory, as we see in the dance of Miriam (Ex. 15:20) and in the dance of the Israelite women after the death of Goliath (1 Sam. 18:6). Apart from general joy and relief at the defeat of the threat, there is a very specific reason for these celebrations, which is revealed to us specifically in Jeremiah 31:4, "Again I will build you, and you shall be rebuilt, O virgin of Israel! Again you shall take up your tambourines and go forth to the dances of the merrymakers." The defeat of the enemy brings about peace and safety from rape, and makes possible the building of a house, with children. Jephthah's daughter, like her father, anticipates the building of his house.

Second, the passage stresses that she was Jephthah's only child. Any possible dynasty had to come through her. We know that Jephthah was interested in a dynasty because he was anxious to be made head of Gilead (11:9). The fact that it was she of all people who met him caused him anguish, for he realized that all his personal hopes were now dashed forever.

Third, Jephthah's mourning was not some mild regret, as those who defend him to the hilt want to make it out. He tore his clothes, an action which has a specific symbolic meaning in the Bible. A covenant is a bond joining two or more people. When those two people are ripped apart, the covenant is torn. Thus, for instance, in marriage man and wife are one flesh, and encircled by one garment (Ruth 3:9; Ezk. 16:8). The garment symbolizes the covenant. Now, death definitively rips two people apart. We know that what causes mourning and grief is the intense feeling of loss, of separation, caused by death. Death, then, rips apart the covenant that exists, whether formally or informally, between people (the close tie of marriage, for instance, or the looser ties of friendship). Thus, ripping the garment as a sign of the rending of a covenant is most appropriate for mourning (for instance, 2 Sam. 1:11; 13:31; Ezra 9:3).

Jephthah's mourning is cast in terms of the ripping of his daughter from him, and the rending of his house. There is no apparent joy in this for him.

He says she has brought him very low. The Hebrew word is actually "caused me to bow down." This word almost always is used for the bowing down of an enemy in humiliation or in death, though it is also used for acts of obeisance. Jephthah states that he is being forced to bow the knee to God's purposes, and forsake his own. This is an act of confession, of yielding to what God now makes clear, that he is to have no abiding house. Also, Jephthah is "troubled." Clearly, then, Jephthah has met with a reversal of his expectations here.

Why didn't Jephthah substitute a money payment for his vow? These monetary substitutes are set out in Leviticus 27:1-8. If a man dedicated a man or a woman to the Lord, such persons could not be accepted as such because only Levites were permitted into the courts to serve at the Lord's house. Accordingly, a monetary substitute was required. A woman was to be redeemed for 30 shekels of silver (Lev. 27:4). Why didn't Jephthah do this? The few commentators who have addressed this particular question have noted that there seems to be no explanation for it, unless we assume that when Jephthah made his vow he mentally excluded this "easy out." I think that the answer is to be found in another direction.

Leviticus 27:28-29 says, "Nevertheless, any proscribed [devoted] thing which a man sets apart [devotes or banishes] to the LORD out of all that he has, of man or animal or of the fields of his own property, shall not be sold or redeemed. Every proscribed [devoted] thing is most holy to the LORD. No proscribed [devoted] person who may have been set apart [devoted or banished] among men shall be ransomed; he shall surely be put to death." The word translated "devoted" in these verses is the same as the word Hormah, which we studied in chapter one. We found that a "Hormah" was a site devoted to destruction, fired from God's altar, and called a whole burnt sacrifice (Dt. 13:16). Thus, to "devote" something to God is the same as to offer it as a whole burnt sacrifice. To set something apart as holy was one thing, and such objects might be redeemed; but to set something apart as devoted was something else, here called "most holy," and such could not be redeemed. Since Jephthah vowed to offer this person as a whole burnt sacrifice, we realize that he was "devoting" him or her to the Lord, and thus no ransom was possible.

Usually this means the death penalty, but it is also possible to "devote" something or someone to God in life. Numbers 18:14 says to the priests, "Every devoted thing in Israel shall be yours" (and see Ezk. 44:29). Thus, the heart and essence of "devotion" was not destruction, but total dedication to the sanctuary of God. We see this also from the fact that to be "devoted" was also to be "*most* holy." Except for Jesus Christ, no man is ever called "most holy" (Dan. 9:24; Mt. 12:6). A concordance study of "most holy" will show that the food of the various sacrifices, and the various articles of furniture in the Tabernacle, were "most holy," and that only the Aaronic priests might have anything to do with them—ordinary Levites would be killed if they approached them (Num. 4:19). Thus, because of sin, no man could be "most holy" or devoted to God; but by eating of the most holy sacrifices, the Aaronic priests were *incorporated* into union with the most holy, just as the Christian is incorporated into the most holy Son of God by eating of His flesh and drinking of His blood in Holy Communion.

What emerges from this all too brief discussion is that any person devoted to God as most holy could not be redeemed, but had to be given totally to the sanctuary, the Tabernacle. Normally, because of sin, this meant death, so that the only persons thus "devoted" were persons who needed to be put to death. To our knowledge, except for Jesus Christ, Jephthah's daughter is the only person ever devoted to God in life. It meant that she could not be redeemed; it also meant that she would spend the rest of her life at the sanctuary of God. Doubtless she was not the only person ever thus devoted to God in life, but she is the only example we know of.

The daughter submits to the inevitable, and only asks that she be given two months to roam around the mountains to bewail her virginity. This would make absolutely no sense if she were about to be put to death, but it makes a lot of sense if she were about to be consigned to perpetual virginity. The whole point of having virginity is to lose it in the joys of marriage. The virgin in the Bible is the one who awaits the bridegroom; perpetual virginity is pure sterility, and is a Greek, not a Biblical, ideal (see Ps. 45). Jephthah's daughter "mourns" her virginity because she is now being torn from any future family life and from any future husband. Her arms will be empty.

She takes her companions. These are the other virgins who would have attended upon her in her wedding (Ps. 45:14). Now they join her in mourning what will never be. She says that she wants to "walk and go down upon the mountains." This is a curious phrase, and conjures in our minds an insane woman with wild hair screaming and running through the hills. Undoubtedly this is the wrong notion, and the action here is symbolic in character, though what it might mean is difficult to say. I should like to take a stab at it, though. We find that men pass, but the mountains remain, so that the mountains are spoken of as eternal or everlasting in Scripture (Gen. 49:26; Dt. 33:15). The dew of heaven is seen to drop down first upon the mountains, and then flow down to the plains where men live (Dt. 33:28; Ps. 133:3; Prov. 3:20). The mountain, a high place, is where God meets with man, and the gracious influences of His peace are brought down the mountain to the nation by His representatives. This was done most dramatically by Moses, who went up and down the mountain several times (Ex. 19, 20, 24, 34).

Corresponding to this mountain home of God is the Tabernacle home of God. The high priest brings the gracious influences of God's dewy peace from the enthroned Cloud out to the people. We find that there were women who ministered at the door of the Tabernacle (Ex. 38:8; 1 Sam. 2:22). These women (perhaps) were involved in passing God's messages to other women who came to the door of the Tabernacle to talk with them. We find (Jud. 11:40) that this was what Jephthah's daughter did for the rest of her life.

Thus, if we are right in our hypothesis, there is a correspondence between her ministry of bringing God's gracious words from His Tabernacle to other women, and her action of "coming down" on the mountains of Israel. At least in terms of the way ancient people thought, this is a valid suggestion. If so, then Jephthah's daughter spent time on the mountain spiritually preparing herself for a life of ministering God's Word to other women, and as part of that preparation she engaged in certain dramatic/symbolic actions that both showed forth and also psychologically reinforced to her the nature of her ministry ("coming down" upon the mountains).

This fits with the overall message of the passage, which is that man's dynasties may be cut short, and are not everlasting, while God's mountain and Tabernacle do endure from age to age. Jephthah's desire for an enduring house, through his daughter, must give way before the primacy of God's enduring house and mountain.

Verse 40 is obscure. The verb translated most often "lament, commemorate" actually means "recount," and occurs only one other place in the Bible, Judges 5:11. Most translators assume that Jephthah killed his daughter, so they are oriented toward translating the word "commemorate," but in fact it most likely means that the young women annually went to visit Jephthah's daughter, and to talk with her. Thus, she sustained a ministry to the other women of Israel.

Why for four days? The number four usually refers to the four corners of the world, and is a number thus for universality. Also, however, a week of seven days is divided into three days and four days. In the Bible, the third day is the day of the first judgment, and the seventh is the day of the final judgment (see Numbers 19:12ff.). My guess (and it is, again, only a guess) is that there is a connection between the two months of mourning (Jud. 11:37) and the four days spoken of in verse 40. If we think in terms of the Biblical symbolism of the week, a young woman is a virgin for two days, and then she is married on the third day. That gives her four days of married life and productivity before death. Jephthah's daughter lamented her virginity for *two* months, but when the third month (day) came, instead of passing into the married state, she was consigned as a sacrifice to virginity. Her marriage is what was sacrificed. Thus, the remaining four days of her life were also lived as a virgin.

In a sense, as we shall see, her sacrifice of marriage and fruitfulness is what made possible the marriages and fruitfulness of the other women of Israel. This is parallel to the work of Jesus Christ, for He did not marry and have children, nor did He exercise dominion, but His forfeiture of these things is what makes possible our enjoyment of them. He took the punishment that we deserve. I believe that the perpetual virginity of Jephthah's daughter was a sign to Israel that the fall of man, and their own sin and rebellion, brought upon them the curse of sterility and barrenness, and that only if this curse were taken by a willing substitute could they hope to have life and fruitfulness in the earth.

Thus, when the women of Israel came to talk with her four days in the year, they were confessing that they deserved four "days" of barrenness, and they were confessing that she had taken their curse upon her, as their substitute. This is the first way in which Jephthah's daughter was a continuing sign to Israel. She was a sign that they deserved perpetual sterility for their sins, and deserved to be in mourning, but that God had given them fertility because Someone had taken upon Himself the curse that they deserved. Jephthah's daughter can indeed be a type of Christ, because as He represented the Church, He stood in union with the Bride, and thus assumed a feminine role.

But there is a second aspect to the ministry of Jephthah's daughter. She served as a type of the Old Covenant church, waiting for the Lord to come and consummate the marriage. The Bride of the Lord had to be "most holy," lest she die (Dt. 22:13-21), and a picture of that is virginity. The high priest, representing the Lord to the people, had to marry a virgin (Lev. 21:13). Paul compares Satan's seduction of Eve with loss of virginity in 2 Corinthians 11:3, and says that the Church has been reconstituted a pure virgin by the work of Christ, and thus a fit bride for Him. (In a sense, the New Covenant Church is already married to Christ, and bears fruit for Him; but in another sense, she is still a virgin, awaiting His final coming.)

Israel did not want to wait for the coming of their true Lord, King, and Husband. They kept wandering off to fornicate with the Baals (and "baal" means lord, husband), and they kept wanting to go ahead and set up a human king. God kept telling them to trust Him, and to wait. Jephthah, like the rest of Israel, was impatient. With good motives, desiring to lead God's people in righteousness, Jephthah wanted to establish a kingdom and a dynasty. God turned him down. The perpetual virginity of Jephthah's daughter was a sign to Jephthah and to all Israel that the Lord alone was King and Husband, and that He had not yet come to marry the Bride and establish the Kingdom. Year after year, the presence of Jephthah's daughter at the Tabernacle door was a reminder of this fact to Israel. If they understood her message aright, Jephthah's daughter was the gospel for Israel.

Some day their Prince would come.

Let us pull together what we have seen thus far. First, the households of Israel were established on the substitutionary death of God's firstborn, at Passover. Apart from this, all their houses would be destroyed. Jephthah wanted to extend this principle further to the establishment of his kingdom and dynasty, but God did not permit it.

Second, the fertility of the households of Israel were established on the substitutionary sacrifice of God's Virgin. The foxes had holes, but Jesus had no home, no dominion. He took no wife, and had no children (Is. 53:8); rather, He was cut off. He sacrificed His normal human fruitfulness, taking the curse upon Himself, in order that His people might be fruitful. Jephthah's daughter pictured this for Israel.

Third, the perpetual virginity of Jephthah's daughter was a reminder to Israel that they had better not grow impatient and seek another Husband and King. The King is coming some day, and the wise *virgins* will take along enough oil (faith) to wait until that midnight when the Bridegroom suddenly arrives.

Finally, there is a fourth message to Israel in the virginity of Jephthah's daughter. It is that their political security as a nation did not depend on the might of arms, or on the power of a human kingly house, but on the inviolable moral virginity of the Church. This is part of the heart of the message of the book of Judges, and even though it will take us into some byways if we want to understand it, it is important that we see the whole message found in this remarkable story.

In order to understand this, we have to think like ancient Hebrews, and not like modern people. For the ancient world, a garden, a house, a city, or a temple was like a woman. Adam was supposed to guard the garden, and he was also supposed to guard his wife. The Song of Solomon compares the woman to a garden several times in the course of the book. In all languages, the words for city, garden, and the like are feminine, and we speak of a city as "she" in English today.

Let us take a look at the city in the Bible, remembering that what is said of the city is also true of the house, tent, Temple, Tabernacle, and other enclosed homes for humanity. The city has walls and gates. The purpose of these walls and gates is to keep the enemy out. The goal is that the city be impregnable, and note that English word—it directly connects the city with the woman. Thus, the city has to be a virgin, sealed against attack.

Jerusalem is referred to as an impregnable virgin repeatedly in Scripture (2 Kings 19:21; Is. 37:22; Jer. 14:17; 18:13; Jer. 31:21; Amos 5:2). The attack on Jerusalem is thus the rape of a city (Lam. 1:15; 2:13). Other "impregnable" or sealed cities are also called virgins (Sidon: Is. 23:13; Babylon: Is. 47:1-3). Just as Eve was "built" from Adam (using an architectural term, Gen. 2:22), so Jerusalem would be rebuilt as a virgin (Jer. 31:4).

Similarly, a woman is described as a house or city, so that the girl in Song of Solomon is either a "wall" or a "door," and since she is a virgin, she is a "wall" (Cant. 8:9-10). She is like a walled and locked garden (Cant. 4:12; 5:1).

An invading army, which breaks through the gates of the city, also rapes the virgins. When the city gates are impregnable, so are the virgins of the city. Thus, the safety and security of the virgin daughters of Israel was a symbol of the safety and security of the whole land. Their inviolability corresponded to the inviolability of the whole culture (Lam. 1:4; 2:10).

Similarly, the book of Judith (part of the religious literature of Old Testament times, found in the Apocrypha) is an extended allegory in which Judith, like Deborah a mother in Israel, acts to defend and protect her daughter, the city Bethulia ("Virgin"). The opening paragraph of Judith establishes the book as a work of fiction, in that it contains obvious and deliberate mistakes designed to point the reader to its allegorical character (such as that Nebuchadnezzar was king of Assyria, which any Jewish child would know was wrong). When Holofernes attacks Bethulia, Judith goes out to him. He is ravished with her beauty, and she strings him along until he is drunk. Then she chops off his head, and the Assyrian army flees in panic. The symbolism in the story depends on our understanding the connection between Holofernes's assault on the town "Virgin" and his desire to possess Judith, and the connection between the virginal inviolability of the town "Virgin" and the moral inviolability of Judith which gives her the strength to crush the serpent's head. This is but one more example of a common "way of thinking" found in the Bible, in popular Jewish literature, and throughout the ancient, medieval, and early modern world. We don't have walled cities any more, and so we don't think this way any longer.

Thus, the sealed gates of the city correspond to the sealed status of the virgin. The gates of the city are opened to receive the king and lord of the city, just as the virgin gives herself to her lord on the wedding night.

Just as the serving women at the door of the Tabernacle generally signified the fruitfulness of God's kingdom, so also the special presence of virgins at the doorway of the Tabernacle was a symbol of the sealed impregnability of God's holy kingdom. When God's house was kept pure from moral defilement, a sealed virgin, then also the land of Israel would be protected from assault. If God's house were defiled, or left unprotected due to the failure of the Levite guardians to shield her, then so also the nation would be unprotected.

When we see this we get a new dimension on what is found in 1 Samuel 2:22, "Now Eli was very old; and he heard all that his sons were doing to all Israel, and how they lay with the women who served at the doorway of the tent of meeting." Not only was this an act of moral outrage, sure to bring the curse of God; it was also a picture of how the priestly guardians of Israel were failing to protect the virginal integrity of God's holy bride. They themselves were "penetrating the veil," and leaving the "gates of the city" wide open to attack. As a result, Israel was defenseless against the Philistines, who ravaged the land and even took the Ark into captivity, and who killed Eli's sons (1 Sam. 4).

Thus, the fourth aspect of the ministry of Jephthah's daughter was this: She was an abiding sign to Israel that their protection from the enemy came from their moral purity and faithful virginity, as they awaited the coming true King. If they feared attack, if they feared the rape of their cities and land, they should act to protect the house of God, not to build up their own. If they would guard the most holy things, they would be safe, but if they looked to politics and the might of arms to save them, they would be destroyed.

Conclusion

Jephthah had hoped to build his own house and dynasty. This was not for purely selfish motives, but rather because like all of the rest of Israel, he had come to believe that a strong visi-

Judges

ble state, a human kingship, was needed for the protection of
Israel. With love for God in his heart, he believed that he was
the one to establish such a protection. He was wrong, for he dis-
regarded the laws concerning bastards and the prophecy that the
king had to come from Judah.

God gently reproved him, and in reproving him reproved all
Israel as well. God said to Jephthah, "Not your house, but My
house must be built. I accept your sacrifice of your firstborn,
but I have arranged it so that this sacrifice will end your house,
and build Mine. Your daughter will be a continuing sign to My
people that their safety depends on how well they guard themselves against moral and spiritual fornication, and on how well
they guard My house." Jephthah bowed to God's will, and
resumed his place as a judge.

11

JEPHTHAH: DESTROYING THE ENVIOUS
(Judges 12:1-7)

12:1. Then the men of Ephraim were summoned, and they crossed to Zaphon and said to Jephthah, "Why did you cross over to fight against the sons of Ammon without calling us to go with you? We will burn your house down on you."

2. And Jephthah said to them, "I and my people were at great strife with the sons of Ammon; when I called you, you did not deliver (*yasha'*) me from their hand.

3. "And when I saw that you would not deliver (*yasha'*) me, I took my life in my hands and crossed over against the sons of Ammon, and the LORD gave them into my hand. Why then have you come up to me this day, to fight against me?"

4. Then Jephthah gathered all the men of Gilead and fought Ephraim; and the men of Gilead smote Ephraim, because they said, "You are fugitives of Ephraim, O Gileadites, in the midst of Ephraim and in the midst of Manasseh."

This passage has also occasioned criticism of Jephthah. Criticism, however, is out of place. Jephthah here acts as the sword of the Lord, and Ephraim has gotten totally out of hand. Both Deuteronomy 17:12 and Joshua 1:18 specify the death penalty for those who rebel against the judge.

In the story of Ephraim and Gideon (Jud. 8:1-3) we saw the selfishness of Ephraim, and that they did not glory in the Lord's victory, but wanted glory for themselves. The same thing is seen here, only it has gotten worse. This time, Ephraim attacks the Lord's anointed messiah. This is equivalent to attacking the Lord, and marks them as enemies of God.

They threaten to burn Jephthah's house down on him, not a very wise thing to threaten him with in view of the immediate circumstances, as we have seen. This immediately reminds us of Abimelech (Jud. 9:48f., 52). In saying this, they threaten not only God's judge, but also the place of judgment. Theirs is a total revolt against the Divine order.

Jephthah says that he did call them, and that they did not come. We see here just a bit about the actual battle, in that apparently Jephthah was hard pressed at one point. Ephraim failed to come when summoned. It is interesting to note that these men, who present such a brave and threatening front now that the battle is over, apparently were cowards when it came to the real fighting. God had said that Israel was to learn to fight (Jud. 3:2), and to fight by faith. Those who did not trust God and respect His messiah not only refused to fight, but did not have the courage to fight either. But like cowards and bullies of all ages, Ephraim is now ready to fight.

Jephthah informs them that the battle was not his, but the Lord's. It was the Lord Who had delivered Ammon into his hand, says Jephthah. Jephthah thus admonishes them, and in so doing preaches the gospel to them, giving them an opportunity to repent. He tells them that when they complain about the victory, they are complaining about the Lord. Rather, they should give thanks for the deliverance.

Ephraim, however, does not repent. Instead they go out of their way to insult the Lord's anointed and his men. Pointing to Jephthah's band, they call them and all Gilead "fugitives from Ephraim." They say that the Gileadites are fugitives from justice, criminals. Ephraim says that they are justified in attacking Gilead, since they are just a bunch of criminals. Clearly, Ephraim struck the first blow, because they crossed the Jordan to attack Jephthah, and in verses 5 and 6 we see them trying to get back.

What we see here is unfortunately all too common in daily life and in the Church. After the victory against the real enemy, the righteous have to face complaining and insurrection from within the Church itself. There is always something, it seems, to criticize, and those offering the criticism are always people who could not be bothered with the real battle. Did the Church picket an abortion chamber? Did the clinic shut down? Wonderful, but now be prepared for a revolt in the Church itself. The people who were too busy to fight the Lord's battle will now, to justify themselves, attack the leadership in the Church. Be prepared, as Jephthah was, to deal severely with such people, for they are the worst enemies of all.

Notice also that Ephraim makes it easy on themselves by pretending that the righteous are wicked. They declare that Jephthah is an antichrist, that his people are a false church, and thus they are justified in going to war against him. There is no moderation in their behavior, no willingness to listen or be conciliated. This is another common tactic used by wicked people within society and within the Church. Once they have refused to listen to reason, and are determined to destroy God's good work, they seek to justify their actions by accusing the righteous of some great evil.

> 5. And the Gileadites captured the fords of the Jordan opposite Ephraim. And it happened when any of the fugitives of Ephraim said, "Let me cross over," the men of Gilead would say to him, "Are you an Ephraimite?" If he said, "No,"
> 6. Then they would say to him, "Say now 'Shibboleth.'" But he said "Sibboleth," for he could not speak so. Then they seized him and slew him at the fords of the Jordan. Thus there fell at that time 42,000 of Ephraim.

God's heavy humor is seen here again. Jephthah's men captured the fords of the Jordan, where the Ephraimites would have to cross to get home. This was the same tactic Ephraim had used against Midian (Jud. 7:24), and for which Gideon had praised them. Now it is used against them, for they have become spiritual Midianites, attacking God's people. Similarly, Amalek had been allied with Midian (Jud. 6:3). Now, however, Ephraim is showing itself to be a second Amalek, true to their roots (Jud. 5:14; 12:15), and they receive the judgment of Amalek. Moreover, in another humorous twist, it is now the Ephraimites who are the fugitives, as verse 5 pointedly brings out by using the same phrase as verse 4.

Numbers 26:37 gives 32,000 men as the number of Ephraimites who entered Canaan 300 years earlier. 42,000 of the cream of the warriors of the tribe of Ephraim are killed at the fords. This must have pretty well wiped out Ephraim as a political force for several generations to come. Continued belligerence meets its reward here. (The number 42 is possibly significant. It is seven times six, a sevenfold inadequacy. Forty-two youths mocked the ascension of Elijah to Elisha in 2 Kings

2:23f. In Revelation, 42 months is the period of oppression [11:2; 13:5].)

The purpose of the period of the judges was to teach Israel to war by faith. The Gileadites had tried to make war by finding a hero, not by faith in God (Jud. 10:18). Jephthah had believed that a strong kingly house was needed, another mistake. Ephraim wanted to make war to glorify themselves, not to glorify the Lord (Jud. 12:3). By these three negative examples, God was teaching Israel how *not* to make war.

The destruction of Ephraim shows the end results of pride and envy. The elimination of Ephraim as an opponent and competitor made possible the ascendency of Judah, the royal tribe, under David a couple of generations later. Even so, when David became king, Ephraim and Gilead joined in opposing him (2 Sam. 2:9). They were not able to succeed, however. Later, under Jeroboam, they rebelled against Solomon (1 Kings 11:26), but God forestalled it. God offered Jeroboam, and Ephraim, an opportunity to repent and serve Him. They could have the northern part of Israel, if they would serve the Lord (1 Kings 11:29ff.) Jeroboam and Ephraim, however, wanted a kingdom on their own terms, and the history of Northern Israel became a history of apostasy unrelieved by any revival.

Ephraim thought that they should be the leaders of all Israel. Yet, they did not even speak the same dialect as the rest of the land. They were way out of touch, and in no position to lead. They were unable to make a "sh" sound, and when asked to say "Shibboleth" (which means "ear of corn" or "flowing stream," scholars are unsure), they could only say "Sibboleth."

Once again, judgment took place at the Jordan river. This was the boundary of the land proper. It was the place of judgment, of transition from wilderness to Eden. Because some of the tribes had chosen to live across the Jordan (in Gilead), an altar of sanctuary had been erected as a sign of the unity of Israel (Josh. 22). Ephraim had denied that unity, despising the altar, committing the very sin the altar had been set up to prevent. "And the sons of Reuben and the sons of Gad called the altar Witness, 'For,' they said, 'it is a witness between us that the LORD is God' " (Josh. 22:34). In despising that witness, Ephraim had despised the Lord. Those who seek thus to split and destroy the Church must always be met with severe chastisement. For such people, their baptism (in the Jordan) will become their destruction (as it happened to Ephraim). The sign of unity (baptism) will become a sign of obliteration.

> 7. And Jephthah judged Israel six years. Then Jephthah the Gileadite died and was buried in the cities of Gilead.

Perhaps the fact that Jephthah only judged six years is designed to show one more time that man's rule does not reach to the sabbath, and thus that a True and Future Judge and King must come to bring in the everlasting, sabbatical kingdom. We also see something else here. The other judges are said to be buried with their fathers, or in their cities. Jephthah's father was (almost certainly) unknown, and here we see that his burial site is also unknown. He emerged from "Gilead," and he returns to "Gilead." He emerged as a man with no family name, and he left no family name. Thus, he was a sign to Israel that ultimately their trust for such things must be in the Lord alone. The bastard and the eunuch (and Jephthah is in some sense both) might not have been full citizens of the earthly kingdom in the Old Covenant, but they had a heavenly home, from which they could never be driven, and which will endure forever.

12

SAMSON THE NAZIRITE
(Judges 13)

Before considering the story of Samson, we have to get some background. Samson was a Nazirite, indeed the preeminent Nazirite in the Bible. To understand his life and work, we have to look back at Numbers 6 to find the Command/Promise of the Lord as regards the Nazirite vow. Then we can see how Samson responds to this, and God's evaluation. The word *nazir* primarily means "separated," though it is tied to other concepts as we shall see. It is a seldom used word, and thus each time it is used it is important for us to consider the light it sheds on the Nazirite.

We cannot take the space to go into all the details of the Nazirite vow, but we can briefly survey the parts most relevant for us. Basically, the Nazirite was an Israelite who took a special vow, and became a special temporary priest. Since a priest is a guardian of the Bride/Land, usually the Nazirite vow was taken in wartime, as we saw in Judges 5:1. God's war camp was like His Tabernacle, a holy place, and the men who were in it had to be holy, like the priests. Holy war was the main idea in the Nazirite vow, though "holy war" might easily include any battle against sin, so that the vow might be appropriate for any number of occasions. Let us look at the laws governing this.

Alcohol and Grapes

Numbers 6:2. . . . When a man or woman makes a special vow, the vow of a Nazirite, to dedicate himself to the LORD,
3a. He shall abstain from wine and strong drink; he shall drink no vinegar, whether made from wine or strong drink.

Leviticus 10:9 prohibits the priest from drinking alcohol when in the Tabernacle. The reason given is so that a distinction

221

might be made between the holy and the profane, and between the clean and the unclean. We might think that this means alcohol is profane or unclean, but the reverse is actually the case. It is because men are unclean that they may not relax with alcohol in the presence of God. In the New Covenant, men are commanded to drink wine in the sacrament of the Lord's Supper, with God, in the holiest of all times, the time of worship.

To understand this we must set aside our 19th century Unitarian prejudices against alcohol, which unfortunately have infected the Christian Churches to a great degree, at least in America. In the Bible, wine is for joy (Jud. 9:13; Ps. 104:15). It is a picture of future blessings, when the curse on the ground (thorns; brambles) is overcome and the vine flourishes. It thus has a close tie to the Sabbath, to the time when a man's work is finished, and he can relax in the presence of God.

The Biblical example of this is Noah. Sadly, the common understanding of Noah is misguided. Lamech prophesied when Noah was born that he would give rest and comfort "from our work and from the toil of our hands from the ground which the LORD has cursed" (Gen. 5:29). After the Flood, in sabbath rest, Noah planted a vineyard, and drank of the wine. He got "drunk," but all this means is that he became relaxed and went to sleep. Noah was certainly no drunkard! Noah uncovered himself in the privacy of his tent, laying aside the robe of his office and duties. It was a time for sabbath relaxation.[1]

Later, as a sign that he had completed the task set before him for the moment, Abram was given wine by Melchizedek (Gen. 14:18). Similarly, at the annual feast in the seventh month, the Feast of Tabernacles, Israel was encouraged to drink wine and strong drink in God's presence (Dt. 14:26).

So, why was the priest forbidden to enjoy a little sabbath wine in God's presence? It was to show that the Aaronic priesthood was inadequate, and that the sabbath had not come. One of the most important tasks of the priesthood was to *exclude* Israel from God, to guard His holy places from

---

1. Notice that Ham is the one who sins, by invading Noah's privacy, and it is Ham's son who is cursed. There is a "second fall" here in this passage, but it is in Ham, not in Noah. See my essay, "Rebellion, Tyranny, and Dominion in the Book of Genesis," in Gary North, ed., *Tactics of Christian Resistance* (Tyler, TX: Geneva Ministries, 1983).

defilement. The priests were like cherubim, guarding the door of Eden; and indeed, cherubim were embroidered on all the doors of the Tabernacle. The prohibition against alcohol was a sign to Israel that they had not come to sabbath in the final sense, and the inclusion of alcohol in the Lord's Supper is a sign that in the New Covenant the Church has come to that sabbath in Christ, for He has completed man's task. In the Old Covenant, the labor of the priest was never finished, so he never sat down (Heb. 10:11); but Christ has sat down. The priest took upon himself the curse of endless toil, so that God's people might rest. Because the priest did not sit down, and did not drink wine in the Tabernacle, Israel could sit down at Passover and drink wine (as Jesus did at the Last Supper) and for the same reason they could drink at the Feast of Tabernacles.

The Nazirite, as a temporary priest, had a holy task to perform. Until he had completed it, he was not to sit down and enjoy the sabbath blessing of alcohol.

> 3b. Neither shall he drink any grape juice, nor eat fresh or dried grapes [raisins].
> 4. All the days of his separation he shall not eat anything that is produced by the grape vine, from seeds even to skins.

Grapes were forbidden for the same reason alcohol was. To understand this more fully, we have to go to Leviticus 25. During the sabbath year, and during the year of Jubilee, Israel was not to plant, nor to harvest. They might eat whatever they found growing, and God promised a triple harvest the year before the sabbath so that they would have food stored up. They were not allowed to eat any wild grapes, however. God said, "Your grapes of trimmed vines you shall not gather" (Lev. 25:5), and "You shall not . . . gather in from its untrimmed vines" (Lev. 25:11). What is of interest is that the word "untrimmed" is the word *nazir,* from which we get Nazirite. The grape vines growing everywhere during this year are like the hair on the head of the Nazirite. Both are "separated" from trimming.

The grape was a symbol of the fertility and blessing of the land. As noted above, it was a sign that the curse of thorns had been replaced with the blessing of the vine. When Israel came to Canaan, they were impressed right off by the riches of grapes they found there (Num. 13:20, 23). The grape was a sign, once again, of the arrival of sabbath blessing, and of the end of the curse. When the sabbath year came, however, Israel was not allowed to eat the grapes! This was a sign to them that the sabbath had not really come, and was still really in the future. They were not ready to enter into this privilege. (Similarly, the word *nazir* is used in Lev. 22:2 to show that when the priests were unclean, they were not allowed to eat the holy food.) In the New Covenant, the highlight of the Lord's Day is the meal with God, drinking the juice of the grape. For us, the sabbath has come in Christ.

Once he had finished his work and had dedicated it to the Lord, "afterward the Nazirite may drink wine." Just so, when Jesus finished His work, He sat down at the Father's right hand, and now drinks wine anew with us in the Kingdom (Matt. 26:29).

Long Hair

5. All the days of his vow of separation no razor shall pass over his head. He shall be holy until the days are fulfilled for which he separated himself to the LORD; he shall let the locks of hair on his head grow long.

The third separation demanded of the Nazirite is that he not use a razor during the time of his vow. If he becomes defiled, he must shave his head, and let the hair grow back, starting over as it were (Num. 6:9, 11). At the end of his vow:

18. The Nazirite shall then shave his dedicated head at the doorway of the tent of meeting, and take the dedicated hair of his head and put it on the fire which is under the sacrifice of peace offerings.
19. And the priest shall take the ram's shoulder, boiled, and one unleavened cake out of the basket, and one unleavened wafer, and shall put them in the palms of the Nazirite after he has shaved his Nazir [his "untrimmed"].

Let us note initially three things here. First, the hair is referred to as the Nazir (v. 19). This connects it up with the untrimmed grape vines of Leviticus 25. Second, throughout this passage what is dedicated is the "head," and what is shaved is the "head."

We remember that Satan's head is to be crushed. We have an opposition here between the crushed head and the dedicated head. Third, at the end of the vow, the head is shaved, and it is all dedicated to God by burning it up. It is put in the fire with the Peace Sacrifice, and we realize that this hair is "food for God."

How are we to understand this? Well, remember that the luxuriant grape vine is a symbol of the fertility and bounty of God's land. Similarly, the hair on the head is a sign of life and power and glory (as we shall see). It is the consecrated land that produces grape vines, and it is the consecrated head that produces this hair, a sign of man's works. The bounty of the land is all there, waiting for man to eat, but man may not eat of it on the sabbath until his own work is completed and is acceptable to God. The sign of the Nazirite's work is his hair. When it is completed, and is acceptable to God, then the Nazirite may enter into sabbath and eat grapes.

This is a picture of the work of humanity, defiled in Adam, but accomplished by Christ. The people of God are His vine (Is. 5:1-7). God has a right to "eat" of this vine, which means tasting of man's works and approving of them, and drawing man into closer and more glorified fellowship with Himself. (See Revelation 3:16 for a picture of Christ tasting the works of the Church.) Accordingly, every sacrifice burned up as food for God was accompanied by a libation of wine for God to drink (Num. 15:1-10). When God came to His vine, however, He found that the grapes were bad (Is. 5:1-7). The works of man were unclean, tasted foul, and thus man could not enter into sabbath rest. Jesus, however, is the True Vine (John 15:1-6), and in union with Him our works do taste good to God. Thus, we may enter into sabbath rest with Christ, and drink wine with Him in the Lord's Supper.

Man may not eat of the Nazir-grapes of the land until his own Nazir-hair is acceptable to God. When God is pleased, man may enter into sabbath. The Nazirite's long hair, thus, was a picture of the good labors of humanity, performed in the power of the Holy Spirit. At the end of his labors, the Nazirite devoted his hair to God, returning to Him the power that He had given, and asking God to taste his works. God's approval of the work of the Nazirite is seen in God's letting him drink wine. It is just so with Christ, the Greatest Nazirite.

As a sign that it was the power of the Spirit that produced the long hair — life and power — the Nazirite braided his hair into seven locks (Jud. 16:13). Seven is the number of fulness, and the number of the Spirit (Rev. 1:4; 3:1, etc.).

This long hair is a crown. The word *nazir* is used for the crown worn by the high priest and the crown worn by the kings of Israel. These crowns set apart their wearers to a special task, a task of showing what man's labors are supposed to be, a task fulfilled by Christ. Just as the Nazirite cuts off his hair and offers it to God, as a sign that his labors are ended, so the saints take off their crowns and cast them at the foot of God's throne (Rev. 4:10). Both the high priest and the king were crowned by anointing with oil, as well as with physical crowns. These crowns were for life, and not cast down before God until death. The Nazirite's crown had to be temporary, something that could be dedicated at the end of his vow. The hair was suitable for this.

Long hair was not suitable for a man unless it was a sign of something specially given to God. The rebel prince Absalom wore his hair long as a sign of his glory and power (2 Sam. 14:26). Since he did not dedicate it to the Lord, but used it for his own glory, God hanged him from the neck by it, destroying his Satanic head (2 Sam. 18:9).

1 Corinthians 11:1-10 tells us that long hair is a sign of power and glory in a woman, but not in a man. The long hair is her crown of authority. A man's hair is to be short. Why, then, did the Nazirite male have long hair? I believe the best and simplest explanation is this: When the priest/Nazirite represented God to the people (in the Tabernacle or in the war camp), he was a male before the Bride. Thus, only men might be priests, and only men might lead in war (so Deborah sought out Barak). When, however, the priest or Nazirite stood before God, he stood as a representative of the Bride, and thus as the woman par excellence. The hair of the high priest was also *nazir,* but in a different way. Instead of growing long, it was consecrated by being anointed with holy oil (Lev. 21:10-12; *nazir* is usually translated "consecrated" in v. 12). We might notice, for instance, that the oil of the bride in Song of Solomon is described in much the same language as the anointing oil of the high priest (Ex. 30:22-25; Cant. 4:10, 14).

In a sense all of man's work is labor performed for the Bride to please her Husband. When the man presents his labors to God for approval, this is precisely the Bride (humanity) presenting her works to the Lord. The man normally wears short hair, because his fundamental "imaging" of God is to represent the Divine Husband in all of life. The woman wears long hair, for she pictures the Bride in all her fulness. When the man takes the role of representing the Bride before the face of God, an exceptional role for him, he may join the woman in letting his hair grow long or in anointing it with oil; but such a role is only temporary for him, and he is to go back to being a man when it is over.

Permanent Nazirites such as Samson, Samuel, and John the Baptist were pictures of humanity as a whole for their whole lives, and thus pictures of Christ, Who accomplished the labor of the Bride that Eve (and Adam) failed to do.

Death

6. All the days of his separation to the LORD he shall not go near to a dead person.

7. He shall not make himself unclean [ceremonially dead] for his father or for his mother, for his brother or for his sister, when they die, because his separation to God is on his head.

8. All the days of his separation he is holy to the LORD.

Death is the curse upon man. Since man is made of dust, the curse is that to dust he shall return (Gen. 3:19). The ground is cursed with death. Thus, anything that gets dirt on it can be see as having the curse of death on it. Accordingly, "dirty" or "unclean" means (symbolically) "death."[2] The reasoning works the other way also. Getting dirty means getting death on you, but also contacting death in any form is equivalent to getting dirty, or "unclean." Thus, anything resembling death in the Bible is called "dirty, dusty, un-clean." All the laws of cleanness and uncleanness have to do, one way or another, with death.

---

2. Note, for instance, that in the Old Covenant men always wear shoes or sandals. This is to avoid contact with the cursed soil. Only the serpent travels with his belly or flesh in the cursed soil. Clean land animals wear shoes (hooves). Men only take their shoes off on "holy ground" (Ex. 3:5; Josh. 5:15). Entering someone's house, you washed your feet, to avoid bringing contamination into the house (Gen. 18:4; 19:2; 43:24; Jud. 19:21; Luke 7:44). In the death and resurrection of Christ, the curse has been removed from the soil.

Adam should never have faced uncleanness, for he should never have faced death. The Nazirite, taking the role of Adam in guarding the Garden/Bride of Israel, is not to come in contact with death either. He is assiduously to avoid it.

Now the Nazirite, with his consecrated head, is set aside to be a holy warrior, to be a "head-crusher extraordinaire." He will constantly come into contact with death, and according to the laws of the war camp, he will have to purify himself (Num. 31:19; Num. 19:11ff.). Normally, however, the holy war only lasts for a few days, so that after the battle, the shaving of the head because of defilement is the same as the shaving of it at the end of the vow (as in Num. 6:9-21). A man who takes a Nazirite vow for some other reason, or a woman who takes it, might have to shave his or her hair during the course of the vow if he or she comes in contact with a dead person, and then continue on with the vow.

Now, what about the permanent Nazirite? Numbers 6 does not say anything about him. Perhaps Samson shaved his head and started over after each battle. Or, perhaps his was a lifelong battle, so that the battle was never really over, and so he did not ever have to shave because of wartime defilement. We do not know. We are not told, and I can find no hint of an answer. Thus, it probably is not important (or God would have told us).

We cannot take the space to go into the rest of Numbers 6, about the sacrifices offered by the Nazirite, interesting though they are. We now have an idea of what the Nazirite was supposed to be, however. He was a picture of what Israel as a whole should be, indeed of humanity as a whole. He was singlemindedly dedicated to a particular dominion task. He confessed that he was excluded from God's bounty because of sin, but he confessed that God was giving him the power to perform this task. He expected at the end of this task to enter into rest and relaxation.

Thus, Samson as a Nazirite was a picture of what Israel should have been doing. They should have been singlemindedly dedicated to the Lord, and they would then have had power to deal with the Philistines. Each of them would have been as powerful as Samson (Lev. 26:8; Dt. 32:30; Josh 23:10). They had sinned and compromised, however, and so they had become blind and weak. Samson was a picture of both aspects: strong in the Lord, but weak in his compromises.

The following is an outline of the Samson narrative:

I. The Prophecy of Samson's Birth (Judges 13:1-23)
   A. The Angel's Appearance to Samson's Mother (13:2-7)
   B. The Angel's Appearance to Manoah (13:8-14)
   C. The Angel's Refusal to Commune (13:15-23)

II. Samson's Early Ministry (13:24 - 15:20)
   A. Samson's Birth and Growth (13:24-25)
   B. Samson's Offer of Marriage (14:1 - 15:8)
      1. Samson Seeks a Philistine Wife (14:1-4)
      2. Samson Defeats "Philistine" Lion (14:5-9)
      3. Samson's Wife Betrays His Trust (14:10-20)
      4. Samson's Wife Given to Another (15:1-5)
      5. Samson's Wife Destroyed (15:6-8)
   C. Israel's Betrayal of Samson (15:9-19)
      1. Israel Turns Samson over to Philistia (15:9-13)
      2. Samson Destroys more Philistines (15:14-17)
      3. God Gives Samson Water (15:18-19)
   D. Samson's 20-Year Judgeship (15:20)

III. Samson's Old Age Compromise (16)
   A. The Harlot at Gaza (16:1-3)
   B. Seduced by Delilah (16:4-20)
   C. Chastisement and Repentance (16:21-22)
   D. Victory through Death (16:23-31)

Pure Grace from God

13.1 Now the sons of Israel again did evil in the sight of the LORD, so that the LORD gave them into the hands of the Philistines forty years.

We see oppression here, summarizing what has already been stated in Judges 10:6-7; but there is nothing about repentance or crying to the Lord for deliverance. Maybe we are supposed to assume that Judges 10:7-16 applies also to the Philistine oppression, but all it directly speaks about is the Ammonite. Here in Judges 13, the passage by its silence emphasizes that man simply does not have it in himself even to repent. Salvation is all of grace. Ultimately that has been true each time, but we are now at the end of the decline of the period of Judges, and it is as if we hit rock bottom. The same point is made in the first chapters of 1 Samuel, concerning the birth of Samuel, the killing of Eli's house, and the capture of the Ark. A third witness to this truth is found in the Book of Ruth. At the end of this chapter of our study we shall take a look at the birth of Obed and the joint ministries of Samuel and Samson at this stage in the history of Israel.

The First Visitation

2. And there was a certain man of Zorah, of the family of the Danites, whose name was Manoah; and his wife was barren and had borne no children.

3. Then the angel of the LORD appeared to the woman, and said to her, "Behold now, you are barren and have borne no children, but you shall conceive and give birth to a son.

4. "Now therefore, be careful not to drink wine or strong drink, nor any unclean thing.

5. "For behold, you shall conceive and give birth to a son, and no razor shall come upon his head, for the boy shall be a Nazirite to God from the womb; and he shall begin to deliver (*yasha'*) Israel from the hands of the Philistines."

6. Then the woman came and told her husband, saying, "A man of God came to me and his appearance was like the appearance of the angel of God, very awesome. And I did not ask where he came from, nor did he tell me his name.

7. But he said to me, 'Behold, you shall conceive and give birth to a son, and now you shall not drink wine or strong drink nor eat any unclean thing, for the boy shall be a Nazirite to God from the womb to the day of his death.' "

At this time, most of the tribe of Dan had apostatized and moved north, refusing to worship the Lord properly and refusing to conquer the territory God had given them (Jud. 17, 18). Manoah and his wife were among the faithful remnant still living in the proper territory of Dan.

As mentioned above, there is a theme of new beginnings in this chapter, and verse 5 highlights this by saying that Samson will *begin* to deliver Israel from the Philistines. Full deliverance would await the coming of David.

Why did God appear to the woman rather than to her husband? Is it because Manoah was a bad man, so God had to bypass him? Not at all. It is because the theme, again, is the Seed of the Woman. God appears to the mother, to instruct her how to raise up the Seed. Similarly, God appeared to Rebekah, not to Isaac, to give instruction about the primacy of Jacob over Esau (Gen. 25:22f.).

Manoah's wife was barren. The salvation of the world is to come through the Seed of the woman, but because of sin, the woman is barren. How can the Seed be born? Only by means of a miracle. Thus, all three wives of the patriarchs in Genesis were barren. God had to open the wombs of Sarah, of Rebekah, and of Rachel. The child born on the other side of the miracle, in each case, was the Seed (note especially how Joseph delivers his older brethren).

All three mothers of permanent Nazirites in the Bible were barren. The mother of Samson we have before us. Samuel's mother was barren, and a miracle was needed (1 Sam. 1:6, 11). The mother of John the Baptist was both barren and past menopause (Luke 1:7, 15). In each case, a son who is set apart for extraordinary work, and given especial power of the Spirit (signified by long hair), is born of a barren woman.

The fulfillment of this theme comes when the Ultimate Seed and Nazirite, Jesus Christ, is born of the ultimately barren womb, the womb of a virgin. The genealogy of Matthew 1:1-17 points to the impotence of the natural line of Adam. The genealogy issues in Joseph, who is not the father of Jesus.[3] The genealogy shows the need for a total miracle, a wholly new beginning, for the salvation of the world. This is also the meaning of the births of Samson, Samuel, and Obed (which may well have been the same year).

Why didn't Gabriel appear to this woman, as he did to Mary? It is because it is important for the "angel of the Lord" to be the one bringing the message. This is because the angel of the Lord is the Captain of the Lord's hosts (Josh 5:15 - 6:2). This Divine war captain is also the One Who appeared to Gideon (Jud. 6:11ff.). God is going to war, and He is raising up yet another Joshua, another Savior who brings *yasha‘* to His people.

The child is to be a Nazirite, and this is specified in terms of alcohol, avoiding all ceremonial death (unclean food), and long

---

3. Numerologically, this genealogy is 42 generations long, seven *sixes*, a fulness of *human inadequacy*. Of course, this genealogy also shows that Jesus inherited the official status of Isaac and Solomon, the seed/sacrifice and the son/king, from Joseph.

hair. What makes certain foods unclean is the fact that the unclean animals resemble the serpent in having their feet in contact
with the now cursed dust — crawling on their bellies as it were,
and in eating "dirt" — manure, carrion, and the like. Avoiding
unclean (dirty, Satanic) food was a sign to Israel not to eat, and
thus make alliances with, the pagan (Satanic) nations round
about. (See Lev. 11; 20:22-26.) Samson's involvement with three
Philistine women seems to involve "eating unclean food," that
is, forming alliances with the wicked. (As we shall see, his offer
of marriage to a Philistine girl in his youth has a different meaning; and we may question whether or not Delilah was a
Philistine.)

We may add as a note that Samson's mother was not to drink
alcohol or eat grapes, etc., while she was pregnant. The Bible
assumes that Samson is already alive in the womb, and thus
already set apart. This is one more line of evidence to show that
from the moment of conception, there is a new life in the womb,
and so abortion is murder. Also, we may say on the basis of this
passage that if the fetus is to avoid sacramentally unclean food
in the womb, then the fetus also participates in the sacramental
food of Holy Communion in the womb. When Samson's
mother ate grapes, they went to her baby as well as to her. When
a Christian woman eats Christ's flesh and drinks His blood,
these go to her baby also. When the baby is born, he is
separated from the spiritual protection of the womb, excommunicated as it were, and must be baptized into the Church before he can once again partake of the Lord's Supper.

One other thing to notice in this paragraph. The woman
already recognizes Who the Messenger is, even if she cannot put
a name to Him (v. 6). It takes Manoah, as we shall see, a while
to figure it out. The woman is more alert to the Spirit here. If we
simply moralize or psychologize on the text, we might say that
Manoah is just not a very spiritual man. We ought to take a
theological explanation, however. Manoah as the father stands
in Adam, and his wife stands in Eve. She is the mother of the
Seed. Manoah's blindness is a sign of the blindness of Adam in
sin, and Adam was much more guilty than Eve (2 Cor. 11:3; 1
Tim. 2:14). Adam must be set aside, and replaced by a son who
will be a Second Adam, a Son of Man (Adam), who will do the
work Adam failed to do, and who will turn around and save his

father. Manoah is not personally a wicked man, but his spiritual slowness is a sign of the inadequacy of the first Adam due to sin, and of the failure of the Old Israel.

The Second Visitation

8. Then Manoah entreated the LORD and said, "O Lord, please let the man of God whom Thou hast sent come to us again that he may teach us what to do for the boy who is to be born."

9. And God listened to the voice of Manoah; and the angel of God came again to the woman as she was sitting in the field, but Manoah her husband was not with her.

10. So the woman ran quickly and told her husband, and said to him, "Behold, the man who came to me the other day has appeared to me."

11. Then Manoah arose and followed his wife, and when he came to the man he said to him, "Are you the man who spoke to the woman?" And he said, "I am."

12. And Manoah said, "Now when your words come to pass, what shall be the boy's mode of life and his vocation?"

13. So the angel of the LORD said to Manoah, "Let the woman pay attention to all that I said.

14. "She should not eat anything that comes from the vine, nor drink wine or strong drink, nor eat any unclean thing; let her observe all that I commanded."

This section of the chapter consists of five questions or requests made by Manoah to the Angel of the Lord. The answers he receives are in four instances rebukes. Manoah's wife had been spiritually sensitive enough not to ask questions, but simply to receive the Word of the Lord. Manoah was much farther from sensing what was really going on.

In case we have missed the point, this second visitation reinforces the fact that the message is for the woman. Though God hearkens to Manoah's prayer that the visitor "come to us," the Angel appears to the woman alone, not to him (v. 9). The Angel is gracious, however, in waiting for Manoah to arrive, and is willing to talk with him. In answer to Manoah's question about his son, the Angel says that the duties are for the woman, and in describing them says less to Manoah than He had said to the woman (v. 13f.). It seems as if there is nothing for the father to do; he is not involved. It seems as if Manoah is snubbed. Theologically, Manoah simply has nothing to do with this new birth and new beginning. When the Angel appears to the woman, she is once again alone in the field, Manoah not with her (v. 9). Theologically speaking, the Miracle Child is begotten of God's Angel in the womb of the mother, and the first Adam's lineage is set aside. Physically, of course, this was only true of Jesus Christ, and physically Manoah did beget Samson. The text, however, emphasizes that it is God's miracle that brings this to pass, and thus stresses the total impotence of the fallen first Adam.

No Peace with God

15. Then Manoah said to the angel of the LORD, "Please let us detain you so that we may prepare a kid for you."

16. And the angel of the LORD said to Manoah, "Though you detain me, I will not eat your bread, but if you prepare a burnt offering, offer it to the LORD." For Manoah did not know that he was the angel of the LORD.

17. And Manoah said to the angel of the LORD, "What is your name, so that when your words come to pass, we may honor you?"

18. But the angel of the LORD said to him, "Why do you ask my name, seeing it is Wonderful?"

19. So Manoah took the kid with the grain offering and offered it on the rock to the LORD, and He performed wonders while Manoah and his wife looked on.

20. For it came about when the flame went up from the altar toward heaven, that the angel of the LORD ascended in the flame of the altar. When Manoah and his wife saw this, they fell on their faces to the ground.

21. Now the angel of the LORD appeared no more to Manoah or his wife. Then Manoah knew that he was the angel of the LORD.

22. So Manoah said to his wife, "We shall surely die, for we have seen God."

23. But his wife said to him, "If the LORD had desired to kill us, He would not have accepted a burnt offering and a grain offering from our hands, nor would He have showed us all these things, nor would He have let us hear things like this at this time."

With the final two questions of Manoah, there is a shift of focus from the message to the Messenger. We might have outlined the chapter accordingly: Message (13:2-14); Messenger (13:15-23).

The author of Judges wants us to contrast this scene with Judges 6. Gideon makes the same offer, and God is willing to eat with him. Gideon sacrifices a kid, an animal that symbolizes a youth, just as Manoah offers a kid. Gideon is fearful after seeing the Angel of the Lord, just as Manoah is. After the sacrifice, God states that there is peace between them, affirming for us that this was a Peace Sacrifice, and thus a communion meal. Here, however, God refuses to eat with Manoah, and thus with Israel. God is frankly at war, not at peace, with a sinful Israel. What is needed is a whole burnt sacrifice, a confession of sin and judgment. Communion can only come after the re-consecration of person (whole burnt sacrifice) and works (grain offering). With Gideon, God ignited the fire, ate the food, and vanished from sight. Here, however, something more amazing happens.

While the kid is being burned up, the Angel steps onto the altar and goes up in flames! This is a picture of the substitutionary death of Jesus Christ. This is the great turning point we are needing at this time in history. Because God has sent his Son/Angel to be the Substitute, history can turn around and Israel can be delivered from the Philistines. Because Christ has died, Samson can live. God's holy Kid (Child) substitutes for the kid (child) of Manoah and his wife. When the Angel goes up in flames, it is a picture that God Himself will take the punishment that men deserve!

The Angel will not give His Name. This shows that He is God. The only Name He gives is "Wonderful," and this is explained in the next verse in that "He performed wonders." Wonders are miracles, the unexpected surprises that God humorously brings into history in order to reverse the expectations of both the wicked and the righteous. God did wonders in Egypt (Ps. 78:12). God here does wonders again. There will be a new exodus from this new bondage.

Because God is a God of wonders, we cannot put Him in a box. We cannot have a "name" for Him that completely describes Him, so that we can say we understand Him fully. (The reason Jehovah's Witnesses are so insistent on the name "Jehovah" is precisely because they think they can control God by using that name.) God is always a God of surprises, and the more truly childlike our faith is, the more delighted we shall be at His daily newness and His continuing surprises. Samson, the surprise child, will do one funny wondrous thing after another, as a sign to Israel of God's holy humor. Like Jesus Himself, Samson's name will be "wonderful" (Is. 9:6).[4]

Neo-orthodox theologians may say that God's wonderfulness means that man cannot understand Him at all, but that is not what we find here. God did wonders, but Manoah and his wife "looked on." We can indeed see God's wonders, and we can know much about Him, but we can never put Him in a box.

When Manoah sees this, he realizes Who it is he has been speaking with. His response is a proper one: fear. Up to now he has been spiritually blind, and so no communion has been possible. Now, however, on the other side of the miracle, his eyes are opened, and he is surprised that judgment does not fall. We realize that, because of the sacrifice, peace has been restored. His wife, spiritually more aware, realizes that God has a purpose for them, and is not going to curse them.

Samson's Birth

24. Then the woman gave birth to a son and named him Samson; and the child grew up and the LORD blessed him.

25. And the Spirit of the LORD began to stir him in Mahaneh-Dan, between Zorah and Eshtaol.

Samson comes from *shemesh,* and means "sun." Thus, Samson is another fulfillment of Deborah's prayer that God's children be like the sun in its *might* (Jud. 5:31). Psalm 19 gives us a vignette of the life of Samson in verse 5 when, commenting on the sun, it says, "which is as a bridegroom coming out of his chamber; it rejoices as a strong man to run his course." Samson, the strong man, will also be the mighty bridegroom.

---

4. This is as good a place as any to point out that the book of Judges lies behind Isaiah 9:1-7. The stories of Deborah and Gideon lie behind 9:1 (Zebulun and Naphtali). Barak is referred to in 9:2 (the great lightning bolt). Gideon's dividing the spoil of Midian is referred to in 9:3-4. The theme of government resting on a man's shoulders, prominent in the Jephthah story, is referred to in 9:6, and the perpetuity of that reign, in contrast to Jephthah, in 9:7. The names "Wonderful" and "Mighty" in 9:6 allude to Samson. We can, in fact, continue with this and point out that the arrogance of Ephraim comes up in 9:8-10, and the idea of two enemies at once, from Judges 10, comes up in 9:11-12.

We are told that God blessed Samson as he grew up, and we are told that the Spirit stirred him up to his great work. We need to bear this in mind when we read the next two chapters of Judges, for at first glance some of his actions seem morally wrong. At this point, however, as we shall see, Samson is under the guidance of the Spirit, and his actions are pure.

Samson, Samuel, and Obed

We see in Judges 13 again the theme of God's initiative. Man is lost in sin, but God takes steps to save him. To get the full picture of what is going on in the history of redemption at this point, we have to put Samson together with Samuel and Obed.

According to Judges 13:1, Israel was in bondage to Philistia for 40 years. This bondage ended at the battle of Mizpah (1 Sam. 7:7-13). The battle of Mizpah happened 20 years after the battle of Aphek (1 Sam. 7:2), when the Ark was briefly captured. Samuel was a youth, just coming into his ministry at the time of the battle of Aphek, when Eli died (1 Sam. 3, 4).

Putting all these things together, we get the following clear chronology. About the time the Philistine bondage began, God appeared to the mother of Samson, and she conceived. Simultaneously God answered the prayer of barren Hannah, and she conceived. Both children were Nazirites, born of dead wombs. They formed a testimony of two witnesses to Israel that God was doing a new work to save them.

When Samson was about 20 years old, God began to stir him up, and he offered marriage to a Philistine girl. This would have to be about the time of the battle of Aphek, when the Philistines took a much stronger hold over Israel. At this very time, Eli died and Samuel began his public ministry.

God restrained the severity of the Philistine oppression during the second 20 years by two means. The first was Samson's wild and unpredictable activity in harassing Philistia. The second was the capture of the Ark, which frightened the Philistines greatly, and made them treat Israel more carefully (1 Sam. 5, 6).

At this time, when Israel was so thoroughly compromised in sin, a new birth was needed. We have looked at the new birth theme in Judges 13. Let us look at it briefly in 1 Samuel 1-3. We have noted the barrenness of Hannah and the miracle birth of

Samuel. We also find the problem pictured symbolically in the Tabernacle in 1 Samuel 3. Eli was going blind, and at the same time the lamp in the Tabernacle was about to go out (3:2, 3). These two things go together, and they are explained by the phrase "the word of the LORD was rare in those days; visions were infrequent" (v. 1). The light was going out, and the Word was not going forth.

One night, the Lord visited Samuel in the dark "womb" of the Tabernacle. God gave His Word to Samuel. Up until that time, Samuel did not "know the LORD" (3:7). This experience was a new birth for Samuel, and enabled him to give a new word to Israel. Just as the doors of Hannah's "house" had been closed until opened by God's miracle, so Samuel is the one who opens the doors of God's house (v. 15), and when Samuel comes out of the Tabernacle-womb through the doors, he comes out as one born a second time. Now there is a message from God, and it is a message of judgment on the old Adams, Eli and his house.[5]

Thus, the theme of a radically new beginning is present with Samuel as with Samson. There is a third aspect to God's work at this time, and it is the capture of the Ark (1 Sam. 4 - 6). As a Substitute for His people, God Himself goes into captivity to Philistia. All the parallels here are with the exodus from Egypt, as God wars against and disgraces the false gods, as He visits plagues upon Philistia, and as the Ark is sent away adorned with spoils. The Philistines understood this fully (1 Sam. 6:6). This new bondage and exodus makes possible a new beginning for Israel. Just as the Angel offered Himself as a sacrifice to make possible the birth of Samson, so the Ark goes into captivity and oppression to make possible the freedom of Israel. It is the beginning of a deliverance that will culminate with David and Solomon.

All this is going on while Samson judges Israel. It is not all brought into the theology of Judges, but it is part of Biblical theology as a whole, and so it is well that we take some notice of it. It is entirely possible, given the chronology, that Samson's youthful offer of marriage (salvation) to Philistia comes at the same time as the captivity of the Ark. It is certain that Samson's

---

5. See J. Gerald Janzen, " 'Samuel Opened the Doors of the House of Yahweh' (1 Samuel 3:15)," in *Journal for the Study of the Old Testament* 26 (1983):89-96.

destruction of the five lords of the Philistines and of much of the Philistine nobility happens just before Israel's defeat of Philistia at the battle of Mizpah. From the perspective of 1 Samuel, Israel is able to defeat Philistia because of a whole burnt sacrifice that takes away their sin (1 Sam. 7:8-11). From the perspective of Judges, that same victory is due to the final and mightiest work of Samson, the Savior, who shattered Philistia and made their defeat certain. Both perspectives are true, and both are necessary.

The book of Ruth gives us a third perspective on the death and resurrection of Israel at this time. The birth of Obed was at about the same time as that of Samson and Samuel. According to 2 Samuel 5:4, David was 30 years old when Saul died, and according to Acts 13:21, Saul reigned for 40 years. Thus, David was born in the tenth year of Saul's reign. We know that Samuel judged for 20 years, until the end of the first Philistine oppression at the battle of Aphek (1 Sam. 7:2). We also know that Samuel was "old" when he appointed his sons judges over Israel (1 Sam. 8:1). If Samuel was 40 years old at the battle of Aphek, he might have been called "old" at the age of 60. This gives us a 40-year judgeship for Samuel, which is eminently reasonable. David was, then, born about 50 years after Samuel began to judge, or when Samuel was about 70 years old.

David was the eighth of Jesse's sons (1 Sam. 16:11), so let us assume that Jesse was 50 years old when David was born. That means Jesse was born when Samuel was 20 years old. We have every reason to believe that Jesse was Obed's firstborn (1 Chron. 2:12), so Jesse could have been born when Obed was 20 years old. Jesse's father, Obed, thus was born about the same time as Samuel. Even if we are off by several years, we have established that Obed was born roughly the same time as Samson and Samuel.

What does this mean? A study of the genealogy of Ruth 4:18-22 shows that David, God's planned true king, was descended from Obed. No Obed, no David. Obed, though, was heir to Elimelech (by levirate marriage, born on Naomi's knee), and Elimelech's line had died out under the curse of God. No Elimelech, no David, no king. The king had to come from Judah, and not until the tenth generation, as we have seen. The God-appointed kingly line, however, had apostatized and been wiped out. Only the levirate marriage of Ruth (as Naomi's surrogate) to Boaz (as Elimelech's surrogate) made possible the coming of the true kingship. Thus, the book of Ruth presents us with the death and re-creation motif in a form different from that either of Judges 13 or 1 Samuel 1–7.

Elimelech, a Judahite from Bethlehem, refused to accept the judgment of God when famine came, and fled the land of promise to the land of Moab. To see the apostasy and stupidity of this, we need to remember that Moab had *refused* bread to Israel in the wilderness. Elimelech left the land of milk and honey for Moab! Predictably, he died there. Meanwhile, God had granted new life to Israel (Ruth 1)

Naomi returned to Israel in bitterness, and changed her name to Mary, which means "bitter" (Ruth 1:20). Her womb was dead, her sons were dead, her husband was dead — a striking picture of the death of the first Adam under the curse of being cast out from the Garden of Eden (land of milk and honey). God, however, graciously provided Naomi a surrogate in Ruth, and the levirate law made possible a rebirth to her family. Obed, indeed, is called Naomi's redeemer (Ruth 4:14f.).

In all three of these stories, which happened simultaneously in the history of redemption, we see God working to grant resurrection out of judgment and death. Israel had not repented, but God gave them Samson. Israel was in moral blindness, but God wiped out Eli, took the judgment upon Himself (in Philistine exile), and raised up Samuel. Israel was dead, having cast herself out of the land, but God raised up a true king (Obed–David) in spite of man's sin.

As a brief appendix to this discussion, I should like to suggest that just as Judges was written, most probably by Samuel, to argue against humanistic kingship, so Ruth was written in part to display the qualities of a true Godly king. Boaz is the example of a true king, and his descendant David becomes the first true king of Israel. Note also that Elimelech means "God is king," which is ironic since he did not honor God's kingship in his life — but this establishes kingship as a theme in Ruth. Also, the son granted by the "miracle" of rebirth is named Obed, "servant," another indication of what a true king is like. Possibly, Ruth was written during the time Saul was in apostasy and David was already anointed, as a pro-David "tract for the times."

13

SAMSON: THE MIGHTY BRIDEGROOM
(Judges 14-15)

The labors of Samson can be considered in four dimensions: his involvement with "Philistine" women, his Nazirite vow, his work of stirring up Israel, and his ministry to Israel.

All three stories about Samson have to do with Philistine women (and even if Delilah was not a Philistine, she associated herself with them, so may be counted as one). At the beginning of his life, he offers marriage and salvation to a Philistine girl. This is a picture of how Israel should relate to the nations, for Israel was to be priest to the nations. Israel was to preach the Word to the nations, and as a priest portray the Divine Husband to them. Israel was not doing so, but instead was conforming itself to the nations. Samson's early work is a positive portrayal of the gospel, which Philistia rejects, with dire consequences.

At the end of his life, we have two stories about Samson fornicating with Philistine women. This is a negative picture, showing how Israel should not relate to the nations. Whoring after Philistine culture leads to impotence, blindness, and death, as Samson found out. In this, he was an object lesson to Israel.

Second, as a Nazirite, Samson pictures to Israel that tremendous strength was available to them if they would live faithfully to God. If they would separate from uncleanness, they could all be Samsons, and the Philistines would be wiped out overnight. If they compromised their priestly status, however, they would wind up as Samson did.

Third, since Israel was at ease under the generally benevolent rule of the Philistines, it was necessary for someone to stir them up. God took the initiative, and with Samson provoked an ascending series of confrontations with Philistia. This made Israel embarrassed and fearful, and they even bound Samson over to the Philistines at one point. Eventually, however, Samson succeeded in sharpening the antithesis to the point where co-operation was no longer possible, and Israel could no longer compromise. Samson forced Israel to act.

Finally, Samson's ministry to Israel was accomplished primarily through his wild and extraordinary acts. Samson was God's big joke on the Philistines. He did not look strong, but he was. Humor, as we have noted, involves the unexpected. The gospel is the great specimen of God's humor, for just when Satan thought he had won, he lost. Samson keeps doing funny things that turn the tables against the Philistines.

"Have you heard the latest thing Samson has done?" Such would be the talk at the watering places of Israel (see Jud. 5:11). There is nothing prosaic about the things Samson did. The striking character of the stories meant that they would be talked about everywhere, and this would help stir Israel up to its duties. Moreover, Samson went around making up little poems, jingles, which would circulate around. (These remind me of Muhammed Ali's little poems, and like the champ, Samson was no dummy, even if he pretended to be one.) Third, Samson stuck funny memorial names on things, like "Jawbone Hill" (15:17), or more serious names like "The Caller's Spring" (15:19). These also would poke into the consciousness of Israel.

Let's listen in to some conversations. First, one from Samson's early ministry:

Jared: "Did you hear about what Samson did the other day?"

Eliezar: "No, what? Tell me!"

Jared: "He got 300 foxes, can you believe it? Then he tied their tails together, put torches between them, and set them out in the Philistine's wheat. It was all burned down!"

Eliezar: "Boy, I guess the Philistines are going to be mad now. They'll probably come steal all our barley. Thanks a whole lot, Samson!"

Jared: "Yeah, maybe. But it sure is funny to think about all those foxes."

Now let's listen to another conversation 20 years later:

Uriah: "Did you hear that Samson went to visit a Philistine whore in Gaza the other night?"

Saul: "No, really? What's he doing that for? He's a judge. He's supposed to set a good example, and keep himself pure from people like that. He's a Nazirite. He's supposed to keep a stricter rule than the rest of us."

Uriah: "Well, I don't know. Maybe he's just a man like everybody else."

Saul: "Yeah, but that's compromise, and he's the one that's not supposed to compromise."

Uriah: "Well, uh, that's right, but maybe none of us ought to be compromising. . . ."

We can take one more example:

Abner: "Did you hear about Samson carrying off the gates of the city?"

Amnon: "Yeah, he left the city wide open. We could have moved in and conquered it."

Abner: "That's true. How come we didn't?"

A Philistine Wife

14:1. Then Samson went down to Timnah and saw a woman in Timnah, of the daughters of the Philistines.

2. So he came up and told his father and mother, saying, "I saw a woman in Timnah, of the daughters of the Philistines; now therefore, get her for me as a wife."

3. Then his father and his mother said to him, "Is there no woman among the daughters of your brothers [relatives], or among all our people, that you go to take a wife from the uncircumcised Philistines?" But Samson said to his father, "Get her for me, for she is right in my eyes."

4. However, his father and mother did not know that it was of the LORD, for he [or, He] was seeking an occasion against the Philistines. Now at that time the Philistines were ruling over Israel.

Samson goes *down* to Timnah, and comes back *up* to his parents. Israel is living in the hills; Philistia controls the plains. Timnah was two miles west of Beth-Shemesh, the house of the Sun God. Samson is God's true sun, God's replacement for the false Canaanite worship of the sun.

Samson's parents call his attention to the basic Biblical principle that believers do not marry unbelievers. It seems that they are correct, but we are told in verse 4 that God was guiding Samson; indeed, it was not simply "God" superintending Samson by Divine providence, but it was the Lord, the Covenant God of

Israel, who was guiding him. We know from Judges 13:24-25 that the Spirit was guiding Samson at this time. He says in verse 3, "she is right in my eyes," which means that he judges that this is the right thing to do.

God had forbidden intermarriage with the Canaanites (Ex. 34:11-17; Dt. 7:1-4). The Philistines were not actually Canaanites, however, but cousins of the Egyptians, and there was no explicit prohibition on marrying Egyptians. Generally speaking, however, God's people were certainly not to marry unbelievers.

Moses had married an outsider, and Aaron and Miriam had complained about it (Num. 12). Indeed, we see intermarriage later on as well. Uriah the Hittite was married to Bathsheba. If Bathsheba was an Israelite, then this was a mixed marriage (except that Uriah was a convert). If Bathsheba was also a Hittite, then David's marriage to her was a mixed marriage (except again she was a convert). Note that the Hittites were indeed a branch of the Canaanites. Thus, God's prohibition on intermarriage has to be taken in a covenantal sense. If a Canaanite man or woman converted, he or she might intermarry with Israel.

What Samson's parents did not realize is that this was a missionary task. An offer of marriage to a woman outside Israel would ordinarily be a bad thing, but when it is the messiah who makes the offer, it is an act of evangelism. God offers to incorporate Philistia into His bride, and the sign of that is Samson's offer of marriage to this girl. This will become clearer as we go along, because the test put before this girl is whether she will put her trust in Samson, the Lord's messiah, or in the power of the Philistines. Her failure to trust Samson results in her destruction, and similarly the failure of Philistia to repent results in theirs.

There is an ambiguity in verse 4. Was it God or Samson who was seeking an occasion against the Philistines? Indeed, the Hebrew indicates a constant seeking. Commentators, assuming Samson to be blinded by lust at this point, have generally moved in the direction of seeing God as the one seeking occasion. More likely, however, it was Samson who was actively seeking occasion. We have already shown that he was being guided by the Spirit at this point. Rev. G. M. Ophoff has commented on this to good effect: "It cannot be that he truly loved that woman and that as some interpreters maintain, he actually expected to find a covenant of true love and fidelity in a Philistine family. What he expected to find was hatred and infidelity. For he was seeking occasion. It is not true that he put forth his riddle in a most peaceful spirit and that he meant not to bring the hidden antagonism to light. He meant to do exactly that; for he sought occasion. It is not true that he did not foresee that the wedding would give rise to conflict. He did foresee. It is not true that he was bent on avoiding conflict; he wanted conflict and was eager for it. If he did not want conflict and was not even expecting it, if he did think to find love and fidelity in that heathen family, we would not know what to make of the man. Then certainly his expliots were solely of the flesh. But this they were not. He wanted conflict because God had commanded him. And his obedience was the obedience of love—love of God and His people."[1]

As we shall see, Samson had this whole event planned out from the beginning. Ophoff probably goes too far in saying that Samson had no love for the young woman. I think he misses the evangelistic aspect of the passage, the genuine offer of salvation to Philistia as signified by Samson's offer of marriage to the Philistine girl.

This brings up the question, why did Samson want an occasion? Why not just start out killing Philistines? It would certainly have been morally proper, since God had raised him up as a judge and deliverer, and the Philistines had no business in Israel's land. A state of occupation is a state of war, and it would have been all right for Samson simply to have declared war on the Philistines and had at them. Why, then, seek an occasion?

I believe there are two reasons for this. First, as noted above, there is a genuine offer of conversion and salvation made to Philistia in all this. Had they accepted the gospel, the war could have ended that way. Second, however, Samson acted in such a way as to expose the true character of the Philistines, and to stir Israel up. Israel was asleep in Philistia. The Philistines were not all that bad, and Israel was happily intermarrying with them. What happens to Samson is designed to expose the fact that the

---

1. From an essay by G. M. Ophoff in *The Standard Bearer,* volume 21; as cited by H. C. Hoeksema, *Era of the Judges* (Grandville, Michigan: Theological School of the Protestant Reformed Churches, 1981), p. 238f.

Philistines are not trustworthy. They are oppressors. They are betrayers. They don't accept Israelites as equals. If you try to intermarry with them, you get burned. Thus, by seeking an occasion, Samson was looking for something that would get his countrymen to see what was really going on, something that would rile them up.

The Philistines were Egyptians, as Genesis 10:14 shows us. Captivity to the Philistines is, then, theologically equivalent to captivity to Egypt. This is very important in understanding the capture and exodus of the Ark in 1 Samuel, and it is important here. The guardian of Egypt was the lion-like Sphinx, and it is a lion that attacks Samson as he goes down to the Philistine town. The Sphinx was the master of riddles, and in defeating the Philistines with his riddle, Samson defeats the Sphinx. The Egyptian Sphinx represented the sun-god, so that the face of the Sphinx could be a Pharaoh, also a representative of the sun. Samson as the true sun defeats the false sun of the lion-Sphinx. These are underlying motifs in the story, but they would have been understood at the time. For their sins, God's people had been returned to Egypt, but God was defeating Egypt once again.[2]

A Philistine Lion

5. Then Samson went down to Timnah with his father and mother, and came as far as the vineyards of Timnah; and behold, a young lion came roaring toward him.

6. And the Spirit of the LORD rushed upon him mightily, so that he tore him as one tears a kid though he had nothing in his hand; but he did not tell his father or mother what he had done.

7. So he went down and talked to the woman; and she was right in Samson's eyes.

8. When he returned later to take her, he turned aside to look at the carcass of the lion; and behold, a swarm of bees and honey were in the body of the lion.

9. So he scraped it into his palms and went on, eating as he

---

2. "The original idea of the Egyptian sphinx was that of an imaginary quadruped, human-headed, living in the desert, and assumed by the sun-god Ra as his incarnation, for the purpose of protecting his friends. Out of this conception grew the idea of the sphinx as the guardian of a temple, a deity, or a tomb. . . ." James Baikie, "Sphinx," in James Hastings, ed., *Encyclopedia of Religion and Ethics* (Edinburgh: T. & T. Clark, 1920).

went. When he came to his father and mother, he gave some to them and they ate it; but he did not tell them that he had scraped the honey out of the body of the lion.

What happens here is a picture of the attack of Philistia against Israel. The lion signifies strength and often represents mighty powers that attack Israel. Just as David kills a lion before killing the uncircumcised Philistine Goliath, so Samson fights a lion first (1 Sam. 17:33-37). Samson kills the lion of Philistia. Once the lion is dead, the land once again becomes a land of milk and honey. It is the death of the lion that makes this possible.

(While in a general way it is obvious that the lion's attack pictures the Philistine/Egyptian assault on Israel, we can see that the author of this narrative has made it fairly explicit by means of literary parallelism. Note this comparison between Judges 14:5f. and 15:14:

14:5f. And behold, a young lion came *roaring* toward him.
And the Spirit of the LORD came upon him mightily,
So that he tore him as one tears a kid. . . .
15:14 The Philistines *shouted* as they met him.
And the Spirit of the LORD came upon him mightily,
So that the ropes that were on his arms were as flax that
is burned with fire. . . .

In both cases, they roar/shout as they meet Samson, the Spirit rushes on Samson, and Samson tears something apart. Clearly the roaring of the lion parallels the shouting of the Philistines. In addition, as noted above, the lion guarding the entrance into Philistine territory proper is parallel to the Sphinx that guards Egypt. Samson's destruction of the lion is his destruction of the guardian of Philistia/Egypt, and lays Philistia/Egypt open to invasion by God's people.)

Deuteronomy 33:22 says of Dan, "Dan is a lion's whelp, that leaps forth from Bashan." Just as Samson is the true sun to replace Beth-Shemesh, so he is the true lion who defeats the false lion of Philistia. He is a picture of the Most Perfect Danite, the very Lion of God, Jesus Christ.

If we assume that Samson used his hands to scrape the honey out, then we have to assume that he made himself unclean. The text does not say this, however. We ought to assume that this Spirit-led man used a tool to scrape the honey out into his palm. Giving the honey to his parents meant that the land would again become a land of milk and honey once the Philistine lion had been slain (and compare Ps. 19:5 and 10).

Why didn't he tell his parents? Because he was ashamed because he had broken his vow? There is no reason to think he broke his vow, though. We find out later on why Samson did not tell them. Under the guidance of the Spirit, Samson recognized the meaning of the lion's attack. He planned to use it against the Philistines. In order for his riddle to be a real test of his wife, no one else might know about it. The girl alone will know, and so he will know exactly who betrayed him, if she does betray him.

A Riddle for the Philistines

10. Then his father went down to the woman; and Samson made a feast there, for the young men customarily did this.

11. And it came about when they saw him that they brought 30 companions to be with him.

12. Then Samson said to them, "Let me now propound a riddle to you; if you will indeed tell it to me within the seven days of the feast, and find it out, then I will give you 30 linen wraps and 30 changes of clothes.

13. "But if you are unable to tell me, then you shall give me 30 linen wraps and 30 changes of clothes." And they said to him, "Propound your riddle, that we may hear it."

14. So he said to them,
"Out of the eater came something to eat;
"And out of the strong came something sweet."
But they could not tell the riddle in three days.

Back in those days, a truly "macho" man was not only physically strong, he was also clever. Contests of songs and riddles were as important as contests of strength. Samson seeks to defeat (and even convert) Philistia by words before going out to battle against them. If they had realized the threat implied in the riddle, that the defeat of the Philistine lion would bring sweetness to Israel, and that Israel would consume those who sought to consume them, they might have repented.

Also, riddles were keys. The Sphinx guarded his territory by means of a riddle. If a man could not tell the riddle, the Sphinx would kill him. The classic example of this comes from the story of the Theban Sphinx. The riddle was, "What has four legs in the morning, two legs at noon, and three legs in the evening?" The Sphinx killed travellers who did not know the answer, until Oedipus solved the riddle.. A greater than the Sphinx is here, however, for Samson has already slain the lion-guardian. If the Philistines can solve the riddle, they will have the key to Samson's secret, and they will have power over him.

The wedding feast always involved freely flowing wine, as at Cana (John 2:1-11). Did Samson violate his Nazirite vow? We are not told so, and there is no reason to think so. Since his hair was long, everybody knew he was "weird" anyway. They would have known he was under a vow (for the pagans had similar vows), and he could gracefully have refused alcohol.

Not being a wealthy Philistine, Samson could not provide the retinue that a wedding feast should have, so the Philistines provided it. This was a sign of Israel's weakness and humility in the face of Philistine domination. Thirty men were provided as "friends of the groom." The number 3 and multiples of it occur throughout this passage, and except for the numbers 7 (14:12, 15, 17) and 1000 (15:15f.) no other number occurs:

14:6 "the Spirit of the LORD rushed upon him mightily" three
        times, 14:19; 15:14
14:11 30 companions
14:12 30 linen wraps and 30 changes of clothing
14:13 30 linen wraps and 30 changes of clothing
14:14 3 days
14:19 30 slain Philistines
15:4   300 foxes
15:11 3000 men of Judah

The clue to understanding this use of the number three is in Judges 14:14. As we have noted before, the third day is the day of preliminary judgment, which puts men back on the track and makes it possible for them to do good works and come to the final judgment of the seventh day. It is precisely such a preliminary judgment that Samson brings upon Philistia, since he is only *beginning* to deliver Israel (Jud. 13:5). Moreover, the judgment of the third day is an opportunity to repent, before the final judgment of the seventh day. Thus, Samson's judgments against Philistia always contained grace, because they were not final. In order to stress that this is the nature of the situation, God providentially arranged for the number 3 to occur repeatedly in the events, and the writer of Judges highlighted it.

Clothing in the Bible is a sign of dignity and office. A contest for clothing was a kind of contest for honor. If Samson won, they would have to honor him with a gift of clothing, according him dignity. This would have been a sign of salvation to them, for they might have seen in it the need to submit themselves to the wisdom of Israel's young judge. On the other hand, if they won, Samson would have to give them clothing, a sign of their domination over Israel. While the symbolism here is not everything, and the men could have given clothes to Samson without thinking any more highly of him, all the same the symbolism would not have been lost on them either. They were determined not to lose.

Samson gives them the seven days of the feast. At the end, on the day of judgment, there must be a reckoning.

A Philistine Betrayal

15. Then it came about on the seventh day that they said to Samson's wife, "Entice your husband, that he may tell us the riddle, lest we burn you and your father's house with fire. Have you invited us to impoverish us? Is this not so?"

16. And Samson's wife wept before him and said, "You only hate me, and you do not love me; you have propounded a riddle to the sons of my people, and have not told it to me." And he said to her, "Behold, I have not told it to my father or mother; so should I tell you?"

17. However, she wept before him seven days while their feast lasted. And it came about on the seventh day that he told her because she pressed him so hard. She then told the riddle to the sons of her people.

18. So the men of the city said to him on the seventh day before the sun went down, "What is sweeter than honey? And what is stronger than a lion?" And he said to them,

"If you had not plowed with my heifer,
"You would not have found out my riddle."

19. Then the Spirit of the Lord rushed upon him mightily, and he went down to Ashkelon and killed 30 of them and took

their spoil, and gave the changes of clothes to those who told the riddle. And his anger burned, and he went up to his father's house.

20. But Samson's wife was given to his companion who had been his friend [best man].

This paragraph is not quite in chronological order. Apparently the 30 men came to the bride on the first day and threatened her, so that she wept all seven days of the feast (v. 17), but they came again and really put the fear into her on the seventh day (v. 15) so that she pressed Samson hard on that day (v. 17). Since this is so, why does verse 14 call attention to the fact that they could not tell the riddle on the third day? The reason is to call attention to the third-day symbolism in this passage, as discussed above.

I believe that Samson knew exactly what he was doing in all of this. He was testing her. He had not told the riddle to his parents, so if the 30 men found out, he would know exactly who had told them. He wanted to see if she would fear and trust him and his strength, or if she would fear and trust the men of Philistia. She would have to decide which was the stronger, and would have to cast her lot with one side or the other. If the reader has any question about whether this is really what is going on, it becomes crystal clear in Judges 15:6 — she feared the Philistines when they threatened to burn her house down, and the consequence of her action was that her house was burned down. She feared the wrong party, and trusted in the strength of the weaker force.

The men come up with the answer, before the sun goes down. The word for sun here is not the same as the one used in Samson's name, but the point is clear: The sun of Samson's glory is setting. The sun was rising on Gideon after his victory (Jud. 8:13, same word as here), but it sets on Samson here in his defeat.

The 30 men ask "What is sweeter than honey? And what is stronger than a lion?" Good questions. We already know that Samson is stronger than a lion. While the Philistines have gotten the answer to the riddle, they have missed its point. They are going to find out what is stronger than a lion! When we see this, we are moved to ask what is sweeter than honey. The Bible answers this also (Ps. 19:10): the law of the Lord.

Now we can come full circle. Samson the messiah is the strong one who offers something sweet to Israel and to Philistia: the word of God. Samson the messiah is the eater (of honey) who offers something to eat (the honey-word of God). The Philistines really do miss the point. We can hope that the Israelites at the watering places did not.

Samson views his wife's betrayal as adultery. It is not hard to see sexual overtones in the phrase, "plowing with the heifer (female)." Eve's hearkening to Satan's voice is pictured as adultery in 2 Corinthians 11:1-3. The wife is to hear and obey her husband, and to fear him. Failure to do so is adultery in one sense, and that faithlessness is what Samson points to here.

In the background is once again the riddle. If you get the riddle right, the Sphinx has to let you pass, so that the riddle is a key. Samson really won the contest—they could not figure out the riddle. Thus, he and his "heifer" should have been inviolable. The Philistines, however, had forced the "heifer" to tell them the riddle's answer. They had broken in in order to steal the key. This is analogous to a rape, since no man's wife should ever be forced to betray her husband.

By bringing these sorry events to pass, Samson and the Lord are making clear to Israel what the Philistines are really like. They cheat. Their sphinx-guardian-lion had been defeated, but they could not defeat Israel's true sphinx, Samson. So, they had to attack his wife in order to win.

Samson then goes and steal clothes to give them. Is this immoral? Samson says in Judges 15:11, "As they did to me, so I have done to them." As a judge, he lives by the strict rule "eye for eye, tooth for tooth." What Samson does in Judges 14:19 is a direct payback for what was done to him. How is this so? Just as the 30 men did not themselves figure out the riddle, but got the answer elsewhere, so Samson does not give them clothing himself, but gets it elsewhere. As far as Samson's killing the 30 men of Ashkelon is concerned, we need only remember that this is a time of war.

We should note the language of verse 19, "his anger *burned*." There is a contest of fires in these chapters, on which we shall have occasion to comment below.

The Structure of the Gospel Offered to Philistia

We now come to the second half of the story, and before looking at it, it would be well to examine the literary form of these two chapters. Chapter 14 has four episodes, each of which begins with someone going down. Chapter 15 also has four episodes, each of which begins with someone going somewhere. In the four episodes of Chapter 14, what is at the center of things is "telling." In the four episodes of Chapter 15, what is at the center of things is "doing." The episodes are parallel to one another, as follows:

Episode 1: Samson and Parents
    a. 14:1-4. "Samson went down to Timnah" (v. 1)
    Samson "*told* his father and mother" (v. 2)
    b. 15:1-3. "Samson visited his wife" (v. 1)
    "Her father said" (v. 2)
    Samson said, ". . . when I *do* them harm" (v. 3)

Episode 2: Samson's Prowess shown over animals
    a. 14:5-6. "Samson went down to Timnah" (v. 5)
    Samson "did not *tell* his father or mother" about the lion
    (v. 6)
    b. 15:4-6a "Samson went and caught 300 foxes" (v. 4)
    The Philistines said, "Who *did* this?" (v. 6a)

Episode 3: Transition to Longest Episode
    a. 14:7-9. "So he went down" (v. 7)
    Samson "did not *tell* them" about where he got the honey
    (v. 9)
    b. 15:6b-8. "So the Philistines came up" (v. 6b)
    Samson said "Since you act *[do]* this way" (v. 7)

Episode 4: Climax and Expansion of Theme
    a. 14:10-20 "Then his father went down" (v. 10)
    "I have not *told* it to my father or mother; so should I *tell*
    you?" (v. 16)
    b. 15:9-19 "Then the Philistines went up" (v. 9)
    The Philistines want to "*do* to him as he *did* to us."
    The Judahites say, "what have you *done* to us?"
    Samson says, "As they *did* to me, so I have *done* to them"
    (vv. 10-11)

The fourth episode in each case is the climax of the story. In Chapter 14, we have a whole series of conversations; in Chapter 15, a whole series of actions. In both cases "three characters are involved: Samson as protagonist, the Philistines as antagonist, and a third party, whom the Philistines draft to enable them to gain advantage over Samson. The third party in 14:10-20 is the Timnite; in 15:9-19 the Judahites assume this role."[3] In each case, "the Philistines succeed at what they had wanted. The Timnite tells them the answer to the riddle; the Judahites deliver over Samson to them. In each episode, at the point where the Philistines appear to have the upper hand, the spirit of Yhwh impels Samson to go to Ashkelon, where he *smites (nkh)* thirty Philistines. In Ch. 15, when Samson arrives at Lehi, the spirit comes upon him and he *smites* a thousand Philistines!"[4]

Theologically, the passage moves from the verbal to the physical, from word to act. This is liturgical order, from the declaration of the Word, to the sacramental act. Here, of course, both are negative. Samson did not tell his parents or his wife his secret, until his wife prevailed upon him. At that point, the real contest was joined. Privy to the truth at last, how would she respond? Her negative response to the messiah's secret sealed her own doom, and the abuse of that secret by the Philistines sealed theirs. The negative side of the sacrament follows: a series of visitations of judgment in the second half of the story.

This same order is seen in the book of Revelation. In the first half of the book, we have seven trumpets proclaiming the Word of judgment against the nations and Israel. When they do not repent, the second half of the book shows seven chalices of anti-sacramental judgment poured out against them.

It is important to see that Samson was not ultimately concealing the truth from the Philistines or his parents. That he had killed the lion was gospel to Israel, and also to Philistia if they would listen. Samson created a situation in which people greatly desired to hear the truth, and then he told it. We should not psychologize the text here, as if Samson had been brow-beaten by his beloved wife into revealing something he really did not

---

3. J. Cheryl Exum, "Aspects of Symmetry and Balance in the Samson Saga," *Journal for the Study of the Old Testament* 19 (1981):17. I am indebted to Exum for this entire schema.
4. *Ibid.*, p. 18.

want to tell. Samson calculated all along to tell his wife the answer, as a test to her and to the Philistines. Had she responded with proper fear, she would never have passed it on. Had they responded with proper fear upon hearing about the lion, they would have respected Samson. Their lack of fear was damning to them all: They did not fear God's messiah, and so they did not fear the Lord.

Even so, the gospel continues to come to them. None of the judgments visited upon the Philistines is final. Each one, as we have seen, is a "3," a partial judgment that leaves time for repentance. Philistia's refusal to repent and bow the knee is what ultimately destroys her.

Philistine Infertility

15:1. But after a while, in the time of the wheat harvest, it came about that Samson visited his wife with a young goat [kid]; and said, "I will go in to my wife in her room." But her father did not let him enter.

2. And her father said, "I really thought that you hated her intensely; so I gave her to your companion. Is not her younger sister better than she? Please let her be yours instead of her."

3. Samson then said to them, "This time I shall be blameless in regard to the Philistines when I do them harm."

4. And Samson went and caught 300 foxes [or, jackals], and took torches, and turned them tail to tail, and put one torch in the middle between two tails.

5. When he had set fire to the torches, he released them into the standing grain of the Philistines, thus burning up both the shocks and the standing grain, along with the vineyards and groves.

Samson's marriage was of an odd sort. The woman remained with her father, and was visited by her husband from time to time. This was because the husband did not have the money to pay the *mohar* or dowry. The *mohar* was money given by the groom to the bride as her future insurance. The amount was negotiated by her older brother or father (see Gen. 24:50-60; 34:12; Ex. 22:16f.; 1 Sam. 18:25-27). Samson apparently did not have the money to negotiate a proper marriage, and so the girl stayed with her father. Here is another picture of Israel's weakness and humility in the face of Philistine dominance. Yet, had the girl trusted in the messiah's might, she might have been delivered from her father's house and its doom; but she chose to remain, and was given to another.

Samson does not attack his former father-in-law, realizing that he has made an honest mistake. He sees the cause of it as lying with the Philistines who had threatened his wife and caused it all in the first place, and he takes revenge on them. Again, the principle has to be "eye for eye." Thus, we ask the question, what does burning up wheat have to do with the offense? The answer involves two factors: the grain harvest, and the pairing of the 300 foxes.

Harvest time was a time when a man's fancy turned to love, in the ancient world. This was probably because the fertility of the soil brought to mind the fertility of the wife, and a desire for children. We notice, for instance, that Ruth approached Boaz on the threshing floor during the harvest (Ruth 3). At any rate, Samson is expressing here a desire for a child. The kid of the goats is a regular symbol for a child, and by bringing a kid, Samson made his intentions known.

The father-in-law informs Samson that he really believed Samson did not want the girl, and gave her to another. He makes an honorable offer, but Samson is not interested. The Philistines, by wrecking his marriage, have prevented him from enjoying the seed that would be lawfully his. In response, then, Samson destroys their harvest, their standing grain. They have ruined his harvest, so he ruins theirs.

The number in the text is 300. Yet, by tieing the foxes together in pairs, Samson created 150 teams. The number 150 is five times 30. We find in Exodus 22:1 that if a man steals and kills an ox, five-fold restitution is required. We cannot take the space to prove this here, but laws about animals have their ultimate application in relations among men. Four-fold restitution is required when a powerful man oppresses a weaker brother, and destroys his property; and five-fold is required when a weaker person attacks and destroys the property of a leader.[5] We might think, in view of the weakness of Israel, that four-fold vengeance would be in view. We know, however, that Samson is

---

5. See my book, *The Law of the Covenant: A Commentary on Exodus 21–23* (Tyler, TX: Institute for Christian Economics, 1984), Appendix G: "Four and Five-fold Restitution."

actually the stronger party, and the true judge and ruler of this land. By acting against him, the Philistines had assaulted a leader. The Philistines had unlawfully stolen 30 changes of garments from Samson, which was now the value of his wife. By giving his wife to another, they had robbed Samson of something worth "30." His vengeance, then, is strictly according to law, five-fold, involving 150 teams of foxes. Thus, while the number 300 points to the non-final character of this judgment, the pairing of the foxes and the resultant number 150 shows that it was strictly according to the law of "eye for eye, tooth for tooth."

Vengeance on the Philistines

6. Then the Philistines said, "Who did this?" And they said, "Samson, the son-in-law of the Timnite, because he took his wife and gave her to his companion." So the Philistines came up and burned her and her father with fire.

7. And Samson said to them, "Since you act like this, I will surely take revenge on you, but after that I will quit."

8. And he struck them ruthlessly [shoulder on thigh] with a great slaughter; and he went down and lived in the cleft of the rock of Etam.

A heap of corpses lying on each other, with their limbs cut off at shoulder and hip and piled up, is a grotesque but powerful image. Samson killed a large number this time.

Samson's wife had feared the fire of Philistia more than she trusted the strength of her lord and husband, who represented the Lord God of Israel. By siding against God, she hoped to avoid being burned. She received the very judgment she had hoped to escape.

There is a contest of fires in these two chapters. The Philistines threaten fire against Samson's wife, and eventually they bring it upon her. Samson's anger burns, and he brings fire to the wheat of the Philistines. Fire is the sign of judgment, man's or God's (as we saw in Judges 1:8 and 17). Whose fire is stronger? As the fires go back and forth, the battle escalates. Whose fire will win? The answer will come at the end of the story.

How does this square with the lex talionis? The phrase

"shoulder on thigh" (v. 8) easily connects to the shoulder portion of the sacrifices, which was given to the priests (Lev. 7:32ff.; 8:25f.; etc.). An animal has four shoulders, but a man has two shoulders and two hips. The use of this expression here draws our attention to the notion that Samson sacrificed these men to the Lord. Their deaths were sacrificial.

They had burned Samson's wife and father with fire. This is also sacrificial language. Here we have the lex talionis, then: eye for eye, sacrifice for sacrifice. The Philistines had in essence sacrificed Samson's in-laws to their gods, to their culture, to preserve themselves and to take revenge. In return, Samson sacrificed a great number of Philistines to the Lord, "shoulder on thigh." The war is a war of religions, of Gods.

Judah's Betrayal

9. Then the Philistines went up and camped in Judah, and spread out in Lehi.

10. And the men of Judah said, "Why have you come up against us?" And they said, "We have come up to bind Samson in order to do to him as he did to us."

11. Then 3000 men of Judah went down to the cleft of the rock of Etam and said to Samson, "Do you not know that the Philistines are rulers over us? What then is this that you have done to us?" And he said to them, "As they did to me, so I have done to them."

12. And they said to him, "We have come down to bind you so that we may give you into the hands of the Philistines." And Samson said to them, "Swear to me that you will not fall upon me yourselves."

13. So they said to him, "No, but we will bind you fast and give you into their hands; yet surely we will not kill you." Then they bound him with two new ropes and brought him up from the rock.

The men of Judah, like Samson's wife, fear the wrong side. They think that Philistia is stronger than the Lord's Anointed. They will soon find out otherwise, but for now Samson is patient with them. He makes them swear that they will not attack him, not because he fears them but because he does not want to have to do them any harm.

It is the royal tribe, no less, that fears Philistia more than the Lord, and that seeks to turn Samson in. The cowardly Judahites take 3000 men along to deliver Samson into the hands of only 1000 Philistines, as we see in verse 15. Clearly, Judah is unfit to produce a true king at this stage in history. We might bear in mind that by this time the Ark has surely been taken captive by the Philistines. In their superstition, the men of Judah think that there can be no deliverance without the presence of the Ark.

We are reminded of another story when a young deliverer was betrayed by fellow Israelites. In another Egypt, the real one this time, Moses sought to deliver his people, but they would have none of it. As a result, Moses had to flee (Ex. 2:11-15).

Philistine Asses

14. When he came to Lehi [Jawbone], the Philistines shouted as they met him. And the Spirit of the LORD rushed upon him mightily so that the ropes that were on his arms were as flax that is burned with fire, and his bonds were melted from his hands.

15. And he found a fresh jawbone of a donkey, so he stretched out his hand and took it and smote 1000 men with it.

16. Then Samson said,

"With the jawbone of an ass,

"One heap, two heaps,

"With the jawbone of an ass,

"I have smitten a thousand men."

17. And it came about when he had finished speaking, that he threw the jawbone from his hand; and he named that place Ramath-Lehi [Jawbone Hill].

Whose fire is stronger? God's fire, of course. The fresh, new ropes snap as if they were but flax "that is burned with fire." God's fire frees Samson, and His fire defeats the Philistines once again.

In battle, the Nazirite comes into contact with death, as we noted in the previous chapter of our study. Thus, there is nothing objectionable about Samson's using a fresh jawbone of an ass as a weapon. Ordinarily he would not have touched it, but this is battle. (The fresh jawbone may or may not have had meat still on it, but it was not yet dried out and brittle.) The Philistines had an iron monopoly in Israel, and so the Israelites were compelled to use other things as weapons, like Shamgar's oxgoad and Samson's jawbone.

After the battle, Samson hurls the jawbone from him, immediately separating himself from the unclean object. He is the Nazirite warrior par excellence.

The Hebrew word for "heap" is spelled and sounds exactly the same as the Hebrew word for "ass." The poem is a very funny pun, comparing the Philistines to asses:

> "With the jawbone of an ass,
>   "One ass, two asses,
> "With the jawbone of an ass,
>   "Have I slain a thousand men."

In terms of the parallelism, lines two and four refer to the same thing. Samson kills these asses one at a time: one ass, two asses, three asses, and so forth up to 1000. The ass is an unclean animal, and a perfect symbol for the Philistines.

The sea monster in the Bible is pictured as having jaws that hold and grip God's people, which God breaks (Ezk. 29:4; 38:4). Here the jaws are of the Philistine asses. Samson breaks them, and hurls them away. It is a vivid symbol of the shattering of the Philistine hold upon Israel.

Spiritual Water

18. Then he became very thirsty, and he called to the LORD and said, "Thou hast given this great deliverance by the hand of Thy servant, and now I shall die of thirst and fall into the hands of the uncircumcised."

19. But God split the hollow place that is in Lehi so that water came out of it. When he drank, his spirit returned and he revived. Therefore, he named it En-Hakkore [The Caller's Spring], which is in Lehi to this day.

20. So he judged Israel 20 years in the days of the Philistines.

Samson's strength came from the Lord, and that Spiritual strength is pictured as water time and again in Scripture. Having expended all his strength, Samson prays for more, that he not fall into the hands of the Philistines. As He did for Moses in the wilderness, God splits a rock and provides water to Samson.

The deliverance from Philistia is a new exodus, as 1 Samuel 1–7 makes clear; here that motif is only hinted at, but water from the rock is a clear reminder to Israel of Moses in the wilderness. The Philistine oppression lasted 40 years, the same as the wilderness wanderings. If Israel would follow the lead of their new judge, Samson like Moses would give them water, and lead them to the restoration of the promised land.

It is God's way to humble us immediately after a great victory, lest we be proud and trust in our own strength. It is, thus, of the grace of God that he humbles Samson right after his victory. Samson is reminded that God alone is the Source of his strength. He would die, were it not for God's grace to him.

Samson inaugurates his ministry with a glorious series of victories. I think that there is nothing to criticize in these early actions of Samson. They were followed up by 20 years of wise and dynamic leadership and judging. At the end of those 20 years, however, Samson fell into sin, a sin that was a picture of Israel's sin.

It was the sin of whoring after Philistine culture, signified by whoring after Philistine whores. Maybe we should see Samson already falling into this sin in the story we have just considered. It might be that this story shows Samson (Israel) wrongly looking to marry Philistine culture. If we take such an approach, then we see God showing Israel the faithlessness of the Philistines as Samson's wife refuses to trust him, and the cruelty of the Philistines as they murder her and her father. We might see Samson "defiled" at the beginning of the story by scraping honey out of the carcass of the lion with his hands, and see him hurling away this defilement when he throws away the fresh jawbone. Between these two actions, we might see Samson making a series of mistakes, which God graciously delivers him from, and from which he repents.

This is a possible interpretation, but I do not think it is the correct one. I have attempted to show how each of Samson's actions can be seen as morally and spiritually sound. The overall reason why I think we need to take this approach is that nothing in the passage *says* that Samson was in sin, or that he was stupid. Rather, what the passage *says* is that the Lord blessed him, that the Spirit stirred him up, and that his desire to marry the Philistine girl was from the Lord (13:24, 25; 14:4). Unless we want to believe that the Spirit worked with Samson by completely bypassing his brain (which certainly would make Samson unique in the history of the world!), we have to say that Samson knew what was going on, and was in moral control of the situation.

Thus, in my opinion the parallels between Samson's youthful offer of marriage and his later involvement with Delilah are not indications that Samson was in the same moral state. Rather, they are inversions. In the first story, Samson dynamically moves out to the gentiles to offer them the gospel; in the second, Samson is seduced by the sins of the gentiles and becomes blind to the gospel. In the first story, the girl hounds Samson into giving up a secret, but Samson is in complete control of the situation and this is but a way of testing her, with the result that he overcomes the Philistines; in the second, Delilah hounds Samson into giving up a secret, but Samson winds up in her control and power, with the result that the Philistines overcome him. Finally, we should note that in the first story the Spirit repeatedly rushes upon Samson mightily; while in the second the Spirit departs from him, leaving him powerless. If Samson had been in sin in the first story, the Spirit would also have departed from him then.

In conclusion we should see that this story anticipates certain interesting characteristics of our Lord's ministry, which revolve around what is sometimes called "the Messianic secret." Anyone familiar with the gospels can remember that Jesus on several occasions enjoined people not to tell what they had seen Him do. Also, Jesus told parables that were secrets only for the inner circle of believers (Mark 4:11-12). Repeatedly the Jews asked Jesus to say who He was, but He spoke to them in cryptic sayings, and gave them no sign but the sign of Jonah. It was only at the resurrection that it was made unmistakeably clear to all men who He was.

Unquestionably, many things are involved in the "Messianic secret," but the story of Samson gives us one perspective on it. By delaying the revelation of His secret, Jesus created intense interest in it. Such an interest should have led to faith, when the Jews realized that Jesus had indeed slain the lion of Satan and made available once again the milk and honey of the kingdom. Just as Samson's wife was not impressed, however, neither were the Jews impressed with Christ's resurrection. Samson's wife and the Philistines only wanted Samson's secret so that they could betray him, and that is all the Jews and Pharisees wanted from Jesus. In the New Testament, the Jews are the Philistines, Judas is the wife (betraying with a kiss), and the betrayal price is 30 pieces of silver instead of 30 changes of clothing. And just as Samson engineered the whole thing and was in complete control throughout, so was Jesus Christ. Philistia would not repent, and eventually they were destroyed. Just so, when the Jews continued to persecute the Church, God sent ever more severe tribulation among them, until finally Jerusalem was destroyed in A.D. 70.

14

SAMSON: BLINDNESS, JUDGMENT, RESTORATION
(Judges 16)

We now come to the sad end of Samson's life. Like Israel in general, he went a whoring after the Philistine culture, symbolized in its women. The results were destructive to him.

Before looking at the stories in detail, we should get before us their structure and the parallels between chapter 16 on the one hand, and chapters 14 and 15 on the other.[1] In both accounts Samson sees a woman, is persuaded by a woman to reveal a secret, is bound and given over to the Philistines, and calls on the Lord for deliverance. There are specific parallels as well:

1. In both stories, the woman wants to be *told* the secret, and in both cases Samson tells her because she harasses him (14:17; 16:16f.).

2. Both women use love as bait (14:16; 16:15).

3. The Timnite works on Samson for seven days; Delilah works on him every day (14:17; 16:16).

4. The Philistines want the Timnite to "entice" Samson, and they use the same word (*patti*) in persuading Delilah to "entice" him (14:15; 16:5).

5. In both stories the Philistines need the assistance of a third party to capture Samson; their attempt to do so on their own fails (16:1-3).

6. The men of Judah bind Samson in the first story; Delilah binds him in the second (15:12; 16:8, 12). This establishes a parallel between the Judahites and Delilah, as betrayers of the Lord's anointed.

7. The Judahites and Delilah each use "new ropes" (15:13; 16:12).

---

1. I am again indebted to the essay by J. Cheryl Exum, cited in the preceding chapter, for much of this comparison.

265

8. "In the first cycle, the ropes which were upon his arms become as flax which is burned with fire, 15:14. In the second cycle, virtually the same simile appears. Samson snaps the bowstrings as the tow — a stage in the preparation of flax — snaps when it touches fire, 16:9."[2]

9. Twice the Judahites say that they have come to give Samson into the hands of the Philistines (15:12f.), and twice the Philistines say that Dagon has given Samson into their hands (16:23f.). It is at this point in each story when Samson turns and, with the aid of the Lord, kills the Philistines.

10. At the end of both stories, Samson faces death and calls upon God, once to save him, and once to let him die.

This literary parallelism highlights for us several aspects of the message of Samson. First, there is a contrast in the two stories. In the first one, Samson is in complete control. True, his wife was told to entice him to tell a secret. True, she harassed him for many days and used love as bait. Yet, Samson did not fall because of this; rather, the events were of his own staging. Samson was showing Israel what Philistine women and culture were truly like. This sets us up for the second story, for in this one Samson is not in control. Here we see Samson ignoring his own sermon. Delilah acts just like Samson's wife, yet he ignores the message. He thinks he is in control, and plays around with his gift; but in the end he falls (for he has fallen already, having "loved" Delilah). Samson in his forties chooses to forget what he knew full well in his twenties.

Second, the parallelism identifies the Judahites with Delilah. Both are third parties used to betray Samson; both give him over to the Philistines; both bind him with new ropes, which he breaks as if flax. We note that the text does not say Delilah was a Philistine. Maybe she was a traitor from Judah itself. On the other hand, maybe she was a Philistine woman, in which case the parallelism causes us to see the Judahites acting like Philistines in betraying Samson. At any rate, the literary parallelism clearly puts the Judahites into the came category as Delilah, certainly to their eventual and undying shame.

Third, as Exum points out, "Both cycles move toward a theological message: in time of need, Samson calls on Yhwh and

---

2. Exum, p. 6.

Yhwh answers Samson's prayer. The strong man cannot deliver himself. Though the lives of the Philistines appear to be in Samson's hands, 15:15, and ultimately in 16:30, Samson's life and death are in the hands of Yhwh, and Yhwh alone."[3] Thus, both stories bring us in the end to the fact of human impotence, and God's omnipotence.

Philistia Exposed

16:1. Now Samson went to Gaza and saw a harlot there, and went in to her.

2. When it was told to the Gazites, saying, "Samson has come here," they surrounded the place and lay in wait for him all night at the gate of the city. And they kept silent all night, saying, "At the morning light, then we will kill him."

3. Now Samson lay until midnight, and at midnight he arose and took hold of the doors of the city gate and the two posts and pulled them up along with the bars; then he put them on his shoulders and carried them up to the top of the mountain which is opposite Hebron.

The first verse of this chapter has the same form as the formula, "Now Israel played the harlot with some false god" (Jud. 2:17; 8:27, 33; and many other places in Scripture). At the end of each deliverance, we read that the Judge judged Israel for x number of years, and then he died, and then Israel went whoring after some other gods. The same thing is seen here. Samson delivered Israel. Then the text says he judged for 20 years. The next thing we read is that Samson went whoring after a Philistine prostitute. Samson as the anointed judge is a picture of Israel as a whole. His failures are theirs.

There is a literary parallel between this verse and the first verse of chapter 14, a parallel designed to bring out irony:

> 14:1 And Samson went down to Timnah, and he *saw* a woman in Timnah. . . .
> 16:1 And Samson went to Gaza, and he *saw* there a woman, a prostitute. . . .

In the first story, Samson acted honestly, with pure motives. Here the seeing has a different culmination.

---

3. *Ibid.*, p. 8.

The men of Gaza did not think Samson could get out through the gates at night, since they were locked, so they went to sleep. (It was foolish of them to think they could kill one whose name was "Sun" by waiting until *morning*.) The city gates did not stop Samson, however. By removing them a great distance, Samson showed his prowess (it was uphill all the way). Moreover, he left the city wide open to conquest. Philistia was like a harlot, not a virgin, and thus was not sealed against attack. Sadly, however, Samson was not interested in destroying Gaza, but only in playing with it. God had given him strength, and left the city exposed, but he was not interested. Just so, Jesus has destroyed the gates of hell, leaving the kingdoms of Satan wide open for conquest by the Church (Matt. 16:18). How well are we doing?

It happened at midnight. Midnight is sometimes seen in Scripture as the time when the definitive blow is struck against the wicked. Thus, it was about midnight that the Angel of Death struck down the firstborn of Egypt (Ex. 11:4; 12:29; compare Matt. 25:6). At sunrise, Samson the Sun might have been there leading an assault on the city. He was, however, long gone.

There is one other ironical aspect to this passage, and that is seen in its parallel with Joshua 2. The spies entered Jericho, and according to Joshua 2:1, "they entered the house of a woman, a prostitute, and her name was Rahab, and they stayed there." Also, in Joshua 2, the men of Jericho were concerned about their city gate. They shut the gate (Josh. 2:7) to keep the spies in, just in case they had not left the city yet. The parallels between these two stories indicate that Samson might have entered Gaza to spy it out, and come back and conquer it. Such was not, evidently, the case—no conquest followed. Samson was only interested in the woman—he went in to *her*, not simply to her *house* as the Joshua's spies had.

Samson and Delilah

4. After this it came about that he loved a woman in the valley of Sorek, whose name was Delilah.

5. And the lords of the Philistines came to her, and said to her, "Entice him, and see where his great strength lies and by what means we may overpower him that we may bind him to afflict him. Then we will each give you 1100 pieces of silver."

The story of Samson and Delilah is connected to the story of the Gaza prostitute. This is indicated in the text by the connective statement in verse 4, "after this." Samson is continuing on one course, downhill.

We are not expressly told that Delilah was a Philistine woman, though that has usually been assumed. We might also guess, because of the context, that she was a professional prostitute. This may not be so, however. Thomas Kirk comments, "There are several things, however, which may well lead us to doubt the correctness of this opinion, and to believe that she was an Israelite. First of all, there is her residence, which seems to have been within the territory occupied by the tribe of Judah; then there is the confidence placed in her by Samson, which would be highly improbable on the supposition that she was a Philistine; and then there is the largeness of the bribe with which she was tempted by the lords of the Philistines—a fact which can be most easily explained on the supposition that she was an Israelite, whose patriotism had to be overcome."[4] To these arguments we can add that the theme here is betrayal, and we would not expect a betrayal from someone outside the camp. A betrayer has to stand within the inner circle, as Judas did with Jesus. This adds to the likelihood that Delilah was an Israelite. Finally, there is, as we have noted, a parallel between what Delilah does and what Judah did in betraying Samson in Judges 15. This again lends force to the notion that Delilah was an Israelite, indeed perhaps of the royal tribe.

If an Israelite by birth, Delilah was a Philistine in heart. By identifying herself with God's enemies, she came to be counted as one herself. Spiritually, if not in fact, Delilah was a Philistine indeed. Moreover, even if she was not a prostitute by profession, her acceptance of money from the Philistines certainly puts her in the same category.

The five lords of the Philistines prevailed upon her by offering her 5500 pieces of silver, to betray her lover. (We commented on possible meanings of the number 1100 on page 29 above.) This is the second betrayal for money in Judges (see Jud. 9:4).

---

4. Thomas Kirk, *Samson: His Life and Work* (Edinburgh: Andrew Elliot, 1891 [reprint, Minneapolis: Klock & Klock, 1983]), p. 163.

They want to afflict him. This seems a strange way to put it, and it is used three times in this chapter (vv. 5, 6, 19). It is the term usually used for the affliction of the people Israel by a foreign power, such as the affliction in Egypt. The use of this term here brings out Samson's identification with Israel, and Philistia's identification with Egypt.

6. So Delilah said to Samson, "Please tell me where your great strength is and by what means you may be bound to afflict you."

7. And Samson said to her, "If they bind me with seven fresh cords that have not been dried, then I shall become weak and be like any other man."

8. Then the lords of the Philistines brought up to her seven fresh cords that had not been dried, and she bound him with them.

9. Now she had men lying in wait in an inner room. And she said to him, "The Philistines are upon you, Samson!" But he snapped the cords as a string of tow snaps when it touches fire. So his strength was not discovered.

10. Then Delilah said to Samson, "Behold, you have deceived me and told me lies; now please tell me, by what means you may be bound."

11. And he said to her, "If they bind me tightly with new ropes which have never been used [with which work has not been done], then I shall become weak and be like any other man."

12. So Delilah took new ropes and bound him with them and said to him, "The Philistines are upon you, Samson!" For the men were lying in wait in the inner room. But he snapped the ropes from his arms like a thread.

13. Then Delilah said to Samson, "Up to now you have deceived me and told me lies; tell me by what means you may be bound." And he said to her, "If you weave the seven locks of my head with the web."

14. And she fastened it with the pin, and said to him, "The Philistines are upon you, Samson!" But he awoke from his sleep and pulled out the pin of the loom and the web.

Delilah tried and failed three times to find out Samson's secret. Each time she had men hidden in another room, but they never showed themselves. She *said* "The Philistines are upon you," but they remained hidden. After all, if Samson had seen them, he would have known she was betraying him. She kept him thinking that this was just a game.

The Philistines believed in magic, and they believed Samson's strength was magical. Samson has fun ridiculing this belief in magic. He recommends fresh undried cords, never before used ropes, and binding his hair in a loom. Each time she tries these, he breaks free, showing the stupidity of magic. For Samson, it is just a game.

But it is more than that. We see Samson playing around just a bit with his vow. In the first binding, it is *seven* cords that must be used. This has to do with his seven locks of hair, and with the seven-fold Spirit he depends upon. In the third binding, he tells her to do something with his seven locks of hair, again toying with his vow. We see Samson falling through compromise.

The message for Israel? No, magic does not exist, and you need not fear it. But you must fear compromise. Involvement in playing around with evil people will drag you down, until you fall totally, as did Samson. You may get by with messing around for a while, but there are always men lurking in the inner room, waiting to destroy you when you are exposed.

15. Then she said to him, "How can you say, 'I love you,' when your heart is not with me? You have deceived me these three times and have not told me where your great strength is."

16. And it came about when she pressed him daily with her words and urged him, that his soul was impatient to the point of death.

17. So he told her all that was in his heart and said to her, "A razor has never come on my head, for I have been a Nazirite to God from my mother's womb. If I am shaved, then my Strength will leave me, and I shall become weak and be like any other man."

18. When Delilah saw that he had told her all that was in his heart, she sent and called the lords of the Philistines, saying, "Come up once more, for he has told me all that is in his heart." Then the lords of the Philistines came up to her, and brought the money in their hands.

19. And she made him sleep on her knees, and called for a man and had him shave off the seven locks of his head. Then she began to afflict him, and his strength left him.

20. And she said, "The Philistines are upon you, Samson!"

And he awoke from his sleep and said, "I will go out as at other times and shake myself free." But he did not know that the LORD had departed from him.

21. Then the Philistines seized him and gouged out his eyes; and they brought him down to Gaza and bound him with bronze chains, and he was a grinder in the prison.

Samson's wife had worn him down until he told her his riddle. Now Delilah also wears him down and he tells her another, more important secret. Samson should have remembered the earlier incident, how this nagging was a sign of betrayal. He understood it then, but now, blinded by lust, he ignores the danger signals.

She annoyed him "to death." This is not just an hyperbolic expression. Proverbs 2:16ff. tells us that the adulterous woman flatters with her words, but "her house sinks down to death and her tracks lead to the dead." Involvement with Philistia can only lead to death.

When Samson said "my Strength will leave me" (v. 17), he referred to the Spirit. After his head was shorn, we read in verse 20, "the LORD had departed from him." Samson knew where his strength came from. It was not magic. It was a personal gift from the Lord. God had graciously not withdrawn it yet, in spite of Samson's adultery. There was no magical tie between Samson's strength and his hair, but there was a spiritual connection in that God gives strength to those who are dedicated to Him, and in Samson's case, his dedicated head was the sign of his separation to God. In fact, Samson was already in sin, and God was about to pull away His Strength from him, but God chose to do so at the same time as Samson's head was shorn, so that the outward sign would correspond to the reality.

By this time, the five lords have given up their hopes of defeating Samson. Delilah, anxious for the money, sends for them to come up one more time. Once Samson falls asleep (a picture of his spiritual state), she has his head shaved, and then she "afflicts" him. Thus, she displays the true nature of Philistia! The reference to Samson's "sleeping" on Delilah's "knees" is an allusion to his sinful sexual relationship with her, as can be seen from the use of "kneel" in Job 31:10. The connection between knees and legs is obvious, and we are thus back to the harlot of

Proverbs, whose "feet go down to death" (Prov. 5:5).

Here is the secret of Philistia's domination of Israel. It was not because they were stronger, for they were not. It was because of Israel's sin, and God's giving Israel over to them. It is clear from the passage that the Philistines, their warriors and their magic, are utterly powerless. The only reason they have ascended to rule over God's people is that God's people are faithless.

The Philistines blinded Samson so that, if his strength returned, he still would not be able to fight. His blindness also serves as an outward sign of his spiritual condition. Samson, like Israel, and like Eli before him, has been blinded by sin.

He is put to work grinding in the mill. This is a sign of the victory of Dagon, the Philistine god of grain. The Philistines assumed that the fertility of their culture came from Dagon, the god of grain and fertility. The text, however, hints of something else. Grinding is put in parallel with sexual relations in Job 31:10, because of the connection between human and agricultural fertility (compare Is. 47:2; Jer. 25:10). There is an eye for eye, tooth for tooth justice in this. God's principle is, as we have seen, "If you like the gods of the nations, then you will doubtless enjoy being dominated by the cultures of the nations." The same thing is true here. Does Samson (Israel) enjoy "grinding" with Delilah (Philistia)? Well then, let him be put to work grinding!

Also, though, when Samson is grinding for the Philistines, we see that their agricultural fertility and prosperity are actually built upon the slave labor of Israel. Samson's grinding is a picture of Israel's condition, and it is also one more slap at idolatry. It is not Dagon but the Lord who gives prosperity to Philistia, and the only reason God gives prosperity to Philistia is because He is punishing His people by making them slaves of Philistia.

Repentance and Vengeance

22. However, the hair of this head began to grow again after it was shaved off.

This is so obvious that we need to ask why the Spirit bothers to record it here. Do we need to be told that hair grows back after it is shaved off? The point is that in his humiliation, Samson begins to repent and return to the Lord. Simultaneously God gives Him back his miraculous strength, and the sign of that is the return of his hair. This also is a picture to Israel: If they will repent and humble themselves under the grinding oppression of Philistia, God will gradually build them back up to a position of strength.

> 23. Now the lords of the Philistines assembled to offer a great sacrifice to Dagon their god, and to rejoice, for they said, "Our god has given Samson our enemy into our hands."
> 24. When the people saw him, they praised their god, for they said, "Our god has given our enemy into our hands, even the destroyer of our country, who has slain many of us."

The Philistines have now provoked the Lord. They have made the big mistake, for they say *"our* god has given Samson our enemy into our hands." The Lord will now act to avenge His honor. We shall have a war of the gods, and we shall see just Who the True God really is. (Note the parallel between the humiliation of Dagon here and in 1 Sam. 5:2ff.)

Has Israel adopted the Philistine point of view? Does Israel think that it is because Dagon is stronger that they are in misery? Do modern American Christians think that it is because Humanism is strong that we are oppressed? Not so. If the Church is oppressed in America today, it is because the Church has been faithless. It is not the Dagons, the Philistines, the Humanists and Statists with whom we have to deal. It is the Lord with whom we must wrestle. When our ways please Him, the tyrant will be destroyed. Our problems are not political, and neither is the solution to them.

We learn something encouraging about Samson from what the Philistines say. They admit that he has been "the destroyer of our country, who has slain many of us." What a great testimony! We learn from this that Samson did a mighty work indeed during his 20 years of judgeship.

> 25. It so happened when their hearts were merry, that they said, "Call for Samson, that he may amuse us." So they called for Samson from the prison, and he made sport before them. And they made him stand between the pillars.

They brought Samson out to kick him around in his blindness. We are immediately reminded of how the Greater Samson, betrayed by a kiss from another Delilah (Judas) for silver, was treated by the Romans: "And they blindfolded Him and were asking Him, saying, 'Prophesy: Who is the one who hit You?' " (Luke 22:64).

Samson was put between the pillars. Temples in the ancient world were generally symbolic models of the world, and their pillars were symbols of the might of the god who upholds the world. This was also true of the Tabernacle and Temple of the Old Covenant. The ancients knew that the world was round, and that there were not really pillars holding it up, but they used that figure of speech (see for instance Job 38:6). On top of the temple there was frequently a garden, held up by the pillars.

In the Temple of Dagon, the central pillars were like the arms of Dagon, holding up the Philistine world. The Philistines had confidence in the might of Dagon. They were congregated on the roof, certain that Dagon could uphold their garden-civilization. This is the picture we need to have in mind to understand more fully the meaning of what happens next.

> 26. Then Samson said to the boy who was holding his hand, "Let me feel the pillars on which the house rests, that I may lean against them."
> 27. Now the house was full of men and women, and all the lords of the Philistines were there. And about 3000 men and women were on the roof looking on while Samson was amusing them.
> 28. Then Samson called to the LORD and said, "O Master LORD, please remember me and please strengthen me just this time, O God, that I may at once be avenged of the Philistines for my two eyes."
> 29. And Samson grasped the two middle pillars on which the house rested, and braced himself against them, the one with his right hand and the other with his left.
> 30. And Samson said, "Let me die with the Philistines!" And he bent with Strength so that the house fell on the lords and all the people who were in it. So the dead whom he killed at his death were more than those whom he killed in his life.

Samson positioned himself between the two central pillars. When he pulled them down, he symbolically pulled down the entire civilization built upon Dagon. All five of the Philistine

lords were killed, destroying all five heads of that culture. True
to form, their heads were crushed under tons of rock. Moreover, the chief priests of Dagon must also have been present,
and they also got their heads crushed. Once again the number
three shows up, pointing again to the fact that Samson's
deliverance was a "beginning," not the full seven-fold end.
There were many more than 3000 present, for the house was full
in addition to the 3000 on the roof. It must have been a very
large Temple, to have that many people on the roof.

Was Samson's prayer a selfish one? Hardly. Bear in mind
that this is Israel's messiah praying. Jesus also prayed destruction down upon His enemies from the cross, as we see in Psalm
69:20ff. Samson does indeed phrase his prayer in terms of vengeance for his two eyes, but as we have seen, Jesus was also
blindfolded at one point, and in His prayer, He prays, "May
their eyes grow dim so that they cannot see" (Ps. 69:23). The
prayer is in terms of God's perfect standard of justice: eye for
eye. It was Israel's messiah they had blinded, and Samson
knows that there is a price to be paid for attacking the Lord's
anointed.

A careful translation of verse 30 brings out that Samson's
Spiritual Strength had returned, and that Samson used all of
this Strength in pulling down the Temple. He asked to die with
the Philistines, showing that the Messiah would have to die
Himself in order to effect the destruction of His enemies. We
also see that he killed more at this time than at any other time in
his career. (Doubtless his total number over 20 years was higher
than the number killed in his last deed, but this was the greatest
number of any particular occasion.) His greatest and most
definitive victory came with his death. In all of this, he is a picture of the coming Messiah, Jesus Christ.

(If all the people were killed, who got out to tell this story to
the author of Judges? Perhaps the boy who guided Samson to
the pillars. Maybe, being a servant, he was a Hebrew, and
maybe Samson warned him. Maybe. We don't know. Another
question: Was Samson's death a suicide? Yes, in one broad
sense, but compare Matthew 27:50, where Jesus "gave up the
Spirit." We don't regard volunteering for a suicide mission on
the battlefield as immoral, but as an act of self-sacrifice. That is
how we should understand Samson's death.)

31. Then his brothers and all his father's household came down, took him, brought him up, and buried him between Zorah and Eshtaol in the tomb of Manoah his father. Thus he had judged Israel 20 years.

In conclusion, we should see Samson as the representative Danite. Genesis 49:16-18 said that Dan ("Judge") would judge his people. Dan would be like a serpent in the way, striking without warning. Certainly this was true of Samson. Deuteronomy 33:22 said that Dan would be a lion that leaps out of the undergrowth and pounces on his prey. It takes a lion to kill a lion, and Samson began his career by killing a lion.

The story of the fall of Samson should have taught Israel three basic things. First, that even the strongest man will fall if he goes a whoring after pagan culture. Second, that involvement with pagan culture would destroy their lives and calling, blinding them and rendering them impotent in life. And third, that a more perfect Messiah would be needed if Israel was ever fully and finally to be delivered from sin and bondage. What was needed was a Deliverer Who would be both morally pure and also omnipotent.

15

THE LEVITES' FAILURE: RELIGIOUS APOSTASY
(Judges 17-18)

We now arrive at the two appendices to the book of Judges. These two stories happened early in the history, but their placement here serves to bring out the fundamental causes of the disorders of the period. We reach here the climax of the message of Judges, which is that when the fathers and mothers of Israel fail in their tasks, all goes wrong; and when the Levites fail to show forth the true Husband of Israel to the Bride, then the Bride goes whoring after other husbands.

Women need attention, so Paul says, "Husbands, love your wives as Christ loved the Church" (Eph. 5:25). It was the job of the Levites to manifest God's Husbandly attentions to His Bride. Just as an ignored women may seek attention elsewhere, so Israel sought other lovers. She was in sin, but the Levites were in greater sin, just as Adam bore greater responsibility for humanity's fall.

The Lord was to be Husband and King, but Levi failed to make His presence manifest. Thus, as the appendices say five times, there was no king in Israel. The first appendix shows the consequences of this failure in the area of worship, while the second probes the consequences in social life.

The liturgical structure of Judges 17 and 18 is all in the background. The Command/Promise from God centers in two areas. One is the second commandment, forbidding the worship of God through graven images. The second commandment does not prohibit religious art, or even the placement of religious art and symbols in the place of worship. What it forbids is bowing down to images, using them as magical means to communicate with and manipulate God. By extension, it forbids the erection of any competitive place of worship, at least during the Old Covenant. There is only one Mediator between God and man,

279

and He is the very image of God Himself, the Son. All other mediators are false.

The other area of Command/Promise has to do with the Levites. They were to be the priest-guardians of Israel. When they failed in their task, chaos ensued.

Nor does this passage give an explicit evaluation or judgment from the Lord. The reason for this is that the whole history of the period shows God's evaluation. Because of the failure of the Levites, Israel came under judgment time and again. This passage does move to a climax of horror, though. It comes when we find out that the apostate Levite was none other than the grandson of Moses himself! (Judges 18:30.) So horrible is this fact that the Jewish scribes took the letters MSH, which are the Hebrew consonants in the name Moses, and changed them to read "Manasseh" (MNSH) after the apostate king of that name. (In Hebrew, only the consonants are written; the vowels are "understood," and were not written into the text until during the Middle Ages.) But in the margin, the scribes always gave the real name: Moses. This, by the way, is what shows that this event happened early in the period of the judges.

The following is an outline of Judges 17 - 18:

I. The Establishment of a False Sanctuary (17:1-6)

II. The Establishment of a False Priesthood (17:7-13)

III. The Danite Migration (18)
  A. The Spies meet with the Levite (18:1-6)
  B. The Report of the Spies (18:7-10)
  C. The Danites Steal the Idols (18:11-20)
  D. The Danites Drive Micah Away (18:21-26)
  E. The Conquest of Laish and the Full Establishment of an Apostate Sanctuary (18:27-31)

The Establishment of a False Sanctuary

This story is a parody of the story of the establishment of true worship at the exodus from Egypt. Virtually every detail found here is also found there, but here it is perverted.

17:1. Now there was a man of the hill country of Ephraim whose name was Micah.

2. And he said to his mother, "The 1100 pieces of silver which were taken from you, about which you uttered a curse and also spoke it in my ears, behold the silver is with me; I took it." And his mother said, "Blessed be my son by the LORD."

3. And he returned the 1100 pieces of silver to his mother, and his mother said, "I wholly dedicate the silver from my hand to the LORD for my son to make a graven image and a molten image; now therefore I will return it to you."

4. So when he returned the silver to his mother, his mother took 200 pieces of silver and gave them to the silversmith who made it into a graven image and a molten idol, and it was in the house of Micah.

5. And the man Micah had a house of gods and he made an ephod and teraphim [household gods] and consecrated one of his sons, that he might become his priest.

6. In those days there was no king in Israel; every man did what was right in his own eyes.

Just as Samson had been betrayed for 1100 pieces of silver, so here the Lord is betrayed. This betrayal is fundamental to everything that happens. This is the third betrayal for money in Judges (cf. Jud. 9:4). (On 1100, see my comments on p. 29 above.)

When Micah stole the silver from his mother, she cursed the thief. She pretty well knew who had done it, so she made sure to tell Micah about the curse (see Leviticus 5:1). Afraid, he returned it to her, and she undid the curse by use of the formula of blessing at the end of verse 2. We notice that Micah makes none of the required restitution demanded by Leviticus 6:1-7, which was to add 20% to what was stolen and offer a Trespass Offering. The restitution was to satisfy the person who was robbed, and the sacrifice was to satisfy God. Micah ignores the true God.

The mother is not named, indicating that we have to look for the essence of motherhood operative in this paragraph. The mother led her son into idolatry, and perhaps the writer of Judges intends to say something to us by using the word 'mother' six times in this paragraph, six being the number of inadequacy. She stands in contrast to Deborah, the true mother in Israel. She is a picture of the Israelite parent who fails to teach her child about the Lord, and who brings Israel into sin (as we discussed this in chapter 2 of this study).

She says that she will give all 1100 pieces of silver to Micah, but she only gives 200. From this we see that Micah's covetousness was learned at his mother's knee.

The Israelites made the golden calf out of the golden spoils of Egypt, spoils given to the women of Israel (Ex. 3:22). Here another woman contributes to what is in essence another golden calf. As if to stress the decline, however, the passage only speaks in terms of silver, not gold. The word 'silver' also occurs six times in this paragraph. The four world kingdoms described in Daniel chapter 2 run downhill from gold to silver to bronze to iron. The silver kingdom is specifically called inferior in Daniel 2:39.

Every conceivable kind of idolatry is mentioned here, so that we do not miss the point. The graven image was a large statue covered with silver plate. The molten image was a small, portable, solid piece of silver (Jud. 18:20). The ephod was, as we have seen already, a device for answering questions. The teraphim were little statues that represented the heavenly host around the throne of the god, perversions of the angels and departed spirits of men around God's throne.

Micah made his own false tabernacle to be a house for these gods. God's Tabernacle was His earthly Palace/Temple. Micah's was a perverse copy of it. Now all that Micah needed was a priest, and he made one of his sons priest, which was customary.

If the law had been functioning in Israel, Micah would have been put to death (Dt. 13; 17:2-7). But, there was no king in Israel, which means that the Lord was not being respected as King, and so Micah was left alone.

The Establishment of a False Priesthood

7. Now there was a young man from Bethlehem in Judah, of the family of Judah, who was a Levite; and he was sojourning there.

8. Then the man departed from the city, from Bethlehem in Judah, to sojourn wherever he might find a place; and as he made his journey, he came to the hill country of Ephraim to the house of Micah.

9. And Micah said to him, "Where do you come from?" And he said to him, "I am a Levite from Bethlehem in Judah, and I am going to sojourn wherever I may find a place."

10. Micah then said to him, "Dwell with me and be a father and a priest to me, and I will give you ten pieces of silver a year, a suit of clothes, and your maintenance." So the Levite went in.

11. And the Levite agreed to live with the man; and the young man [Levite] became to him [Micah] like one of his sons.

12. So Micah consecrated the Levite, and the young man became his priest and was in the house of Micah.

13. Then Micah said, "Now I know that the LORD will prosper me, seeing I have a Levite as priest."

18:1a. In those days there was no king in Israel.

The Levite is called a young man here, and several times in the passage. In our study of Gideon, we investigated the theme of the young man in the Bible. Like Ham, this young man does not respect the tent of the Father of Israel, and seeks to build his own power base.[1]

The Levites not only lived in Levitical cities, they also were scattered in Israelite towns to serve as local pastors of the local synagogues (Lev. 23:3; Dt. 14:27, 29). They were to be the fathers of Israel, and also represented the Divine Husband to the Bride. The Levites had been consecrated to serve the Lord in this capacity as substitutes for the firstborn sons of Israel, when the latter failed to lead properly at the golden calf incident (Ex. 32:29; Num. 8:16).

If ever there was a "Judas Priest" this Levite is he. He is not named, again, so we look for the essence of what it was supposed to mean to be a Levite. We find nothing but perversion. His entire ministry is built on 1100 pieces of silver that were used to betray the Lord. Like the true Levites he was defiling, this man substituted for a son, Micah's son. Moreover, the Levites were not to be sanctuary priests, but local pastors. This Levite, however, presumes to take a post not his, like Nadab and Abihu who offered strange fire to the Lord (Lev. 10:1, 2).

This Levite was also an opportunist. It might have been proper for him to leave Bethlehem and look for a post, but he proves to be a false spiritual father and husband to Micah. When a better job comes along, with the Danites, he is only too ready to take it.

---

1. On Ham's rebellion, see my essay, "Rebellion, Tyranny, and Dominion in the Book of Genesis," in Gary North, ed., *Tactics of Christian Resistance* (Tyler, TX: Geneva Ministries, 1983).

The "suit of clothes" is mentioned in verse 10 as a parody of Aaron's garments of glory and beauty.

This paragraph also begins the "Bethlehem theme" in the Bible. Beth-Lehem means "house of bread." Bethlehem should have been feeding the True Bread of Life to Judah and Israel. Instead, everything coming out of Bethlehem is defiled. The false Levite of Judges 19 also comes from there, and the traitor Elimelech departs Bethlehem for Moab in Ruth 1. Only with the birth of David is Bethlehem "redeemed," and only in the Greater David does Beth-Lehem truly become a House of Bread.

Like the Philistines ridiculed by Samson, Micah believes in magic. Like a Baalist, Micah believes that the essence of religion is the manipulation of God, not submission to Him. Now that he has some gods under his control, Micah believes that the Lord will bless him for sure. He is about to be relieved of that misconception.

The Danite Migration

The parody continues. After the exodus, God built His house (Exodus 25–40), and invested His priesthood (Leviticus). Then, the people spied out the land (Numbers), and conquered it, burning the first city, Jericho, as a "hormah" (Joshua). The same thing now happens, in a perverse way.

18:1b. And in those days the tribe of the Danites was seeking an inheritance for themselves to live in, for until that day an inheritance had not fallen to them as a possession among the tribes of Israel.
2. So the sons of Dan sent from their family five men out of their whole number, valiant men from Zorah and Eshtaol, to spy out the land and to search it; and they said to them, "Go, search the land." And they came to the hill country of Ephraim, to the house of Micah, and lodged there.

The faithless Danites had failed to conquer the land God gave them. They wanted something easy, something they could conquer in their own puny strength. The writer of Judges pokes fun at the Danites by calling them "valiant men," when in fact they were a bunch of cowards looking for an unguarded city to capture. These "valiant" men were from Zorah and Eshtaol, the same place that produced Samson later on (Jud. 13:2, 25; 16:31). Samson shows where true strength lies, but he was a descendant of the faithful remnant of Dan who did not apostatize.

Five men were sent out, five being the number of a hand, a force, and thus the number used in military formations. We see human strength here, in all its pettiness and weakness.

All the language here is designed to remind us of Moses sending men to spy out Canaan. Moses' spies returned to say that the land was good, but ruled by strong adversaries. These spies are looking for something easy to conquer. Everything here is designed to ridicule the Danites.

God was teaching His people how to war. This story is designed to give a negative illustration. The Danites make war in total faithlessness, and show themselves as ridiculous cowards.

> 3. When they were near the house of Micah, they recognized the voice of the young man, the Levite; and they turned aside there, and said to him, "Who brought you here? And what are you doing in this place? And what do you have here?"
> 4. And he said to them, "Thus and so has Micah done to me, and he has hired me, and I have become his priest."
> 5. And they said to him, "Inquire of God [or, the gods], please, that we may know whether our way on which we are going will be prosperous."
> 6. And the priest said to them, "Go in peace; your way in which you are going has the LORD's approval."

The apostasy of Dan is seen clearly here. Rather than go to where the Tabernacle was located, they ask this false priest to consult his false ephod for an oracle. They knew what God would have told them, had they asked Him: Go conquer the land I gave you. Like apostates of all ages, they are seeking a minister who will tickle their ears with what they want to hear. Verse 5 is ambiguous, because the word "God" can also be rendered "gods." This is a pun, which exposes the apostasy of the Danites once again.

They get what they want. Like palm readers and crystal ball gazers of all ages, Micah knows exactly what to say.

> 7. Then the five men departed and came to Laish and saw the people who were in it living in security, after the manner of the

Sidonians, quiet and secure; for there was no ruler humiliating them for anything in the land, and they were far from the Sidonians and had no dealings with anyone.

8. When they came back to their brothers at Zorah and Eshtaol, their brothers said to them, "What do you report?"

9. And they said, "Arise, and let us go up against them; for we have seen the land, and behold, it is very good. And will you sit still? Do not delay to go, to enter, to possess the land.

10. "When you enter, you shall come to a secure people with a spacious land; for God has given it into your hand, a place where there is no lack of anything that is on the earth."

The spies return. Their report is just like the report of Moses' spies, except that they encourage Dan to make the move. The text stresses that the people of Laish had no defence, in order to point out the cowardice of the Danites. (Laish was indeed part of the land Israel was supposed to conquer, Joshua 13:1-7, but it was not part of Dan's alloted territory.) They wanted the blessings of the Covenant apart from the conditions of the Covenant, which involved faithfulness to the Lord and also holy war.

11. Then from the family of the Danites, from Zorah and from Eshtaol, 600 men armed with weapons of war set out.

12. And they went up and camped at Kiriath-Jearim in Judah. Therefore they called that place Mahaneh-Dan to this day; behold it is west of Kiriath-Jearim.

Again we are reminded of Samson, who was from Mahaneh-Dan (Jud. 13:25), in order once again to make the contrast between that mighty man and these Danites.

13. And they passed from there to the hill country of Ephraim and came to the house of Micah.

14. Then the five men who went to spy out the country of Laish answered and said to their kinsmen, "Do you know that there are in these houses an ephod and teraphim and a graven image and a molten image? Now therefore, consider what you should do."

15. And they turned aside there and came to the house of the young man, the Levite, to the house of Micah, and asked him of his welfare.

16. And the 600 men armed with their weapons of war, who were of the sons of Dan, stood by the entrance of the gate.

17. Now the five men who went to spy out the land went up and entered there, and took the graven image and the ephod and the teraphim and the molten image, while the priest stood by the entrance of the gate with the 600 men armed with weapons of war.

18. And when these went into Micah's house and took the graven image, the ephod and teraphim and the molten image, the priest said to them, "What are you doing?"

19. And they said to him, "Be silent, put your hand over your mouth and come with us, and be to us a father and a priest. Is it better for you to be a priest to the house of one man, or to be priest of a tribe and a family in Israel?"

20. And the priest's heart was glad, and he took the ephod and teraphim and the graven image, and went among the people.

21. Then they turned and departed, and put the little ones and the livestock and the valuables in front of them.

Verse 14 is designed to provoke us to think. "Now consider what you should do." A good question. They should have burned Micah and his house of idols down (Dt. 17:1-7; 13:1ff.). That is not what they do.

This passage lists all four idols over and over again, in order to pile up for us a sense of the comprehensive idolatry involved.

The Levite rejoices at his new opportunity. He gets to move from the small country church to the big city tabernacle. While such a move would not be wrong in all cases, here it clearly is. Glory is what this man seeks, but he does not seek it from God.

Realizing that Micah will pursue them, the Danite army stays at the rear of the column. But maybe the writer of Judges is engaging in more ridicule here, since putting the women and children in front certainly makes them look like cowards!

22. When they had gone some distance from the house of Micah, the men who were in the houses near Micah's house assembled and overtook the sons of Dan.

23. And they cried to the sons of Dan, who turned their faces and said to Micah, "What is the matter with you, that you have assembled together?"

24. And he said, "You have taken away my gods which I made, and the priest, and have gone away, and what do I have

besides? So how can you say to me, 'What is the matter with you?' "

25. And the sons of Dan said to him, "Do not let your voice be heard among us, lest fierce men fall upon you and you lose your life, with the lives of your household."

26. So the sons of Dan went on their way; and when Micah saw that they were too strong for him, he turned and went back to his house.

A little community of apostates had formed around Micah's shrine, and they joined Micah in pursuing the Danites. They didn't want their gods taken away.

There is a lot of humor and irony here. Micah, the thief, is himself robbed. Even more ridiculous is what Micah himself says, "You have taken away my gods which I made." Man-made gods aren't very loyal to their makers, it seems. Here again is the heart of Baalism: gods in the control of men.

The Danites remind us of a motorcycle gang. "Hey, keep your voice down," they say. "There are some real tough guys back in the camp behind us, and if they hear what you say, we might not be able to restrain them. You'd better go your way." Micah gets the message.

27. Then they took what Micah had made and the priest who had belonged to him, and came to Laish, to a people quiet and secure, and struck them with the edge of the sword; and they burned the city with fire.

28. And there was no one to deliver them, because it was far from Sidon and they had no dealings with anyone, and it was in the valley which is near Beth-Rehob. And they rebuilt the city and lived in it.

Beth-Rehob means "House of Rooms" or "Roomy Place." The Danites have found a wide open space, it seems. They have renounced the Lord as their *Yasha'* (Giver of a wide, open space), and have made their own.

They burned the city with fire. This is a parody of the hormah burnings in Joshua and elsewhere in Judges. The fire this time was not from the altar of the Lord, but was strange fire.

Again the passage stresses the peacefulness of these Canaanites. This is not to say that they were not to be driven out, because they were indeed included in God's command that all Canaanites be driven out or exterminated. The point here, however, is that the Danite tough guys were really cowards. Ezekiel later on compares Gog and Magog to these Danites (Ezk. 38:11, 14).

29. And they called the name of the city Dan, after the name of Dan their father who was born in Israel; however, the name of the city formerly was Laish.

We already know that Dan their father "was born in Israel." Why mention it here? Because by doing so the writer is able to introduce a subtle contrast between Dan and his descendants. He was born in Israel. They have, for all intents and purposes, left the nation. In leaving God, they have forsaken the kingdom.

30. And the sons of Dan set up for themselves the graven image; and Jonathan, the son of Gershom, the son of Manasseh [MOSES], he and his sons were priests to the tribe of the Danites until the day of the captivity of the land.
31. So they set up for themselves Micah's graven image which he had made, all the time that the house of God was at Shiloh.

The captivity of the land spoken of here is the Philistine captivity delineated in 1 Samuel 4 and 7:3, 4. This to me is another slight indication that Samuel probably wrote the book of Judges. It was apparently written when he was judging Israel, at least.

The city of Dan became a center of idolatrous worship, under the leadership of Moses' descendants! Jeroboam I of Northern Israel (Ephraim) put one of his golden calves there. Jeroboam's program was as follows: Rather than trust the promise of the Lord for his protection (1 Ki. 11:38), Jeroboam feared that if the people worshipped the Lord in Jerusalem they would eventually reject him as their king and kill him (1 Ki. 12:27). To prevent that, he created a separate religion. He set up two golden calves, one at Bethel near the border with Judah, and one at Dan for obvious reasons (1 Ki. 12:29.). He created a new theology, based on the original golden calf incident. He maintained that the golden calf was the real religion, and that the worship in Jerusalem was false. It was the calf which had brought Israel out of Egypt (1 Ki. 12:28). Jeroboam rewrote history, maintaining that Nadab and Abihu had been the righteous ones, and that they had been wrongly murdered by Moses and Aaron, and so Jeroboam named his sons Nadab and Abihu (1 Ki. 14:1, 20; Abijam is the same as Abihu).

Just so, the Mormons and Jehovah's Witnesses pretend that the true Christian faith is anti-trinitarian. The Council of Nicaea, they say, was the triumph of the false, Trinitarian faith. They want to return to the "true" faith, the anti-trinitarian faith of the heretics, the religion of the golden calf.

Conclusion

This story, as a parody of Israelite history, is a fine presentation of the nature of idolatry. It begins with a false exodus, a Levite leaving his congregation to seek a better place. It continues with the establishment of a false sanctuary, and then a false priesthood. Then comes a false spying out of the land, and a false conquest. The idolatrous civilization is an ape of the true one, according as Martin Luther said, Satan is the ape of God.

It was the job of the Levites to keep Israel pure by setting forth the true faith. They were to guard Israel, as representatives of her True Husband. When they failed, the result was apostasy, idolatry, and corruption. Just so, it is the job of pastors to represent the Groom to the Bride (which is why women may not rule in the Church, 1 Cor. 14:34 in the context of v. 29). When the Church drifts into error, she is indeed at fault, but the primary blame lies with the pastors. Judgment begins at the house of God, and reformation must begin with the Levites.

16

THE LEVITES' FAILURE: MORAL DEPRAVITY
(Judges 19)

The second appendix to Judges has three sections. The first (Jud. 19) is a true horror story, very carefully and dramatically written, delineating the rape and murder of an Israelite woman by a gang of thugs in a Benjamite town. The second part (Jud. 20) reveals the astonishing fact that the entire tribe of Benjamin chose to stand with this gang, rather than punish them, and as a result all Israel went to war against Benjamin. The third part (Jud. 21) concerns the fact that the tribe of Benjamin was virtually wiped out, and the problem of rebuilding the tribe.

As was the case with the first appendix, the various commands and promises of the Lord that are involved in this narrative are not expressed here, but are found in the laws God gave Israel at Sinai. We shall examine them as we come to the sections they apply to. Also, God's evaluation of these incidents is not expressed as such, but events fall out in such a way as to make that evaluation obvious.

Turning now to Judges 19, we find here a very carefully constructed narrative. If we read it as if we had never before heard the story, we find a steady rise in tension in the way the writer has set it out. It is set out as a nightmare. The Levite delays on his journey until late in the day. As the sun goes down, we become uneasy about what may happen. As the scene grows darker, our sense of foreboding increases. No one invites the Levite and his family in to spend the night. The old man who does finally take them in urges them not to spend the night in the square. Sure enough, a gang of Sodomites surrounds the house at which they stay. And then comes the shocker: The Levite kicks his wife out of the house for them to rape and murder. As the day begins to break, the Sodomites leave her alone, and she crawls back to the door. As the sun rises, she dies.

Few stories in the Bible are constructed with as much "literary finesse" as this one. There is a reason for it. The writer piles up in us a sense of outrage. Each stage of the story is filled with drama and meaning. The Levite might have spent the night among the heathen, but chose to lodge among fellow Israelites. The scene of the Levite, a holy man who normally would be accorded especial respect, being studiously ignored in the city square by all passers by, is pregnant in its simplicity. As the story is told, our gorge rises within us. Surely the tribe of Benjamin will punish those responsible for this horror. But then comes the second shocker, in chapter 20, for Benjamin protects its criminal class.

Judges 19 may be outlined as follows:

  I. The Unfaithful Wife (19:1-2)

 II. The Levite and his Father-in-Law (19:3-9)

III. The Nightmare Journey (19:10-28)
    A. Late Afternoon: The Pagans Bypassed (19:10-12)
    B. Sundown: Lodging with Israelites (19:13-15)
    C. Twilight: The Old Man and the City Square (19:15-21)
    D. Dark: The Assault of the Sodomites (19:22-24)
    E. Midnight to Dawn: The Rape and Murder of the Wife (19:25-28)

 IV. The Call for Holy War (19:29-30)

The Unfaithful Wife

19:1. Now it came about in those days, when there was no king in Israel, that there was a certain Levite sojourning in the remote part of the hill country of Ephraim, who took a wife, a concubine for himself in Bethlehem in Judah.

2. But his concubine played the harlot against him, and she went away from him to her father's house in Bethlehem in Judah, and was there for a period of four months.

3. Then her husband arose and went after her to speak to her heart in order to bring her back, taking with him his servant and a pair of donkeys. So she brought him into her father's house, and when the girl's father saw him, he was glad to meet him.

If we can put ourselves back into the position of someone hearing this story for the first time, and having the mindset of an ancient Israelite, we may be delighted at how this story starts out. A girl from a poor family is sold to become the wife of a Levite ministering in a remote place. The dowry goes to her father instead of to her, so that she is an unendowered wife, or concubine.[1]

At some point, this wife commits adultery. When caught, she flees in shame back to her father's house. Because her Levite husband loves her, however, he pursues her. Like Joseph later on, he is unwilling to press for the death penalty (Lev. 20:10; Dt. 22:22-27; Matt. 1:19). When he gets to her father's home, everyone is glad to see him. He speaks tenderly to her heart, to woo her back to himself, and he is successful.

Here is a vignette of Israel and the Lord. Israel is the unendowered wife, who has no possessions of her own. She has played the harlot, but her Lord seeks her out again. The Lord takes along His servants the Levites (v. 2) to help Him.

To this point in the story, the Levite is correctly imaging the Lord to the people. We shall have to see, however, whether he maintains his role properly.

At the Father-in-Law's House

4. And his father-in-law, the girl's father, detained him; and he remained with him three days. So they ate and drank and he lodged there.

5. Now it came about on the fourth day that they got up early in the morning, and he arose to go; and the girl's father said to his son-in-law, "Sustain your heart with a piece of bread, and afterward you may go."

6. So both of them sat down and ate and drank together; and the girl's father said to the man, "Please be willing to spend the night, and let your heart be merry."

7. Then the man arose to go, but his father-in-law urged him so that he spent the night there again.

8. And on the fifth day he arose to go early in the morning, and the girl's father said, "Please sustain your heart, and wait until the day declines"; so both of them ate.

9. When the man arose to go along with his concubine and servant, his father-in-law, the girl's father, said to him, "Behold now, the day has drawn to a close; please spend the night. Lo,

---

1. See my book, *The Law of the Covenant: An Exposition of Exodus 21–23* (Tyler, TX: Institute for Christian Economics, 1984), pp. 84ff.

the day is declining; spend the night here that your heart may be merry. Then tomorrow you may arise early for your journey so that you may go to your tent [home]."

The story seems to bog down and stretch out here. Why this emphasis on lingering at the house of the father-in-law? It does not seem to add any tension to the story, and it does not seem to make any point.

I should like to suggest an overall pattern into which this section of the narrative fits, which I believe explains what we have here. When the girl goes back to her father's house, it is as if Israel had gone back to Egypt or to Ur of the Chaldees. When Israel played the harlot, she rejected the Lord as husband and sought the gods she formerly worshipped in Ur and in Egypt (Josh. 24:2, 14). There is a *formal* parallel between Israel's return to her father's house (idolatry) and the girl's return to her father's house when she plays the harlot. That is not to say that her father was himself a faithless man, only that a formal parallel exists.

We cannot help but notice the way the writer emphasizes how the father-in-law tried to detain the Levite. We might expect the writer to say that the girl's father tried to get the Levite to prolong his stay, but when we read over and over and over again that the father-in-law persuaded him to stay a bit longer, we are alerted to a theme of "detaining." Now, the Levite was a man with a calling, a task. He was supposed to be pastor of a local congregation in the remote part of Ephraim. For him to be gone too long would result in a neglect of his task. Thus, after three days, he wants to depart. The girl's father, however, detains him. Now we are reminded of Laban, how he sought to detain Jacob, and of Pharaoh's detaining of Israel.[2] Once again, there is no indication of a *moral* parallel between this father-in-law and Laban or Pharaoh, but there is a *formal* parallel. After three days is indeed the proper time for a definitive break, to be on one's way; but the father-in-law persuades him to stay. In all, the father-in-law is shown trying to get the Levite to stay five times (v. 4, 5, 6-7, 8, 9).

By doing this, the writer creates in us a sense of urgency.

---

2. See my book, *Law of the Covenant,* pp. 32ff., for a study of this "exodus pattern" in the relationship of Jacob and Laban.

What had been a pleasant stay is turning into a hassle. We want the Levite to go ahead and get back where he belongs. There is something not quite right about remaining too long in the father-in-law's house (compare Gen. 2:24). If there is a message for Israel here, it is that they are being dragged down by too much familiarity with the house of their father-in-law, which is to say, too much familiarity with the house of that paganism from which they had been delivered. The emphasis is on "eating and drinking" with the father-in-law (vv. 4, 5, 6, 8). Again, this is not morally wrong, but in terms of the typology it contains a warning not to be too familiar with one's unsavory past.

I mentioned in the previous chapter of this study that Bethlehem in Judah is presented in a rather unsavory fashion in Judges and Ruth 1. Here, the bread of Bethlehem is shown seducing and preventing this Levite from getting back to his appointed tasks.

Thus, the writer has skillfully created in us an air of tension. The Levite really does have to be going, now. He needs to get on home, where he belongs. He has been delayed from his holy calling long enough.

There is one other matter to note in this section, which has to do with its numerology. The girl stayed with her father 4 months (v. 2), and then they left on the 5th day (v. 8ff.). It might not occur to us to add 4 to 5, but it would have occurred to the ancient reader to do so. We wind up with 9. In some contexts this might not have any meaning, but here it does. The girl has played the harlot. At exactly nine periods of time later, she is killed, raped to death. This is a horrible inversion of what should have taken place. She should have been faithful to her husband, and after nine months borne him a child. This is a picture to Israel of the consequences of sin. The fruit of faithfulness is life, but the fruit of faithlessness is death.

Bypassing Jebus (Jerusalem)

10. But the man was not willing to spend the night, so he arose and departed and came to a place opposite Jebus (that is, Jerusalem). And there were with him a pair of saddled donkeys; his concubine also was with him.

11. When they were near Jebus, the day was almost gone; and the servant said to his master, "Please come, and let us turn

aside into this city of the Jebusites and spend the night in it."

12. However, his master said to him, "We will not turn aside into the city of foreigners who are not of the sons of Israel; but we will go on as far as Gibeah."

13. And he said to his servant, "Come and let us approach one of these places; and we will spend the night in Gibeah or Ramah."

There are two things going on here. First of all, the Levite does not want to spend the night with the heathen. Rather, he will entrust himself to fellow Israelites, who will honor his station as a priest of God. By calling attention to this, the narrator causes us to wonder what will happen when he gets to Gibeah. Knowing the sequel, we realize that Gibeah is presented as far worse than anything they might have encountered in Jebus.

Second, Israel had failed to conquer Jerusalem, as we saw in Judges 1:21. Had Jerusalem been conquered, the Levite might have spent the night there. The narrator calls our attention to this explicitly in verse 10, by reminding us of what we already know, that Jebus is Jerusalem. The holy city, which had been Melchizedek's capital (Gen. 14:18), was not available for sanctuary. Israel's compromise was to blame.

The mention of Ramah here serves to give the theology of the passage a sharper focus. Ramah, as we noted on page 76 above, is where Rachel died giving birth to Benjamin. This helps to clarify and reinforce the "symbolic/allegorical overtones" in this narrative. Rachel and Jacob had been delayed in Laban's house. They had gotten away, with their servants and family. At Ramah, some distance from Bethlehem, Rachel had gone into labor and given birth to Benjamin, and then died.

The story before us parallels and inverts the story of Jacob and Rachel. Here again a woman leaves her father's house, with her husband, after being detained, and she dies near Ramah. She dies after nine periods of time, but there is no birth for Benjamin. Rather, the consequence of her death is a death for the whole tribe of Benjamin. Indeed, the parallels that the narrator has created enable him to point the finger at Benjamin and say, "In killing this poor woman, who represented the bride of the Lord, you have raped and murdered your mother." The narrator can also point the finger at the Levite and say, "You certainly did not love your wife the way Jacob loved Rachel, and the way the Lord loves Israel."

Sodom in Israel

14. So they passed along and went their way, and the sun set on them near Gibeah which belongs to Benjamin.

15. And they turned aside there in order to enter and lodge in Gibeah. When he entered, he sat down in the open square of the city, for no one took them into his house to spend the night.

Sunset forced them to turn aside to Gibeah. They camped in the open square of the city, but we get an ominous feel when we read that no one took them in. So important is hospitality as a characteristic of the believer that it is one of the things explicitly mentioned for judgment on the final day (Matt. 25:35).

But there is more. Had this city loved the Lord, people would have vied with one another to have this Levite in for the night. The Levite calls attention to this in verse 18, when he says "I am one who walks at the house of the LORD, and yet no man will take me into his house." (This is a literal translation of the Hebrew; most English versions mistranslate it.) Gibeah has no interest in the Lord or in His Levites.

16. Then behold, an old man was coming out of the field from his work at evening. Now the man was from the hill country of Ephraim, and he was sojourning in Gibeah, but the men of the place were Benjamites.

17. And he lifted up his eyes and saw the traveler in the open square of the city; and the old man said, "Where are you going, and where do you come from?"

18. And he said to him, "We are passing from Bethlehem in Judah to the remote part of the hill country of Ephraim, for I am from there and I went to Bethlehem in Judah. But I am one who walks at the house of the LORD, and no man will take me into his house.

19. "Yet there is both straw and fodder for our donkeys, and also bread and wine for me, your maidservant, and the young man who is with your servants; there is no lack of anything."

20. And the old man said, "Peace to you. Only let me take care of all your needs; however, do not spend the night in the open square."

The self-sufficiency of the Levite is a further shame and proof against the inhospitality of Gibeah, for he would have been a burden to no one.

The old man here is not named. We have simply an "old man." The younger generation is grossly corrupt, but this older man still has some of the courtesy and decency of his generation. We shall see, however, that he is hardly pure himself, and this points us again to the way in which the sins of the fathers are multiplied in the children.

We are also told that the old man is from Ephraim. Apparently there was absolutely no one native to Gibeah who was righteous. This is a tip-off to the alert reader, for the same thing was true of Sodom. None of the locals were righteous; the only righteous man was a stranger living in the city. He also was the only hospitable man in the place.

By establishing a parallel between the old man and Lot, the narrator also establishes a parallel between the Levite and the angels of the Lord. The angels in their purity protected the daughters of Lot. They acted as proper guardians. How will the Levite behave?

21. So he took him into his house and gave the donkeys fodder, and they washed their feet and ate and drank.

22. While they were making their hearts merry, behold, the men of the city, certain sons of Belial [thugs], surrounded the house, pounding the door; and they spoke to the owner of the house, the old man, saying "Bring out the man who came into your house that we may know [have sex with] him."

23. Then the man, the owner of the house, went out to them and said to them, "No, my fellows, please do not act so wickedly; since this man has come into my house, do not commit this act of folly.

24. "Here is my virgin daughter and his concubine. Please let me bring them out that you may ravish them and do to them what is good in your eyes. But do not commit such an act of folly against this man."

Verse 21 encapsulates what hospitality meant in ancient Israel. The old man took them into his own house. Second, he gave his own food to their beast of burden. Third, he had them wash their feet. Fourth, he gave them food and drink. A moment's reflection will show the reader that this is also how God shows His hospitality to us: He invites us to His house, provides for the details (donkeys) of our lives, washes our feet, and feeds us bread and wine. The only aspect of this that is unclear to us is footwashing. Since the ground was cursed under the Old Covenant, before the coming of Christ, coming in contact with the ground was a sign of coming in contact with dirt and the curse. People wore shoes, normally, to keep them from contact with the ground. Washing the dirt off the feet was, thus, a religious or symbolic act, cleansing the unclean and thereby removing "death" and granting life. (For more on this, see footnote 2 on page 227 above.) These details of hospitality create a gentle scene, and set us up for the shock in the next verse.

Like Lot, this old man has been influenced by his environment, or else he was morally compromised all along, and he offers his virgin daughter to the Sodomites. He also offers the Levite's wife, without asking permission it seems (though he may have gotten permission; we are not told).

To this point in the story, we have not seen anything negative about the Levite. He has imaged the Lord properly in seeking his wayward wife. He has tried to get back to his ministry as soon as possible. He has avoided staying with the heathen, and sought to fellowship with the righteous. What happens next is, in terms of the narration, an unexpected and incredibly shocking turn of events.

25. But the men would not listen to him, so the man [host or Levite] seized his concubine and brought her out to them. And they raped her and abused her all night until morning, then let her go at the approach of dawn.

26. At the turning of the morning, the woman came and fell down at the doorway of the man's house where her master was, until full daylight.

27. When her master arose in the morning and opened the doors of the house and went out to go on his way, then behold his concubine was lying at the doorway of the house, with her hands on the threshold.

28. And he said to her, "Get up and let us go," but there was no answer. Then he placed her on the donkey; and the man arose and went to his place [home].

There are several things to notice here. First we see the cruelty of this Levite. He certainly does not love his wife as Christ loves the Church (Eph. 5:25). He certainly does not image the Lord's love for Israel. Either he kicks her out himself, or he stands by and lets his host give her to the Sodomites. We see this cruelty also in verse 28, where he barks out (in Hebrew): "Get up! Let's go!" It is even shorter in Hebrew than it is in English. The narrator thus reveals to us that this Levite has never really forgiven his wayward wife. He wanted her back, yes, but when the chips were down, he was certainly not going to die for her! After all, she was a whore. Let her go out and do her tricks. And in the morning, "All right, let's go. You've had your fun." No sympathy. She had cheated on him, so he could easily rationalize dealing harshly with her.

Second, we notice that death is the end to which this young woman comes. It is a sad end. We had hoped that she would be saved by a loving husband, as Hosea saved Gomer and as the Lord saved Israel. This was not to be. The wages of sin is death, and so it was for her. (Hosea is the only prophet even to mention the incident at Gibeah, and he does so three times: 5:8; 9:9; 10:9. Hosea's pursuit of wayward Gomer corresponds to this story, except that God guides Hosea to a more honorable performance.)

Third, as we have had occasion to note previously in this book, the doorway is the place of birth. Sunrise is another picture of birth and strength, as we have seen. Here everything is inverted. She dies on the threshold as the sun rises. And as we have noted, this is after nine periods of time, when she might have been giving birth. The narrator portrays this scene with heart-rending pathos and consummate skill. We can see her crawling bleeding back to the man who should have protected her, and dying without ever seeing his face or hearing his voice again. Her mute plea for help and protection sets us up for the sharp language of verse 28: "Get up! Let's go!"

So the message is clear for Israel. They should have been giving birth to all kinds of good works for God, but instead they had been playing the harlot and they were dying. Similarly, the Levites should have been guarding them, but because they were not, social disaster was the result.

We might feel sorry for this Levite, but the fact is that

Biblically speaking what happened was his own fault and the fault of his brethren. Had they been sounding forth the law of God clearly in every place, Gibeah would have been a clean, hospitable city. This nightmare resulted precisely from the failure of the Levites to preach and to guard Israel from sin. What happened to the Levite was, in a sense, one more example of God's ironic "eye for eye" justice.

Finally, the attack of the thugs of Gibeah was not just against a man, it was particularly against a Levite. Initially they refused the two women, one of whom was a virgin, in their lust for this man (v. 25). (Why they accepted the concubine in the end we are not told.) In so doing, they attacked the Lord's anointed. Like Ephraim making war on Jephthah, they assaulted someone who symbolized the Lord in their midst. This simply added to the enormity of their sin. When the men of Sodom attacked the angels, they thought they were mere men. The men of Gibeah were worse, for they knew that this man was a Levite, a symbol of the Lord in their midst.

There is a typological connection here, which is that the attack upon Jesus Christ in the gospels was basically a homosexual or Sodomite attack, in the spiritual sense. Instead of putting His bride out to suffer, He took it upon Himself. There is no reason to think that Christ was physically assaulted by Sodomites, any more than He was really surrounded by wild bulls of Bashan, Ps. 22:12. The point is that this narrative shows us one more dimension of the work of Christ, and of His sufferings, at the spiritual, psychological level at least.

> 29. When he entered his house, he took a knife and laid hold of his concubine and cut her in twelve pieces, limb by limb, and sent her throughout the territory of Israel.
>
> 30. And it came about that all who saw it said, "Nothing like this has ever happened or been seen from the day when the sons of Israel came up from the land of Egypt to this day. Consider it, take counsel, and speak up."

Chopping the woman's body into twelve pieces strikes us as grotesque, but it was a symbolic act. This is the same terminology used, in Hebrew, for cutting up sacrifices. Tearing and ripping animals apart, or one's garment, was a sign of the tearing of the Covenant. The murder of this woman was a breach in

the Covenant, and meant that the land was torn up. To symbolize this, the Levite sent the pieces of this woman's body to
the twelve tribes of Israel. This dead woman now symbolized
the nation, hacked to bits by sin. Action to restore order was
needed. The Levite, who had proven no protector, at least
proved to be an avenger.

17

THE DESTRUCTION OF BENJAMIN
(Judges 20)

Judges 20 records the destruction of the tribe of Benjamin. An outline of the chapter is as follows:

    I. Israel Summoned (20:1-2)

    II. The Levite's Report (20:3-7)

    III. The Inquest (20:8-13)

    IV. The War Against Benjamin (20:14-48)
        A. Preparations and the First Battle (20:14-21)
        B. The Second Battle (20:22-25)
        C. Repentance (20:26-28)
        D. The Third Battle (20:29-47)
            1. The First Account (20:29-36a)
            2. The Second Account (20:36b-47)
        E. The Liquidation of Benjamin (20:48)

The Levite's Report

20:1. Then all the sons of Israel from Dan to Beersheba, including the land of Gilead, came out, and the congregation assembled as one man to the LORD at Mizpah.

2. And the cornerstones of all the people, of all the tribes of Israel, took their stand in the assembly of the people of God, 400,000 foot soldiers who drew the sword.

3. (Now the sons of Benjamin heard that the sons of Israel had gone up to Mizpah.) And the sons of Israel said, "Tell us, how did this wickedness take place?"

4. So the Levite, the husband of the woman who was murdered, answered and said, "I came with my concubine to spend the night at Gibeah which belongs to Benjamin.

5. "But the men of Gibeah rose up against me and surrounded the house at night because of me. They intended to kill me; in-

stead, they ravished my concubine so that she died.

6. "And I took hold of my concubine and cut her in pieces and sent her throughout the land of Israel's inheritance; for they have committed a lewd and disgraceful act in Israel.

7. "Behold, all you sons of Israel, give your advice and counsel here."

In verse 1, the expression "from Dan to Beersheba" probably reflects the hand of the narrator, since the Danites probably had not yet captured Laish at this time. "From Dan to Beersheba" is an expression meaning from the northernmost city to the southernmost. The trans-Jordanian tribes also came. Everyone was there.

They drew up in battle array. The Israelite army was arranged with sergeants over 10s, lieutenants over 50s, captains over 100s, majors over 1000s, and colonels over 10,000s.[1] The "cornerstones" were the tribal generals over each tribal army, and in military formation they probably were positioned at the corners of the assemblies (compare 1 Sam. 14:38; Is. 19:13).

The number 4 is the number of the land and its four corners. Thus, in God's providence, 400,000 men were mustered out to defend the purity of the land. Benjamin heard about the muster, but refused to come.

The Levite gives a somewhat jaundiced account. He glosses over the fact that he gave his wife to the Sodomites of Gibeah, and says that they had intended to kill him. Our estimation of him sinks to new lows as we hear these lies.

The Inquest

8. Then all the people arose as one man, saying, "Not one of us will go to his tent, nor will any of us return to his house.

9. "But now this is the thing which we will do to Gibeah; we will go up against it by lot.

10. "And we will take 10 men out of 100 throughout the tribes of Israel, and 100 out of 1000, and 1000 out of 10,000 to supply food for the people, that when they come to Gibeah of

---

1. See my essay, "How Biblical is Protestant Worship, Part 1," in *The Geneva Papers* No. 25 (Feb. 1984), published by Geneva Ministries, 708 Hamvasy Lane, Tyler, TX. This essay discusses the cross-shaped layout of the Israelite camp at Mount Sinai, and in connection with this explores the nature of Israelite military formation as the Bible sets it forth.

Benjamin, they may punish them for all the disgraceful acts that they have committed in Israel."

11. Thus all the men of Israel were gathered against the city, united as one man.

12. Then the tribes of Israel sent men through the entire tribe of Benjamin, saying, "What is this wickedness that has taken place among you?

13. "Now then, deliver up the men, the sons of Belial in Gibeah, that we may put them to death and burn away this wickedness from Israel." But the sons of Benjamin would not listen to the voice of their brothers, the sons of Israel.

We begin to see the parallels between this last story in Judges and the first. Just as the tribes went up against the Canaanites by lot, so now they go up against Benjamin the same way. The Benjamites are the moral and spiritual Canaanites here.

The offer of peace to Benjamin, which gives them the opportunity to choose whom they will serve, comes from the laws of war given in Deuteronomy 20:10-11. As is so often the case, the Benjamites stood with their sinful relatives against the Lord. How many times in the Church do we see wives standing by rebellious husbands, or parents standing by apostate children. Which is thicker, blood or God's covenant? Such was the issue then, and such is it today. Any church that has had to excommunicate a sinner has seen other people march out, fists raised, because they would not break off their relationship with the excommunicant.

Israel says that the wickedness must be "burned" out (v. 13). The Hebrew verb form used here is relatively rare, and is used for sacred sacrificial fires and for the purging out of sinners by the death penalty. When Benjamin refuses to purge out the thugs of Gibeah, the result is the sacrificial torching of that city (v. 40).

Preparations and the First Battle

14. And the sons of Benjamin gathered from the cities to Gibeah, to go out to battle against the sons of Israel.

15. And from the cities on that day the sons of Benjamin were mustered, 26,000 men who draw the sword, besides the inhabitants of Gibeah who were mustered 700 choice men.

16. Out of all these people 700 choice men were left-handed; each one could sling a stone at a hair and not miss.

At the time Israel came into the land, Benjamin numbered 45,600 men (Num. 26:41). They seem to have declined considerably at this point. We might think that not all of Benjamin came out, but at the end of this battle, virtually none of the tribe is left, creating the problem dealt with in Judges 21. Apparently 26,700 men represented all the men of Benjamin at this point.

Gibeah contributed 700 men, and among the whole Benjamite army there were 700 left-handed slingers. Nothing more is said about these two groups. It appears that the reason for calling attention to them here is to note the number 7, the number of fulness and strength. Symbolically, Benjamin and Gibeah have a strong position at this point.

> 17. Then the men of Israel besides Benjamin were mustered, 400,000 men who draw the sword; all these were men of war.
> 18. Now the sons of Israel arose, went up to Bethel, and inquired of God, and said, "Who shall go up first for us to battle against the sons of Benjamin?" Then the LORD said, "Judah first."
> 19. So the sons of Israel arose in the morning and camped against Gibeah.
> 20. And the men of Israel went out to battle against Benjamin, and the men of Israel arrayed for battle against them at Gibeah.
> 21. Then the sons of Benjamin came out of Gibeah and cut down on that day 22,000 men of Israel.

As in Judges 1, Israel inquired of the ephod who should go up first, and the reply again was Judah. We cannot miss the point that the campaign against Benjamin was just like the campaign against the Canaanites.

Israel is defeated. This is a surprise. Their cause is plainly righteous, yet Benjamin easily defeats them. Obviously there is a terrible problem, and it is equally obvious what it is: All of Israel is generally guilty of the same sin as Gibeah and Benjamin. All their Levites are failing, and all of them are playing the harlot. There is no other reason why they would be defeated in battle.

The Second Battle

> 22. But the people, the men of Israel, encouraged themselves and arrayed for battle again in the place where they had arrayed themselves the first day.

23. And the sons of Israel went up and wept before the LORD until evening, and inquired of the LORD, saying, "Shall we again draw near for battle against the sons of my brother Benjamin?" And the LORD said, "Go up against him."

24. Then the sons of Israel approached the sons of Benjamin the second day.

25. And Benjamin went out to meet them from Gibeah the second day and cut down again 18,000 men of the sons of Israel; all these drew the sword.

Israel arrayed itself for battle "in the place where they had arrayed themselves the first day." We see no repentance, no confession that they also are guilty. Thus, they once again are defeated. Their total loss is 40,000, a tithe of their whole army. The tithe is what the Lord claims, as a token of claiming everything. In taking this tithe, the Lord was judging them all.

Repentance

26. Then all the sons of Israel and all the people went up and came to Bethel and wept; thus they remained there before the LORD and fasted that day until evening. And they offered burnt offerings and peace offerings before the LORD.

27. And the sons of Israel inquired of the LORD (for the Ark of the Covenant of God was there in those days,

28. And Phineas the son of Eleazar, Aaron's son, stood before it to minister in those days), saying, "Shall I yet again go out to battle against the sons of my brother Benjamin, or shall I cease?" And the LORD said, "Go up, for tomorrow I will deliver them into your hand."

Now Israel has gotten the message. First they fasted until evening. The new day began in evening, and fasting for the remainder of the day was a confession that they were cut off from God's blessings of food. Next they sacrificed burnt offerings, which symbolized that they were guilty, and deserved to be burned up by God's fire, but that they trusted in the Substitute. Then they sacrificed peace offerings, which symbolized communion restored. They did this at evening. Since the new day began at evening (as in Genesis 1, "evening and morning"), this is the third day, the day of judgment, resurrection, and new beginnings.

We are told that Aaron's grandson was ministering in those

days. This is how we know that this story happened very early in the period of the judges. The reason why this detail is given at this point rather than earlier in the story is that only now is Israel really and truly approaching God in humility and faith.

The Third Battle, First Account

29. So Israel set men in ambush around Gibeah.

30. And the sons of Israel went up against the sons of Benjamin on the third day and arrayed themselves against Gibeah, as at other times.

This time Israel does not position itself as before, though Benjamin does. This is the third day, the day for a new beginning in righteousness. Rather, Israel uses the tactic it used in defeating the Canaanite city of Ai (Josh. 8). Just as Israel had been defeated initially by Ai because of sin in the camp (Josh. 7), so Israel was initially defeated by Benjamin. Just as the men of Ai knew all was lost when they turned around and saw their city aflame, so it happened to Benjamin. In every respect, the Benjamites, by acting like Canaanites, are treated according to the punishments God handed down against the Canaanites.

31. And the sons of Benjamin went out to meet the people and were drawn away from the city, and they began to strike and kill some of the people, as at other times, on the highways, one of which goes up to Bethel and the other to Gibeah, in the field, about 30 men of Israel.

32. And the sons of Benjamin said, "They are struck down before us, as at the first." But the sons of Israel [had] said, "Let us flee that we may draw them away from the city to the highways."

33. Then all the men of Israel arose from their place and arrayed themselves at Baal-Tamar; and the men of Israel in ambush broke out of their place, even out of the Meadow of Gibeah.

34. When 10,000 choice men from all Israel came against Gibeah, the battle became heavy, but Benjamin did not know that evil was touching them [disaster was close to them].

35. And the LORD struck Benjamin before Israel, so that the sons of Israel destroyed 25,100 men of Benjamin that day, all who draw the sword.

36a. So the sons of Benjamin saw that they were smitten.

Benjamin had started out with 26,000 men, plus 700 from Gibeah. On the third day, 25,100 men fell. After the battle was over, 600 were left (v. 47). This leaves 1000 unaccounted for. We may assume that they died in the first two battles.

It is not clear whether any Israelites died in this third battle. Benjamin *began* to smite about 30 men. It is unclear from the Hebrew whether Benjamin was beginning "to smite and wound," or beginning "to smite the wounded." It may be that Israel lost no men in the battle. The number 30 may be significant, since we are told that it was "about 30" rather than the exact figure, as pointing again to the third day. These 30 men offered themselves as sacrifices to enable the rest of the army to lie in wait. This might be intended by the writer to connect with the sacrifices offered on the third day, which enabled Israel to be restored and to win the war.

A full brigade of 10,000 men of Israel took possession of Gibeah once the Benjamite army had been lured off. At this point, the story breaks off and we are simply given a theological summary of the battle: The *Lord* was the one Who defeated Benjamin, with the result that 25,100 Benjamites died that day.

This paragraph gives the theological perspective. It was on the third day, after the substitutionary sacrifice, that the Lord defeated Benjamin. This is the essence of the victory. Now, however, the narrator tells the story of the battle a second time, in more detail, showing how Israel did the Lord's work. In the second telling of the story, it will be made clear precisely how the Lord struck Benjamin.

The Battle in Detail

36b. When the men of Israel gave ground to Benjamin because they relied on the men in ambush whom they had set against Gibeah,

37. The men in ambush hurried and rushed against Gibeah; the men in ambush also deployed and struck all the city with the edge of the sword.

38. Now the appointed sign between the men of Israel and the men in ambush was that they should make a great cloud of smoke rise from the city.

39. Then the men of Israel turned in the battle, and Benjamin began to strike and kill about 30 men of Israel, for they

said, "Surely they are smitten before us, as in the first battle."

40. But when the cloud began to rise from the city in a column of smoke, Benjamin looked behind them; and behold, the whole burnt sacrifice of the city was going up to heaven.

The Lord struck Benjamin. Naturally this means that He put fear in their hearts, and strengthened the hearts and arms of Israel. Also, however, it means something specific. Just when Benjamin thought once again that they had won another battle, they turned around and saw Gibeah going up in smoke. But it was not just ordinary smoke. The Hebrew uses the word for whole burnt sacrifice. It was fire from God's altar at Bethel that had been used to torch the city. Gibeah became a whole burnt sacrifice to the Lord.

Before looking at this further, let us ask if this action had the Lord's approval. It meant that Israel was conducting holy war against Gibeah, and it meant that all within the city would be slaughtered, as we shall see. We must say, from the passage, that this did indeed have the Lord's approval. First, the Lord had guaranteed them victory when they consulted Him at the Tabernacle. They could not have brought fire from the altar without the approval of Phineas, and thus of the Lord. Second, the parallel between the burning of Gibeah and the statement of verse 35 that it was the Lord Who struck Benjamin, makes it clear that burning Gibeah was God's own appointed means of destroying it.

We took up the sacrifice of a city in our comments on Judges 1:8 and 17. We need to look at it a bit more fully here. The city of Gibeah was clearly a second Sodom, and in Genesis 19:24 and 28 we read that God rained fire on Sodom, and that Lot saw that "the smoke of the land ascended like the smoke of a kiln." Sodom was the first "hormah," the first city burned up by fire from heaven. It is entirely appropriate that Gibeah receive the same treatment.

There is also a parallel, as we have seen, to the defeat of Ai. A study of Joshua 8 shows that Ai was also burned up as a whole burnt sacrifice (Josh. 8:28).

By offering a whole burnt sacrifice on God's altar, Israel had confessed their sin and had put their faith in a Substitute (Jud. 20:26). As a result, they were not consumed. Benjamin, however, had rejected the Substitute, and so they were destroyed.

41. Then the men of Israel turned, and the men of Benjamin were terrified; for they saw that evil was touching them [disaster was close to them].

42. Therefore, they turned their backs before the men of Israel toward the direction of the wilderness, but the battle overtook them while those who came out of the cities destroyed them in the midst of them.

43. They surrounded Benjamin, pursued them without rest and trod them down opposite Gibeah toward the sunrise [east].

44. Thus 18,000 men of Benjamin fell; all these were valiant warriors.

45. And they [the rest] turned and fled toward the wilderness to the rock of Rimmon, but they gleaned 5000 of them on the highways and overtook them at Gidom and smote 2000 of them.

46. So all of Benjamin who fell that day were 25,000 men who draw the sword; all these were valiant warriors.

47. But 600 men turned and fled toward the wilderness to the rock of Rimmon, and they remained at the rock of Rimmon four months.

After the 10,000 men of Israel captured Gibeah, the remaining 350,000 men of the army attacked the Benjamite host. The Benjamite army fled toward the wilderness, and were cut down. Initially, 18,000 were slain, the same number Israel had lost the day before. At the end of the battle, the number of dead, in round numbers, was 25,000 (compare v. 35).

Then, 5000 were "gleaned." This is a very obscure way to describe the slaughter of these men, and the only other time the slaughter of men is called a gleaning is Jeremiah 6:9. The language here has two purposes. First, the very same rare Hebrew verb is used for mocking or abuse, and it used in Judges 19:25 to describe the rape and "abuse" of the wife of the Levite. Here is the eye for eye principle again, then: Just as Benjamin "abused" the poor woman to death, so they are "gleaned" to death. Second, this is the verb for gleaning in Leviticus 19:10 and Deuteronomy 24:21. Benjamin is here pictured as a vineyard, one that is subjected to an awful harvest. Not only is the main crop harvested, but the gleanings as well, so that (virtually) nothing is left.

The connection between the woman's body and a vineyard or field is common in Scripture, particularly in the Song of

Solomon. The men of Gibeah had not only raped this woman, they had "gleaned" her, so that she was not only harmed but killed. Just so, Benjamin is not only to be defeated, but "gleaned," so that it is destroyed. We may say that if the men of Gibeah had only raped her, then Benjamin would have been defeated but not completely destroyed.

All of this is important, as we shall see, in understanding what happens after the battle.

The progressive diminution of Benjamin, as it is described, creates for us a sense that the entire tribe is being liquidated. First 18,000 are killed, then 5000 are "gleaned," and then 2000 are smitten. Obviously, holy war is being conducted, and will not stop until no Benjamites are left.

> 48. The men of Israel then turned back against the sons of Benjamin and struck them with the edge of the sword, both the entire city with the cattle and all that they found; they also set on fire all the cities which they found.

We have now to discuss more fully whether this action was right or wrong. Did Israel break out of bounds and go too far? Is what we read in Judges 21 a punishment for Israel because they exceeded the Lord's requirements? Or do we have to look in another direction to understand what is going on here?

The problem is that there is no explicit statement of evaluation from the Lord in this passage. Commentators generally feel that this entire story is designed to show social anarchy, the result of not having the Lord as King. We don't have to disagree with this general assessment to point out that Israel as a whole had repented before the battle of the third day (Jud. 20:26) and was acting under the guidance of the Lord.

Clearly, to make a moral assessment of the slaughter of Benjamin, we need to take a close look at the laws of war in Deuteronomy. These are the commands of the Lord. We can then ask if Israel was obeying them properly or not. First of all, Deuteronomy 13:

> 12. If you hear in one of your cities which the LORD your God is giving you to live in, anyone saying that
> 13. Some sons of Belial have gone out from among you and have seduced the inhabitants of their city, saying, "Let us go and

serve other gods" (whom you have not known),

14. Then you shall investigate and search out and inquire thoroughly. And if it is true and the matter established that this abomination has been done among you,

15. You shall surely strike the inhabitants of that city with the edge of the sword, putting it under the ban [hormah] and all that is in it and its cattle with the edge of the sword.

16. Then you shall gather all its booty into the middle of its open square and burn the city and all its booty with fire as a whole burnt sacrifice to the LORD your God; and it shall be a ruin forever. It shall never be rebuilt.

There are several things to notice here. First, the apostates are referred to as "sons of Belial." It is not known exactly what "Belial" means, but it seems to mean "worthlessness." Deuteronomy 13 is the first time the expression is used, and the second time is in Judges 19 and 20. This literary connection shows us that the narrator of Judges intended his readers to see the sin of the men of Gibeah along the lines of what is described here in Deuteronomy 13.

Second, the sin was apostasy from the true God. Two details in Judges 19 bring this out. First, the city ignored the Levite, and offered him no hospitality. Second, when the sons of Belial attacked the Levite, they were attacking God. The crime of Gibeah was primarily social in character, at first glance anyway, but it had a clearly religious root. Gibeah was an apostate city, and came under the ban of Deuteronomy 13.

We notice that the law requires that everyone in the city, including cattle and all booty, be utterly destroyed as a whole burnt sacrifice to God.

Before returning to Judges 20, we need also to look at Deuteronomy 20:10-18. Here we have the laws for normal warfare. When a faraway nation declared war on Israel, the Israelite army would go to that city and defeat it. In such a case the women, children, cattle, and goods of the city became spoil for Israel. Such was not to be the case with the Canaanite cities, however. They were to be utterly destroyed, "in order that they may not teach you to do according to all their detestable things which they have done for their gods." Clearly, the action of the Sodomites of Gibeah is in the category just described. Gibeah had identified itself with the Canaanite culture, so it received the judgment commanded for that culture.

In the light of all this, we observe that the sin of Gibeah was plainly religious apostasy and abomination. The law commanded that an investigation be made, and this was followed out. The Benjamites refused to cooperate, and openly sided with the sons of Belial. They sided with the Canaanite culture and went to war with their Lord. Inescapably, then, this was holy war. The total destruction of Benjamin, their women, children, cattle, and goods, was the proper and appropriate action.

Conclusion

One message that comes through loud and clear in this passage is that it is not enough to be in the right. Israel was right, and Benjamin wrong, yet Israel lost the first two battles. To be against evil is not enough. We have to be right with God.

Modern American conservatives and Christians often assume that because they are right on one point or another, and because they oppose the modern sons of Belial (abortionists, homosexuals, communists, etc.), that is enough. Such a mentality is a trap. It is not enough simply to oppose evil. God will not restore America or the Western world until the Church not only holds to what is right, but holds it the right way. God will not honor a merely political opposition to evil. Deliverance from evil will only come when men return to the Church and make her ministry and worship their first love (Jud. 20:26). Such is the only way to defeat secular humanism.

18

THE SALVATION OF BENJAMIN
(Judges 21)

The story before us is generally seen by commentators as an example of the moral chaos that existed in Israel from the earliest times until the reformation under David. Almost universally, Christian commentators (I exclude liberals, who see in this story just an interesting folk tale) use verse 25, which says that "everyone did what was right in his own eyes," to provide a moral evaluation of the entire final three chapters of Judges. They contend that Israel went into excess of vengeance in destroying all of Benjamin, that Israel's vow not to permit their daughters to marry Benjamin was an evil one, that the destruction of Jabesh-Gilead was unwarranted, and that the capture of the daughters of Shiloh was a rape.

I believe that this interpretation misses the point. It is the burden of this chapter to draw quite a different interpretation from the record of the events. For reasons that seem sufficient to me, and that I shall attempt to make clear to you, the reader, I believe that the actions of Israel as recorded here were each right and proper.

In the preceding chapter, I pointed out that this final section of Judges corresponds in certain ways to the first chapter of the book. Benjamin identifies itself with the Canaanites, in its moral and spiritual behavior. As a result, Benjamin comes under the condemnation of Canaan. When this is understood clearly, the events of Judges 21 make more sense.

When Lot lifted up his eyes and considered the circle of the Jordan, the heart of the land of Canaan, it was like the garden of Eden in appearance (Gen. 13:10). At this time, the iniquity of the Canaanites at large was not yet full, and God was not ready to judge them fully (Gen. 15:16). There were, however, four cities in the heart of Canaan, in the circle of the Jordan, that

315

had become sufficiently depraved to be destroyed at this early date: Sodom, Gomorrah, Admah, and Zeboiim. When Sodom was destroyed, Lot escaped and lived in a cave of the ground, signifying a condition near death ("to dust thou shalt return"). His daughters, who had picked up the ways of Sodom, made him drunk on two occasions, and lay with him. Their offspring were the Ammonites and the Moabites (Gen. 19). The Ammonites and Moabites are seen in Scripture as extensions of the culture and ways of Sodom (Zeph. 2:8-10).

The destruction of Canaan under Joshua completed the program of liquidation begun at the burning of Sodom centuries earlier. Thus who, like Gibeah, chose to place themselves in union with Sodom, received the judgment of Sodom. This point has been made already.

Judges 20 and 21, however, also pull out motifs from Israel's war against Moab in the book of Numbers. The tribe of Benjamin, in acting like Sodom and Canaan, was also acting like Moab. We need to get these parallels in mind before reading Judges 21. The Moabites were in alliance with the apostate branch of Midianites, and hired Balaam to curse Israel, in Numbers 22 - 24. When Balaam failed to get God to curse Israel, he hit upon a better scheme. If Israel would sin, God would then curse Israel. Thus, under Balaam's advice, Moabite and Midianite women were sent into the camp of Israel, and Israel played the harlot with them. God sent a plague that killed 24,000 men of Israel. That plague was stopped only when Phineas drove a spear through the bodies of a fornicating couple. As a result, to Phineas was given the hereditary line of the high priesthood (Num. 25). We have already noticed that Judges 20:28 calls attention to Phineas as the Lord's leader in the holy war against Benjamin.

In Numbers 31, Phineas led an army consisting of 12,000 men, 1000 from each tribe, to punish the Moabites and Midianites. In the battle, every man of the Midianite/Moabite host was slain, but the women and children were kept alive, according to the law later recorded in Deuteronomy 20:14. Moses, however, ordered that every male child be killed, as well as every woman who had ever known a man carnally. Only virgin girls were to be kept alive (Num. 31:14-18). We shall notice that this is exactly the procedure that Israel (under Phineas's direction?)

used against Jabesh-Gilead.

What we are now in a position to assert is that the Biblical theology of this story has as its background not only the destruction of Sodom, but also the destruction of the neo-Sodomites of Moab and Midian during the wilderness period.

Turning to God's evaluation of these events, we note that Judges 21:15 says it was the Lord who had made the breach in Israel. This holy war was His doing. This being the case, how shall we justify the ways of God to ourselves? I suggest that the commentators have erred in saying, as they do, that Israel should not have been so rough with Benjamin. After all, they say, Benjamin was a fellow Israelite tribe. To defeat them was one thing, but to exterminate them quite another. This kind of severity was proper against heathen Canaanites, but not against fellow brethren in the Church.

This, I submit, is a completely wrong way to look at it. Judgment begins at the house of God, and the believer is judged by a stricter, not a laxer standard. What was inexcusable among the Canaanites was all the more horrible when done by a tribe of Israel. Moreover, as we noted in our comments on Judges 19, the men of Sodom only wanted homosexual relations with the two "men" who visited their city, while the men of Gibeah were deliberately attacking the representative of the Lord God of Israel. Their sin was, thus, far worse, because they fell from greater privilege, and because their intention was even more directly blasphemous.

The discipline to be maintained within the Church of Jesus Christ is inevitably more strict than the discipline maintained in outward society, even in a Christian land. This must be the case, and it explains the severity of God's war against Benjamin in Judges 20 and 21. We have to say that if it was Israel's duty to destroy all the Canaanites, men, women, and children, so much the more was it their duty to destroy all the Benjamites in their apostasy.

(We must agree with the commentators that in the day to day round of sin and trespass, Christians should deal with each other in a spirit of love, seeking to correct and help one another, and not cutting each other off. When, however, a fellow Christian becomes a total apostate, and goes to war with the Lord, greater severity must be used against him than would be used against ordinary unbelievers. Thus, the New Testament everywhere teaches that Christians must shun excommunicated persons socially, while we may have social fellowship with unbelievers.)

We shall have more to say along these lines as we comment on the chapter. Turning to the literary structure of Judges 21, we find that it is like Judges 20 in that there seems to be a repetition of events, with expansion. An outline of Judges 21 is as follows:

I. The First Presentation of the Problem and Solution (21:1-5)
   A. The Israelite Oath and the Death of Benjamin (21:1-3)
   B. Sacrifice as the Salvation of Benjamin (21:4)
   C. The Israelite Oath against Non-participants (21:5)

II. The Second Presentation of the Problem and Solution (21:6-14)
   A. The Israelite Oath and the Death of Benjamin (21:6-7)
   B. The Israelite Oath against Non-participants (21:8)
   C. The Hormah of Jabesh-Gilead as the Salvation of Benjamin (21:9-14)

III. The Third Presentation of the Problem and Solution (21:15-24)
   A. The Israelite Oath and the Death of Benjamin (21:15-18)
   B. A New Birth as the Salvation of Benjamin (21:19-24)

IV. Summary of Judges (21:25)

In this way, the literary structure of this chapter enables us to see that the salvation of Benjamin is effected by three actions, which are seen as one salvation. Their salvation is made possible because of the death of a substitute under the fiery wrath of God. Their salvation is made possible because God's fiery wrath destroys His enemies, which are their enemies. Their salvation is made possible because God gives them new wives from His palace, making it possible for their tribe to continue.

Sacrifice

21:1. Now the men of Israel had sworn in Mizpah, saying, "None of us shall give his daughter to Benjamin for a wife."

2. So the people came to Bethel and sat there before God until evening, and lifted up their voices and wept with great weeping.

3. And they said, "Why, O LORD, God of Israel, has this come about in Israel, so that one tribe should be missing today in Israel?"

4. And it came about the next day that the people arose early and built an altar there, and offered burnt offerings and peace offerings.

5. Then the sons of Israel said, "Who is there among all the tribes of Israel who did not come up in the assembly to the LORD?" For there was a great oath concerning him who did not come up to the LORD at Mizpah, saying, "He shall surely be put to death."

Why did the Israelites take the vow not to let their daughters marry Benjamites? God had commanded Israel not to inter-marry with Canaanites (Ex. 34:15, 16; Dt. 7:3, 4). Since Benjamin was identifying itself wholly and completely with the Canaanites, Israel would not intermarry with them.

At the same time, the rending of the seamless robe of the Israelite Church was painful to the tribes. They realized that this excommunication was not an occasion for joy. They felt a true spiritual loss and grief. The problem they faced, as set out here, was that the tribe of Benjamin would die out in one generation unless wives were found for the remnant of the Benjamite army. If Benjamin were to be preserved, a new birth would be needed. Theologically, the problem of a new birth for Benjamin is the governing motif in Judges 21.

So, on the next day they built a memorial altar at Bethel, probably next to the one already there, and offered burnt sacrifices on it. Why? In context, there was no reason for them to offer sacrifices for themselves. I suggest it was to atone for the sin of the remaining Benjamites. On the basis of this atonement, salvation could once again be offered to Benjamin. Of course, the Benjamites were not present to lay their hands on the sacrifices, but when peace was proclaimed to them in verse 13, they had opportunity to accept or reject the sacrifice. They apparently accepted the sacrifice, for they were given the fruits thereof.

Then, peace offerings were sacrificed. Israel was already in fellowship with God (Jud. 20:26), so again I take it that these peace sacrifices were offered on Benjamin's behalf. We may connect this with the offer of peace to Benjamin in verse 13. It is also well to bear in mind that all this was done under the direction of Phineas, the prince of peace (Num. 25:10-13).

This is the only interpretation that makes sense of the passage. If Israel were morally bound to exterminate Benjamin, then on what theological basis did they avoid doing so? The answer must be that a substitutionary sacrifice took the punishment Benjamin deserved. This makes a great deal of sense in view of the expressed concern of the Israelites, and in view of the fact that after these sacrifices had been offered, they were able to take steps to restore Benjamin.

The Israelites had sworn another oath, that if any portion of Israel did not support the holy war, they would also be exterminated. This also seems excessive. After all, Deborah did not declare war against the tribes who did not support her, but only ridiculed them. Was Israel justified in this "extreme" vow?

Three aspects of the situation show that they were. First, they were under the guidance of Phineas throughout, and we may presume that their decisions were lawful, for Phineas was an eminently lawful man.

Second, we are concerned here, as we have mentioned already, with internal Church discipline. A temporary neutrality might be possible in social affairs, but not in Church discipline. The law clearly stated that when discipline was measured out against an offender in Israel, every man was to cast a stone. We may note particularly Deuteronomy 17:7. The case here is of a man who apostatizes from the Lord and worships another god. According to verse 7, every man in the city is to cast a stone, and thus "burn" away evil from their midst. We noted in Judges 20:13 that the Benjamites were called upon to "burn" away the sons of Belial from Gibeah, but they refused. As a result, Gibeah and all the cities of Benjamin were literally burned up. And, just as the law required every man to cast a stone, so when it was a whole city that needed dealing with, every single sub-tribe in Israel was required to be present to help with the "stoning/burning" judgment. (Compare Dt. 13:9; Lev. 24:14.) Thus it was entirely right for Israel to make this oath against any non-participants.

Third, we ought to take note of the language, "he shall surely be put to death." Literally it says, "dying, he shall die," just as in Genesis 2:17 and 3:4. Adam was supposed to guard the Garden, on pain of death. Eating or not eating of the fruit of fellowship with the devil was the test of whether or not he would be a true priestly guardian. This is exactly the same as what is going on here in Judges 21. It was the duty of each and every "Adam" (city) in the holy land to guard the "Garden," God's new land flowing with milk and honey. Those who refused to guard showed by their action that they had been fellowshipping with the devil, and so they came under the original curse.

With all of this in mind, we need not be troubled at Israel's destruction of Jabesh-Gilead. In this situation, in this context, the oath that Israel swore was right and proper, and the destruction of Jabesh-Gilead was absolutely necessary.

The Destruction of Jabesh-Gilead

6. And the sons of Israel were sorry for their brother Benjamin and said, "One tribe is cut off from Israel today.

7. "What shall we do for wives for those who are left, since we have sworn by the LORD not to give them any of our daughters in marriage?"

8. And they said, "What one is there of the tribes of Israel who did not come up to the LORD at Mizpah?" And behold, no one had come to the camp from Jabesh-Gilead to the assembly.

9. For when the people were mustered, behold, not one of the inhabitants of Jabesh-Gilead was there.

10. And the congregation sent 12,000 of the valiant warriors there, and commanded them, saying, "Go and strike the inhabitants of Jabesh-Gilead with the edge of the sword, with the women and the little ones.

11. "And this is the thing that you shall do: You shall utterly destroy [hormah] every man and every woman who has known lying with a man."

12. And they found among the inhabitants of Jabesh-Gilead 400 young virgins who had not known a man by lying with him; and they brought them to the camp at Shiloh, which is in the land of Canaan.

13. Then the whole congregation sent word and spoke to the sons of Benjamin who were at the rock of Rimmon, and proclaimed peace to them.

14. And Benjamin returned at that time, and they gave them the women whom they had kept alive from the women of Jabesh-Gilead; yet they were not enough for them.

The sack of Jabesh-Gilead is a copy of the war against Moab and Midian, led by Phineas, in Numbers 31, in that 12,000 men were sent to prosecute it, and in that only virgin girls were taken alive.

How shall we make sense of this? By noticing the relationship between Moab and Canaan. The Moabites were not pure Canaanites, but were like them. The Moabites had hindered Israel, but were not the actual peoples God had ordered wiped out. Thus, the Moabites were subjected to a similar, but not quite as extreme punishment. The situation is the same here. Jabesh-Gilead was not a Benjamite city, but in refusing to war against Benjamin, it was like them. Jabesh-Gilead had not warred against the Lord, but it had hindered His campaign. Thus, Jabesh-Gilead was subjected to a similar, but not quite as extreme punishment.

The city of Jabesh-Gilead was made a "hormah" according to verse 11. We have seen throughout our study of Judges that the hormah is but the reverse side of the sacrifice. All men are standing on God's altar, which is the earth itself, for the altar was made of earth. The fire of His wrath is coming. How can a man be saved? Only if a Substitute takes his place for him on the altar. Thus, the choice before men is this: Either trust in the fire that burns the Substitute on God's altar, or else be burned up yourself. We noted above the literary parallel between Judges 21:1-5 and 6-14. At the heart of each section is an action that makes possible the salvation of Benjamin. In the first section it is the fire of God consuming a substitute. In the second section it is the fire of God consuming His enemies.

Theologically these are one event. The same waters that buoyed up the ark and saved Noah, drowned God's enemies. The same Passover event saw the death of Egypt's firstborn sons, and the salvation of Israel's by means of a substitute lamb. The same Red Sea that parted for Israel, drowned the Egyptian army. God always acts in redemption and vengeance at the same time. The salvation of the saints is correlative to the destruction of God's (and their) enemies. So it is here. From one perspective, the salvation of Benjamin was made possible by the sacrifice (and this is the most basic perspective). From another perspective, their salvation came from the destruction of Jabesh-Gilead and the capture of 400 virgins. The third perspective comes in the third section, below.

This is a convenient place to take note of the numerology that shows up here in the amazing providence of God. The survivors of Benjamin numbered 600, six being the number of humanity in its inadequacy. Just as Adam was created on the sixth day (but did not attain to rest on the seventh), so Benjamin is re-created in terms of the number six.

Four is the number of the earth, with its four corners. Jabesh-Gilead rendered 400 virgins as a sign that Benjamin would now be able once again to take dominion over its land. Moreover, given the parallels between the earth/garden and the woman, and that Adam was to guard both, we can see here 400 new Eves for the restored Adams of Benjamin. The fundamental imagery is of a new creation, and of new helpers meet for the new Adams of Benjamin, in their restored dominion.

The proclamation of peace to Benjamin (v. 13) was possible only on the basis of the peace sacrifice. At the same time, correlative to that, Israel was able to offer Benjamin a practical means of restoration. That Benjamin accepted the Lord's proclamation of peace to them, means that they repented and could be accepted back into Israel.

Four hundred women were not enough for 600 men. Thus, we are set up for the most remarkable sign of God's favor to Benjamin.

The New Birth

15. And the people were sorry for Benjamin because the LORD had made a breach in the tribes of Israel.

16. Then the elders of the congregation said, "What shall we do for wives for those who are left, since the women are destroyed out of Benjamin?"

17. And they said, "There must be an inheritance for the survivors of Benjamin, that a tribe may not be blotted out from Israel.

18. "But we cannot give them wives of our daughters." For the sons of Israel had sworn, saying, "Cursed is he who gives a wife to Benjamin."

19. So they said, "Behold, there is a feast of the LORD from year to year in Shiloh, which is on the north side of Bethel, on the east side of the highway that goes up from Bethel to Shechem, and on the south side of Lebonah."

20. And they commanded the sons of Benjamin, saying, "Go and lie in wait in the vineyards,

21. "And watch; and behold, if the daughters of Shiloh come out to dance [twirl] in the dances [twirlings], then you shall come out of the vineyards and each of you shall catch his wife from the daughters of Shiloh, and go to the land of Benjamin.

22. "And it shall come about, when their fathers or their brothers come to complain to us, that we shall say to them, 'Give them to us voluntarily, because we did not take for each man of Benjamin a wife in battle, nor did you give them to them, else you would now be guilty.' "

23. And the sons of Benjamin did so, and took wives according to their number from those who danced [twirled], whom they carried away. And they went and returned to their inheritance, and rebuilt the cities and lived in them.

24. And the sons of Israel departed from there at that time, every man to his tribe and family, and each one of them went out from there to his inheritance.

As noted, this section is formally parallel to the two preceding sections. In terms of that, the capture of the virgins of Shiloh corresponds to the salvation of Benjamin by substitutionary sacrifice and by the destruction of Jabesh-Gilead. Thus, before we react and condemn what we read here, we should try to put a positive construction on it, and see if our own thinking needs reforming.

Do we have here the Israelite equivalent of the rape of the Sabine women? I think not. First, "Shiloh" means "peace." We have already had a peace offering, and peace offered to Benjamin. Now we have an event that takes place at "Peaceville." Unless this entire chapter is designed as irony, and I think I have shown that it is not, we should allow the peace motif to shine through here.

Looking at it closely, then, we find that the word for "dance" used three times here (vv. 21, 23) is not the usual word for dance. Rather, it is very strange word that is usually used for the writhing or twisting of a woman in labor pains, as in Isaiah 13:8; 23:4; 26:17; 45:10; 54:1; 66:8. (It is also used, by analogy, for painful agonies of several other sorts, but that is not material for understanding the dances performed by these girls.) Judges 21 is the only place in the Bible where this word is translated "dance." Obviously the translation is correct, since we certainly don't have a group of virgins giving birth to children here!

What this indicates, though, is what kind of dance these girls were dancing, and what the purpose was. These were unmarried virgins. They were out to catch husbands. The dance taught to the virgins of Israel involved a kind of twirling or writhing that imitated, to some extent, the labors of childbearing, doubtless in an artistic and tasteful form. By performing these dances, the girls were arguing that they would be good mothers, and would have fruitful wombs. Thus, the whole point of these dances was to catch husbands. When we understand this, then we are not horrified at what the men of Benjamin do. Rather, the situation becomes amusing, and even delightful.

We ought not to read a rape into this. It is not there. My guess is that each year, at the Feast of Tabernacles (at the grape harvest, indicated by verse 20), the virgins would come out and dance, and the young men would "catch" them. If the girl were willing to marry the young man who caught her, then the boy would negotiate with her father or brother, and the marriage would be arranged. Nothing more than this delightful custom is indicated in the text of Judges 21, and we should not read any more into it.

Why would the fathers object? Not because their daughters were getting married (after all, that's what they wanted to happen). The objection would be that they were marrying Benjamites, and they had taken an oath not to permit that to happen.

The plan had to be kept secret, of course. It was concocted by the elders of Israel, and only they and the 200 remaining Benjamites knew about it. Thus, the fathers of the captured girls could honestly say before the Lord that they had not "given" their daughters to the men of Benjamin.

Was this a mere subterfuge? No, it was a profound subterfuge. Considered from one perspective, the gospel is a subterfuge. God really ought to put all men to death for their sins, but He has chosen to save some and punish their sins in a Substitute. God had sworn an oath, "dying thou shalt die," but when it came time to kill Adam, God let him go, anticipating the Substitute. (The formula "dying thou shalt die" is called an oath formula in Hebrews 6:13-18, in that it doubles the verb and forms a testimony of two witnesses.) Thus, God Himself engaged in a "subterfuge" to get around the surface meaning of His oath.

It is just so here. It is the Lord, acting through His appointed officers in state and Church (the elders and Phineas), Who comes up with this subterfuge. Indeed, when we realize that this takes place at a feast of the Lord (v. 19), we see that in a sense, it is the Lord Who gives these new brides to Benjamin, just as He gave Eve to Adam.

And so now we have a comprehensive picture of salvation. Each of the three literary sections of Judges 21 presents part of the total picture. At the foundation of salvation lies the substitutionary burnt and peace sacrifice of Jesus Christ. Because of this, we spiritual Benjamites, who deserve extermination, can be offered peace by Phineas, God's prince of peace, and find it at Shiloh, God's place of peace. Salvation entails the total destruction of God's and our enemies. Salvation means that the good things, virgin and unspoiled, of the wicked are given to the righteous. Salvation means a new birth for us, made possible by the feast of God, His holy Supper. Thus, salvation means that we, like Benjamin, can return to our inheritance and rebuild the cities and live in them (v. 23).

Conclusion

25. In those days there was no king in Israel; everyone did what was right in his own eyes.

It is generally assumed that this verse is a commentary on Judges 19–21 in their entirety. I hope that I have succeeded in showing that such is not the case. It is only a comment on the sins of the Benjamites.

The book of Judges closes with a most positive picture of the goodness of God. In spite of the sins of His people, concentrated in Benjamin, which He has had to chastise most severely, God is still faithful to them. God works out a way of salvation and new life for those under the judgment of death. In spite of sin, there is always grace in judgment, if men will repent. This was the message of the first section of Judges (ch. 1:1 - 2:5), and it is also the message here. When the people weep over their sins (2:4 and 20:26; 21:2) and offer burnt sacrifices (2:5 and 20:26; 21:4), then peace is restored, and God blesses them.

A final note on the phrase, "In those days there was no king in Israel." This is seen by some as a reference to the Davidic monarchy. Israel is in anarchy, and only a strong centralized state can help her. This is exactly the opposite of the message of Judges. Rather, the message is precisely the same as Samuel's message in 1 Samuel 8, which is that the Lord is King. The book of Judges contains a sustained polemic against centralized human government, for it is an expression of man's will to be like God, and is part and parcel of Baalistic humanism. In no way does the author of Judges (probably Samuel) want to see the erection of a human monarch in Israel, at least not until the Lord is ready to bring one out of Judah (which is probably part of the message of the book of Ruth, but we cannot take the space to comment on that here).

The anarchy in Israel resulted, each and every time, from a failure to recognize the Lord as King. When the people took other gods as their kings, they fell into bondage, but when they returned to the Lord, they were delivered. As the people forgot the Lord as King, they began to want mere human kings to rule over them, but God graciously prevented this from happening until the days of Saul. Behind all of this was the fact that the Levites were failing to make manifest the presence of the Lord as True King and Husband, the True Baal of Israel.

On the tomb of Oliver Cromwell is written, "Christ, not man, is King." Is it any wonder that our Puritan forefathers, whether separated from episcopacy or not, insisted that the Lord should be King, and the king of England should be but His prince? Christianity in America has fallen a long way from that early vision. We look to the force of arms more than to Christ for our defense. As a nation we have sought out other gods, and we have also centralized all power into one pagan humanistic state. This is due to one problem, and to one problem only: The Churches (Levites) have failed to set forth clearly the presence of Christ as King. Conservative theologies tell us that we may have Christ as Savior, but that it is optional whether or not we have Him as King. They tell us that Christ is not King today, and will not become King until the Millennium (a serious departure from historic Christian beliefs, even from historic premillennial thought). They fail to make His sacrament visible on a weekly basis, thus pushing the people of God into a search for fellowship with Him along all kinds of fantastic avenues, most prominently seen in the riotous "worship" of certain charismatic churches. Until the Church once again takes seriously the King and His Law, and makes Him manifest in her midst through Bible exposition and weekly sacramental fellowship, we shall continue to live in the days of the judges.

AFTERWORD

THE POLEMIC AGAINST KINGSHIP IN
JUDGES AND THE AUTHORSHIP OF JUDGES

I want finally to tie together some matters dealt with briefly in the Introduction and throughout this study. We are now in a better position to assess these, which have to do with the authorship and immediate purpose of Judges, and with the theme of humanistic kingship.

It has become common in recent years to find commentators taking the last two stories in Judges as arguments in favor of some type of central state presided over by a human king. Without going into who says what (because generally not very much is said), I should simply like to take up the matter in general terms, and summarize here in one place my arguments against this viewpoint.

First, Israel could not have had a king during this period, because the king had to come from Judah, and virtually all of the tribe of Judah were disqualified at this time. Not until the tenth generation could Judah produce a king. Now, it might be argued on the basis of this fact that the book of Judges shows the terrible consequences of Judah's sin, thus: "Suppose Judah had not sinned? Then Israel might have had a king, and then this horrible anarchy would not have come to pass. But, Judah did sin, and so the anarchic nightmare of a decentralized state was brought to pass in order to show the consequences of sin." Such an argument, however, goes against the greatness of grace, for in 1 Corinthians 10:13 we read that "no temptation has overtaken you but such as is common to man; and God is faithful, who will not allow you to be tempted beyond what you are able; but with the temptation will provide the way of escape also, that you may be able to endure it." Thus, with or without a king, Israel did not need to sin, and did not need to experience anarchy.

Second, the story of Gideon argues against monarchy. Gid-

329

eon rebuked those who offered him the crown, saying "the LORD shall rule over you" (8:23). We read in 2:18 concerning the judges themselves that "the LORD was with the judge." It follows then that the True Kingship of the Lord was made manifest through the judges themselves, and no human monarchy was necessary. Accordingly, when the people rejected the judges, they were rejecting the kingship of the Lord, as He told Samuel: "They have not rejected you, but they have rejected Me from being king over them" (1 Sam. 8:7).

Third, the story of Abimelech clearly argues against monarchy. The parable of the trees makes this abundantly clear, expressing only contempt for the idea of human kingship. More sheer anarchy is seen in the history of Israel's first king than in any other story in the book, for it is here we read of unchecked highway robbery and open civil war. There is nothing pro-monarchical here, though the story has an important place in a theology of monarchy, as we shall see.

Fourth, as we saw, the story of Jephthah argues against monarchy. Whatever kind of headship was offered to Jephthah, and whatever kind of house Jephthah was trying to build, it was not approved by the LORD.

Fifth, the book of Judges everywhere presents civil chaos and oppression as the result of sin and apostasy, not as the result of lack of central authority. Indeed, the desire for central authority is presented as the people's alternative to repentance. Rather than serve the Lord and live moral lives, and have social peace as a result of that, the people want to live as they please and have a strong central state to guarantee them social peace. Centralism is thus everywhere presented as a counterfeit to moral virtue.

Sixth, this should be clearly in the reader's mind by the time he gets to the two appendices to the book. When we read there that "there was no king in Israel, and every man did what was right in his own eyes," we are not at liberty to think that the author of Judges was so incapable of maintaining a train of thought as to reverse in his last five chapters the whole polemic developed in the main body of his work. That is hardly credible. The statement, "there was no king in Israel," taken in context, must be taken as a reference to the Kingship of the Lord. As I have sought to demonstrate at length in the last four chapters of this study, it was the task of the Levites to make present among the people an awareness of the reality of God as their King. Ultimately, the social anarchy experienced by Israel was due to the failure of the Church.

Seventh, the fact that events recorded in the two appendices to Judges happen early in the period provides what strikes me as a strong argument against the human kingship interpretation. If what is needed to prevent social anarchy is a human king, why did conditions *improve* later on under the leadership of such judges as Deborah and Gideon? It seems to be assumed that these stories provide a polemic for human kingship based on the horrors of the decline at the end of the period, but these horrors occurred at the beginning of the period.

Eighth, it needs to be asked why the two appendices focus attention on the Levitical ministry if their purpose is to show the need for a powerful state. If the point of these narratives were really to point to the need for a strong civil ruler, then we should expect to see illustrations of the failure of civil rule under the judges. What in fact we see is the failure of the Church. Thus, we are impelled to see that it is the Lord's Kingship that is in question here.

Ninth, many commentators assume that the office of judge in Israel was only intermittent. Between the judges, anarchy reigned. Thus, this was an inadequate system of civil government, and showed the need for a king. On the contrary, however, Deuteronomy 17:9 assumes that there is a permanent office of judge, and the records of the "minor judges" (discussed in chapter 9 of this study) show continuity in office. There was always a judge in office as president, chief executive, and chief judicial officer for the nation.

Tenth, some commentators speak as if the last two stories in judges show that if there had been a king, he could have prevented these horrible things from happening, or at least taken care of the situations once they came about. But how? Did the later kings of Israel prevent anarchy and apostasy? Turning to the story of Micah's house of gods, did the Lord commit into the hands of the civil authority a kind of totalitarian power to inspect the households of all Israelites? Apart from such a power, I don't see what a king could have done to prevent Micah from making his house of gods. And how about preventing the

Danite migration? *Should* a king have prevented it? Could any Israelite king, being a constitutional and not an absolute monarch, have prevented it? I doubt it.

How about the sin at Gibeah? Again, I don't see how any constitutional monarchy could have prevented this from happening. Well, then, it may be said that a king could have taken steps to punish it. To which I reply that the twelve tribes seem to have done a pretty thorough job of punishing Benjamin without the need of a king, and under the guidance of the True King via His high priest, Phineas. How does this last story show that a human king is needed to avenge wrongs? If anything, it shows the effectiveness of the republican system.

Finally, the end of the period of the judges, which comes in 1 Samuel 8, is the people's demand for the king who will be like the kings of the nations. This is clearly and explicitly seen as a rejection of the Lord's kingship. It is hardly credible for an orthodox interpreter to assert that the Bible argues for human kingship in one place, and condemns it in another.

But, that leads us to a question of how there could have been any Davidic kings at all. Is it absolutely and positively wrong at all times and seasons to have a human king? Clearly not. What is required, however, is that such a human king be a viceroy to the Divine king. The period of the judges established clearly the primacy of God as King. Only when this was clearly and unmistakably established was it possible for a man to be placed at the head of the nation as a viceroy to God over the state. Human kingship must always be subordinate to Divine kingship. In the providence of God (the disqualification of Judah during this period), this was made plain by the period of the judges.

The book of Judges does provide an important theological canon for the interpretation of the books of Samuel and Kings. Whenever Israel sinned, they were sold into slavery to a foreign nation and oppressed until they repented and God raised up a deliverer. The only time this did not happen was after the death of Gideon when, as we saw, Israel was sold into the hands of a king from her own midst. Later on in history, after the establishment of a permanent monarchy in Jerusalem, God no longer brought in foreign oppressors upon the people when they sinned. Instead, He gave them bad kings. The story of Abimelech in the context of Judges shows us that the reign of bad kings in Judah and Israel later on is to be seen in the same category as oppressions from foreign nations. Good kings were like the judges; bad kings were like the Ammonites, Amalekites, and so forth.

This is seen immediately in the reign of Saul. The people rejected the Lord, as recorded in 1 Samuel 8, and were thus sold into slavery, this time (again) into slavery to a king from their own midst. Saul began well, but took upon himself more and more of the trappings of an oriental monarch; so much so that his daughter Michal despised David when he danced before the Ark, an action designed to emphasize that David was but a naked slave before the True King of Israel. The climax of Saul's disobedience was his sparing of Agag, king of Amalek. By doing this, Saul virtually identified himself with one of the "kings of the nations"—after all, royalty do not kill one another. At that point, the reign of Saul over Israel comes to be seen as an Amalekite oppression, and Saul as an Amalekite ruler (1 Sam. 15).

Before this, however, Saul had dishonored the Lord. We have seen from the appendices to Judges that the ultimate Kingship of God over Israel was maintained by the ministry of the Church. When the state recognizes the Church, then things are in proper order, for then the viceroy (state) is recognizing the primacy of the Lord (in the Word proclaimed and administered in the Church).[1] When Saul failed to wait for Samuel at Gilgal, and went ahead and offered sacrifices on his own, he was failing to acknowledge the Lord as True King. Thus, Samuel said to Saul, "You have acted foolishly" (1 Sam. 13:13), and to act foolishly is to act as if there is no God (Ps. 14:1; 53:1). God's judgment against Saul at this point was that his dynasty would not endure.

This principle, that Israel is sold into bondage to internal powers (bad kings) analogous to the external powers (nations) that enslaved them during the period of the judges, is seen equally clearly in the history of Solomon and Rehoboam. Solomon used forced labor to mine, quarry, timber, and build the Temple and his own palace. Had this been only a temporary

---

1. I am not arguing for any institutional primacy of the Church over the state. The state, however, must recognize the primacy of the Word, the exposition of which is primarily committed to the institutional Church. The state must, thus, honor the Church and receive her moral teachings as its own.

measure, for the glory of the Lord, it doubtless would not have met with resistance. He kept it up, however, and upon his death, the people demanded of Rehoboam that he "lighten their yoke" (1 Kings 12:4-11). Rehoboam's refusal to do this resulted in the division of the kingdom, according to the principle laid down at the Tower of Babel whereby God splits and shatters centralized statist powers. Thus, so far from uniting the kingdom, the strong centralized state and its king actually split it!

In closing I should like to return to the question of authorship and occasion for the book of Judges. It is easy to see, in the light of all this, that Judges may have been a "tract for the times." Samuel, or else someone in Samuel's circle, emerges more and more as the most likely author for the book. Its message squares precisely with the message of Samuel in 1 Samuel 8, a polemic against humanistic kingship. It is easy also to imagine that the book might have been written in the years of Samuel's ministry, as he saw the people drifting more and more into a desire for kingship. The book of Judges would warn them of what was coming, and help them understand the reign of Saul. Thus, while the question of the authorship and occasion of Judges is not a terribly important one, I believe that on the basis of what we have seen in the book as a whole, we are in a position to hazard a pretty good guess.

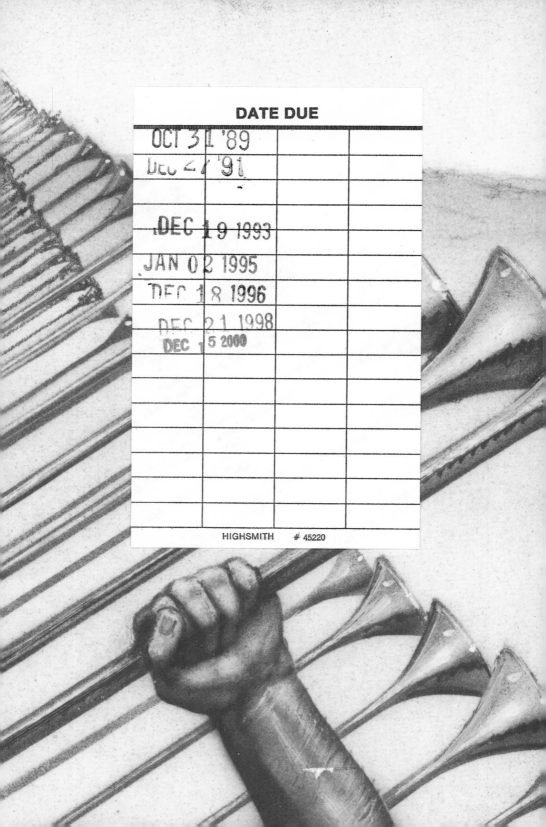